Perpetual Scriptures in Nineteenth-Century America

Perpetual Scriptures in Nineteenth-Century America

Literary, Religious, and Political Quests for Textual Authority

Jeff Smith

BLOOMSBURY ACADEMIC
NEW YORK • LONDON • OXFORD • NEW DELHI • SYDNEY

BLOOMSBURY ACADEMIC
Bloomsbury Publishing Inc
1385 Broadway, New York, NY 10018, USA
50 Bedford Square, London, WC1B 3DP, UK
29 Earlsfort Terrace, Dublin 2, Ireland

BLOOMSBURY, BLOOMSBURY ACADEMIC and the Diana logo
are trademarks of Bloomsbury Publishing Plc

First published in the United States of America 2023
Paperback edition published 2025

Copyright © Jeff Smith, 2023

Cover design by Eleanor Rose
Cover image: First page of the Address delivered by Abraham Lincoln at the dedication of the National Cemetery, Gettysburg, Pennsylvania, November 19th, 1863. The Tudor Press, Inc. 1919, Boston, Mass. Image in the Public Domain

All rights reserved. No part of this publication may be reproduced or transmitted in any form or by any means, electronic or mechanical, including photocopying, recording, or any information storage or retrieval system, without prior permission in writing from the publishers.

Bloomsbury Publishing Inc does not have any control over, or responsibility for, any third-party websites referred to or in this book. All internet addresses given in this book were correct at the time of going to press. The author and publisher regret any inconvenience caused if addresses have changed or sites have ceased to exist, but can accept no responsibility for any such changes.

Library of Congress Cataloging-in-Publication Data
Names: Smith, Jeff, 1958 January 25- author.
Title: "Perpetual scriptures" in nineteenth-century America : literary, religious, and political quests for textual authority / Jeff Smith. Description: New York : Bloomsbury Academic, 2023. | Includes bibliographical references and index. | Summary: "Connecting several crucial developments in America's nationally formative period, this book shows how seemingly separate debates and movements in literature, religion, and politics reflect shared anxieties over the problem of textual authority"–Provided by publisher.
Identifiers: LCCN 2023001433 (print) | LCCN 2023001434 (ebook) | ISBN 9781501398957 (hardback) | ISBN 9781501398995 (paperback) | ISBN 9781501398964 (ebook) | ISBN 9781501398971 (pdf) | ISBN 9781501398988 (ebook other)
Subjects: LCSH: American literature–19th century–History and criticism. | Religion and literature–United States–History–19th century. | Politics and literature–United States–History–19th century. | United States–Religion–19th century. | United States–Politics and government–19th century.
Classification: LCC PS217.R46 S445 2023 (print) | LCC PS217.R46 (ebook) | DDC 810.9/003–dc23/eng/20233088
LC record available at https://lccn.loc.gov/2023001433
LC ebook record available at https://lccn.loc.gov/2023001434

ISBN:	HB:	978-1-5013-9895-7
	PB:	978-1-5013-9899-5
	ePDF:	978-1-5013-9897-1
	eBook:	978-1-5013-9896-4

Typeset by Integra Software Services Pvt. Ltd.

To find out more about our authors and books visit www.bloomsbury.com and sign up for our newsletters.

Gratefully dedicated

to the many excellent teachers, professors, friends, and colleagues who have helped, informed, and guided me, and to the international Fulbright Scholarship Program and the Fulbright Commissions of the UK, Bulgaria, and the Czech Republic, for invaluable career assistance and with the highest regard for the Fulbright mission of promoting international peace and understanding.

CONTENTS

Introduction: A Nation Founded on Writing 1

Part One The Quest for New Prophets

1. The "World's Oldest Book" and the Crisis of Scriptural Authority 9
2. Revivals, Reaction, and the Ultra-Protestants 27
3. Scriptures as Sepulchres: Unitarians and Transcendentalists 55
4. Spirit and Kingdom: Language, Social Action, and the "True Reviving" 81

Part Two The Quest for New Scriptures

5. American Parascriptures: The Making of a National Political Canon 109
6. Sacred Ephemera: News, Literature, and *Uncle Tom's Cabin* 129
7. Walt Whitman's "New Bible" and the Spiritual Vitalizing of Facts 151

Part Three The Quest for National Salvation

8. Slavery, Liberty, and the Three Great Charters 173

9 Lincoln's Miniature Bible: Salvation History in the Gettysburg Address 199

Conclusion: The New American Testaments 223

Notes 228
Bibliography 261
Index 286

Introduction:
A Nation Founded on Writing

The rapid social and cultural changes in America's early years as a nation, between the Founding and the Civil War, included several events and movements that were highly significant but are difficult to see in full because, for the most part, they are analyzed independently of each other. Americans of that era were innovating and experimenting on many fronts at once—developing new religious practices and even new religions; defining the meaning and debating the rules of a new type of constitutional republic; attempting to formulate a distinctive national identity and a suitably powerful means of expressing it; and leading the way into the industrial age, which would bring commodification and mass production to a great many products, including information. Many other things were happening as well, of course, but these particular developments were noteworthy for having centrally involved written texts: religious experiments made frequent use of the Bible and other sacred scriptures; political arguments in the era often focused on the Founding texts, the Declaration of Independence and Constitution; the search for a national identity was closely tied to the urgent need, as many saw it, for a new and original national literature; and the information revolution was most clearly visible in the advent of the "penny press" and the massive growth of printed matter produced on an industrial scale.

The premise of the chapters that follow is that these developments were closely related and mutually interacting, and are better understood when considered together. At issue was both what kinds of authority could be reliably received from written texts, and how to create new texts that would also speak with authority. The background to these problems was a cultural situation in which two especially distinctive kinds of writing offered contrasting models, in fact seemed to represent opposite extremes. On the one hand, a broadly literate America was well accustomed to the notion that some texts were sacred. It had long been under the influence of a Calvinist or "Reformed" Protestantism that emphasized Bible-reading, had a rapidly spreading and relatively democratic system of common schooling, and was awash in Bibles thanks to the growing efforts of missionary and Bible societies to distribute them free or at very low cost. Americans were accustomed to assuming that a particular book could provide absolute, ancient, timeless, and unchanging truth, nothing less than God's own divine Word—and eventually, to assign analogously high prestige to other key documents, beginning with the nation's foundational charters.

But at the same time, the new media of the period were soon producing massive amounts of text of seemingly no higher value whatsoever. Mechanical printing had long produced not just holy books but a wide range of ephemera, but the new industrial presses and the rising institution of "news" vastly increased the amount of printed matter appearing daily, even hourly, and intended for immediacy, with only a very short half-life before it was replaced with further reams of equally cheap and disposable text. Much of this material was mundane and some of it notably tawdry, the very opposite of spiritually elevating or sacred.

Americans of the time navigated their way between these high and low paradigms of the written word, looking to make sense of them but also perhaps turn them to advantage. Much was at stake in all this for America's religious life, for its political future—especially as intractable debates over slavery dismayingly devolved toward Civil War—and for the advancement of particular groups, including the country's large and badly oppressed nonwhite minorities. For men and women of letters, one problem of special and sustained concern was what an American critic early on diagnosed as "literary delinquency": For all its impressive growth and economic vitality, why did the young nation not yet have its own national literature? What would such a literature be like, and when and how would it develop, if at all?[1]

"Where Genius Dies": American Authors and the Problem of Author-ity

In the years after the Revolution, fretful discussions of the state of America's literature, or lack thereof, became virtually a literary genre in itself.[2] It was normal not just for condescending foreigners, but for many chagrined Americans, to charge that the country was a cultural backwater—a place, one Philadelphia poet lamented, "Where Fancy sickens, and where Genius dies."[3] Thomas Jefferson debated the question with French naturalists who claimed that the American continent was simply degenerate, an entire environment of *"rapetissement"* or the shrinking of just about everything. Proceeding scientifically, Jefferson marshaled statistics to show that, no, animals were as large in the New World as the Old. (Later, as president, he would seek more vivid proof, asking the Lewis and Clark expedition to check the far northwest for any living giant mastodons.[4]) As to culture, he granted that as of the 1780s the country had not yet produced any good poets, but insisted it was not lacking in great achievements overall if compared fairly with Britain and France *per capita*.[5]

The "anxious collective hand-wringing" continued past the Civil War and arguably into the twentieth century. Besides *rapetissement* there were other proposed explanations.[6] America was said to need no literature of its own because it could so easily import Great Britain's, and could not effectively compete without a system of international copyrights. It was said to be too busy with the crudely material aspects of nation-building to pursue the finer things, which would follow only centuries later. A crass, "business-doing, money-making people" always acting "with railroad speed" was too undisciplined and "hasty" to produce greatness.[7] Such a people was adolescent, burning with convictions but still struggling to find its voice. Or, contrarily, it was too sunk in timeworn corruptions, having yielded to the received aesthetic standards and styles of the old countries. Some said Americans were too blandly alike, too seldom beset by the troubles and conflicts that are fodder for great literature—though Alexis de Tocqueville's observation that they had "witnessed no great political catastrophes" would prove true, if it ever was, for only a few more years.[8]

"In the four quarters of the globe," a leading English critic, Sydney Smith, insultingly asked in 1820, "who reads an American book? or goes to an American play? or looks at an American picture or statue?" The question stung badly enough that Americans long continued quoting it, whether indignantly or, sometimes, in reluctant agreement. In "the whole annals of this self-adulating race," said Smith, there were "no indications of genius."[9] When the group that would become the Transcendentalist movement began meeting in 1836, the announced topic of its very first discussion was, "American Genius: The Causes Which Hinder Its Growth, Giving Us No First-Rate Productions."[10] It was widely assumed that every nation had a unique "genius," a distinctive, elemental national talent—a certain spirit and force it could channel better than other nations and possibly to the world's benefit. So what was America's? Perhaps its democratic impulse, its deference to the common folk? But maybe catering to the common taste meant vulgarization and a lowering of standards. Then again, trying to meet conventional "standards" would yoke America's writers and artists to forms imposed from the past and abroad. Seemingly higher levels of refinement might be as bad as excessive vulgarity, in fact might even be a variant of it.[11]

An authentically American literature would do what other national literatures did, yet somehow by and through a considered effort *not* to do what they did but something else entirely. The problem was one of both message and medium: What would be a non-imitative, uniquely American mode of expression, and what kinds of uniquely American thoughts or experiences would it best express? Harriet Martineau, another foreign observer who, like Tocqueville, chronicled an extended American tour in the 1830s, noted that America's culture was borrowed and blended from other civilized nations, much as an orchestra blends many instruments. Eventually it would strike a great chord, but the conductor was not in place yet, and the awkward sounds heard so far were merely the "tuning for the concert."[12] But Martineau, like Tocqueville, also anticipated one possible answer to this tangle of anxieties and cultural defensiveness. At the same time the penny newspapers were first appearing, she saw a hopeful prophecy of an American literature and its future great "creator" in the vigor with which America "applies herself to the produce of her press, to find the imperishable in what is just as transient as all that has gone before."[13]

A similar solution came from Ralph Waldo Emerson. Emerson and the Transcendentalists were originally a group of young ministers, dissatisfied with religious convention, who would turn to literature as one means of religious revival.[14] Preoccupied with interlinked failures in religion, literature, and culture, Transcendentalists saw one key source of the problem as books. That might seem odd, coming from a coterie of the nation's most elite readers and writers—the movement began as a kind of book club—but books were channels to the old authorities of the past. These were the chains that had to be broken, starting with excessive reverence for that prototypical book, the Bible. Emerson argued that Bibles were needed, but each age and each nation in essence had to write its own. America had all the raw materials needed for great literature in its ordinary common life, so the new, vital, and authentic national expression would give supreme, even divine poetic voice to the kinds of events and daily contentions that filled the pages of newspapers.[15] It would find the imperishable in the transient by marrying the sacred and disposable, the high and the low—or better, putting them into a dialectical relationship in which the key features of each enabled the other.

A new nation's authors, then, could hope to speak with genuine "authority" by writing the "bibles" of their busy, politically rambunctious, money-making society. These, however, must be "no dead letter," like inherited bibles and literatures, but—in Emerson's provocative phrase—"a perpetual Scripture."[16] Determining how, and how far, such a thing might be possible would be the goal of a number of subsequent American writers.

The Plan of This Book

In critical analysis the issues outlined above have largely been "siloed," separately treated as distinct matters of literary, religious, political, and even industrial history. The chapters that follow are meant to enhance our understanding of them by treating them as different manifestations of the same broad cultural project.

Part 1, "The Quest for New Prophets," explores the crisis over biblical authority and some of the key responses to it. Chapter 1 reviews the makings of the crisis. Chapter 2 describes the revivalism of the "Second Great Awaking" and some of the controversies over authority it provoked, then turns for close attention to three related movements of the 1820s–40s: the Millerite or "Adventist" movement, the Campbellite or "Primitivist" movement, and the Mormon movement, sometimes called "Restorationist" (as were the Campbellites). These movements are grouped here under the term "ultra-protestant," since they each represent intensifications of the biblicist logic that defined much of Protestantism in the first place. Each was addressed to a different spiritual anxiety, but eventually found itself re-creating the problem it set out to solve—a self-canceling logic that illustrates the difficulties of founding high authority on written texts.

Chapters 3 and 4 turn to the different set of responses conventionally known as "liberal" Protestantism. Key movements and figures here are the Unitarians; their dissenting offshoot, the Transcendentalists; and the even more dissident theologians Theodore Parker and Horace Bushnell. Dissociating themselves from traditional claims for the Bible's authority and its literal truth, the liberals raised a number of probing questions about the sources of spiritual power, its relationship to social action, and whether it could be conveyed through language at all. The tendency of language to fossilize thought and fix meanings onto the page was troubling not just for religion, with its scriptures and written creeds, but for any high hopes one might attach to books or literature, including the hope that a nation like America could have a powerful literature of its own.

Part 2, "The Quest for New Scriptures," considers the parallel emergence of the new varieties of high and low text and some of the literary experiments they inspired. Chapter 5 examines the "canonizing" of the Founding and its core documents. America was more reliant than most nations on written charters, but the Declaration of Independence and Constitution were initially more controversial than is usually remembered, attaining quasi-sacred or "parascriptural" status only over the course of decades of re-evaluation and political struggle. As they did, they followed the Bible in becoming templates for other writings, widely mimicked and mined for resonant phrases, as well as the bases of further contention, with debates over how to read them as vexed as—and intersecting with—debates over interpreting the Bible.

Chapters 6 and 7 discuss the "news revolution" and some early efforts to synthesize high and low, to create a literature rooted in both sacred text and the new culture of commodified and mass-produced print. What Lawrence Buell has called "literary scripturism" helps explain the work of both Herman Melville and Harriet Beecher Stowe, whose *Uncle Tom's Cabin* was not just a novel but a large, multifaceted project with elements of both journalism and Christian liturgy. Chapter 7 examines Walt Whitman's equally large, in fact lifelong poetic project, which also resembled journalism, the field in which his career began, and which he called "the Great Construction of the New Bible."

Part 3, "The Quest for National Salvation," applies questions about textual authority to the great political crises of the 1850s and '60s. Arguments both for and against slavery were grounded in the Bible and the parascriptures of the "national compact," demonstrating not just the difficulty of extracting determinate meanings from each text in itself but the special interpretive problem of reading them in combination. Alongside the slavery debate, therefore, were a number of related debates that merged political and religious questions in complex and sometimes surprising ways. These struggles, involving such figures as William Lloyd Garrison, Frederick Douglass, John Brown, and Martin Delany, are the subject of chapter 8. Different ways of reading the core texts of the national compact and defining national "missions" involved interpretive problems long familiar to readers of Scripture, extending concepts like "heresy" and "infidelity" into politics.

Chapter 9 considers Abraham Lincoln's appropriations of the Founding texts, first in his pre-presidential statements and then, above all, in the Gettysburg Address, a recapitulation of the Bible's dual-testament "salvation history" but centered on America and the struggle to realize its historical mission. This remarkable parascriptural text, along with the larger mythography built around Lincoln, was also eventually elevated to the national canon, and the chapter reviews the significant role of fictional storytelling in that development as well.

The question of textual authority was not a new one in a human affairs, but it engaged Americans, in large numbers, as both an especially puzzling and a distinctively national problem, one that needed their urgent attention if their remarkable new enterprise—a very large and consequential experiment in deliberate nation-making—was not to fail. Emerson and Whitman both suggested that America, itself, was a "poem," perhaps the greatest of all poems. In a culture of sacred text, it was also a kind of gospel. Writing that poem, proclaiming that gospel, and composing its new "testaments" have been among the ongoing, essential projects of American literature and culture.

PART ONE

The Quest for New Prophets

1

The "World's Oldest Book" and the Crisis of Scriptural Authority

"The value of Scripture history, as the only authentic account we possess of the earliest ages, and the most instructive mirror of man, is not yet estimated as it ought to be; for in it alone, we contemplate character and events, recorded without prejudice or partiality. ... The subject is exceedingly interesting, for the Bible is not only the oldest book in existence, but it contains an account of the creation of all things, and a history of mankind from the beginning."
SARAH HALL, *CONVERSATIONS ON THE BIBLE, BETWEEN A MOTHER AND HER CHILDREN*, 1818/1827[1]

Sarah Hall's maternal advice on teaching biblical stories to children was one of many religious handbooks that sold widely in the early years of the American republic. Looking at it today, we find a view of the Bible that is difficult to classify. At first glance it might seem to resemble Fundamentalism, the later movement that sought to counter modernizing theologies with reassertions of the Bible's "inerrancy"—including the literal truth of such vivid legends as the Garden of Eden, Noah's Ark, the Tower of Babel, and the Parting of the Red Sea. Hall, however, while in many ways a progressive and even an early feminist, actually outdoes modern biblical conservatives. By comparison, their defenses of Scripture are narrower and more hedged: Today's Southern Baptist Convention, for instance, describes the Bible as "without any mixture of error, *for its matter*" and "the supreme standard by which all human conduct, creeds, and religious opinions should be tried." These are large claims, but they are carefully limited to the Bible's "matter," its religious and moral content—and even so, the SBC has found them somewhat difficult to sustain and in need of shoring up.[2] Unlike Sarah Hall,

Christians nowadays who call themselves "Bible-believing" would not think to treat the Bible as either a comprehensive world history or the oldest book in existence. Where it was once possible to imagine that the biblical writings were unique, that Old Testament Hebrew was the world's first language and the source of all others (as Hall and many others supposed), such beliefs are no longer conserved even at very conservative institutions that advertise themselves today as "Bible-based."[3]

Also odd-sounding nowadays is Hall's idea that the Bible alone records things "without prejudice or partiality," as if its value lay in straight reportage like that of an almanac or news magazine. We can find claims like this here and there in other nineteenth-century sources as well, sometimes in remarks made in passing, as if it were well known that Scripture is uniquely objective, plain, simple, and universally understandable.[4] Many readers of the time apparently felt, nonetheless, that they needed help with it; there was a large market for expository manuals, including Hall's, and if a Bible was sold as "Self-Interpreting," that meant it came stuffed with explanatory essays, notes, and appendices. Still, it was apparently possible at one time to view the Bible as not merely the proverbial "Good Book," not even merely the greatest book, but also the clearest and the single most informative book, perhaps the only book one would ever need.

As many historians have noted, assumptions like these were long a commonplace among Christians. "The first millennium of Christianity knew only one Book," says Arthur McCalla. "The Bible, as the Word of God, was the authoritative source of religious knowledge, and indeed, of all knowledge on the matters of which it spoke." As a world history, it was complete—"not a detailed history, to be sure, but all major events and peoples were present and accounted for."[5] Containing the entire "structure and aim of world history and human destiny, " according to J. Samuel Preus, the biblical epic "had for centuries stood guard over knowledge in every social, political and cultural domain," providing "the most comprehensive available framework for understanding the totality of things."[6] American Puritans, says Emory Elliott, "believed that the words of the Bible literally contained all truth" and therefore overrode the "fallen" or sin-corrupted reasoning power of human beings.[7] This view demanded that all other knowledge be enclosed within the biblical narrative, which "*was* the history of the world—at least within broad brushstrokes," says Terence Keel. "Knowledge derived from nonbiblical sources was cast into the general conceptual framework established by scripture."[8] As Hans W. Frei puts it, the Bible reader in this era, which he calls "precritical," had to fit himself into the biblical world, "since the world truly rendered by combining biblical narratives into one was indeed the one and only real world."[9]

The quests for textual authority that will concern us in this study came about in large part because the Bible lost that reputation. Over the course of about two centuries, from the mid-seventeenth to the mid-nineteenth—and with rapidly intensifying force during the years when America was organizing its new republic—serious new questions arose about what kind of book the Bible was and what kinds of questions it could and could not answer. These were complicated and cross-cutting developments that reflected changes both in intellectual fashions and in the broader society. They did challenge the Bible's former authority, but simply calling them a loss of authority, as if they followed a single, linear downward track, is too simple. Instead, we might usefully regard them as multiple broad and overlapping movements, a matrix of new relationships between believer and text that undercut scriptural authority in some ways while at the same time enhancing it in others.

Relativizing the Bible in the Sixteenth to Eighteenth Centuries

The Bible is voluminous, a large anthology of several dozen writings of quite different kinds, composed, compiled, and multiply edited in various communities and for many different purposes over the course of about a thousand years. That fact in itself poses challenges for anyone looking to it for authority. On the one hand, the book's great breadth and comprehensiveness make it seem a likely source of answers to a very wide range of questions. Especially in earlier eras, believers would have assumed it contained not just spiritual guidance but information on many topics: the origins and history of the world and its peoples, the right ways of ordering societies and framing legal systems, and much else. On the other hand, the sheer multiplicity of the Bible's writings, including as they do a wide variety genres—stories, proverbs, sermons, poetry, law codes, letters of instruction, and others—can make it difficult to extract answers and even more difficult to agree on them. The varied contents will often be obscure, oblique, hard to interpret, or seemingly quite different for different readers, even readers who come to the text with broadly similar premises. These differences can easily become large sources of division. That the Bible is read in many different ways and to very different ends is obvious today, but in fact this difficulty goes back to the very beginning. Rabbinical debates over the meaning of the Hebrew Scriptures were already in progress even before Christianity began, and records of disagreements among the first Christian apostles appear in the pages of the New Testament itself. Differences over even the most fundamental claims of the faith have recurred in every Christian generation; as one striking example, one of the New Testament's own first and most important compilers, Marcion of Sinope, was himself declared a heretic and excommunicated from the second-century church.

What kept the disagreements somewhat in bounds, at least in the Latin West, were the councils and "magisterium" of the Roman Catholic Church—its system for settling disputes and making authoritative decisions on questions of doctrine and correct Christian practice. Subject to this system, the average believer was neither expected nor urged to consult the Bible directly, both because of the danger of misreading it (from the Church's standpoint) and because it was not the ultimate authority in the first place: For the Catholic Church, Scripture stood alongside "Tradition" and the Church's own authority as just one route through which the original, "apostolic" faith reached down the centuries to later Christians.

It was this system that the Protestant Reformation by and large rejected. Incensed with what they saw as the Church's corruptions, early reformers broke with the Roman hierarchy and refused to accept the authority of Church councils later than the early Christian centuries. In a momentous decision, however, they accepted the continuing authority of the Church's book. Indeed, the rejection of other authorities greatly enhanced the importance of the Bible, which some Protestants came to view as nearly identical to Christianity itself. Until the Enlightenment upset this view, wrote C.H. Dodd in 1929, the Bible was regarded as "divine in origin and consequently infallible":

> Historic Christianity has been a religion of revelation. This has been held to mean that the ultimate truths of religion are not discoverable by the unaided faculties of the human mind, but must have been directly communicated by God in a "supernatural" way, and that the Bible is the "Word of God" in this unique sense.[10]

Though they labeled a few books "apocryphal," Protestants accepted most of the biblical "canon," the list of writings approved for inclusion in the Bible by about 400 CE. Thus the lines of religious authority were effectively reversed. A canon means a measure, and what was now to be measured were the very institutions that had constructed the canon in the first place. As Peter J. Thuesen puts it, the prevailing Protestant formula would be "Book over Church."[11]

Embraced as the Word of God, apart from and bypassing any church, the Bible served reformers as a standard for judging Catholic and, eventually, any other doctrines. In his famous 1521 declaration, "Here I stand," Martin Luther had demanded that the bishops accusing him show from Scripture how he was wrong and Church teachings were right. Implicit in that demand is the view that Scripture's authority is an independent fact and not, itself, one of those Church teachings. The Bible must be its own, self-sufficient witness, as indeed a few key verses in it are often taken to suggest.[12] John Calvin, one of the founding Reformers, made the point explicit: "the Scriptures obtain full authority among believers only when men regard them as having sprung from heaven, as if there the living words of God were heard." They did not need authenticating from the Church and its "precarious" human authority, but just the opposite. Manifestly superior to all other books, "Scripture exhibits fully as clear evidence of its own truth as white and black things do of their color, or sweet and bitter things do of their taste."[13] It was completely harmonious, with all its parts in "beautiful agreement," was effectively the oldest book in existence, and was clearly "crammed with thoughts that could not be humanly conceived."[14]

While some Protestants even more given to questioning old authorities de-emphasized the Bible as well—Quakers, for instance, rely less on any one book than on a divine "Light Within"—the largest Protestant churches, those descending from Luther, Calvin, and their followers, looked to Scripture to replace the hierarchical, priestly, and tradition-based authority they had rejected. This was especially the case for Protestants of the various Calvinist or "Reformed" churches that would long predominate in the future United States. Lutheran and Calvinist churches claimed a faith founded on *sola scriptura*: the Bible alone. Like every other Christian claim, this formula too was contested, with different Protestant factions assigning it different weights and meanings. *Sola scriptura* is not, by definition, at odds with church authority; it could simply mean that the church in question claims that authority from no source other than Scripture. A given faith community can still have an internal system for deciding and enforcing what it deems truly "biblical." Professional theologians, trained and accredited clergy—even sometimes "bishops"—and settled doctrines, creeds, catechisms, and codified "confessions" are to varying degrees still important features of most Protestant churches. Some believers, however, would carry the Protestant principle to its logical extreme: For them, "the Bible alone" came to mean not just relying solely on the Bible but, literally, reading it alone—by itself, and by themselves.

Of course, a "priesthood of all believers" (another Protestant credo) would need a Bible that is broadly intelligible. Catholic biblical interpretation over the centuries had built up a complex body of allegorical, figurative, and "typological" readings of biblical events, especially those in the Old Testament. The Reformers discarded much of this. Freeing the Bible from the guardianship of the Latin-speaking doctors of the Catholic Church, they invited the people at large to hear its words for themselves, issuing vernacular translations in Bibles printed without the former apparatus of Catholic notes and commentaries.[15] They also read the text in a basically different way. "If the Bible alone was to be the sole authority for Christian belief and life," says McCalla, "then every sentence in it must have a single, clear meaning intended by the apostles and prophets and that is understandable to every reader without the aid of a special class of privileged interpreters."[16] This quest for "the 'plain sense' of Scripture" had an important corollary, because it

> meant that only passages which at a common-sense level contain moral or theological teachings could be read for a moral or theological message. All other biblical passages must have some other primary referent. As a result, many biblical passages, and above all the narrative sections of Genesis and Exodus, were now construed as conveying cosmological or historical knowledge. The narratives of the Flood or of the forty years in the wilderness, which for patristic and medieval interpreters contained spiritual meanings in addition to their literal sense, now were to be understood as, and only as, true accounts of things that had happened in the distant past.[17]

Protestant interpretation thereby added further weight to what was already a heavy emphasis on the Bible's authority across wide expanses of human knowledge, including geography, history, and cosmology. Also, necessarily, the biblical text was assumed to lack any history of its own. It could not be a "merely human composition," compiled and handed down like other ancient writings through human agencies and subject to critical analysis in light of other sources and information.[18] To outrank church authorities, it had to be a book like no other, not just inspirational but "inspired" in a technical sense that made it, for some Protestants, something like direct dictation from God.

For obvious reasons, enormously high estimations like these are also vulnerabilities. For believers, new information at odds with the Bible's histories or chronologies would pose an anxious problem, calling at minimum for efforts to explain or excuse the seeming contradictions. Perhaps even more disturbing would be a compelling story of the Bible's own origins—of what its writing and compiling owed to contingent events and human decisions. Protestant biblicism made understanding the text vitally important, encouraging microscopic attention to its every detail. Faithful devotion to such understanding could itself, then, lead to discoveries that would challenge faith.

Textualizing the Bible in the Eighteenth and Nineteenth Centuries

In fact, questions about the Bible's historical reliability were mounting rapidly even as the first Protestants were organizing their new churches. Christopher Columbus, an avid student of scriptural prophecies, had sold his westward voyage to the East Indies partly as a Christian mission: Bringing the Gospel to the furthest reaches would complete the biblical schematics, inaugurating history's final phase.[19] Instead, he and other explorers opened a whole new epoch by stumbling onto worlds not encompassed in the Bible at all. Here were elaborate human societies situated on great landmasses that were not among the three "soils"—Asia, Africa, and Europa—previously thought to constitute the world, each supposedly peopled after the biblical Flood by descendants of one of Noah's three sons (Genesis 9:18-19). Borrowing explorer Amerigo Vespucci's name in feminine form, "America," German mapmakers did their best to line up this "fourth soil" with the existing scheme—but they could not go back and rewrite Scripture to give Noah a fourth son. Who were the native Americans, then? What was their place in the biblical plan of "salvation history"? European and American Christians would worry themselves over those questions for at least the next three hundred years.

Also startling were the Mesoamerican societies' unknown religions and rituals. Europeans already knew that distant societies were not Christian, and of course unfamiliar beliefs could always be dismissed as superstition, idol-worship, or even witchcraft. Nonetheless, on Christian assumptions it was hard to explain why the God of all creation, and the Savior of the whole, fallen world, would have let so many centuries go by without revealing themselves across large parts of the planet. Moreover, the intricate Mesoamerican calendars, along with records emerging from China and, eventually, new insights into the histories of ancient Egypt, Assyria, and Babylon, implied a world much too old to fit the Bible's Genesis account.[20]

The humanist scholars of the Renaissance, followed by such distinguished successors as Sir Isaac Newton, labored to reconcile a biblical "sacred chronology" with information from these secular or "Gentile" sources. By their very nature, though, such efforts had an unintended effect: Whereas previously, "interpretation was a matter of incorporating information about world history into the framework provided by the biblical narrative," it would instead become a matter of relativizing Scripture, "fitting the biblical stories into a more comprehensive historical narrative," as McCalla puts it. Reversing these "frameworks of interpretation" was, in itself, "an epochal moment in the intellectual history of the West."[21] It was becoming increasingly clear that "the Bible is not the sole source of true history; there are people in the world not descended from Noah; the Bible does not contain the history of all peoples; and the Bible is the local history of one people only."[22]

At the same time, other new discoveries posing challenges to the biblical view were arising from early modern science. The "scientific revolution" owed much to earlier Christian scholarship and speculation—Copernicus held various church appointments, Galileo and Johannes Kepler both considered careers in the clergy, Newton spent his later years obsessed with interpreting biblical prophecy—but its emphasis on systematic, observation-based assessments of the tangible and measurable gradually developed into a competing epistemology, a different way of understanding the world altogether. Galileo's telescope, which famously got him into so much trouble with Catholic officials, produced discoveries that seemed to refute not only traditional, Ptolemaic geocentrism but the received idea that the heavens were a realm of perfection, different in kind from the fallen, "sublunary" world below. Earth was another planet, like the bodies moving through the sky, and was not the center of the cosmos—hence, perhaps, not the focal point of a human-centered Creation, divinely arranged as a stage setting for the great moral drama of human life. Demotions like this from special positions in a divine scheme would recur in one field of knowledge after another. Thus geologists, for instance, would gradually come to recognize that Earth itself also had a natural history, that this included very slow events like the raising of mountains, that the planet must therefore be millions of years old, and that certain unusual rocks were actually the fossilized imprints of unknown plant and animal species that had, apparently, once lived but long since disappeared. What the Book of Genesis presented as a few brief days of Creation preceding Adam and Eve, and then a period of Edenic perfection, would come to look like vast and utterly strange prior ages, an entirely different world of alien and even monstrous beings that Adam had never seen or named, assuming any "Adam" had ever even existed.

Scientific discovery also posed a challenge not just to the Bible but to other ancient authorities, including such long-dominant figures as Aristotle and Ptolemy. Early on, Aristotle and other classical authors had become the subject of new and closer attention, reflecting another goal of the Renaissance humanists: recovering and critically analyzing the stories and philosophies of the ancient world—which in turn meant reading them in the original texts and languages. That project in textual restoration had prepared the way for Protestant efforts to reconstruct an original, corrected text of Scripture, one that would free it from earlier translators' mistakes and the supposed theological corruptions of the Catholic Church. In another case of unintended consequences, this endeavor, starting from pious intentions and the highest possible estimation of the Bible's authority, unwittingly "began the process that dethroned 'the Book' from its inerrant, universal, and ahistorical exceptional status and made it one more fallible, particular, and historical book," says McCalla.[23] Cleaning up textual inaccuracies necessarily meant noting inconsistencies among ancient copies, allowing that some of these must be errors, and making corrections that might also extend at times to judging the contents of the passages in dispute. Furthermore, textual criticism drew attention to the complex history of authorship, redaction, transmission, and canonization that might originally have allowed the errors to creep in; and it required understanding the nature of the writings in question, which obliged close readers to notice the genres, poetic conventions, oral traditions, and underlying sources that tended to assimilate biblical literature to the similar legends and writings of other cultures of the ancient Near East.

The broad results of these efforts are summed up in such phrases from recent titles as *The Death of Scripture* by Michael G. Legaspi and *The Erosion of Biblical Certainty* by Michael J. Lee. Legaspi describes a movement "from scripture to text," a "textualizing trajectory" that began in response to the sixteenth-century division of the church and eventually replaced a "scriptural" with an "academic" Bible. Thus reconceived, the book "could no longer function unproblematically as Scripture" and, in effect, ceased to be a "Bible" at all.[24] Lee, in a similar vein, notes that interpreting Scripture "by the same rules they used for ordinary ancient texts" guided seventeenth-century skeptics like Thomas Hobbes, Baruch Spinoza, Richard Simon, and others toward what would eventually become the "higher" criticism, a major innovation of the Enlightenment era that still guides academic biblical studies today.[25] By the early nineteenth century, higher critics were scandalizing public opinion with various faith-shattering claims: the Pentateuch was a complex composite, not the work of Moses; Jesus was a mortal man whose miracle-making reflected the legends of the early church.

Shattering faith, however, had not been the purpose. Unlike some Enlightenment rationalists who were hostile to religion, the higher critics were apt to count themselves among the faithful. Hoping to enrich, not diminish, their engagement with Christianity's core documents, they were simply applying the best available methods, "the ordinary principles by which history is judged and evidence estimated," as one of them would later insist.[26] What had made those principles "ordinary," though, was an intellectual sea-change. As Peter J. Thuesen explains it,

> higher criticism was simply the byproduct of that more fundamental revolution in human thought, the dawn of historical consciousness. The emergence of the modern concept of history, with its realization that societies and their texts are conditioned by time and circumstance, meant that Bible-readers never again would be oblivious to the truth question.[27]

Of course, Bible-readers were a very large group, among whom these modern, scholarly ways of thinking were less than universally known, let alone embraced—not by the early nineteenth century, and indeed not yet today. Popular "precritical" commentaries like Sarah Hall's attest to a certain abiding credulousness, a readiness among ordinary believers either to dismiss the more troubling truth questions or to meet them with reassertions of the traditional teachings of the faith. If anything, insistence on the Bible as a clear and reliable charter not just for that faith, but for social attitudes and life in general, seemed to be taking ever-firmer root in heavily Protestant early America. It would be yet another historical irony when this development, too, helped raise further doubts about the Bible's truth.[28]

Democratizing the Bible in the Nineteenth Century

The rapid and immense cultural transformation of the United States in its so-called early national period had many dimensions and causes: the early stages of industrialization and westward expansion, the further penetration into American life of democratic ideas, and not least a large degree of religious experimentation and upheaval, notably but not only that of revival movements like the "Second Great Awakening." How these varied developments would affect Americans' relationship to the Bible would have been difficult to predict at the time of the Revolution. Throughout the West, the longstanding powers of "Throne and Altar" were under new pressures from a rising republicanism and a general revolt against received traditions. In the same skeptical vein as influential writers like Voltaire and David Hume, a number of prominent American patriots took aim at traditional Christian faith. Colonel Ethan Allen, a Revolutionary War hero and one of the founders of Vermont, published an anticlerical treatise promoting *Reason, the Only Oracle of Man* in 1784. Thomas Paine, having attacked monarchy in his famous pro-independence pamphlet *Common Sense*, went on to attack "priestcraft" and what he viewed as the Bible's more odious teachings in three volumes, *The Age of Reason,* published between 1794 and 1807. In the same years, Thomas Jefferson, with the encouragement of such friends of the Revolution as Joseph Priestley and Benjamin Rush, was privately undertaking a radical, rationalistic re-editing of the Gospels. His aim, he would later tell John Adams, was a "euthanasia for Platonic Christianity," the overly elaborate, official faith of the churches.[29] Fashionable opinion of the time was hostile enough to the old faith that the German theologian Friedrich Schleiermacher gave *On Religion,* his landmark 1799 treatise, the subtitle *Speeches to Its Cultured Despisers*—a group he apparently saw as large and influential.

Extreme skepticism, moreover, was not confined to Enlightenment rationalists. The Romantic movement, emerging in these years with its critiques of "pure reason" and vindications of the non-rational, intuitive and historically particular against Enlightenment universalism, quantification, and logic, also confronted religion with unsettling questions: where it originally came from, how any teaching could be universally true, how religious experience was related to feeling as compared to intellect. For Romantic-era philosophers like Immanuel Kant, Samuel Taylor Coleridge, and Thomas Carlyle, the value, if any, of an old book like the Bible was a matter of considerable doubt. By and large, what interested the Romantics was religion as one of many expressions of the human spirit, not traditional, doctrinal faith as delivered through institutional churches and their approved texts.

In a revolutionary age, and with these political and intellectual forces arrayed against it, one would not expect the Bible to gain in stature and influence. Yet as some historians see it, that is essentially what happened. In Michael J. Lee's words, Americans emerged from their years of political revolution "less deferential and more independent" than before, inclined to reject "the authority of tradition, of mediating elites, and of organizations that were perpetual rather than volitional."[30] For a Protestant public, that meant a higher standing for the one source of truth that anyone could consult and no institution seemed to control. "The Bible was the one traditional authority to emerge from the revolutionary period even stronger than before," says McCalla. "This was so because of a uniquely American synthesis of Evangelical Protestantism, political republicanism, and common-sense moral philosophy"—a group of ideas, associated with the Scottish Enlightenment, that held that people relate to the world through an innate faculty of "common sense" that includes reliable moral intuitions. Because this common moral sense "replicated" moral principles known from Christian revelation, it reinforced American Protestants' belief that they could trust their own moral and theological instincts, and therefore did not need the help of "a state church or a privileged class of religious specialists."[31]

According to Mark A. Noll, a leading historian of American Protestantism, what thus emerged from the revolutionary period, and with great force, was a principle he calls "Bible-onlyism." Americans' "post-Revolutionary tide of antiformalism, antitraditionalism, democratization, and decentralization," based on a growing "paranoia about power," produced "a churning sea of demographic, social, and political turmoil," against which the Bible was a kind of anchor:

> Deference to inherited authority of bishops and presbyters was largely gone, obeisance to received creeds was largely gone, willingness to heed the example of the past was largely gone. What remained was the power of intuitive reason, the authority of written documents that the people approved for themselves, and the Bible alone.

Reliance on the Bible could also seem like the democratic way.[32] Scottish Common Sense thinking, merged with Calvinism, led to a broadly shared mode of reading that Noll calls a "Reformed, literal hermeneutic."[33] Believers were encouraged to think that anyone could clearly see what Scripture was saying. Extracting its meanings should therefore be "simple," as many witnesses of the time insisted. There was a "simple original form of Christianity, expressly exhibited on the sacred page," said one; freedom of conscience was underwritten by "the simple truths of the Bible," said another; the "simple" question was "what is the fair and legitimate meaning of the words—a matter-of-fact investigation—no theorising, no speculations," said a third.[34] The leading revivalist Charles Finney, having just left a nascent career in law for the ministry, declared that even as a "novice" he could settle complex theological questions from his own scriptural reading just as he would by consulting a law book. Sarah Grimké, a prominent abolitionist and early feminist, insisted she could "depend solely on the Bible" to establish the equality of the sexes, and could judge the meaning of the text herself without help from the authority of men.[35]

Ironically, then, Americans' detachment from other traditions increased their attachment to an ancient book. As it became a standard companion to private worship, the Bible also resonated publicly, with citations to it regularly featuring in legal and political debates. In all, the effect of what Noll describes as "a broadly based and widely shared biblicism" was nothing less than the "scripturalizing" of the United States:

> Scripture had become the national book par excellence. Confidence in the ability of ordinary people to understand it fueled the formation of many new sects. The revitalization and expansion of Protestantism in the early republic rested upon a widely shared confidence in the trustworthiness of the Bible. Broad familiarity with its contents characterized both ordinary people and elites.[36]

Determined to make that familiarity universal, entrepreneurial souls of the early industrial age set out to mass-produce Bibles on an industrial scale. Hundreds of new editions appeared, some of them printed at low cost by the millions and distributed free, or on penny-a-week payment plans, through "Bible societies" and missionary organizations that aimed to get copies to everyone in the country—not least those out settling the distant frontiers, where the scarcity of religion in both preaching and print was compared to a "famine" and "destitution."[37] Attempts to remedy such conditions were rapidly carrying variants of the Reformed faith to every corner of the expanding nation, and with it went its principal text. One observer during the period, Robert Baird, surveying evangelical churches for a major report on *Religion in America*, identified them all as "churches whose religion is the Bible, the whole Bible, and nothing but the Bible."[38]

If Scripture provided a common frame of reference and was thought to yield to "Common Sense," however, it seemed incapable of getting Americans to settle on common opinions. Perhaps the opposite: Baird's report also found American evangelicals separated into four or five "great families" of church types and at least two dozen distinct denominations.[39] As it always had done for Protestants, relying heavily on the Bible seemed as likely to divide Christians as unite them. Thomas Paine had remarked on this phenomenon in a passage sardonically answering his own critics. Christian preachers and commentators, he said, have disputed and wrangled, and anathematized each other about the supposed meaning of particular parts and passages therein; one has said and insisted that such a passage meant such a thing; another that it meant directly the contrary; and a third, that it meant neither one nor the other, but something different from both; and this they call *understanding* the Bible.

... these pious men, like their predecessors, contend and wrangle, and pretend to *understand* the Bible; each understands it differently, but each understands it best; and they have agreed in nothing but in telling their readers that Thomas Paine understands it not.[40]

Here, of course, was a major reason that Protestantism was so varied and diverse. Having declared independence from a common institutional authority, Protestants found themselves emerging from their Bibles, or their self-guided spiritual quests, with vastly different and often incompatible ideas on virtually every point touching Christian life. Never a single movement, Protestantism had flowed from various points of origin into many streams, among them the Anglican and (in America) Episcopalian; the Lutheran; the Calvinist, Evangelical, and "Reformed," which would eventually include Presbyterians, Puritans or Congregationalists, Baptists, Unitarians, and some Methodists; and the Quaker, Shaker, Anabaptist, Amish, and other movements of the so-called "Radical Reformation," groups that sought to remove themselves even further from the old lines of authority. "High Church" denominations differed sharply from "Low Church," with variations in worship that ranged from elaborate rituals in grand cathedrals to austere "meetings" presided over by clergy in plain clothes, or no clergy at all. As time went on, dissent within Protestant groups often led to new divisions, sometimes featuring opposed groups with names like "Old Lights" and "New Lights," sometimes prompting dissenters to break away and start new denominations of their own.

All these divisions, schisms, and occasional mergers created a religious landscape of bewildering variety and complexity. Religious pluralism had arrived in the country early, simply by virtue of its settlement by different and often competing groups. Already in sparsely populated seventeenth-century America, the low-church Puritans of New England had fought off challenges from the even lower-church Quakers, while one radical separatist, Roger Williams, concluding that Puritanism itself was insufficiently pure, had emigrated from the emigrants to the new colony of Rhode Island, where he founded America's first Baptist church—until he rejected even that limited authority and made himself, in effect, a denomination of one.

The fact of religious diversity in early America meant that social peace would require policies of pluralism and toleration, whether individual churches liked it or not. When a federal government was eventually created, it promptly wrote religious neutrality into its Constitution. States were still free to maintain established churches, but a "disestablishment" movement coinciding with the Second Great Awakening soon abolished these. American churches could not call upon secular authorities to enforce their doctrines, and every church's teaching was implicitly hedged: everyone knew that other churches in the vicinity taught something different. Since conflicting statements of ultimate truth cannot all be true, they inevitably weaken if not discredit each other, as well as the source from which they all claim to be drawn. As skeptics like Paine sneered, "anything may be proved from the Bible."[41]

And as religiously pluralistic as America already was compared to most European countries, the Awakening was about to make it considerably more so. The role of biblical faith in this development was, as usual, complex and double-sided. Revivalism relied on emotional appeals, often in mass meetings, not mainly on the more cerebral activity of Bible-reading—but it also called on people to re-engage with the faith personally, not through rote rituals, and to know and seriously follow God's directions for their lives. That could mean discovering the right reading of the Bible, or being guided to it. But with many, sometimes competing revivals in progress at once, guidance was on offer from many quarters. This variety, says Lee, "accelerated the erosion of traditional religious authority":

> New religious sects proliferated with seemingly endless variety, often led by charismatic figures who claimed a more authentic interpretation of Holy Writ. Americans were increasingly free to choose their religious leaders and, in effect, choose their interpretation of the Bible. Hermeneutical options seemed to grow without limits.[42]

Another historian, Nathan O. Hatch, equating the great movement he calls *The Democratization of American Christianity* with a "splintering of American Protestantism," puts it even more vividly:

> The first third of the nineteenth century experienced a period of religious ferment, chaos, and originality unmatched in American history. Few traditional claims to religious authority could weather such a relentless beating. There were competing claims of old denominations and a host of new ones. Wandering prophets appeared dramatically, and supremely heterodox religious movements gained followings. People veered from one church to another. Religious competitors wrangled unceasingly, traditional clergy and self-appointed preachers foremost in the fray.[43]

Or, in the words of one satirist at the time:

> Ten thousand Reformers like so many moles
> Have plowed all the Bible and cut it [in] holes
> And each has his church at the end of his trace
> Built up as he thinks of the subjects of grace.[44]

As this bit of mockery suggests, "Bible-onlyism's" proliferating sects and freedom for individual readers predictably made biblical belief more difficult. It soon became apparent, says Lee, that "unbridled interpretations were spinning out of control."[45] A Methodist visitor in early Kentucky reported seeing disorder that brought to mind the French Revolution. Revivalist entrepreneurs of religion who were "inclined to a fretful impatience" had broken with established churches, claiming the Bible as their only guide, "but it was, in fact, turning every one foot-loose, as every individual had an equal right to put his own construction." So "they ran wild," succumbing at times to "abominable heresy" and "*soul stupifying creeds.*"[46] A missionary to the Illinois frontier in 1829 likewise found himself "plunged" into a "realm of confusion and religious anarchy"—"a sea of sectarian rivalries" that was "kept in constant agitation," while "ignorant" Christians, divided into "little cliques," listened with admiration to a ranting, ill-trained local minister and his "shower of emptiness and stupidity."[47]

Here was one of the logical conundrums that arose from believing that Scripture's message was simple, or as Hatch identifies Americans' hope, "self-evident." To assume that biblical authority could emerge "from below," from a democracy of independent readers, without help from creeds or theologians who would only get in the way, was to authorize private judgment—and although believers found it hard to accept, "a commitment to private judgment could drive people apart, even as it raised beyond measure their hopes for unity."[48] The truth would thus become more elusive, not less. Independent judgment was not authority but a rejection of it, and setting readers free to find what was self-evident could produce "as many bibles as there are men," as some critics observed.[49]

Noting issues like these, Alexis de Tocqueville's famous report on *Democracy in America*, composed in light of his 1831–2 fact-finding tour, concluded that even the intensely Protestant United States might see a surprising flight back to the unifying hierarchy of Roman Catholicism. Presumably struck by the contrast with the centralized and official religious establishments of Europe, Tocqueville wrote that in "democratic times," people are

> very prone to shake off all religious authority; but if they consent to subject themselves to any authority of this kind, they choose at least that it should be single and uniform. Religious powers not radiating from a common center are naturally repugnant to their minds; and they almost as readily conceive that there should be no religion as that there should be several.

Since it was doubtful that Americans could forever "keep their minds floating at random between liberty and obedience," Tocqueville saw the alternatives as either becoming Catholic again or giving up Christianity altogether.[50]

Although that prediction did not hold up well, Tocqueville was right in supposing that the conditions he observed would strike many as repugnant. Having been "left to adjudicate for themselves what would constitute persuasive proof of biblical truth," says Laurie F. Maffly-Kipp, American Christians of the time faced "a huge problem." The King James Bible "as a religious object was revered and protected in public schools and courthouses," and its influence was enormous—"But what, exactly, was it? And what verifiable evidence did believers have for its authority as a sacred text?"[51]

Attempts to answer questions of this kind generated a large secondary industry in Bible guides and handbooks. Some of these, like Sarah Hall's, simply reviewed the text's contents, as if—in her case, literally—explaining it for children. Others, like Leicester A. Sawyer's 1836 *The Elements of Biblical Interpretation*, took up questions of interpretation and correct modes of reading in a more theoretical vein. Sawyer was a Presbyterian and then Unitarian minister who would later attempt to incorporate the results of biblical criticism into a new Bible translation. *Elements* began from the familiar premise that the Bible is "a supernatural communication of Divine truth":

> This singular book, exceeding all others in the importance and variety of its communications, containing the most ancient and well authenticated history; the most remarkable and undoubted prophecy; the purest morality; and the only rational system of religious worship; is given us by God as the only authoritative rule of faith and practice.[52]

At the same time,

> It is an independent source of knowledge, by which God has undertaken to correct the errors and supply the deficiencies of reason and experience. It is of itself alone, an independent witness, of a character so high, and so entitled to confidence, that it does not need the confirmation of collateral evidence to make its declarations certain, however strange, and singular, and surprising some of them may appear.[53]

While terms like *rational, knowledge, evidence,* and *authenticated* echo the Enlightenment and Common Sense thinking as well as Noll's Reformed, literal hermeneutic, here—as in many of the era's Scriptural apologetics—they are deployed to establish the perfection of this "supernatural" text. The Bible is all things: rational yet surpassing reason, implausible at times yet impossible to doubt, and well authenticated yet not needing "collateral evidence" because it is, "of itself alone," the only witness required for its own claims.

From there, Sawyer goes on to explain that correct biblical interpretation is a "demonstrative science," which like other sciences follows systematic "laws"—yet it goes wrong if overly "Rationalistic," just as it does if overly "Mystic." The text, he asserts, contains "a determinate sense," which ordinary readers are "competent" to grasp "with certainty." Yet the whole premise of his handbook was that this might not spontaneously happen. The Bible may be God's direct address to the faithful, clearly understandable with no help needed from priests or professional theologians. Even so, there was apparently still room for generous quantities of instruction and guidance.[54]

For certain religious dissenters and outsiders, the inability of Christians and their churches to come to agreement was an advantage, an opportunity for vindication. In 1855 Charles Linton, an advocate of Spiritualism—the popular nineteenth-century traffic in mediums, séances, and the spirit world—replied to charges that such pursuits were "unbiblical" by turning the accusation around: What business did the churches have defining this? Their own bitter disputes about what was orthodox cast doubt on all their claims. Noting their radical disagreements over even Christianity's most basic tenets, Linton scoffed that "all the various doctrines of the different religious sects and denominations" were said "to be found in the Bible, however inconsistent or antagonistic they may be." He pointed with amazement to Galatians 3:20, a single brief sentence which alone, he said, had been subject to no fewer than 243 different interpretations. Given "so enormous a discrepancy," unlike anything else in classical literature, it was absurd for the churchmen to try to enforce "truths about which they themselves can not begin to agree!" Yes, the truths of salvation were, in theory, fully contained in Scripture, and perhaps were even left obscure as part of God's design—but "in this conflict of religious opinions it is impossible to ascertain what those truths are."[55]

What that meant, Linton suggested, was no less than this: The apparent ubiquity of Christian faith might itself be a kind of illusion. Probably more people were just giving up, lapsing into deism or infidelity, than anyone could see, least of all their own preachers.[56] As the writer of another *Key to the Bible,* David Dobie, noted at about the same time, "inconsistent methods of interpretation" had "given birth to the proverb, as mischievous as it is untrue":

In the Bible every man his opinion seeks;
In the Bible every man his opinion finds.

Dobie disputed that satirical claim, calling it a "libel on the Bible." Like Sawyer, he set out to vindicate the Bible amid all the interpretive chaos. There was, in the end, a reasonable system of "right interpretation," one that would enable the reader's freedom of judgment yet also "make sure of the sense of the Bible," thus reliably revealing God's will. But Dobie then proceeded to place that system "in the reader's own hands"—a job of painstaking elaboration that required about 300 pages.[57] The supposedly simple messages that many hoped, and claimed, to find in Scripture remained a very difficult thing to pin down.

2

Revivals, Reaction, and the Ultra-Protestants

As paradoxical as it may seem, the growing doubts about the Bible in the early nineteenth century coincided with a remarkable burst of religious energy and enthusiasm, one of the greatest in the history of Christendom. Some find much to admire in the revivalist mass movements collectively known today as the Second Great Awakening: historian Nathan O. Hatch, for instance, credits them as "deeply religious and genuinely democratic at the same time," giving wide scope to "upstarts" who were "radically innovative" in pioneering new, more freewheeling worship and preaching styles, supporting "bold experiments" like Gospel music, and mobilizing new converts through methods whose efficiency reminded one observer of early industrial America's impressive new steam-driven engines. Revivals, says Hatch, were "populist" movements, promising to "exalt those of low estate." In affirming people's right to think for themselves, without "the mediations of an educated elite," they extended into spiritual affairs the broader promise of America's democratic revolution.[1]

To many observers of the time, however, especially leading churchmen invested in conservative standards of churchly decorum, these very qualities made them shocking and scandalous. During the "First" Great Awakening, in the 1740s, Charles Chauncy, minister of the august First Church of Boston, had warned against the new "religious Phrenzy"—the highly emotive "Stir" and "Commotion," including "*violent histeric Fits*" among young women, which he and his colleagues had seen producing

> *strange Effects* upon the *Body*, such as *swooning away* and *falling to the Ground*, where Persons have lain, for a time, speechless and motionless; bitter *Shriekings* and *Screamings*; *Convulsion-like Tremblings* and *Agitations, Strugglings* and *Tumblings*, which, in some Instances, have been attended with Indecencies I shan't mention ... Numbers in a

Congregation, 10, 20, 30, would be in this Condition at a Time; Nay, Hundreds in some Places, to the opening such a *horrible Scene* as can scarce be described in Words.[2]

The new wave of revivals that began in the 1790s also revived reactions like Chauncy's. Thomas S. Hinde, a Methodist whose advocacy of the makeshift format known as the "camp meeting" helped spread evangelical religion on the early frontier, and who favored the movement's tendency toward social leveling, nonetheless deplored the "humiliating exercises of involuntary *dancing, jirking, barking, rolling,* &c." he sometimes saw in "the West" (which in 1819 meant Kentucky).[3] Another critic of what he called *Methodist Error,* John F. Watson, said he had "seen and known several persons who have been exercised with *falling down, jumping up, clapping of hands,* and *screaming,* all in a manner to disturb the whole congregation." Especially disturbing was what was happening to church music. Eerily foreshadowing the early criticisms of rock 'n' roll a century and a half later, the appalled Watson blamed some of the "gross perversions of true religion" he was reporting on the influence of high-energy African American musical styles. Worshipers were moving and dancing in rhythm to repetitive choruses, in ways that mimicked the "husking frolic-method, of the slave blacks; and also very greatly like the Indian dances." Especially worrisome, as it had been for Charles Chauncy, was the jumping and screaming of young, unmarried women: "the most indelicate female attitudes" were strewing temptation before upright men of God. In all, the new-style worshipers made religion "*a business of passion and emotion,*" when it ought to be a matter of thoughtful contemplation, not "mere animal spirits."[4]

From Revivalism to "Ultraism"

Gendered and racialized complaints like these joined a variety of other theories that emerged as both critics and defenders of revivals debated what to make of them. Charles G. Finney, the Presbyterian often called the "father of modern revivalism" and one of the century's most influential preachers, freely admitted that they deliberately played on people's "excitability," but that was God's own way, he argued. Finney called them "new measures," yet nonetheless defended revivals as ancient and time-honored: "Almost all the religion in the world has been produced by revivals."[5] To make religion something that people could viscerally feel, overcoming a "sluggish" faith of mere intellectual assent, was simply recalling its origins—that great, perennial Protestant goal of getting back to basics. True, Finney conceded, the movement had made mistakes, but if the establishment had fully backed it instead of looking to find fault, every sinner would already have been reached, and America would have ushered in the "millennium": the final, thousand-year reign of Christ forecast in the Bible's last book and a major focus of Protestant hopes.[6]

Finney imputed revivalism's excesses to the usual human failings: "It could not be expected that, in an excitement of this extent, among *human beings*, there should be nothing to deplore."[7] Another defender of revivals, looking back later in the century, hinted at something darker—the malign influence of forces beyond the human:

> Revivals, whatever else they are, are profound agitations of human passions. The depravity of man is stirred to its depths, and the wiles of Satan are tasked to use it to the worst. Good and evil, God and Satan, come then into visible and extreme conflict. It is no marvel that in the heat of the excitement, great truths should become entangled with great errors.[8]

Theodore Parker, the prominent abolitionist preacher, saw the problem as more mundane. Also writing some years later, Parker sneered that revivals had devolved into "a business operation" with its own predictable "machinery":

> The means of getting up a revival are as well known as the means for getting up a mechanics' fair, a country muster, a cattle show, or a political convention. They have only to advertise in the newspapers, and say, "The Rev. Mr. Great-talk is to be here to-day. He is exceedingly interesting, and has already converted men by the score or the hundred." Then they hang out their placards at the corners of the streets.[9]

An old-line Lutheran theologian, Philip Schaff, who wrote extensively on American religion after immigrating from Germany, likewise described the problem through analogies to business: "Every theological vagabond and peddler may drive here his bungling trade, without passport or license, and sell his false ware at pleasure." Untrained illiterates, "with all their rant and noise and animal excitement," would mistake the "fantastic soap bubbles of their own poor brain" for divine inspiration. America became "a motley sampler" of "all conceivable religious chimeras and dreams."[10]

Schaff and John W. Nevin, his even more harshly anti-revivalist colleague, were particularly struck by what seemed like America's horrid arrogance. Americans had an astonishing confidence they could somehow find Christ outside a church that exists over time and spiritually develops Christians over lifetimes, not just in isolated fits.[11] They seemed to imagine that their "practical, money loving" country had somehow rekindled the true light of Christianity after eighteen centuries of error, as if the greatest Christians of the past—Anselm and Aquinas, Dante, Petrarch, Leonardo da Vinci,

Francis of Assisi—would do well to take lessons at American seminaries and camp meetings.[12] Nevin criticized American Protestants' faith in "no creed but the Bible" for entrusting interpretation to "the exercises of the single mind": "Every congregation has power to originate a new Christianity for its own use."[13] The claims to a peculiarly "*American* christianity" in effect "puritanized" all Protestant churches, argued Schaff. The resulting "sect-plague" of "numberless popes" threatened to re-enslave Protestants to human authority—not Rome's this time, but that of "private will." Schaff called this dismaying style of religiosity "pseudo-protestant."[14]

A more illuminating term might be borrowed from debates of the time in Britain over church authority and Catholicism. At one extreme in these debates were "ultra-protestants," a group whose "outcry," said the English philosopher Isaac Taylor, was "Oh, the Bible, and the Bible alone; I care nothing for what cannot be proved by texts of scripture."[15] (The term "ultraism" was in regular use at the time for religious extremes.[16]) Taylor scoffed at the idea that "the individual Christian, with his pocket bible in his hand, need fix his eyes upon nothing but the little eddy of his personal emotions." Relying on the Bible in this way, he pointed out, was self-contradictory, since it necessarily meant trusting the judgment of the Church Fathers who had compiled the book in the first place. Christianity was "a religion of history," not just of existential belief, and the Bible could be viewed properly only within the continuity and universality of the church that produced it.[17]

Yet that was precisely what many Protestants denied. Taylor wanted respect for the "ancient" Church Fathers and councils, but the ultras saw this as not going back far enough. Ancient, for them, meant the practices of the first century, as supposedly described in the Bible's own pages. Trusting the text alone and nothing outside it meant searching for a fully authentic church life and organization, which could not be those developed and handed down through existing institutions. Since the sixteenth century, Protestant Reformers had claimed to be casting off Catholic corruptions, but the ultra-protestants believed the Reformation was incomplete. It had not yet reached the *truly* ancient gospel or "primitive church," a pristine original that was still awaiting "restoration."

Here, then, would be explicit goals for a number of movements, not identical to revivalism but overlapping with it, often drawing on the same energies but also at times reacting against it. While radically overturning the conservative institutionalism of establishment churchmen like Chauncy, Watson, and Schaff, the ultra-protestants who called themselves "primitivists" and "restorationists" differed from the liberals we will consider in later chapters in that they remained conservative on the issue of textual authority.[18] Ultra-protestants, that is, were "biblicists" or "scripturalists," although these terms too are sometimes difficult to apply because the meanings given to them in this era varied widely.[19] Regardless, the quite different pursuits in question converged on the common project of vindicating a biblically based faith.

Moreover, while emerging from a revivalist culture, the ultra-protestants did not necessarily favor either revivalists' emotionalism—as one might expect, biblicists were often studious and bookish—nor revivalism's freewheeling, entrepreneurial semi-chaos. While taking advantage of it, their own entrepreneurial projects were addressed in large part to the confusions it was creating. These, it is reasonable to suppose, were widespread. As revivals and organized missions extended the Bible's reach, putting it in the hands of millions, increasing numbers of Christians encountered the problems endemic to biblical faith, problems that had beset Protestant biblicism all along. Spreading a text in crisis more widely also spread the crisis more widely. Three problems in particular, distinct but interconnected, each gave rise to a dramatic new movement in this period. The problems may be summed up as *doubt, disagreement,* and *dullness.* They are logically related in that each builds on the last, and in America they were also related historically: responses to them in the 1820s and 1830s each led to extraordinary re-readings of the biblical text as well as to the founding of new American churches.

Against Doubt: William Miller's Adventism

Doubt was a natural result of the loss of the old biblical certainties. It weighed especially heavily on certain sensitive souls—like William Miller, a farmer in upstate New York and former officer in the War of 1812. In the company of local notables, he encountered the works of such eighteenth-century skeptics as Voltaire, David Hume, Thomas Paine, and Ethan Allen, and at first tried taking guidance from the fashionable Deists. He soon found, though, that skepticism gave him "no assurance of happiness" in the "dim and uncertain" fate beyond death.[20] The worry became all-consuming:

> The more I reasoned, the further I was from demonstration. The more I thought, the more scattered were my conclusions. I tried to stop thinking; but my thoughts would not be controlled. I was truly wretched ... I mourned, but without hope.[21]

In this fretful state, Miller wished for belief in a being as "lovely" as the Christian Savior. But, "I felt that to believe in such a Savior without evidence, would be visionary in the extreme."[22]

Proof would come, Miller decided, if the biblical inconsistencies that critics mocked could all be made to "harmonize." A God who was actually there must be sending some comprehensible message. This message, in classic Protestant fashion, Miller "determined to read and try to understand for myself." In 1816, not long after converting and joining the Baptists, he launched what became a long effort to decode the grand hidden meaning of the Bible.

To insulate himself from the influence of any "traditionary belief" and partisan or "preconceived opinions," Miller set aside all books of commentary, and worked—so he thought—directly with the biblical text. He was "determined to lay aside all my prepossessions, to thoroughly compare Scripture with Scripture, and to pursue its study in a regular and methodical manner." On this basis, Miller read the Bible from start to finish, verse by verse. "Whenever I found anything obscure," he explained, "my practice was to compare it with all collateral passages; and, by the help of Cruden [a standard concordance], I examined all the texts of Scripture in which were found any of the prominent words contained in any obscure portion." Seeming difficulties disappeared as collateral passages were made to harmonize.[23]

According to Miller's early biographer, this program was an attempt "to receive, with child-like simplicity, the natural and obvious meaning of Scripture." In the end, Miller believed he had discovered an entire "system of revealed truths" in fifteen parts, based on fourteen distinct analytical rules and eventually requiring nineteen lectures to develop in full.[24] Such complexity scarcely seems natural and obvious, but Miller explained that his system freed the text's meaning from "all the various figures, metaphors, parables, similitudes, &c." that had left it obscure.[25] Sophisticated exegetes typically answered such puzzles with insubstantial "mists" of spiritualized allegories, whereas Scripture's own "pure light," he was convinced, should be real information about real events.[26]

So it proved, he thought. After about two years, Miller had satisfied himself that the Bible was "indeed a feast of reason," its key message was "so clearly and simply given" that even a "fool" could see it.[27] The central meaning, he concluded, was simply this: Christ would return, ending the world, no later than October 1843.[28]

Fully convinced that the facts and the text's own "plain" rules "constrained" his readings, Miller was surprised when others he showed his calculations to were not instantly impressed. He spent five more years double-checking them, and for years after that kept them largely private, but by 1831 his friends had persuaded him that if he was right, he could no longer avoid his great duty to notify the public.[29] So he began lecturing on his discoveries and then, the following year, publishing them.[30]

The public reactions included widespread ridicule, but also substantial interest leading to a mass movement. As the last dates approached, Miller's equations, diagrams, and schematics—despite their complexity or, perhaps, because of it—turned out to have a populist appeal. His "interpretations were the logical absolute of popular biblicism," persuasive to thousands because they came from "a man whose mind was loaded with historical events" and who knew virtually the whole Bible by heart, says one modern historian.[31] Another points out that the Millerite movement was broader than just those who believed the prediction. With its rootedness in ways of reading the Bible that were themselves seemingly orthodox, it drew followers of widely varying beliefs from across a range of different churches, including some who might not have fully trusted the date-setting but "who simply hung on to the crusade just in case Miller was right."[32] Even after he was proven wrong, Miller's predictions retained a significant following of "Adventists"—as has the whole enterprise of End Times calculation, despite its (obviously) unbroken record of failure.[33]

A self-taught layman, Miller apparently failed to notice that his method had certain incurable flaws. First, of course, was the assumption that the Bible offered a comprehensive history of everything. In an 1842 pamphlet explaining his prediction, Miller assured a hypothetical questioner that the end date could be calculated from Daniel's prophetic vision in the Old Testament, "which embraced all the important events in the world's history, from its commencement down to the end of time."[34] His analytical scheme depended heavily on fitting events that Daniel and other biblical prophets had never heard of into a detailed timeline based on that vision. Miller pursued this effort with unusual mathematical rigor, but it was a premise already familiar to his era's Bible-readers: *of course* the Bible, a compendium of all knowledge that mattered, embraced all of human history. The same goes for Miller's use of various well-established "Year-Day" schemes (a biblical "day" counting as a year), which is what allowed his timeline to stretch all the way across recorded history right up to his own era.

On these points, Miller had the dubious assistance of his Bibles' marginal notes, which in his day included dates and chronologies for the ancient events described in the text. Though presenting themselves as simple factual annotations, many of these dates were just some earlier commentator's best guesses—which means that Miller's faith in them unwittingly belied his determination to set aside all traditions and commentaries. Invisibly present in the materials he took as mere background, prior interpretations were insinuating themselves unbidden into his purportedly direct and unmediated reading.[35]

This was even more true of Miller's use of his "Cruden" and the naïve perception of the Bible it implied. The Cruden biblical concordances, still in use today, treat the Bible as a single textual corpus, listing all the words appearing in it alphabetically and indicating in which books, chapters, and verses each one can be found. The problem with using them as Miller did is not difficult to guess:

> For *raiment,* the psalmist, speaking of the church, says, "She shall be brought to the king in raiment of needlework; her clothing is wrought gold." The angel to the seven churches says, "He that overcometh, the same shall be clothed in white raiment."

Here, by way of demonstrating some point "conclusively," Miller links Psalm 45:14 to Revelation 3:5, because both verses appeared in his Cruden under the word "raiment."[36] Of course, this matchup is an illusion: that word is a particular English translation of the Hebrew phrasing of the one verse and the Greek of the other. Alternative translations come out differently; the scholarly 1978 New International Version, for instance, refers to a princess "in embroidered garments" and a victor "dressed in white." Miller's concordance-based method implicitly imported the linguistic preferences of the translators, and along with these their historical and theological assumptions. Perhaps Miller would have linked these two verses regardless, but hundreds of semantic leaps of this kind, combined with many speculative reasons for assigning certain meanings to words or images—that an Old Testament psalmist was really speaking of the Christian church, for instance—multiply the likely errors toward a final result that will be anything but conclusive.

Far from laying aside all "prepossessions," then, Miller's method unwittingly brought several in its train. It assumed that God had encoded the great hidden message not into the original writings, but into the English Bible most familiar in his time. It also suffered from construing the word "Scripture" in the popular sense, whereby the Bible is received as effectively a single long text. "If you wish to understand" the Bible's writings, said Miller, "you must combine them all in one."[37] In jumping about in it based on word associations, Miller believed he was comparing "Scripture with Scripture" and had found a reassuring redundancy: "the same things are oftentimes revealed again and again." What he was actually seeing were reflections in a hall of mirrors that continually showed him images of his own faulty postulates. Positioning himself about as far as one could from the fact that the biblical writings have their own distinct textual qualities and identities, Miller simply collapsed the whole into the one grand scheme which, he imagined, had been delivered at long last into his own hands in the final days.

Against Disagreement: Alexander Campbell's Primitivism

In some ways Alexander Campbell was Miller's opposite. A religious leader by family tradition, he was a university-educated intellectual and, if anything, all too acutely aware of the importance of examining originals and correctly understanding Greek words. This concern would go the heart of his life's work.

The son of another prominent minister, Thomas Campbell, young Alexander was raised in the Scottish-Presbyterian north of Ireland, where his childhood household was one of intensive Bible reading and memorizing. He recalled seeing his father working in a study that was filled with books, none of which he seemed to have the slightest interest in except for the two on his desk, a Bible and a concordance.[38] Thomas Campbell was a member of the

"Seceders," a faction born of an earlier dispute among Scottish Presbyterians, and he served congregants who at the turn of the nineteenth century were entangled in Ireland's sectarian agitations and political "risings"—a time of secret societies, of churches and ministers caught in the political crossfire, and of widespread worries that success for one side could mean religious persecution of the other.[39]

Following some of his congregants, who had been moving to America to escape these and other troubles, the elder Campbell emigrated as well in 1807 and agreed to minister to Presbyterian settlers on the western Pennsylvania frontier. This environment turned out to be almost as rife with controversy as northern Ireland. Lacking accredited ministers like himself, "the various fragments of religious parties, which, having floated off from the Old World upon the tide of emigration, had been thrown together in the circling eddies of these new settlements" were seldom able to receive Communion. Campbell's solution was to try patching the fragments together, organizing church services to which all the "pious" were invited "without respect to party differences." But doing this meant disregarding "sectarian prejudices" and their "division walls"—a liberality that promptly won him the censure of his Seceder synod and a threat of removal from the ministry.

In defiance, Campbell seceded from the Seceders, setting out to found a new and broader group, an "association" or "society." This would not, he insisted, be a new church or party of its own, but would welcome anyone prepared to treat seriously the old Protestant claim that "the Scriptures alone, without note or comment" were the only rule of faith and practice. This, he hoped, was the effort that would put an end to "partyism" and "induce the different denominations to unite together" under the Bible and its sole authority.[40]

Granting the Bible as the only rule, however, what specifically did it require? Campbell offered this credo: "Where the Scriptures speak, we speak; where these are silent, we are silent." Yet members of his society immediately fell into angry and weeping acrimony over whether this meant that newborns could not receive baptism—the sacramental rite of initiation into Christian life, which the Bible models only for adults—or whether infant baptism was tacitly approved in Christ's famous words, "Suffer little children to come unto me, and forbid them not."[41] The "virulence of the party spirit" in this period was hard to imagine, says Campbell's early biographer; people were so "rigid" and "uncompromising" that any statement or position seemed likely to offend: "the most trivial things would produce a schism, so that old members were known to break off from their congregations, simply because the clerk presumed to give out, before singing, *two* lines of a psalm instead of *one,* as had been the usual custom."[42] At one point Campbell tried to limit the fracturing by stating as policy that verbal discussions would always be friendly, with points of dispute conveyed only in writing.[43]

After studies at the University of Glasgow, 21-year-old Alexander Campbell joined other members of his family in 1809 to follow his father to America. He was soon assisting with and then taking over leadership of Thomas Campbell's projects, including the great effort to "put an end to religious controversy" by reasserting "the great fundamental principle of Protestantism itself": that no one was a heretic who sincerely strove to stay true to Scripture alone.[44] In 1812, again as a family, the Campbells left Presbyterianism and were re-baptized as adults in the Baptist church. Alexander, possibly repenting of a youthful role as an intellectual critic and sometime enforcer of church doctrine, apparently provoked this move, which conflicting reports attributed to his reconsideration of baptism. Regardless, both Alexander and Thomas Campbell came to see several ideas as all of a piece: anti-sectarianism, fidelity to the Bible alone, and baptism as a central issue, one whose divisiveness had previously persuaded them to "let it *slip*."[45]

The Baptists were attractive to Christian primitivists because their very name, from *baptisma* in Greek, referred to first things. Baptism was both the first important milestone in the life of most Christian converts and the first ritual mentioned in the Gospels, the one that began the adult life and ministry even of Jesus Christ himself. Baptist practices were rustic, unembellished, and very "low-church," which not only suited them well to frontier conditions but, making theology of necessity, could also be seen as matching them to the straitened circumstances of the first Christians in the New Testament. Along with this, Baptists claimed an unusually strong commitment to doctrinal freedom, a further attraction for those like the Campbells who associated closely policed creeds with Protestantism's proliferating rifts and "division walls."

Even so, on a number of issues Baptists, too, were at odds not only with other sects but with each other, not least over longstanding questions about baptism itself. In the Gospels, John the Baptist apparently bathes or immerses adult supplicants in the River Jordan. So, was immersion required, as the Campbells came to believe, or was any use of water sufficient, even a sprinkling, as was done with newborns in many Presbyterian and other churches? How could infant or "pedobaptism" be meaningful at all without an informed, adult confession of faith—and did such a confession need to include a detailed account of one's religious experience, or was it better as a simple, one-line statement? What role did baptism play in securing salvation? Did it forgive sins? Did it create a new spiritual state, or ratify one already achieved? Could adults baptized as infants, or in other churches with different teachings, be received as members of Baptist churches? Which congregations could exchange ministers with which others? If Baptists were Christians of the most original type, did that mean that no other churches were valid? Did it mean they could trace an unbroken line of succession back to New Testament times, or was "apostolic succession" of this historical kind a Catholic concept, inapplicable to believers who claimed to take their practices directly from Scripture?[46] Immersed, as it were, in controversies like these during his Baptist years, and having himself renounced membership in his original denomination, Alexander Campbell continued his father's quest for answers to the dismaying and seemingly intractable problem of Christian dissensus.

For Campbell, that problem was closely related to problems of language and text. He worried that despite being the greatest good news that ever was, the Gospel message seemed puzzlingly lacking in power.[47] It should be compelling and uniting: readers should have no trouble not only embracing the message but embracing each other in a fellowship based on it. Yet in reality, Christians continually quarreled over matters large and small. Even when they nominally agreed on doctrinal points, they were apt to fall out over any number of other things, from the hotly contested Adams-Jackson presidential contests to the local arrangements for a wedding or christening. This in turn could make them suspicious of each other's faith commitments, thus encouraging new doctrinal divisions. Somehow the Gospel was not fostering "the bonds of peace and affection" that Campbell thought it obviously should.[48]

In Campbell's analysis, the problem was not that believers were neglecting the biblical text. To the contrary, they tended to respond to the "familiar *sound*" of biblical words, making the text's over-familiarity a problem in itself.[49] That familiar sound, of course, arose from particular translations. Even the King James or "Authorized" Version was, as that term suggested, the handiwork of a particular church establishment with a specific doctrinal agenda. For Campbell, this further meant that too many of those crowd-pleasing phrasings were fossilized bits of dogma, chosen to reflect received doctrine rather than what the original words actually said.

Distortions in meaning, then, were likely already embedded in the text, and proof-texting—the "textuary system"—made them worse. Preachers were too prone to constructing sermons from isolated verses that allegedly proved their specialized creedal arguments. Scripture thus wound up sandwiched between two layers of abstract theorizing, the translators' and the contemporary minister's. As a result, listeners seldom even heard the authentic, broader message, whether that of the biblical book in question, the Gospels, or the Bible as a whole.[50] Instead most of the text was, in effect, discarded—"neutralized" and "rendered absolutely worthless," as Campbell sadly put it.[51]

Compounding these many troubles, the filtering of the text through translations and creeds necessarily relied on inference, which meant "logic and philosophy," whose results the authority of a church then imposed on the ignorant faithful. If what was needed were bonds of affection, an "intellectual operation" like this was exactly the wrong thing. Instead of bringing people together it would guarantee continued subdividing, which had already reached the point of absurdity: "Behold the seven sects of Presbyterians, and the fourteen sects of Baptists!"[52] The creedal theories of the different sects were "*extremes* begotten by each other," which meant that division would forever cause more division.[53] The worrisome implications were, in fact, potentially cosmic. Like many evangelicals, Campbell believed in the millennium, the expected conclusion of history and onset of God's final, perfected reign.[54] For some Christians, millennial hopes might make division a kind of promise: Here would be the moment when God would finally and fully separate those true to the faith, presumably themselves and their own favored group, from everyone else. To Campbell, on the contrary, disunity threatened to postpone the millennium altogether. To complete the great plan of history, "the union of christians, and the destruction of sects, are indispensable prerequisites."[55]

Campbell had eventually taken to lowercasing the word "christian" as a gesture of unity, hoping to nip "in the bud" any possibility that "the name *Christian* will be as much a *sectarian name* as *Lutheran, Methodist,* or *Presbyterian.*"[56] Like his father protesting that a new association was not a "church," he would also deny that his own ideas were "Campbellism," as some called them, or amounted to a new sect or theory of any kind.[57] It was simply sticking to facts, the one sure basis for union: "All christian sects acknowledge the same gospel facts. Every notable fact is so plain and evident from the record, that no one crediting the record can mistake the facts." That record was the "scripture evidence"—the Bible and the "ancient order of things" it conveys from "the primitive saints." This revelation was complete, so the facts were all at hand, and once christians saw them clearly they would not only stop disagreeing but would join in unity to convert and "happify" the whole world.[58]

What this analysis called for was a purification of the sacred text. Like his father, Campbell believed that to overcome partyism, it would be necessary "to begin at the *beginning*," disregarding all previous church teachings "as though they had never been," and return to the "pristine purity and perfection" of that "primitive and simple apostolic gospel" and ancient order that supposedly could be "disentangled" from the corruptions, perversions, conflicting claims, and "controversies of eighteen centuries."[59] The means of this disentangling would be mainly linguistic. Creeds, catechisms, and church decrees are statements, and therefore language. What shocked and offended the scholarly Campbell was the way they borrowed the Bible's language but did not stick to it, instead extracting some words, transposing them, and inserting them into new contexts where they were "confound[ed]" with other words, phrases, and technical terms brought in from outside the sacred text.[60] Such statements were necessarily not God's own expressions but "a human vocabulary of religious words, phrases, and technicalities," which explained why christians could not agree: in positioning themselves somewhere amid the "countless creeds, formularies, liturgies, and books of discipline," the "synodical covenants, conventional articles of belief, and rules of ecclesiastical polity," they were adhering not to God but to other people.

As Campbell acknowledged, it might intuitively seem that believers disagreed anyway, just because people are different and have different views, and that the creeds and church formulas were simply where those disagreements were then formally codified. But no, he argued, that was backwards. "Discords and debates," he wrote, "originated *from* the words which man's wisdom teaches." Agreement, accordingly, would come from recovering the right words: "speaking the same things in the same style, is the only certain way to thinking the same things."[61] Let them "speak and hear the same things, and there would not be a Trinitarian, Arian, Semiarian, Sabellian, Unitarian, Socinian, or anything else but a christian on this subject, or an infidel in the world."[62] This happified state could be achieved if "our wild reveries, our orthodox jargon, or our heterodox paradoxes," theology's technicalities and artificial language of "human contrivance," were expunged, leaving only what Campbell called "sacred diction" and "pure speech," the very "language and dialect of the heavenly Father."[63] Like so many Protestants, Campbell believed that "the Scriptures are to be their own interpreter," and he set out to read them "as though no one had read them before me."[64] Where he radically departed even from other primitivists of a similar mind was in his understanding of concepts like *read, Scriptures, their own,* and *as no one before*. To read Scripture, he thought, one must be looking only at actual Scripture—which meant a kind of infra-text, the real words that were hidden beneath and needed releasing from the bondage of received and familiar language; and to read it for oneself meant putting aside not just the readings of others, the innumerable secondary books and commentaries, but even the very words on the Bible's own page if these, too, were later glosses on the authentic originals.

The university-educated Campbell, however, knew things that the self-taught William Miller did not. He knew very well that the authentic "language of Canaan" he was seeking was not Jacobean English, but Hebrew and Greek. This in itself was not a problem; he even suggested that it might be a good thing, inasmuch as ancient languages, "being dead, have long since ceased to change." They are therefore "immortal conservators" of God's meanings, "fixed and immutable" until the end of time.[65] Still, for a world of English-speakers, clearing away eighteen centuries of accumulated dogma would require scholarly rigor—not just setting commentaries aside, as Miller had meant but failed to do, but choosing words that "would not give one turn to the meaning of an adverb, preposition, or interjection, to aid any sectarian cause in the world."[66] Believers would also need help in defeating the textuary system, which, like Miller's, treated Scripture as a giant quarry of fragmented verses whose interconnecting logic depended on the interpreter rather than the text itself. If each biblical book's design and "special purpose" were acknowledged and explained, readers would be better able to "understand the divine revelations without the aid of priests."[67]

With all that in mind, Campbell borrowed, revised, and wrote new introductions to the recent work of three British translators, and in 1826 published *The Sacred Writings of the Apostles and Evangelists of Jesus Christ, Commonly Styled the New Testament.* Besides correcting some errors and outdated phrasings in the King James Version and modernizing the style (eliminating, for instance, archaisms like "-eth" endings on verbs), this translation differed from conventional Bibles in presenting the text in one rather than two columns, and without verse numbers, thus making verse-based proof-texting harder and encouraging readers to read the biblical books as they would other books, as connected wholes.[68] This new plan therefore "had use for every word the Holy Spirit had spoken," and it would foster, said its proponents, a new, superior method of studying Scripture that "commended the truth to every man's conscience." It would rescue the text from dogma and rote familiarity and make it, as it had originally been, "THE LIVING ORACLES," as Campbell emphasized by adding that title to later editions.[69]

Commercially, Campbell's project succeeded; over the course of several decades, his New Testament would become the bestselling American Bible after the King James.[70] A hymnbook that Campbell helped compile, likewise aimed at cleansing psalms and church songs of unscriptural language, would also continue to appear in many editions and printings. Yet in a culture and market overwhelmingly dominated by the King James Bible, Campbell knew that a new translation would meet resistance, so he prefaced his with an "Apology" justifying many of his changes. Before they judge, he urged, critics "had better read all [George] Campbell's Preliminary Dissertations and Notes, Critical and Explanatory; and particularly his fourth dissertation," as well as "Macknight's disquisitions and criticisms on the minor terms—such as adverbs, prepositions, and conjunctions." Only then could the Living Oracles and the KJV be fairly compared.[71] It seems an unwitting irony that for Campbell, arriving at the simplicity of "pure speech" might require one to wade through dissertations on Greek and disquisitions on adverbs. He also failed to notice that technical concerns of this kind, rather than restoring "bonds of affection" as his project aimed to do, would provide still further occasions for disagreement. But to rely on a sacred book for authority is to obligate oneself to understand it fully, and in this case that meant "critical study of the sacred scripture," which Campbell was forthright enough to embrace. Indeed he held it a virtue, for it would help accomplish his purpose: to "subvert the dominion of the metaphysical theology of the schoolmen, with all its interminable questions, cobweb distinctions, and wars of words."[72]

What Campbell further seemed to miss, though, was the possibility that the schoolmen had been engaged in critical study themselves, and that the interminable questions and wars of words were among the predictable results. Thomas Campbell's dream had been "to form a union upon a basis to which no valid objection could possibly be offered," but the immense difficulty of doing this continued to trouble his son's efforts as it had his own.[73] Even as some congregations, following Alexander Campbell's lead, renounced all creeds but the New Testament and embraced what they took to be the "ancient order," the program suffered the discredit of continued dissension and "inquisitorial scrutiny" as members remained determined to police each other's views. The new "order" was also strikingly disorderly, with religious meetings drowned in unprofitable talk as too many participants tried to take up St. Paul's offer: "Ye may all prophesy, one by one" (I Corinthians 14:31). Campbell was reluctant to accredit a special class of ministers with titles and salaries—he took none himself, having sufficient income from farming—but as he recognized, "In overthrowing clerical power" he would need "to check the tendency to an extreme in the direction of individual independency." To that end, he answered Paul's dictum on prophesying with what he called the "higher" one a few verses earlier, "Let all things be done to edification" (14:26), and he called for strengthening the authority of church elders by paying them. No, this practice was not explicit in the New Testament, he agreed, but it was clearly "hinted" there.[74]

More serious were controversies that went to fundamental points of theology, like the intractable disagreements over baptism. Campbell's New Testament not only did not resolve these but in some ways inflamed them. *"In those days appeared John the Immerser ... immersing in the wilderness, and publishing the immersion of reformation for the remission of sins."*[75] Seeing baptism transliterated as "immersion" in these otherwise famous passages was a defamiliarizing shock that some readers refused to abide, and not only because adult immersion was assumed to rule out infant baptism. Adjacent to the baptism issue were a number of others that had perennially divided the faithful: how conversion and salvation work, the right ways to proselytize, the nature and meaning of the Trinity, the limits of human reason in understanding the divine.[76] Issues like these were not subsumed in small-c christian bonds of affection, and "the pitiful and pigmy efforts to discredit and oppose" Campbell's work continued, with one outraged church elder going so far as to burn a copy of the Living Oracles.[77]

Campbell himself would be kept busy arguing for the rest of his days. A particular sore point was, again, the seemingly simple question of what Gospel primitivists should be called. Campbell may have detested sectarian labels, but many Baptists were fond of theirs, even if they agreed that "immersion" was correct English for the ritual itself. Adopting that word validated their practice, but it seemed to deprive them of their name, which is literally to say, their "denomination"; why were they called "Baptists," then?[78] Moreover, most of them believed they were already following the ancient order. Campbell's own descriptions of "restoration" provoked the question of whether and why it should be needed. Many Baptists were Baptists on the premise that theirs was, in fact, the authentic New Testament church, so what was there to restore?[79] If they seemed to be just one of many "sects," that was only because all the non-Baptists had at various points let the ancient gospel be lost. The "controversies of eighteen centuries" were the corruptions of everyone else. It was a claim that most churches implicitly made: To Campbell, sectarianism looked like a single massive error shared across all groups, but from the standpoint of any one group, it was simply being true to God's commands while rejecting the errors of all the others.

Divided to the point of schism over Campbell's teachings, Baptist churches and associations set out on a long effort to regroup and re-establish their distinctiveness, while in the years around 1830 the Campbellites ceased to be Baptist and reorganized as the "Disciples of Christ."[80] By 1832 they had merged with a parallel movement, also calling itself "Christian," that revivalist Barton W. Stone had been leading toward similar goals since an important early revival at Cane Ridge, Kentucky. Eventually the merged groups came to be known as the "Stone-Campbell" or "Restorationist" movement, and its descendants today are three affiliated churches with names based on those attached to Christians in the New Testament: the "Churches of Christ," "Christian Churches/Churches of Christ," and "Christian Church (Disciples of Christ)." Characteristically, Campbell refused to be called a "founder" of any new group, and was so determined to avoid denominationalism that he refused to attend the merged movement's first national convention, which nonetheless went ahead and made him its president.[81] Regardless, complete unity has never been achieved. The Campbellite churches still differ on some points, including the eligibility of women to preach and the use of instrumental music in church. One disagreement that has interestingly persisted is over this question: Does following the practices of the New Testament mean permitting whatever it does not clearly forbid, or forbidding whatever it does not clearly permit?

Against Dullness: Joseph Smith's Restorationism

Compared to the raging emotionalism of the Second Great Awakening, both Miller's and Campbell's projects come across as remarkably dispassionate. Miller confessed to "delight" at uncovering his coded message, while Campbell hoped his own work would promote "pure christian affection," with christians learning "to appreciate and love one another"—but in both cases, the way to these attenuated emotions was through the intellect.[82] Both exegetes also shrank from stirring up emotions in others. To Miller, who sought the comfort of certainty, God seemed to be saying, *"Fear not, for behold, I have sent thee my schedule,"* but having received this message he was reluctant even to make it public. Campbell, meanwhile, might call his New Testament the "Living" Oracles, but he was a student of dead languages and even believed they served a good purpose, in effect preserving the primitive teachings under glass. As a translator he sought a purely factual text not only impervious to change, but geared toward agreeability and simple acceptance rather than the strong reactions that would set christians to arguing. Intense feeling, as he had seen, often meant powerful disputes, which were exactly what he hoped to prevent. Some believers, he seemed aware, might find his vision of religious life rather chilly and yearn for more, but there were limits to the novelty and excitement a faith could provide when its era of revelation had closed many centuries earlier.

It was this kind of fixity that young Joseph or "Joe" Smith, as the future founder of Mormonism was known, was unwilling to accept. Like Miller, Smith yearned to know that he had a Supreme Being's favor, but he ran athwart a Campbellesque discovery: there was too much disagreement over what the Bible said. Revivals, like one he recalled near his home in New York State's heavily revivalist "Burned-Over District," confused matters further. In "this extraordinary scene of religious feeling," there was much excitement but, he remembered, also an unseemly and disturbing spirit of mutual hostility and denunciation. Churches joined the revivals competing for converts as businesses did for customers, with "priest contending against priest, and convert against convert" in "a strife of words and a contest about opinions" that managed only to discredit them all. Smith, still in his early teens then, found it "impossible for a person young as I was" to decide "who was right and who was wrong."[83] Disagreement, that is, was diabolically feeding doubt.

What most worried Smith, however, was a third problem. Troubled over the state of his soul, and with his mind "wrought up" and "greatly excited," he "wanted to get Religion too, wanted to feel and shout like the rest." Yet, finding no answers amid all the confusion, he "could feel nothing."[84] This problem, he later reported, was solved when, like so many Protestants, he set out to find answers by reading the Bible for himself. Miller and Campbell had done the same, but they had their insights while sitting at their desks. Smith's came in the nearby wilderness, where he went to meditate alone, and in visions, in which, he reported, he experienced the presence of two indescribably glorious "Personages" of "marvelous power." These confirmed to him that all existing sects were in error, that "they teach for doctrines the commandments of men, having a form of godliness, but they deny the power thereof" (a near-quotation of 2 Timothy 3:5). Smith said he felt "seized upon," receiving a "shock that affected the whole body" and pushed "into every feeling of my heart" with a "great force," something that no Scripture passage had ever done. The problem that had been harrowing young Joe, dullness, was banished—as it would be for all, he was certain, when the Gospel was finally "preached in power" again.[85]

For Mormonism, this rhetoric of power, intensity, and irresistible force was foundational. As Brigham Young and other leaders later put it, Latter-day Saints reject "dead" prophets, including the Bible's, in favor of those living among us now.[86] Mormonism's premise is that Joseph Smith was such a living prophet, and in his time, divine power returned to the world—and with it the ancient gifts: "inspiration, revelations, prophecy, angels, visions, healings, &c.," as Campbellite-turned-Mormon Parley Pratt put it; "the gift of tongues, prophecy, revelation, visions, healing, interpretation of tongues &c.," as Smith put it himself.[87] The "&c.'s" are significant: They represent the open-endedness of the Mormon claim, the refusal to allow the revelation to stop, the canon to close, the gifts to be limited by being too fully specified.

Mormonism, then, trained its guns on over-spiritualization, the Platonic disembodiment of faith that had dulled and deadened the message of every other Christian church. The Bible's promises, said Oliver Cowdery, another leading early Mormon, were looked upon as having been given of old to some other people, and as merely "figurative" in the present—in need of "*spiritualizing,* notwithstanding they are as conspicuously plain, and are meant to be understood according to their *literal* reading."[88] For Smith, the over-spiritualizing included the conventional but, he said, false Christian claim that the Father and Son somehow vaguely "dwell in a man's heart." Against this "old sectarian notion," he taught that the Persons of the Godhead were genuinely persons, and have actual bodies that he had directly encountered.[89] Conversely, the faithful have bodies that would not actually die, but simply ascend like some ancient prophets'.[90] In the meantime they would wield divine powers themselves. Newly "strengthened by the power of God," Smith testified, early Mormons "saw visions and prophesied, devils were cast out, and the sick [were] healed by the laying on of hands."[91] Echoes of the Bible's own phrases are obviously intended: what Smith claimed to give his converts was a chance not merely to better understand or model their lives on Scripture, but to enter into it, to *become* the powerful beings they had met on the sacred page. Smith promised them a living and felt reality, unlike traditional faiths that were satisfied with metaphors and mere words. Like him, his people would at last feel they were fully experiencing a "time of great excitement."[92]

Of course, it is widely supposed among non-Mormons that Smith's reports include large measures of fantasy or fabrication. Young Joe allegedly had a checkered history as a "money digger," practicing a dubious and possibly dishonest art that involved hunting for buried treasure with the help of a "seer stone."[93] To "find" the Book of Mormon, inscribed in "Reformed Egyptian" and visible only through mystical "Urim and Thummim," could be explained as a bid for respectability: from buried gold to golden plates, from small-time "divining" to a revelation of the divine. Smith's Mormon defenders downplay his interest in conjuration, divination, magical amulets, and the like, while champions of Smith as a kind of religious artist-genius point to them as aspects of his eclectic brilliance: Here were bold strokes drawn from a palette holding every shade of popular supernaturalism, ancient and modern, Jewish, Christian, pagan, gnostic, and Masonic.[94] In any case, from the standpoint of overcoming dullness, Smith's youthful and mature careers were of a piece. Magical rituals are appropriations of spiritual power by other means, attempts to infuse life and animation into the otherwise inert. When Smith graduated from everyday superstition to Mormonism's creative collage of Jewish and Christian motifs, it was a movement "upmarket" but still with the same aims.

In light of Smith's freewheeling, seemingly *ad hoc* approach to religion-founding, it is all the more noteworthy that Mormonism relies as heavily as it does on the authority of texts—and especially on the borrowed authority of the biblical text. As a schoolboy, Smith had probably encountered a history of the War of 1812 written in a *faux*-Jacobean biblical or "ancient historical style," an early effort on the part of patriotic writers to celebrate America's wartime exploits by making them sound like Scripture.[95] It is likely that Smith was following their lead, producing a "translation" of "Reformed Egyptian" that mimicked the phrasings and rhythms most familiar to Bible-readers of his time. Either God Almighty spoke, through Smith, in the seventeenth-century English of King James I, or Smith believed that his followers would suppose as much and would receive such phrasings as more suitably godlike. The Book of Mormon, published under Smith's name in 1830, reflects this linguistic peculiarity throughout. Numerous verses, sometimes in close succession, begin with "yea" or "And it came to pass," include many redundancies ("there were beasts in the forests of every kind, both the cow, and the ox, and the ass, and the horse, and the goat, and the wild goat, and all manner of wild animals ..."), and proceed to mix familiar biblical themes—chosen peoples, captivity, wanderings, smitings, scatterings, great and marvelous works, wars and rumors of wars, a journey to a "Land of Promise"—with ideas apparently drawn from early nineteenth-century anthropological speculations about pre-Columbian America.[96] The notion that America's indigenous tribes might be remnants of the "lost tribes" of the Old Testament was a popular theory of their origins, at least two centuries old by Smith's time, known to the broader public from other works that have been identified as likely further inspirations for the Book of Mormon, notably an 1823 book titled *View of the Hebrews*.[97]

Conveniently, the basic Mormon premise that God was still speaking through prophets and Bible-writers in the present allowed Smith to claim authority for whatever position he hoped to advance at a given moment. For instance, at one point he found that his advocacy of "plural marriage"—that is, multiple wives, in the manner of the Old Testament patriarchs—was running into opposition from some of his followers, especially those who found their own wives on the list of Smith's divinely betrothed. Even Smith's own wife, Emma Hale Smith, was unsurprisingly resisting it. Smith responded by bringing forth new, legitimating prophecies, including one directly targeted at Emma, warning that "she shall be destroyed" if she refuses to "cleave" to Joseph.[98] These crude threats, along with Smith's other prophecies, maintained the practice of semantic cribbing from the KJV, and officially remain part of the Mormon scriptural canon today.

If Mormonism's themes and phrasings, however, were unoriginal by design, the theological and textual project they announced was a striking innovation. The shared project of primitivists was to cut through the religious confusions of their times, peeling away the obscurities of centuries that churches, creeds, and theological systems had wrought, and thus to reconnect with the core of the faith at its original source. For those who supposed that the best route back was to read the Bible anew, apart from received teachings, the lost core might be a message, or a language: the unified meaning of the whole, as for Miller, or a unifying "pure speech," as for Campbell. For Smith it would be the scripture-making power itself, the prophetic energies that were the Bible's own original wellspring. Others might *read* Scripture for themselves; he would do nothing less than *write* it for himself, and continue writing and revising it thereafter. The new "revelations" would include his prophetic pronouncements and those of his successors, but also a collection of newly presented sacred texts, which would modify while basically reaffirming those that Christians already knew perhaps too well. Indeed they would have the same sounds and rhythms as familiar Bibles (and eventually, the same chapter-and-verse structure and double-column printed format), and the angels, prophets, and estimable ancient figures that readers now met in them for the first time would confirm and continue the stories of the great prophets and apostles of old.

The Book of Mormon was thus, at the same time, both startlingly new and reassuringly traditional. Here were new, living prophecies, but written down and safely bound between hard covers like any other religious book. Soon it would be overseen by new "apostles," as Mormon officials are called, and a new "priesthood"—or a new-old priesthood, allegedly traceable back to the Old Testament figures of Aaron and Melchizedek—along with a full panoply of rites, symbols, liturgies, vestments, and impressive temples. At the same time, besides the Jacobean locutions, the simple and even naïve quality of Smith's sacred prose probably helped authenticate it for believers as genuinely primitive. During the long centuries of the supposed "Great Apostasy," which had seen the world given over to a new Babel of confounding sects and a "great and abominable" church of the Devil (1 Nephi 13), the all-too-available public Scriptures had suffered untold sophisticated corruptions. The Book of Mormon, though, was a scripture that had miraculously escaped, pristinely inscribed in gold in a lost language, and safely hidden for many generations on a remote American hillside.

America, furthermore, was at the heart of the story this lost gospel told—a deeply flattering fact for American Christians. Even more than the patriotic *faux* bibles he likely read in his youth, Smith had found a way to incorporate America into the great and ancient Judeo-Christian epic. He could reassure his followers that the New World was indeed included in the old sacred chronology after all, had preserved and now produced a Bible of its own, and had even hosted a late post-Resurrection appearance of the Savior (3 Nephi 11). Americans had long been inclined to see themselves as a chosen people, a latter-day analogue of ancient Israel, but always at one remove because America was not known of old. The Mormon revelation filled that gap. It was in and through America that the Gospel would be restored, the world proselytized and saved for Christ, and the old Bible's "New Jerusalem" brought to earth—perhaps in Missouri—at the end of time.[99] America not only had a role in sacred history, it had the climactic and, perhaps, most glorious role of all.

If all that seems audacious enough, Smith was just getting started. Soon to follow would be several further projects in textual invention. One of these was his "Inspired Version" or "Joseph Smith Translation" (JST) of the King James Bible itself. Early in the Book of Mormon, an angel had revealed "that there are many plain and precious things taken away from the Book" as it "hath gone forth through the hands of the great and abominable church."[100] Unfinished at the time of Smith's death, the JST would rectify this through Smith's prophetic insight, repairing hundreds of passages through more than 3,400 additions, deletions, and rephrasings to bring the KJV into line with Mormon doctrine.[101]

Another textual adventure was "The Book of Abraham," newly uncovered writings of the biblical Abraham and Joseph, which Smith claimed to have translated from Egyptian papyri that he bought (along with a collection of mummies) from a traveling showman in 1835. For a time believed lost in the Chicago fire of 1871, the papyri were partly rediscovered in the 1960s and are now known to be ordinary funerary texts, unconnected to anything in the Bible.[102] In Smith's hands, though, they became testaments to various new teachings, notably the pre-existence of souls before their earthly lives and the plurality of gods, an idea helpful to Smith at a time when he was assigning his followers to various stations in the afterlife, including godhood, depending on their obedience to him. Abraham 1:26-27 later supported the notorious "Negro Doctrine," a long-held policy of racial discrimination within the LDS church, which echoed the old racist readings of the "mark of Cain" and "curse of Ham" in Genesis 4 and 9—as well as the Book of Mormon's association of a "skin of blackness" with idleness and mischief (2 Nephi 5:21-24) and its promise (2 Nephi 30:6) of "a white and a delightsome people." (A 1981 revision replaced *white* with *pure*.)

Claims like these have since put the LDS church on the defensive. In 1978 it announced a new prophecy undoing the Negro Doctrine, and in 2013 it changed its official description of the Book of Abraham: instead of a "translation from some Egyptian papyri," it is now "an inspired translation" that Smith made "after obtaining some Egyptian papyri."[103] About one-third of the Inspired Version's textual emendations were eventually attached as notes and appendices to Mormon editions of the King James Bible, though the canonical text remains the KJV itself, and the JST is avoided for use in Mormon missions out of fear that it could put off potential converts.[104] One commentator has complained that Smith's corrections were so widely neglected as to be "essentially lost," treated for a long time as best discussed only where "the blinds would be drawn and the door would be locked."[105] That it must still struggle for acceptance irritates some Mormons; one asks why there is less enthusiasm for verses newly recovered through Joseph Smith than for other lost texts like the Dead Sea Scrolls, while a onetime dean at Brigham Young University argued that it is "backwards" to "want to test Joseph Smith" by checking whether ancient manuscripts support his textual changes. Instead, Smith's own prophetic authority should be the standard against which the Bible itself is tested.[106] It offended the dean that even some of Smith's own adherents still hesitate over his basic premise: that he was hearing directly from God, just like—but more recently and freshly than—the prophets and "revelators" of old.[107]

A final and, perhaps, fatal venture of Smith's was his attempt to inaugurate a Mormon "Kingdom of God" under his own kingship, encompassing initially all of the Americas and ultimately the whole earth. Alongside this effort, he announced a run for the U.S. presidency in 1844.[108] Smith had meant to provide his followers with "a time of great excitement," and his final year was certainly full of excitements, including the mob attack in which he was killed. After that, the Mormons would sojourn to the Great Salt Lake, where they would build a temple to rival King Solomon's while founding a desert community that became the state of Utah. Like Moses, though, Smith was denied the chance to reach this new promised land himself. Having threatened his wife's destruction over the issue of plural marriage, or "spiritual wifery" as it was scoffingly called, he was himself destroyed in part because of local conflicts arising from that same issue.[109] While his gift for such grand planning never left him, Smith found himself something of a victim of his own success. Having originated in his private visions, the Mormon movement had taken on a life and institutional gravity of its own. Smith was confronted not only with the fears it provoked in others, but with the fact that in wanting to feel deeply, to restore and re-activate the ancient power of religion-making, he had unleashed powers that were beyond his control.

Institutional Successes, Conceptual Failures

Similar points can be made about all the American ultra-protestants. Miller, Smith, and Campbell did not endorse each other's work; Campbell, for instance, wrote one of the first sustained critiques of Mormonism.[110] What they have in common, though, is that all three gathered substantial followings, with churches descended from each of the three movements still operating with relative vigor today—yet also, in their different ways, all failed in their original goals. Each found itself re-enacting the very problems of textual authority it had set out to solve.

Beset by doubt, William Miller had sought proof that God existed and the Bible's message was true. The ironic result was one of the most dramatic disproofs in religious history. Miller had also hoped that reducing the Bible to a single system would pierce through its "mysteries" and "obscurities." What it actually did was create new mysteries and obscurities, like the notion that his final revised date, October 22, 1844, marked a hidden occurrence in the "second apartment" of an unseen "cosmic sanctuary," the claim of today's Seventh-day Adventists.[111] In his last years, Miller found himself at odds with new teachings put forward precisely in order to rescue his own, while another Millerite remnant, the Jehovah's Witnesses, arose to continue the age-old Christian enterprise of trying to calculate end dates, propounding several over the decades that came and went no more eventfully than Miller's. Miller had baffled himself with arbitrary word associations that were artifacts of his own method. Intended to pierce through obscurities, that method made the interpreter an obscurantist himself.

For Alexander Campbell the goal was to defeat disagreement, ending sectarian divisions and bringing lowercased "christians" together as one. The fact that his movement produced enduring new denominations was therefore a Pyrrhic victory. Campbell found himself embroiled in controversies throughout his career, including some that were brought on precisely by his efforts to end controversy. Given what a close student he was of the New Testament and the ancient, primitive church, it is surprising how unaware he seemed to be that dispute was a feature of Christianity from the start, setting its earliest figures—Peter, James, and Paul; "Hebrew" and the "Grecian" disciples; preachers of "other" and "different" gospels—at odds with each other.[112] Many New Testament epistles were written to address disagreements within the first congregations. There was never a "christian" unity of the kind that Campbell imagined. Nor is there any Christian text that precedes and is free of the doctrines of some church or "party." The books that make up the canon had to be chosen for it, and given what we now know about the vast range of excluded and noncanonical writings, those choices themselves were an instance of history being written by the winners. The New Testament text is already an assertion of contested beliefs, the outcome of many arguments involving ancient churches and Catholic councils, even before anyone reads, translates, or argues over a single line.

Moreover, having taken what the Scottish Common Sense philosophy held up as a scientific interest in Scripture's plain facts, Campbellism then further divided over what to do as scientific inquiries into the biblical text advanced. Is historical criticism, with its ever more sophisticated insights into ancient Greek and Middle Eastern sources and contexts, true to Campbell's own spirit? Is it also revealing plain facts, albeit through somewhat specialized methods? Or, as some argued, is its very sophistication a threat to the simple believer's direct, unmediated access to the sacred words? Campbell's successors were also chased in circles by logic of the "all Cretans are liars" variety: Is the Campbellite slogan "no creed but Christ" not a creed in itself? Is "opposition to the introduction of opinions," one Campbellite writer asked in 1916, not "based on opinion merely?"[113] At odds over such riddling questions, the Disciples of Christ underwent schism, the very thing that Campbell had labored to overcome. A movement launched in opposition to "partyism" and "factionists" became, in the end, another group of factions contesting each other's claims to the Bible's meaning.

In one sense, Joseph Smith's remarkable solution to the problem of textual authority worked extremely well. Mormonism spread, survived, and seemingly thrives in the present, fixing its place in American life while aggressively pursuing converts abroad. Smith's original aims, however, were never quite achieved and in some crucial ways were negated. Rather than break free of the dulling weight of church institutions and canons, his efforts had the effect of reinventing them. When Robert Matthews insists that Smith's insights should "test" and "measure" existing Scriptures, not the other way around, he is conceding their failure to become their own canon—an ancient Greek term for a measuring standard. Smith himself fell victim in part to resistance from within the church he himself had founded, whose growing power eventually overwhelmed his ability to command it even in the name of God. As he continued to issue new and more startling prophecies, his followers had to choose between the revelator and the revelation to which they had already signed on.

The LDS community also gradually lost its appetite for the contentious, extra-legal existence it had struggled through while Smith was alive. After emigrating from what was then the United States, it evolved into a businesslike going concern, asked to re-enter the Union as a new state, and accepted the condition of renouncing plural marriage. Having acquired a vast portfolio of commercial and real-estate investments, the Mormon Church today is in many respects another gray-suited corporate establishment. Members of its ruling Quorum of the Twelve Apostles are officially still "prophets, seers, and revelators" like Joseph Smith, but their occasional pronouncements do little to generate public excitement. To the contrary, Mormons are widely seen as sober, clean-living and reliable, and their institution as a pillar of social and political conservatism. Having spent their early years fighting with state and U.S. authorities, today they make a point of professing a patriotism so strong that it extends to suggesting that America's Founding and Constitution were nothing less than divinely inspired themselves.

As to the Book of Mormon, in recent years it has itself come under the kind of critical scrutiny long familiar in biblical studies. A "Critical Text Project" has been at work comparing editions and manuscripts, much as Erasmus and the early Reformers did for the Bible.[114] Inevitably, such efforts tend to raise the same troubling questions as biblical criticism. Some contemporary Mormons express doubts about the Book of Mormon's authenticity; others continue to honor the book, but issue the familiar Protestant demand for new freedom in interpreting it.[115] Still others answer that demand by denouncing such freedom as "revisionist legerdemain."[116] The upshot is that Mormonism, like modern, liberalizing Christianity, has in recent times produced its own fundamentalists—which is to say, a movement is now underway to restore a faith that was, itself, meant to restore an earlier faith.[117] The conservative tilt in Mormonism prompts some Latter-day Saints to try to reform it anew, while others treat it, like any establishment, as a sanctuary for resistance to change.

Miller and Campbell were both focused on retrieving the biblical text's true meaning, and Smith on finding and appropriating its original power. Broadly, these are the two great responses to doubts about the Bible's authority, and we will see further examples ahead. But all three ultra-protestants worked from basic misunderstandings. Miller and Campbell assumed that Scripture spoke with a single voice. Smith believed he could add his own voice and that the text was still subject to change, but like Campbell, he overlooked certain features of social psychology. Campbell supposed that disagreement is text-induced, ignoring the possibility that it is endemic to human communities, with arguments over texts merely one of its many manifestations. Smith assumed that a new church could maintain its originating enthusiasms over the long haul. More likely, any institution that lasts will do so in part by settling again into dull routines. Latter-day Saints gathered today are often hard to distinguish from any old-line, conventional Protestants.

But the ironic, partly self-canceling outcomes of all three ultra-protestant projects are also results of a conundrum enfolded in Protestant biblicism all along. To reject the authority of the late-medieval Catholic Church and its bishops, and instead advert to the Bible, was in effect to embrace the authority of earlier bishops—those under whose aegis the Bible had been compiled. Scripture was, among other things, a charter of the Catholic Church, its contents and claims to sacredness matters of church doctrine themselves, not an independent way around it. It has never had any existence separable from the authority of institutions, past if not present, implied if not expressed. Furthermore, it is a collection of writings, and anything conveyed at length in language is subject to wrong or conflicting interpretations.

The faulty but shared premise of the ultra-protestants was that the spiritual seeker could evade these problems, could receive the Word without error straight from the written text. An exegete's labors might be needed briefly—Miller's to disclose the text's occluded meaning, Campbell's to undo its creedal distortions, and Smith's to correct and supplement it with the further words not yet received—but from then on the faithful would know God at first hand. Going back to the original source would obviate disputes and misunderstandings, eliminating the need for further interpretations or ensuring they would all converge, or in Smith's case putting further questions into the hands of a new, authoritative "priesthood." The mystifications and dogmas, the divisiveness and the dull, rote rituals would at last be purged even from Protestantism, which for its first three centuries had seemed to be multiplying rather than dispelling them.

Even faith might not really be needed, if by that we mean, in the New Testament's famous phrase, "the evidence of things not seen" (Heb. 11:1). On the page, they would be seen. Cleared of doctrinal debris, the Word would prove to be a matter of simple facts and obvious meanings, readily available to any unschooled reader. Making it so would therefore check the "erosion of biblical certainty" that Michael J. Lee sees as having spread among Protestants, often in similarly ironic ways, since the early eighteenth century.[118] In their efforts to resist that erosion, the ultra-protestants might qualify as "conservative biblicists," as long as we recall, again, that their claims were also shockingly radical, not just theologically but also socially. What Nathan O. Hatch says of the Campbellites could apply to them all: their efforts involved "dethroning hierarchy and static religious forms" and calling for "common folk to read the New Testament as if mortal man had never seen it before," a democracy of interpretation "without any mediation from creeds, theologians, or clergymen not of their own choosing." This "exhilarating" hope was piously conservative but, at the same time, anti-traditional and highly unorthodox.[119]

Meanwhile, growing awareness of historical criticism was beginning to make the question of textual faithfulness itself exceedingly difficult. However "biblicist" they may have been, the ultra-protestants were largely indifferent to many features of the Bible's text, especially its internal multiplicity. Smith saw that to look like the old Bible, the Book of Mormon would need internal "books" named after prophets and sometimes numbered 1, 2, and 3, but otherwise, Miller, Campbell, and even Smith treated the received canon as essentially a single writing. "Bible-believing" Protestants have continued looking to it for instructions pertinent to the world today, often without regard to the different materials' origins or contexts. On that point, the ultra-protestants were as devoutly traditional as any conventional expositor or churchman. Primitivists may have thought the Bible's antiquity important, but only insofar as it reinforced the authority of the message, not as a condition affecting what that message was or whether there even was one of any current use.

Just as paradoxically, where intense biblicism meant ignoring the biblicial books as books, some of the more skeptical approaches called for the closest possible attention to them. The very different assumption behind the "higher" criticism was that ancient texts, including the Bible's, were written by ancient authors for ancient, not modern, readers on different occasions and probably for quite varied purposes, often quite alien to any issues in our world today. Even to know what "the text" basically was required painstaking research to reconstruct those occasions and purposes. From the late eighteenth century on, says the biblical scholar James Barr, it was becoming clear that "one main effect of historical study was to break down the conception of the religion as one great system of truths and beliefs, more or less perpetually so existing, and introduce essential distinctions between successive layers of material."[120] The text of interest to most historical scholars was not the canonized writing as such but its underlying components. That meant not just the separate books, but their prior traditions and sources, the ancient "redactions" or editing decisions that gradually molded these into the books we have, and hence the long evolution over time of the religious ideas they contained. Only considerable parsing, says Barr, would end up "enabling the text itself to be heard" apart from received tradition.[121] Obviously, "liberal" assumptions like these broke sharply from the pieties of received faith, as conservatives of all kinds instantly saw and are still in some quarters decrying to this day.

Yet in another sense, historical-critical approaches were a primitivism to outdo the primitivists—a deep search for the actual events, statements, and social conditions that first gave rise to the faith and the texts conveying it, even before it had taken shape as the faith we now know. A quest of this kind had two key implications. First, it suggested that there might be ways to reconnect not just with an "ancient church," but with something even more profoundly original: the creative force driving religion in the first place, the spiritual energies that animated the cosmos itself. Such a project might vaguely resemble Joseph Smith's but be even grander, and need not be limited by the traditional Jewish and Christian ideas and iconography on which Mormonism still heavily relied. Second, its results might well include new bibles—again, not necessarily as studiedly "biblical" as the Book of Mormon, perhaps not resembling the canonical Bible at all, but writings that would do for America and the modern world what the Bible had once done for other societies, giving brilliant expression to their deepest needs and aspirations. Perhaps these new bibles would be, or inaugurate, an entirely new literature. For many at the time, that was something a new nation like America badly needed.

3

Scriptures as Sepulchres: Unitarians and Transcendentalists

In formulating the answers they did to the crisis of the text, the ultra-protestants were all, in their different ways, deeply unorthodox. All three projects—William Miller's intricate interpretive schemas, Alexander Campbell's reduction of New Testament language to a supposedly unarguable "pure speech," and obviously Joseph Smith's claim to prophesy like the Bible's original writers—were self-authorizing, carried out apart from the structures, and with little regard for the doctrines, of any organized church. To the extent they eventually had institutional settings, these were the new churches that the projects themselves helped create. "Traditionary" belief, as the ultra-protestants put it, was by and large seen as the seedbed of doubt, disagreement and dullness, part of the problem to be solved, and their solutions were expressions of frustration about this and impatience with the Christian authorities of their time—combined with a radical, yet quintessentially Protestant, insistence that important spiritual breakthroughs might well be found through the single believer's lone heroic efforts.

At the same time, Miller, Campbell, and Smith all worked within the terms and retained many of the core elements of long-established Christian faith and practice. Not least of these was the concept of "Scripture" itself, which if anything became even more central to their thinking than it already was in Protestant thought in general. Adventism, Primitivism, and Mormonism all presumed a basically traditional, very high status for the Bible and its picture of an all-powerful God who organized and intervenes in human history. Miller further surmised that this collection of writings offered a map—or timeline—of God's intentions. Campbell believed that a text pried loose from doctrinal additions would be God's own language, a window onto an original and ideal church. Smith, for all his dramatic innovations, kept the old scriptures, and whatever the boldness of his "Inspired Version," it was based on Christian apologists' standard claim that biblical errors were later corruptions. God might still be speaking through prophets today, but in the same familiar, antique English.

In other words, though institutional conservatives viewed them as ludicrous, outrageous, or both, such answers to the crisis of the biblical text were still, in their way, "conservative." In this, they contrasted with another class of responses—very different from but, in some interesting ways, also parallel to the ultra-protestants'—that have been known both then and since as "liberal." Nineteenth-century liberals included Unitarians but also some Presbyterians and even occasional Baptists. What they shared was a willingness to break with traditional orthodoxy over various issues, not least the nature of the Bible itself.

Put simply, the liberal view was newly skeptical, but within bounds that its proponents, though often not its critics, would still argue for calling "Christian." Where the old orthodoxies had been "authority-based," says Gary Dorrien in his detailed history of this movement, liberal Christianity appealed to "the authority of critical rationality and religious experience." In doing this, it was attempting "to create a modernist Christian third way between a regnant orthodoxy and an ascending 'infidelism'" associated with the French Revolution. The liberal goal was to reconcile religion with "modern knowledge and experience," moving churches to embrace "the best parts of the Enlightenment legacy, especially its ethical humanism and its emphasis on the liberating value of reason."

By way of at least partial replacements for the old authorities, theological liberals would emphasize "imagination and the metaphorical nature of religious language."[1] Largely accepting the results of the newly developing textual criticism, they acknowledged that the Scriptures were a collection of ancient books, amenable to analysis in essentially the same ways as any others. They assumed that God not only allowed but expected believers to bring to them their powers of reasoning. Doing this, however, would also require readers to recognize that not only many traditional church teachings, but some of the contents of the Bible itself, were products of historical circumstances and even of the idiosyncracies of their authors. Though the Scriptures broadly cohered around certain key themes, there was no single message that infused itself into every verse; indeed some verses and books contradicted or even corrected others. Above all, the New Testament heavily amended the Old, undercutting Old Testament authority to an extent that neither the churches' traditionalists nor the ultra-protestants were prepared to concede.

Hence the disturbing question with which liberals found themselves confronted: "Can Christianity claim to be religiously true if the Bible contains myths and historical errors?"[2] Traditionalists might deny that such a question existed, while at the other extreme, "infidels"—a group generally, if not altogether fairly, seen as including militant skeptics like Thomas Paine—might dismiss it with the simple answer that received religion was a giant fraud. In their search for a third way, liberals faced the more complex problem of trying to reconcile apparent error with essential truth, of finding whatever there was of spiritual value that the Bible could still be seen as reliably teaching. With worries of their own over the crisis of the text, they too were looking to retrieve some usable spiritual core from beneath the dead weight of centuries of institutional and doctrinal malpractice.

For some, what emerged from these efforts was the view that Scripture was still a uniquely valuable resource, full of moral wisdom and the best guide to God's will and plan and the means of salvation. However, one had to separate the wheat from the chaff: particular stories and teachings had to be rationally assessed, not assumed to be correct, let alone edifying, simply because they were in the Bible. It was not clear that there even was a single story that embraced all of humankind. Different cultures had different religious traditions and, thus, their own very different stories, and many of these deserved at least some degree of respect as well. Moreover, while America would continue to loom large, even—in some ways, especially—in liberal thinking, it would not necessarily sit at the apex of a single providential history. Whatever story the Bible did tell was not necessarily continuous, a single arc reaching through subsequent history toward a cosmic fulfillment, let alone one that would centrally feature the United States.

Nor was there any such thing as biblical pure speech, whether conveyed in King James' English or even in Hebrew and Greek. Modern biblical criticism had begun as an effort to correct the text, in the seemingly simple sense of carefully comparing ancient sources to reconstruct the actual words that the first authors had written down on the page—the contents, that is, of the Bible's original or "autograph" manuscripts, all of which were lost in antiquity. That effort resembled Alexander Campbell's, but by the early nineteenth century it was becoming difficult to see how it could ever produce a pristine original, let alone one that avoided the need for interpretation or that settled any serious disputes. To the contrary, this enterprise of textual or "lower" criticism had raised the many new questions that led to historical, or "higher" criticism—a whole, vast arena for further debate—while also opening onto difficult philosophical issues of language, truth, narrative, and meaning.

All these problems seemed certain to frustrate any effort to achieve agreement, let alone certainty, through anything received in speech or writing. Even if the original manuscripts somehow suddenly reappeared, the most important questions would still be unanswered, and Christians would in all likelihood just keep on arguing. Liberals, however, were generally more comfortable than biblicists with uncertainty, dissensus, and change. This perhaps is why, though they loom large in American religious history, liberal efforts were less likely to birth entirely new churches. Instead they helped relocate some of the functions of churches to other institutions and social practices, expanding the range of experiences considered "religious" and redefining sacred scripture itself.

Unitarianism: The Break with Creeds and the Assertion of Reason

A Christianity meant to incorporate Enlightenment reason would necessarily be directed against unreason—which, however, could mean several things. Most obviously, it would set itself in contrast to what appeared even to the liberal-minded as the crazed emotionalism of revivals, the *"Tremblings* and *Agitations"* and *"jirking, barking, rolling,* &c.," that Charles Chauncy and other observers complained of in the thick of both the First and Second Great Awakenings.[3] The more overpowering and immediate the experience, the less it seems to point to a faith that has been thought through.

But reason might also be thwarted through being overly respectful and not immediate enough. This was the danger, warned Jonathan Mayhew in 1748, when ideas or practices were justified on grounds of tradition:

> There is nothing more foolish and superstitious than a veneration for *ancient* creeds and doctrines, *as such,* and nothing more unworthy a reasonable creature than to value *principles* by their *age,* as some do their *wines.* But indeed this is as common as it is ridiculous. With many people, "Antiquity! Antiquity!" is the cry, and, "Who will be so hardy as to dispute the truth of what was believed a thousand years ago?" just as if what was false formerly were not so still, but might be ripened and refined by age into *a doctrine of grace.*[4]

As Mayhew suggested, antiquity was likely to exert its unreasoning influence through "creeds and doctrines." These were especially deadly since they rolled many errors into one. Mayhew's harshest criticism was aimed at what he called "tyranny" and "slavery" over the conscience, the handiwork of "ecclesiastics," whom he denounced as the "spiritual tyrants and lordly bigots of the earth ... those vain conceited men who set themselves up for the oracles of truth and the standard of orthodoxy, and then call their neighbours hard names." With their doctrinal rigidity over "trifles" and "indifferent things," the arrogant and authoritarian ecclesiastics took advantage of "the ignorant and assuming, the enthusiastic and superstitious," preying upon the emotions of the unthinking faithful—thus "fomenting a furious party spirit and exciting ignorant bigots to rail at sober peaceable Christians."

Churchly creeds, in this view, were an abuse of power, and one that both divided Christianity and drove people away from it. They were intellectualizations that, perversely, also produced the unwelcome emotions, not only substituting for one's own reason but also replacing it with "angry debates" and "mutual rage." In so doing, they supported the tyranny of those who wanted to shout reason down by way of serving their own power.[5]

Unfortunately (as the liberals saw it), these dynamics had been in play for a very long time; the creedalists' "novel inventions" dated back to the Church Fathers themselves, who were already busy in the early Christian centuries "coining new articles of faith, new modes and rites of worship, making new canons, and prescribing new rules for the regulation of the church." These were all departures from "scripture orthodoxy," of which early liberals like Mayhew claimed to be defenders. For Mayhew, "Christian teachers in after ages are (or at least ought to be) only *commentators* upon the scriptures, and we cannot suppose their *commentaries* have greater weight and authority than the *text* itself."[6] As Dorrien explains, however, even while championing reasoned interpretation, "Chauncy and Mayhew were careful to emphasize the scriptural basis of their thinking and took for granted the canonical form of the biblical text and the traditional view of scripture as revelation."[7] Early liberals would continue insisting that theirs was the true textual orthodoxy—a stance they would frequently need in their own defense, as the spreading of their ideas through the old Puritan Congregationalist churches of New England, and their takeover of Harvard College around the turn of the nineteenth century, would inevitably bring them under sometimes fierce attack.

An early example of such a defense was William Ellery Channing's landmark 1819 Baltimore Sermon, a founding manifesto of "Unitarianism"—a term coined by critics, but embraced as the official name for a leading liberal movement. "We are particularly accused of making an unwarrantable use of reason in the interpretation of Scripture," Channing began. "We are said to exalt reason above revelation, to prefer our own wisdom to God's." However:

> Our leading principle in interpreting Scripture is this, that the Bible is a book written for men, in the language of men, and that its meaning is to be sought in the same manner as that of other books. We believe that God, when he speaks to the human race, conforms, if we may so say, to the established rules of speaking and writing. How else would the Scriptures avail us more, than if communicated in an unknown tongue?

Reason is called for, Channing argued, because of the Bible's complexity: "It has infinite connexions and dependences. Every proposition is linked with others, and is to be compared with others; that its full and precise import may be understood." He clearly did not mean William Miller-type word associations, but a judicious weighing of meanings: some statements are only "of temporary and local application," not universal truths. But that fact itself reflects God's care and concern. "A wise teacher discovers his wisdom in adapting himself to the capacities of his pupils," not perplexing and distressing them, and the Scriptures were meant to teach.[8]

Since those capacities had developed over time, moreover, the "records of God's successive revelations" were also necessarily timebound. Recognizing the biblical authors' human, historical limitations, and seeking the Bible's meaning "in the same manner as that of other books," does not diminish it but is, in fact, the best way of defending its "divine authority" against "the almost endless errors, which have darkened theology." In fact, though written in ordinary human language, the Bible for that very reason demands interpretation, because ordinary words do not have "a single sense" but take their meanings from context, from "the purposes, feelings, circumstances, and principles of the writer," and from what is known from other sources about the subjects to which they refer—an important caveat, because it will lead a reasonable reader "to restrain and modify" the Bible's language in light of truths known from "observation and experience." Indeed the Bible "demands a more frequent exercise of reason" and "more continual exercise of judgment" than any other book. Some errors arise from not applying reason, but others from a kind of reason run amok:

> None reason more frequently than those from whom we differ. It is astonishing what a fabric they rear from a few slight hints about the fall of our first parents; and how ingeniously they extract, from detached passages, mysterious doctrines about the divine nature. We do not blame them for reasoning so abundantly, but for violating the fundamental rules of reasoning, for sacrificing the plain to the obscure, and the general strain of Scripture to a scanty number of insulated texts.

Channing alluded here to two doctrines that Unitarians rejected, Original Sin and the Trinity. Theological errors like these, he suggested, arose from the prior error of faulty reading—of not understanding what kinds of texts the Bible gives us, what approaches they call for, and what kinds of meanings can be expected from them.

Having established these textual postulates, Channing spent much of the Baltimore Sermon critiquing the errors themselves, the wrong conclusions that follow from those misunderstandings. In addition to the Trinity, or the teaching that God is three "Persons" in one (as opposed to the Unity that gave Unitarians their name), the other "mysterious doctrines" of Calvinist orthodoxy that Unitarians objected to included two in particular: the divinity of Christ, and the saving nature of his death as an "Atonement" for Original Sin—the fundamental human flaw and "fallenness" of the cosmos supposedly passed down from Adam and Eve's disobedience in eating forbidden fruit. Such teachings were not just "unscriptural and absurd" but bad for people's character, denying them the guidance they could gain from seeing moral perfection in terms they could recognize. God was not distant or vengeful but "Parental," like a good father who wished the best for his children and would help them to achieve it.

The Bible's true purpose, then, was to provide that help. "We look upon this world as a place of education," said Channing, which it cannot be under the orthodox doctrine that all, even children, are innately depraved. The Gospel is valuable "chiefly as it abounds in effectual aids, motives, excitements to a generous and divine virtue," providing "the means of purifying the mind, of changing it into the likeness of [God's] celestial excellence." God's goal for us is not mere piety, let alone obedience to authorities, but what Channing variously referred to as "true holiness," the "benevolent virtues," and "practical piety." Terms like "benevolent" and "practical," along with "philanthropic," would continue to appear frequently in the works of liberal Christians, as would an emphasis like Channing's on moral development and improvement over time, both in biblical history writ large and in the lives of individual Christians.

Above all, Channing insisted that Unitarianism was not an effort to replace wrong doctrines with better doctrines of its own. Instead it was opposed to doctrines altogether. Its goal was to put an end to "the habit of denouncing and condemning other denominations," to curtail the power of religious tyrants to set ordinary believers in one church against those in others. Because "on no subject have men, and even good men, ingrafted so many strange conceits, wild theories, and fictions of fancy, as on religion," Channing called for the reverse, an ethos of charity and forebearance. Like other idealistic liberals, he hoped that mutual tolerance was possible, even if the protracted "pamphlet wars" his sermon touched off would soon suggest otherwise.[9] But more than that, he thought he was describing a kind of default state, an obvious and original unity that Christianity could naturally reassume once the dead weight of doctrinal authority was lifted.

Also characteristically Protestant was Channing's belief that this uncomplicated, less contentious Christianity was readily available from Scripture, if everyone would just look at what was actually there on the page. The doctrines that he and other Unitarians rejected, he charged, came from efforts "to abuse and confound language," to read common words in other than their "usual sense" and outside the "universal language of men," and to invent new "phraseology" that could not be found in any "plain, direct passage." For instance, some verses speak of Jesus as human and some as divine, and so a strange and difficult new doctrine is invented—the dual nature of Christ—that imposes "an enormous tax on human credulity." It was ironic that the effort to reconcile difficult passages in the text would lead some to "invent an hypothesis vastly more difficult, and involving gross absurdity. We are to find our way out of a labyrinth, by a clue which conducts us into mazes infinitely more inextricable."

Thus the "false philosophy" that comes from relying on creeds was not just offensive to common sense, but self-defeating. Supposedly aimed at "the harmony of the Scriptures," it instead made a mystery of them. Like other textual restorers, Channing claimed to reject later human additions in favor of the biblical text itself, to clear away mystery so as to reveal its "simple truth." There was a common meaning that did make for harmony—"the general strain of Scripture," as he repeatedly called it—but it was forever being overread and overwrritten.[10]

Many years later, Channing wrote a widely circulated "Letter on Creeds" that put the point more harshly. What are creeds? he asked. "Skeletons, freezing abstractions, metaphysical expressions of unintelligible dogmas"—again, though, in sharp contrast to Scripture itself. If we turn to the New Testament we can hear Jesus directly, no longer drowned out by the shouting voices of "the creed-makers" and "creed-monger."[11] The "skeletons" were the remains of dead and deadening elaborations and controversies, not the ancient writings as such, and the "freezing" was an early but still correctible wrong turn. It was not, he insisted, an inevitable result of staking one's faith on written texts. For mainstream Unitarians the Bible remained the solution, not part of the problem.

Transcendentalists: The Break with Scripture and Assertion of the Higher Reason

By the time of Channing's "Letter on Creeds," however, a further movement had been launched, one that would suggest that to separate Scripture from church doctrine was to draw the line in the wrong place. Transcendentalism was and would lead to many things, including major developments in American literature, but it began as a rupture within Unitarianism—a recognition on the part of some liberal Christians that a restorationist logic like Channing's could be taken still further: it need not necessarily stop with reading the Bible unfiltered through dogma, but might call into question all attempts to get spiritual truth from books.

When liberal Christianity first took shape in the late eighteenth century, some of the freethinking "infidels" it defined itself against had already been making this point. Even Thomas Paine—who said he had no church but his own mind, and who was unsparing in his attacks on the Bible's "horrid," "bungling," and "foolishly told" tales featuring "detestable villains" like Moses—presented himself as merely trying to recover "the true theology," to clear away the "redundancies" that religion of any kind piled atop the true "*canonical book.*"[12] That book was "the scripture called the Creation," the "real word of God existing in the universe," which outshone "a printed book that any man might make."[13] It was not doctrinal additions but biblical faith as such that replaced godly deism with "man-ism," the worship of an "opaque" human redeemer figure, making even Christianity "a species of atheism; a sort of religious denial of God."[14] While not going that far, Paine's fellow radical Joseph Priestley, who helped bring Unitarianism to the new United States after fleeing political reprisals in England, believed that dogmatic corruptions had been infiltrating the biblical text itself almost from the start. Hence, restoring the "original scheme" of a "pure Christianity" that had nearly been lost to history would require something more drastic than just reading Scripture's plain words. The words themselves would first need their intended meanings restored, and to that end Priestley urged a program of "continually improving translation," together with "conjectural" revisions that would make the actual Bible, in effect, finally available to a world that had not really ever had a chance to see it yet.[15]

To the Unitarians' detractors, approaches like Priestly's and Channing's served only to drain the Bible of whatever higher authority it still had. An early opponent of Priestley's conjectural criticism said it would encourage infidelity, producing "an irreverence for the Divine oracles" and even giving "some colour" to "Popery," the Catholic view that interpreting Scripture was best left to a centralized church.[16] Moses Stuart, a leading theologian and professor of sacred literature at Andover Seminary—founded in response to Harvard's Unitarian turn—also warned of such a drift. Responding at length to Channing's Baltimore Sermon, he worried that its interpretive methods would lead "eventually to the conclusion that the Bible is not of divine origin, and does not oblige us to belief or obedience." The next generation would be liable to see it as no different from any other religious or moral text.[17]

The drift of Channing's own later thought seemed to bear this out. Though he continued to affirm the importance of Scripture, he increasingly came to emphasize more direct routes to spiritual truth, while detaching faith from anything transmissible in writing. Eventually his "Letter on Creeds" would argue that Christianity "cannot be comprehended in a set of precise ideas. It is to be felt rather than described," an experience to which words can offer only "brief, rude hints." Words are a poor medium that spiritual impressions "overflow."[18] This was not to endorse revival-style emotionalism: "Religion is something different from strong feelings," Channing cautioned, and is not acquired in a single ecstatic moment of conversion. The notion of "overflow," rather, was a theory of how feelings inform the mind. Although he did not take this idea as far as the Transcendentalists would, in his last years Channing called on the Christian minister to speak "from his own soul" in a way "true to his inward thoughts," warned that borrowing words from others would "cloud the intellectual eye," and professed appreciation for any "transcendental, philanthropic, or religious" enthusiasm that countered the "worldliness" of an era "engulfed in matter and business."[19] In his late works, Channing sounded like someone who had been reading the early works of Ralph Waldo Emerson.

Hence the revolutionary next step was not a very long one. Arguably it was the step that Emerson took in 1832 when, resigning from the ministry after just three and a half years, he launched his long career as a philosopher, critic, and public intellectual. The way had been prepared, however, over the decades in which Western intellectual and artistic circles had increasingly come under the influence of the Romantic movement. Transcendentalism's debts to European Romantic and idealist philosophies have been well chronicled, but what is not often emphasized is that those movements were themselves expressions of a crisis over religion in general and biblical authority in particular. With its new stress on art, nature, feeling, intuition, and "genius," Romantic thinking sought access to the higher things of the spirit, direct routes that would bypass the impediments of tradition, institutional authority, and received beliefs. Accordingly, in their wide-ranging philosophical writings, two of the founding figures of Romanticism and German Idealism, Baruch Spinoza and Immanuel Kant, brought new scrutiny to the Bible, pioneering ideas and methods that would become the higher criticism.[20]

As noted earlier, Scottish "Common Sense" philosophy had held that certain axioms, including basic moral ideas, are part of an inborn sense "common" to all. Romanticism would take a similar premise much further. To the Romantic philosophers, *Reason*—a word they often capitalized—had come to mean something more like intuition, "a faculty of spiritual insight." Unlike what is usually called "reason" today, which in Romantic terms was the mere "understanding" that arose from conventional analysis of facts, Reason offered a powerful route of access to higher realities in general. It was the "organ of the Supersensuous," said one of its early American expositors, James Marsh—a "mind's eye" designed for inward perception of "moral and spiritual truths," much as the physical eyes and other organs of "outward sense" perceive material objects.[21] Reason could serve in this way because, Romantic philosophers believed, nature, human nature, and the divine are similarly structured; each "corresponds" with and supports the others.

America's younger theologians and divinity students were absorbing this "new thought," as they called it, from a variety of sources, including in some cases first-hand travel and study abroad. After leaving the ministry, Emerson toured Europe, meeting several of the most prominent English Romantics, and beginning a long correspondence with one of them, Thomas Carlyle. The influence of another, Samuel Taylor Coleridge, had been spreading in America since his writings began to appear in Marsh's annotated editions in 1829. "The key work was Coleridge's *Aids to Reflection,* which convinced a host of American transcendentalists and Bushnellians that religion belongs to the faculty of imagination," says Gary Dorrien.[22] ("Bushnellians" were followers of Horace Bushnell, whose work will be further discussed in chapter 4.) Marsh, the president of the University of Vermont and a Congregationalist minister, introduced and explained Coleridge in the hope that Romantic redefinitions of reason might reconcile Unitarian rational analysis with both orthodox faith and the emotionalism of revivals.

Unsurprisingly, this was not easy to do; in the judgment of one modern critic, Marsh's efforts were an exercise in strategic ambiguity.[23] If spiritual truth could be readily perceived through a "mind's eye," and if human nature was already structured in accord with divinity—instead of "fallen" and at war with it—then it was not clear what institutional churches, or even revealed religion as such, could contribute to spiritual insight. Their doctrines and even their scriptures would likely be less a help than a hindrance, further thickets of received authority standing in the way of direct spiritual perception. Emerson was one of a new generation of liberals taking note of this problem; in his private journal in 1833, he wrote that traditional Christianity, "the popular faith of many millions," was full of "errors" that obscured "the divine beauty of moral truth." To fixate on its "dry, lifeless, unsightly" doctrines and dogmas "is strange, is pitiful"; it is to make "a fuss about the case & never open it to see the jewel." He was "pledged," he said, to try to demonstrate "that no doctrine of God need appeal to a book."[24]

To that end, he helped organize what would become one of the most famous discussion groups in American history. While the Transcendentalist movement is easy to remember today as an epochal event in American literature and thought, it began much more modestly, and originally in response to concerns that are much less familiar to secular twenty-first-century readers. The movement's founders were mostly younger Unitarian ministers, in their twenties and early thirties, who had already been meeting— but in the overly restrictive confines of the church's regular ministerial conferences. Barbara L. Packer, whose history of Transcendentalism does note this connection, explains that these official gatherings

> were increasingly irksome to the younger clergy, who were reluctant to raise subjects their seniors disapproved of yet who felt frustrated at not being able to discuss freely the moral and theological issues that concerned them ... Why was such [a new] association necessary? Because the "lamentable want of courage" shown at regular conventions of Unitarian ministers and the diffidence of younger ministers in the presence of their "elders & betters" made candid discussion of theological issues impossible.[25]

In the view of one historian looking back from fifty years later, there was a "crust that was beginning to form on the chilly current of liberal theology."[26] The young Rev. Emerson, having closely analyzed the relevant

Gospel texts, had resigned from his parish when he found he could not reconcile them with a central feature of church liturgy, Communion or "the Lord's Supper." Thus he could not carry out his duties.[27] George Ripley, another founding member—like Emerson, not yet 34—who hosted the new group's first meeting, was also a Unitarian minister who would resign within a few years. Having embraced the new thought, he would then found the Brook Farm commune in hopes of proving that it could remake society altogether.

In short, the impetus for what would later be known as "the Transcendental Club" came from the shared professional concerns of a group of dissident junior clergymen. Their gathering in hopes of a "free discussion of theological & moral subjects" was not billed as "Transcendentalist"—that term came from a reviewer of *Nature,* Emerson's first major treatise—but at first was just "the Symposium" (or, in a joking reference to its members' propensity to disagree, "the brotherhood of the Like-Minded"). Members also referred to themselves as the "New School" or "Disciples of Newness."[28] Over the course of the club's thirty or so meetings, scriptural and church-specific matters were frequent topics, with the last two spent considering "the organization of a new church."[29]

The group's more radical potential nonetheless came into public view early. Emerson's *Nature* appeared in September 1836, the same month that the Symposium first met. *Nature* was not an overt attack on either churches or Scripture, but it could easily leave a reader wondering what value those old authorities could possibly still have. It was possible, Emerson wrote, to see nature and God "face to face" and "enjoy an original relation to the universe." Past generations had done so, but the present was relying on the history of their revelations, building only "the sepulchres of the fathers." It was failing to produce "a poetry and philosophy of insight and not of tradition, and a religion by revelation to us." Rather than "demand our own works and laws and worship," the current generation was inclined to "grope among the dry bones of the past."[30]

Much of the rest of Emerson's short book was an argument that setting the old aside and receiving revelation anew was not just necessary but feasible. Nature would support the effort because it was also a wellspring of values: "The laws of moral nature answer to those of matter as face to face in a glass ... every natural process is a version of a moral sentence." Hence, "All things with which we deal, preach to us. What is a farm"—with its great variety of natural processes—"but a mute gospel?" Spiritual truth was a (capitalized) "Unity" that "Reason" enabled human beings to see in everything, including themselves. Religions were founded by people who could see that in every way, nature

> shall hint or thunder to man the laws of right and wrong, and echo the Ten Commandments. Therefore is nature ever the ally of Religion: lends

all her pomp and riches to the religious sentiment. Prophet and priest, David, Isaiah, Jesus, have drawn deeply from this source.

The point, however, was not to learn what such founding figures had seen, but to see *as* they had seen. As normally practiced, religion and ethics devalued the boundlessly changing material world, assigning true reality only to the unseen and eternal. This was to "put nature under foot."[31]

Emerson devoted one section of *Nature* to "Language." This was a matter of continuing interest for liberal theologians confronting the loss of the old biblical certitudes. Scripture was composed of words, and if these were not simply transparent windows onto truth, literally God's own handwriting, then what were they? How does language work, and what is it capable of conveying? Emerson's theory tied language to "visible things," images and analogies based on "natural facts" that are also symbols of spiritual facts. Corrupting that original link perverts meaning and produces "rotten diction," but when it is tightly fastened, language has power: "good writing and brilliant discourse are perpetual allegories." Words can "break, chop, and impoverish" the central Unity, but they begin as poetry—and "not the dreams of a few poets, here and there, but man is an analogist, and studies relations in all objects." Here were several recurring Transcendentalist themes: that what matters spiritually is profoundly original insight and expression, that these come not from churches or preachers but from "poets," and that the true poet is not the mere scribbler of verse but anyone who channels the universal Spirit to speak in profoundly original ways. Emerson's analysis echoed the Unitarian attack on creeds, but generalized it to apply beyond religious doctrine to all human expression on virtually any subject.[32]

With arguments like these, the "Disciples of Newness" were setting themselves against old authorities, implicitly including the Bible. A few weeks after *Nature* appeared, George Ripley made the point explicit. In an article aimed at other Unitarians, Ripley affirmed that even the Gospels must be submitted to "unreserved" rational analysis, then judged on their "intrinsic evidence and merits," with a willingness to discard whatever proved to be an "absurdity." The freedom actually to do this, however, had never yet been experienced:

> The Reformers emancipated the Bible from Catholic theology, but it was only to enslave it to their own. With all their boasting, not a book exists of which Protestants are so much afraid as the Bible. Hence, they take care to keep it surrounded with a whole atmosphere of commentary, invisible in itself, but coloring everything.

Like other Transcendentalists, Ripley believed that the truth of religious claims was known through an innate, inward sense, a "light of the soul," which "is of a kindred nature with the light of the spiritual sun." This meant that Christian belief did not depend on external "evidence"; the doctrine of Christ "bore its own evidence on its face."[33]

Liberal though Unitarians aimed to be, claims like these went too far for many of them. Andrews Norton, an influential figure in the faith and former professor of sacred literature at Harvard, charged that views like Ripley's were seriously wrong. In their subsequent exchange—another "pamphlet war"—Norton would emerge as one of Transcendentalism's leading early critics. To undermine Scripture as the Transcendentalists did was "vitally injurious to the cause of religion, because tending to destroy faith in the only evidence on which the truth of Christianity *as a revelation* must ultimately rest."[34] This was textual evidence, which Norton would go on to publish in three large volumes.[35] Ripley counter-replied at length, bemused at the "ludicrous" picture of two liberals trading what amounted to charges of heresy, but reiterating that the proof of Christianity was its coincidence with "our spiritual nature," not "evidence" of the kind to which Norton referred. Norton, he said, had it backwards: "The evidence of miracles depends on a previous belief in Christianity, rather than the evidence of Christianity on a previous belief in miracles."[36]

Looking back at the "Miracles Controversy," as this debate came to be known, it seems paradoxical to find a staid figure like Norton defending the miraculous, while Ripley and his fellow visionaries seemed to downplay it. This was so, however, because what was really at issue was the biblical text. How essential was the book through which Christianity was typically received? The miracles that Norton promoted were those known from ancient written reports in the Bible. But if one supposed, with the Transcendentalists, that religion was not something to be acquired from ancient books, then whether the New Testament miracles really happened or not was beside the point. Like other Romantics, the Transcendentalists favored a much more expansive notion of *miracle*, one that would reinstate miracles in the midst of present-day life: "The invariable mark of wisdom is to see the miraculous in the common," Emerson had written in *Nature*.[37] Over the next two years, in two of his most famous addresses, he would explain that this necessarily meant looking for miracles close to home, in present-day America.

Emerson on Books, America, and the New Teacher

Though arising in part from concerns about Scripture and ritual of special interest to Christian ministers, early Transcendentalism implied and drew much of its energy from a powerful sense of broader social disquiet. In *Nature*, Emerson had suggested as much with his laments for a generation left to grope among the dry bones of the past. Invited on two occasions to speak at his *alma mater,* Harvard, Emerson took the opportunity to spell out what he meant for the benefit of America's rising leaders—new ministers and other young men at the start of careers that would position them to turn the new thought into treatment for the ills of a suffering nation.

"The American Scholar," Emerson's 1837 address to Harvard's chapter of the Phi Beta Kappa honor society, is most famous for its calls for original American thinking. "We have listened too long to the courtly muses of Europe," Emerson declaimed, but now at last, "Our day of dependence, our long apprenticeship to the learning of other lands, draws to a close." In accounting for "the sluggard intellect of this continent," Emerson blamed various bad influences—fashion, avarice, reclusiveness, faintness of heart, the narrowness and drudgery of labor endemic to a society run on business principles and devoted to "exertions of mechanical skill"—but one of his major antagonists was the written word. Much of the address, with its vivid evocation of "Man Thinking," was a classic in the Transcendentalist genre of polemics against books. There is such a thing as a book with real power, as Emerson found on occasions when he was "warped by its attraction clean out of my own orbit," but mostly, books dull the intellect and spirit and are obstructions in the way of "the active soul."[38] They capture "pure thought" only inefficiently and perishably, and they give rise to "a grave mischief":

> The sacredness which attaches to the act of creation, the act of thought, is instantly transferred to the record. The poet chanting was felt to be a divine man. Henceforth the chant is divine also. ... The sluggish and perverted mind of the multitude, always slow to open to the incursions of Reason, having once so opened, having once received this book, stands upon it, and makes an outcry if it is disparaged. Colleges are built on it. ...
>
> ... The book, the college, the school of art, the institution of any kind, stop with some past utterance of genius. This is good, say they,—let us hold by this. They pin me down. They look backward and not forward. But genius always looks forward.

To his bookish young audience, Emerson criticized "the bookworm" and "the book-learned class, who value books, as such." He urged them to turn their vision of themselves right-side-up: "Meek young men grow up in libraries, believing it their duty to accept the views which Cicero, which Locke, which Bacon, have given; forgetful that Cicero, Locke and Bacon were only young men in libraries when they wrote these books."[39]

In laying claim to their own intellectual authority, moreover, Emerson's listeners would enable and model what America had to do in asserting its own cultural authority. Here, more clearly than in *Nature,* Emerson articulated a key premise that Transcendentalism would bring to the effort to create a distinctive American culture:

> I ask not for the great, the remote, the romantic; what is doing in Italy or Arabia; what is Greek art, or Provençal minstrelsy; I embrace the common, I explore and sit at the feet of the familiar, the low. Give me insight into to-day, and you may have the antique and future worlds.

Rhetorically asking, "What would we really know the meaning of?", Emerson offered a sampling of things familiar and low: "The meal in the firkin; the milk in the pan; the ballad in the street; the news of the boat; the glance of the eye; the form and the gait of the body." If these are explained in terms of spiritual causes and eternal laws, and everyday utilities like "the shop, the plow, and the ledger [are] referred to the like cause by which light undulates and poets sing," then "the world lies no longer a dull miscellany and lumber-room, but has form and order," reflecting the great cosmic design.[40] It went without saying that America, a young and still developing nation, could not furnish the ancient or faraway or the high achievements of the past—but it had plenty of shops and plows and ledgers.

The following year, Emerson would further extend and deepen his social critique, making explicit what it means to reduce a society to a spiritless, meaningless "lumber-room." His 1838 address to the graduating class of Harvard's Divinity School was a catalog of complaints about the dire state of the culture. Among the problems that Emerson listed were doubt, dullness, and "dogma," the same anxieties we have seen motivating the work of the ultra-protestants. Emerson did leave out disagreement, which, after all, his controversial address was courting, but he went on to name dozens more: degradation, depreciation, distortion, deformity, docility, defectiveness, disconsolation, dreariness, decay; coldness, corruption, conformity; ignorance, indolence, imitation, inactivity, injustice; falsehood, fraud, the finite, and a "hollow, dry, creaking formality." Very little was going right in what Emerson summed up as "these desponding days."[41]

That recondite phrase apparently alluded to the "Slough of Despond," an image made famous in John Bunyan's classic Protestant parable *The Pilgrim's Progress* of 1678. Rare today, *desponding* seems to have entered general use thanks to *Pilgrim's Progress*, but gradually disappeared over the course of the liberalizing and secularizing nineteenth century.[42] If there is a reason that Emerson chose it over the more common "despairing" as his general term for the sorry state of things, it may be that "desponding" is despairing in a particularly Protestant Reformed way. It is not a simple emotion, but an activity of the soul, an echo of the old Calvinist doctrine that sinners are simultaneously doing things—making free choices—yet (without God's grace) helpless, and suffering in their helplessness. Thus it is, all at once, an individual feeling, a failing action, and a reflection of the personal soul's submergence in the fallen state, the human condition in its entirety. Passed along to a post-Calvinist like Emerson, it lost some of those meanings, but still touched both the failures and the unearned miseries of individuals while gathering them in and raising them to a larger, collective scale: "desponding days," a condition from which the whole society was suffering.

According to Emerson, much of the blame for this dismal situation—essentially, a crisis of spirit—lay with religion. For his audience of young aspiring ministers, the task ahead would be to address the failures of what Emerson called "historical Christianity" from within their expected roles in Christian institutions. Having failed to square that circle in his own early ministry, Emerson suggested that the solution was to recover and reapply at first hand the authority from which religion originally comes, the "laws of the soul" that are "the essence of all religion." These are the laws of the cosmic order itself, a great resource of "astonishment and power," but they "refuse to be adequately stated. They will not be written out on paper, or spoken by the tongue." Historical Christianity fails for the same reason as "all attempts to communicate religion." It takes Jesus, "whose name is not so much written as ploughed into the history of this world," and petrifies him into a "traditionary and limited" figure surrounded by "official titles": "The idioms of his language, and the figures of his rhetoric, have usurped the place of his truth; and churches are not built on his principles, but on his tropes."[43]

The spiritual crisis of the times, then, owed much to a network of obstacles that separated people from the true experience of religion—one of which, Emerson strongly hinted, was the Bible itself. "Men have come to speak of the revelation as somewhat long ago given and done, as if God were dead," he complained, and therefore they found themselves not "conversing with God" but awaiting a "new revelation." To take guidance from any past prophet—even St. Paul, the writer at the core of the New Testament—was to rely on a "secondary form" and thus "get wide from God." For most people, "Miracles, prophecy, poetry; the ideal life, the holy life, exist as ancient history merely; they are not in the belief, nor in the aspiration of society; but, when suggested, seem ridiculous." People assume "that the age of inspiration is past, that the Bible is closed." This loss of the "true Christianity,—a faith like Christ's in the infinitude of man," was the greatest possible calamity for a nation, because it meant that "all things go to decay. Genius leaves the temple, to haunt the senate, or the market. Literature becomes frivolous."[44]

The great task was to put miracles, prophecy, and the other higher things back into "the aspiration of society," the range of goals and experiences that people actually took seriously, as against the "near-sighted" and "comic or pitiful" pursuits that marked the desponding reality. A minister must learn to speak as "a newborn bard of the Holy Ghost," acquainting his own listeners "at first hand with Deity"—just as the writers of the Bible and the figures depicted in it, including Jesus, had done: "It is the office of a true teacher to show us that God is, not was; that He speaketh, not spake." This effort, however, should not involve inventing new doctrines or rituals, which would be "pasteboard and fillagree, and ending to-morrow in madness and murder." Instead, the old forms needed "the breath of new life," which could "vivify" a "whole popedom of forms." This rousing hope, that Christianity's old practices could still convey speech of real spiritual power, would suitably conclude the address, allowing Emerson's listeners to go forth believing that they could "cheer the waiting, fainting hearts" of a desponding world even while taking up careers within conventional parishes.[45]

It is interesting, therefore, that Emerson did not conclude there. In a final paragraph, he held out a further and quite different hope. There was a "supreme Beauty," he said, that "ravished the souls" of the ancient East and now needs to speak in the West. It produced the Hebrew and Greek Scriptures, which "contain immortal sentences" but "have no epical integrity; are fragmentary; are not shown in their order to the intellect." Therefore:

> I look for the new Teacher, that shall follow so far those shining laws, that he shall see them come full circle; shall see their rounding complete grace; shall see the world to be the mirror of the soul; shall see the identity of the law of gravitation with purity of heart; and shall show that the Ought, that Duty, is one thing with Science, with Beauty, and with Joy.[46]

In this final sentence, almost as an afterthought, Emerson was repeating what the Transcendentalists thought to be their key insights, but assigning the role of unfolding these neither to the Bible nor to parish pastors. The Teacher with a capital "T" to whom Emerson was pointing would be a culture-making figure of singular genius, a prophet on the order of Moses or Christ himself.

Closing on that note without explaining further, Emerson may well have left the divinity students a mite bewildered. It did not seem that he was calling for any of them to be this Teacher, nor that anything of the sort would be possible within the confines of even the most revitalized conventional ministry. Nor was he staking his own claim to the role. The Teacher's teaching, apparently, would go beyond Emerson's own exhortations to spiritual renewal, and would speak to a desponding society in a way more profound than the cogitations so far on offer from anyone in the Transcendental Club. A Teacher that Emerson had to "look for" was one that had not yet been found.

"We Too Must Write Bibles"

Emerson's provocations were bound to raise the ire of institutionalists, starting once again with Andrews Norton—or "Pope Andrews" as Theodore Parker, an Emerson protégé, would mockingly call him. Apparently at the behest of Harvard alumni, Norton issued a shocked reply to Emerson, charging him with "the latest form of infidelity" and an "abuse of religious language" aimed at disguising the "Antichristian" as Christian.[47] Emerson himself declined to reply, again leaving it to George Ripley to prosecute the pamphlet wars with Norton.[48] Writing to Thomas Carlyle, Emerson reported merely that his Divinity School address "has been the occasion of an outcry in all our leading local newspapers against my 'infidelity,' 'pantheism,' and 'atheism,'" but he belittled this "foolish clamor" as just a "storm in our washbowl."[49]

Taking up the challenge, Ripley resumed his debate with Norton in an exchange which, even more so than Miracles Controversy, made clear what was at issue between Transcendentalists and traditionalists. For Norton, the champion of religious "evidences," the "Natural Religion" that the Transcendentalists were promoting was "unintelligible," a "cloud of mysticism" that most people would be unable understand. It presupposed "disciplined minds" of a "peculiar cast" prepared to receive speculations so abstruse. Norton and other (relative) conservatives saw reason, as commonly understood, as a way of knowing that was more inclusive. If readers could be confident in reports of miracles, they were bound to find them vivid and persuasive evidence of God's works.[50]

Such confidence, Norton repeated, could be established in the Bible. The careful analysis and rational assessment needed for this might require, like other sciences, the specialized study of learned professors like Norton—but from their demonstrations would come the assurance, available through normal reason to all ordinary believers, that the sacred book was indeed a revelation of the divine. Establishing philosophical truths might be the work of a few, but the truths themselves could still be "a common property and a common blessing."[51]

Behind the question of textual evidence, in other words, was the question, very germane in an age of rising democracy, of which spiritual approach was more democratic. To Norton, the Transcendentalists were elitists, channels for "the influence of the depraving literature and noxious speculations which flow in among us from Europe"—Spinoza, Hume, and the theologians of the "modern German school of infidelity."[52] Ripley's reply argued just the reverse: Relying on written records, alleged proofs of miracles and the like, "removes Christianity from its stronghold in the common mind and puts it into the keeping of scholars and antiquaries." It amounted to handing ordinary, uneducated seekers a book that was sealed to them until they became conversant with "the subtlest questions of literary criticism." The effect would be to make the saving faith dependent on tutelage from a "learned class." Norton, Ripley scolded, seemed to have forgotten their original shared goal as Unitarians, "the very Protestants of the Protestants": to vitalize a barren Christianity by bringing the Bible out of the "dusty corners" of learned speculation, boldly appealing "to the sense of truth in every man to SEE and JUDGE for himself what is right."[53] Romantic "Reason" with a capital "R" was prior to any mere, mundane reasoning of the kind that one might engage in through books and writing; it was a faculty inherent in human nature, miraculous in itself and in principle available to all. For Ripley, Emerson, and others of the New School, it was the power of prophecy democratized—or as close to such a thing as was likely to emerge from Harvard's precincts and the fashionable salons of New England.

Norton and others were right to see that the Transcendentalists' textual skepticism cut very deeply. Emerson might have moderated it for purposes of a seminary commencement, holding out hope that "new revelation" might still come through young ministers, their churches, and the Bibles from which they were now trained to preach. In its basic premises, though, his critique was quite different than that of the "German school" to which Norton tried to link him. The German higher critics hoped to learn how and for what historical reasons the Bible had originally been composed, which meant treating it like other ancient books and, inevitably, exposing parts of it as pious legend. Yet one could do this and still accept it as the highest source of spiritual truth. Emerson's position made that impossible. In its way, it challenged scriptural authority even more radically than the harshest criticisms from unbelievers or "cultured despisers," or even those from angry rationalists like Tom Paine who had found it difficult "to read the Bible without horror."[54]

The problem, Emerson was suggesting, was not that the Bible was false, but that it could never be true *enough*. It would always, by definition, be an inert record of the past, not a living expression of the fully experienced present. As a religion of revelation, Christianity assumed that a record could have real and even ultimate authority, that what this record in fact recorded was nothing less than God's own Word to humankind. Emerson's view implied that such a conception was just ontologically wrong, that the Bible could never be such a thing. At best, it could only describe the revelation that others believed they had received long ago. It was bound to present God not directly, but always at one remove. People of the present could not rely on the Bible alone but must still receive the revelation themselves, must find a way of "conversing with" as opposed to just reading about God. Even "holy writ" was, by definition, a writ, and therefore too limiting.

Nonetheless, even the essential direct revelation would still in some sense be mediated. Just as there would still be a Teacher pronouncing the message, there would apparently still be sacred writings. Part of what the revelation did was make the message readable: "The teacher of the coming age," said Emerson's earlier journal entries, would work "in the conviction that the Scripture[s] can only be interpreted by the same spirit that uttered them." The power to read Scripture was inseparable from the power that allowed it to be written. This power would forever be needed because, presumably, the same tendencies that fragmented even the Bible's immortal sentences would ossify any new Teacher's as well, eventually reducing the new and inspired teachings to just another batch of dismally conventional formulas. Even Jesus' own instruction in glorious moral truth would not be "the last affirmation," noted Emerson: "There shall be a thousand more." A true Bible could not be a fixed canon, but must be a continuing process—"no dead letter," as Emerson put it, "but a perpetual Scripture."[55]

Emerson was certainly not the first to speak of new Bibles, or to broaden the definition of "scripture" beyond traditional Jewish and Christian sacred texts. There was, of course, the recent example of Joseph Smith and the Book of Mormon. Some Mormons today favor this comparison, recalling Emerson's imagined Teacher in connection with Smith's convention-defying career.[56] The two movements do present some interesting similarities. Emerson's "desponding" might be construed as the same dullness that alarmed Smith, but broadened and elaborated into an erudite cultural critique. Smith wanted "to get Religion" and was worried when he "could feel nothing"; Emerson suggested that this was the sorry state of the whole society. The basic fault, for both, was depending in spiritual matters on ancestral legacies of the distant past.[57]

Both, too, found no answer in revivalism. Revivals were one way to regenerate religious feeling, and those who joined them might gain a new sense of participating, of being able "to sing and shout with the rest," in Smith's words. As Smith had noticed, though, revivalist claims tended to cancel each other out, while liberal Christians increasingly complained that revivals were themselves degenerating into mere rituals, a series of formulaic gestures whose predictability had its own dulling effect.[58] What was needed was participation of a more profound kind, a re-infusion of feeling not in the sense of ostentatious emotion but as ecstatically experienced in the inspired visions and prophecies of old.

For both Emerson and Smith, this meant new revelations in the present day. What made Emerson sometimes sound like Smith were his calls for restoration of "wonderwork[ing]" and conversing with God in the present age, and his worry that received Christianity had lost touch with these "resources of astonishment and power," as he put it in the Divinity School address—that it was not feeling the old "throbs of desire and hope."[59] His goal was not to recover the Bible's meaning, as William Miller and Alexander Campbell were seeking to do, but, like Smith, to recover and reapply the original sources of its power.

On the other hand, Emerson was less attached than Smith to Christian imagery, and far less vividly literal than Smith about the wonders newly to be worked and what conversing with God would be like. Nowhere did he suggest that it meant issuing prophecies of his own, taking audible commands from embodied beings in actual visions, nor anointing himself, like Smith, the new revelation's high priest. In the Transcendentalist circle it was Jones Very, a poet and young Emerson protégé given to seeming bouts of insanity, who claimed to be literally channeling the Holy Spirit, and who at times presented himself as God or Christ while writing "Epistles" in a New Testament style.[60] Emerson liked and supported Very, but his own intellectual demeanor was always more cerebral and circumspect. Far from a high priest, he was not even clearly the leader of the Transcendentalists. As one associate put it, he "was admired as a lecturer," but not "received as a master or authority in either philosophy or religion" because his ideas were too hard to classify.[61]

What we have here, very likely, are differences not just of personal temperament but of class. The frontier-based, revival-inspired faith of the self-educated Smith promised transcendence in a package designed for relative unsophisticates. It might aptly be seen as a backwoods, folkish cousin to Transcendentalism, with a distinctly populist, proselytizing appeal not to be found in an elite club of cosmopolitans with links to Europe's Romantic intelligentsia.

More clearly a forerunner of Emerson was Emanuel Swedenborg (1688–1772), the Swedish scientist-turned-mystic whose followers organized a "New Church" and brought its ideas to America around 1790. The visions that Swedenborg claimed, and the many volumes of writings he based on them, were an influence on many in the century that followed. A subject of particular fascination to Emerson—he is mentioned in the Divinity School address in the same breath as St. Paul and George Fox, the Quaker founder—Swedenborg produced something like a new Bible, discarding some of the old books and reinterpreting others according to what he saw in visions as their underlying message.[62] Still, he was not quite the Teacher whom Emerson hoped to see. Emerson warned the divinity students against relying on such figures for "secondary knowledge," and explained in a later essay that Swedenborg was still too bound to the terms and *mythos* of Christianity. While he pointed down the right path, Swedenborg might better be thought of as "the last Father in the Church."[63]

At any rate, the idea of new bibles yet to be written was a familiar Romantic conceit. Ambitions of this kind were obvious in William Blake's work, and the influential German poet and critic Novalis, in the late 1790s, had called writing a bible an author's highest task (as Carlyle would later remind Emerson). Contrasting such a work with the "dead, earthbound, equivocal letter," Novalis had also written that every "genuine" book is biblical when the spirit sanctifies it.[64]

What that meant in practice, though, was always somewhat elusive. What books were "genuine" or "sanctified"? Transcendentalists were inclined to equate the word *book* with banality and the dead hand of the past, but Emerson allowed a major exception for those books that, as he said, warped him clean out of his orbit. Presumably on that basis, he had written in his journal:

> Make your own Bible. Select & Collect all those words & sentences that in all your reading have been to you like the blast of trumpet out of Shakspear, Seneca, Moses, John, & Paul.

This entry ended with a little picture that Emerson drew of a trumpet.[65] One's "own" Bible, on this account, would be a kind of private canon—the sum of an individual's choices of especially powerful, orbit-warping works, drawn from both Testaments but also from the classical and English canons.

In later writings, Emerson also acknowledged a high regard for "the Bibles of the world, or the sacred books of each nation, which express for each the supreme result of their experience."[66] Here the terms of selection were not individual but national. Emerson's specific examples included the great works of Eastern religions and spirituality, which the Transcendentalists were ahead of most Westerners in taking seriously.[67] He apparently meant the term *nation* in an old-fashioned usage like the Bible's own—a people or cultural collective (like the Persians or "Hindoos") not confined to a given state on the political map, but known through its shared, probably ancient history and its cultural productions themselves. Of these, its "bibles" would be the pinnacle: bibles produce nations as much as the other way around.

Moreover, "All these books are the majestic expressions of the universal conscience, and are more to our daily purpose than this year's almanac or this day's newspaper." If they are true, then their message is both real and current; in fact it merges back into and takes the form of immediate events, such that the world's bibles are not meant for isolated book-reading and "are not to be held by letters printed on a page, but are living characters translatable into every tongue and form of life." They are experience itself, according to Emerson, and are "read" in the living of life in nature and with other people. We think of bibles as "Asiatic" and "primeval" not because the experience they represent was better perceived in the distant past—"there are as good eyes and ears now in the planet as ever were"—but only because "these ejaculations of the soul are uttered one or a few at a time, at long intervals, and it takes millenniums to make a Bible."[68]

What, in this view, would be involved in making bibles in America, a young nation still in cultural formation in the very earliest years of its own "millenniums"? In an essay on "The Poet," Emerson had called poets "liberating gods," capable of making their fellows "dance and run about happily, like children. We are like persons who come out of a cave or cellar into the open air. This is the effect on us of tropes, fables, oracles, and all poetic forms." Poets "are free, and they make free." It is not the works' propositional meaning that does this, but the immediate impact of poetic language itself, the "tropes" encountered even before "we arrive at the precise sense of the author. I think nothing is of any value in books, excepting the transcendental and extraordinary," the outflow of the author's "one dream, which holds him like an insanity." For Emerson, "all symbols are fluxional; all language is vehicular and transitive, and is good, as ferries and horses are, for conveyance, not as farms and houses are, for homestead." The "metamorphosis" of things into words and thoughts can never be finished but must be continually in process, as it was in Swedenborg.[69]

Emerson was seeking a figure capable of this—"the timely man, the new religion, the reconciler, whom all things await." But, "I look in vain for the poet whom I describe. We do not, with sufficient plainness, or sufficient profoundness, address ourselves to life, nor dare we [chant] our own times and social circumstance." The true American poet—the "reconciler" of a new religion—would see classical greatness in Americans' ordinary affairs: "Banks and tariffs, the newspaper and caucus, Methodism and Unitarianism, are flat and dull to dull people, but rest on the same foundations of wonder as the town of Troy, and the temple of Delphi, and are as swiftly passing away." After a further list of everyday phenomena that "are yet unsung," Emerson declares, "Yet America is a poem in our eyes; its ample geography dazzles the imagination, and it will not wait long for metres."[70] The true poet would celebrate the local, but in some way that was universal; in his journal, Emerson wrote that it was "high time we should have a bible that should be no provincial record, but should open the history of the planet, and bind all tendencies and dwarf all the Epics & philosophies we have."[71] It should transcend even the nation and be greater than any of the world's great national epics.

Yet how could it do that and still attend to the particulars of everyday life, the otherwise "dull miscellany and lumber-room" that Emerson had spoken of in "The American Scholar"? America's "materials" might be incomparable, but if they were characteristically American they would also necessarily be provincial, more limited in space and time than "the history of the planet." Emerson sketched an answer to this problem in his conclusion to an essay on Goethe, another influence on the Transcendentalists and, like Swedenborg, a subject of their club discussions:

> We too must write Bibles, to unite again the heavens and the earthly world. The secret of genius is to suffer no fiction to exist for us; to realize all that we know; in the high refinement of modern life, in arts, in sciences, in books, in men, to exact good faith, reality and a purpose; and first, last, midst and without end, to honor every truth by use.[72]

One could write abstractly about the heavens or truth, but the great task was to "bind all tendencies," to unite these higher things with "purpose" and "use," to bring them into the world in which we live and act. This would be "to realize all that we know," to imbue the everyday things with the higher reality. The quotidian and the spiritual each needed the other in order to achieve Novalis' "genuineness."

As a reconciler, then, "the timely man" could make a new bible detailed and specific, yet not provincial, by joining the plain and profound. This would give it the immediacy and practical value of the newspaper and almanac, would convey the facts of national projects like "the northern trade, the southern planting and the western clearing," while also chanting them as the ancient bards had chanted the epics deeds of heroes and gods.[73] Goethe had shown the way, Emerson said, in response to a distinctly modern problem: the "rolling miscellany of facts and sciences," expanding in all directions, that threatened to make the world incomprehensible. He may not have reached the highest unity, but he had "brought back to a book some of its ancient might and dignity"—and as both scientist and poet, had produced an encyclopedic, if partly dated, lifetime output that grapples with the "distracting" multiplicity, "this plague of microscopes," yet still "strikes the harp with a hero's strength and grace."[74] Presumably America, where busy immersion in the modern miscellany was most intense, needed something of this kind even more.

All this still left the vision of new bibles lacking clear definition. On that question, as on many others, Emerson had offered only what he sought from other writers: "not instruction, but provocation."[75] Bible-creating could not really be reduced to a particular program for the same reason that inspiration itself could never fully be captured in creeds or texts. It would remain for future writers to take the broad hint and act on it in various inspired ways of their own.

But it seemed that whatever quality made a spiritual insight or utterance worthy of a bible would also make it impossible to pin down in writing—and therefore, not available to include in a bible. The phrase "perpetual scripture" was, in that sense, at least mildly oxymoronic. Scriptures would be "perpetual" because books, language, and symbols are limited, mere means of conveyance, and therefore have to be continually replaced or transformed in order not to become dead letters. Yet this meant that no particular writing, with its particular words and images, could ever carry the kind of authority that the word "scripture" traditionally implied, at least in Western religions. Instead the particular text would forever be dissolving back into the original sources of inspiration, would always, by definition, need revision and re-imagining, and would therefore be worse than useless as a fixed point for belief. Like the day's news—a significant comparison, given other developments we will turn to later—it would be a revelation fit only for today. It could never help form a canon, a reliable route to the higher things and a measure for judging other spiritual claims. In this respect, the Transcendentalist solution to the problem of biblical authority, like those of the ultra-protestants, risked its own cancellation. It envisioned a program that seemingly could not be pursued without re-creating the same dire needs that called for it in the first place.

4

Spirit and Kingdom: Language, Social Action, and the "True Reviving"

Ralph Waldo Emerson called for a new Teacher but did not claim to be that figure himself, nor did he describe his own voluminous writings as any kind of new scripture. Nonetheless, his modern reputation as a kind of prophet reaches back to the first years of his public career. Already in "The American Scholar" and the Divinity School Address, said one early profile, "he announced himself not as a reasoner, but a prophet," the "organ of his own visions."[1] By 1840 Margaret Fuller, the Transcendentalists' literary editor, was noting a public demand for a "Gospel of Transcendentalism."[2] Theodore Parker praised Emerson for doing far more than any revivalist preacher "to waken this [true] religion in the great Saxon heart of the Americans and Britons," and credited this to his fearlessness, the creedless originality of his message, and "the poetic power of pictured speech" that marked his "genius for literature."[3] Some of Emerson's later admirers, including visual artists he influenced, said they found reading his writings to be like reading the Bible.[4]

Praise like this, however, also highlights a further question, one with which critics confronted Transcendentalists from the beginning. Did their movement address problems in the real world, which were many and severe, or was it a spiritualizing, mystifying way of avoiding these? Did being the "organ of his own visions" make a prophet socially myopic, unable to see the plight of the suffering masses? True, Emerson's early addresses had taken aim at a kind of collective, social-spiritual despondency, and had argued that the mundane affairs of life in society gained order and meaning if they were linked in certain ways to matters of the spirit. Even as he was presenting that thesis to Harvard students, though, Americans were in the first years of a lengthy and very serious economic depression, the "Hard Times" that followed the financial panic of 1837. It would be difficult to detect from Emerson's long train of laments that for ordinary citizens, "desponding" had ceased to be strictly a spiritual concern; at that point millions of people were simply despairing, as banks failed, prices collapsed, and businesses and employment vanished. Compared even to some of his close colleagues, Emerson's concern for the victims of these developments appeared muted at best.[5] Also missing from Emerson's list of the era's woes was slavery, another issue that had been roiling the Harvard community in the weeks just before his Divinity School appearance, and that would take its place in the years just ahead as the nation's most contentious social problem.[6]

Nor was this just a case of scanting social concerns to focus on spiritual questions. In Emerson's hands, at least, Transcendentalism could easily seem positively antisocial: "Society everywhere is in conspiracy against the manhood of every one of its members. Society is a joint-stock company, in which the members agree, for the better securing of his bread to each shareholder, to surrender the liberty and culture of the eater."[7] The virtue it most demands is conformity, against which Emerson set "Self-Reliance," the title subject of this famous essay, and a quality he presented as the antidote to "large societies and dead institutions." As examples, Emerson made rhetorical foils of those who agitated for social relief or reform. He advised an abolitionist decrying the plight of slaves in Barbados to attend to those close to him, not "varnish your hard, uncharitable ambition with this incredible tenderness for black folk a thousand miles off. Thy love afar is spite at home." Against love thus converted to yet another "doctrine," one "that pules and whines," he declared, "I shun father and mother and wife and brother, when my genius calls me":

> Then, again, do not tell me, as a good man did to-day, of my obligation to put all poor men in good situations. Are they *my* poor? I tell thee, thou foolish philanthropist, that I grudge the dollar, the dime, the cent, I give to such men as do not belong to me and to whom I do not belong.[8]

Grounding this seeming heartlessness was Emerson's spiritualized theory of how people "belong" to each other. In "The Over-Soul," often read today alongside "Self-Reliance," Emerson extolled "that Unity, that Over-soul, within which every man's particular being is contained and made one with all other." Although, he said, "We live in succession, in division, in parts, in particles," the parts are all "equally related" in "that common heart" or "soul of the whole." What really joins people, then, is not society—the "common nature is not social"—but the shared soul, "to which all right action is submission." One cannot submit to it, though, and therefore do right by others, in "habitual and mean service to the world," but only by receiving it privately, as one would receive God.[9]

On its face, this austere vision was a formula for social inaction. It was not universal even among Transcendentalists, who kept busy with many projects that were hardly private: utopian communes, like George Ripley's Brook Farm and the short-lived "Fruitlands" that Bronson Alcott helped found; education reform and experimental schools, under Alcott and Elizabeth Peabody; Peabody's bookstore and circulating library in Boston; a literary journal, *The Dial*, whose founding editor was Margaret Fuller; Orestes Brownson's proposals for a Christian program to combat inequality, with Jesus envisioned as "the prophet of the workingmen."[10] Emerson viewed all this activity with bemusement, writing to Thomas Carlyle:

> We are all a little wild here with numberless projects of social reform. Not a reading man but has a draft of a new Community in his waistcoat pocket. I am gently mad myself, and am resolved to live cleanly. George Ripley is talking up a colony of agriculturists and scholars, with whom he threatens to take the field and the book. One man renounces the use of animal food; and another of coin; and another of domestic hired service; and another of the State; and on the whole we have a commendable share of reason and hope.[11]

On the other hand, among the movement's best known real-life experiments today is Henry David Thoreau's retreat from society to private seclusion at Walden Pond.[12] Brownson repudiated the Transcendentalists and converted to Catholicism, and Elizabeth Peabody obliquely criticized the Transcendentalists for an atheistic tendency toward "Egotheism."[13] Transcendentalist impulses continued to cut both ways.

Critics on the outside, among them the prominent Unitarian Andrews Norton, were even harsher, judging the Transcendentalists to be atheists, "mystagogues," and vehicles for the "noxious" European influences. One critic suggested that "the hyper-*spiritual*, neo-super-visionary" Emerson be sent in a balloon to the North Pole.[14] Carlyle, though a friend to the movement, suggested that the Transcendentalists were missing other possible meanings of "transcend," causing Emerson to come across as

> a Speaker indeed, but as it were a *Soliloquizer* on the eternal mountain-tops only, in vast solitudes where men and their affairs lie all hushed in a very dim remoteness, and only *the man* and the stars and the earth are visible,—whom, so fine a fellow seems he, we could perpetually punch into, and say, "Why won't you come and help us, then? We have terrible need of one man like you down among us! It is cold and vacant up there; nothing paintable but rainbows and emotions; come down, and you shall do life-pictures, passions, facts,—which *transcend* all thought, and leave it stuttering and stammering!"

Emerson's epigrammatic writing style, he added, did not "always entirely cohere for me," with the typical paragraph holding together "not as a beaten *ingot,* but as a beautiful square *bag of duck-shot* held together by canvas!"[15]

If such a philosophy included a hope for new bibles, it was fair to ask, what would those bibles, or any other "genuine" book or inspired new literature, be meant to achieve for the world and not just the reader? What could it command, apart from self-reliantly refusing the commands of any book, including itself? Presumably it would go beyond collecting quotable aphorisms. Though the Christian Bible includes proverbs and some parts that might also be compared to duckshot—Emerson's style resembles some sections of Paul's Epistles—it was more than just a square bag of spiritual insights bound in canvas (or leather). To invert one of Emerson's own phrases, what it aimed for was not just provocation but instruction. Certainly that was how it had long been understood, to the point of driving people to schism and war over disagreements about just what it instructed. The Exodus, for instance, was an ancient national epic, one that had been recently appropriated in defense of America's escape from British "bondage" and that would soon inspire efforts to end the literal bondage of African Americans. The Gospels, too, were stories, not just statements, centered on a Teacher whose teachings were expected to be followed. What would be the equivalent in Emersonian terms? Would the new Teacher likewise comfort the poor and the outcast, confront the privileged, overturn the tables of moneychangers, challenge the high priests and rulers of the present age?

Radicals, Mystics, and the Question of Social Responsibility

Ultimately forcing this issue on the Transcendentalists was the growing agitation over slavery, which made it increasingly difficult to treat spiritual freedom as the only kind that mattered.[16] Emerson had the question of social responsibility put to him squarely through the efforts of his own wife, Lidian Jackson Emerson, an anti-slavery agitator years before he was. In a journal entry of 1837, Emerson noted that "Lidian grieves aloud about the wretched negro in the horrors of the middle passage; and they are bad enough," but he then went on to suggest that her attitude was selective and overstated.[17] Gradually, however, she influenced his growing engagement with the slavery question.[18] In a short, unpublished satire from about 1841, Lidian Emerson wryly made fun of the Transcendentalist social ethos, implicitly contrasting it with Christianity's. For those whose aspirations to "Perfection" were focused entirely on "your whole duty to your noble self-sustained, impeccable, infallible Self," and who "care not that a benign Divinity shapes your ends (though you seek a good tailor to shape your coat)," this "Transcendental Bible" or "Abstract of New Bible" [*sic*] offered guidance mimicking but upending that of the Gospels—for instance:

> Loathe and shun the sick. They are in bad taste, and may untune us for writing the poem floating through our mind.
>
> ...
>
> Despise the unintellectual, and make them feel that you do by not noticing their remark and question lest they presume to intrude into your conversation.
>
> ...
>
> Great souls are self-sustained and stand ever erect, saying only to the prostrate sufferer "Get up, and stop your complaining."
>
> ...
>
> If you have refused all sympathy to the sorrowful, all pity and aid to the sick, all toleration to the infirm of character, if you have condemned the unintellectual and loathed such sinners as have discovered want of intellect by their sin, then are you a perfect specimen of Humanity.

Phrased as commands or rules for living, Emersonian self-reliance sounded cruel and absurd. Emerson himself, though, took the point, calling Lidian's lampoon "a good squib."[19]

Transcendentalism was explicitly a quest for new prophets, but the problem that Lidian Emerson's New Bible exposed was that "prophecy" must be seen in two dimensions. We might think of these as vertical and horizontal: Moses goes up the mountain to receive God's message, then comes back down and delivers it so it can spread among the people. When, as if often the case, the nation is not conducting itself as it should, the second function is that of a political or social critic. Prophets exercise a "twofold faculty—the hearing ear and the speaking mouth; the ear to hear God, the mouth to speak to man," wrote Lyman Abbott, a leading liberal theologian, later in the century. They receive a message "from the Eternal" and become the messenger "of the Eternal," translating its "unknown tongue" to "make legible the before invisible writing," with a purpose "always to lead the people forth, to enable them to understand God's will in order that they may do God's work. The prophet, therefore, is always a combination of piety and sympathy." Emerson, in effect, was accused of acknowledging only one of the two.

Abbott explicitly likened the prophet's translating function to art: "The poet, the artist, the musician, are each a kind of prophet"; the poet "brings forth this hidden and sub-conscious life into consciousness, enables the soul to perceive what it could not perceive without this poetic interpreter." Prophets must live both in eternity and in their own time: "What ye hear in the ear, that proclaim ye upon the housetops."[20] The revelation compels the proclamation, which is a social act. What distinguishes and perhaps even defines a bible, then—or any writing or art with a similar function—is its key role at that point of vertical-horizontal intersection. It is the medium through which the message above becomes the message abroad.

Liberal Christianity had been founded on this dual awareness. Its goals, as William Ellery Channing had put it, were not strictly spiritual but included the "benevolent virtues" and "practical piety," meaning piety put into real-world practice. Each of the two prophetic modes therefore exerted powerful yet distinct pressures. Looking back on his own career from late in the century, one prominent liberal minister, Rufus Ellis, saw the two functions as parallel streams running through the Christianity of his time. For one-third of the century, from 1853 to 1885, Ellis was minister of Boston's First Church—called "First" because it literally was, founded by the original Puritan settlers as soon as they landed in 1630. In this prestigious office he was the parish pastor to such luminaries as Edward Everett and Charles Francis Adams, and a direct successor of both Charles Chauncy, the Unitarian founder, and Emerson's own father William. Even earlier, as part of a circle of Harvard students curious about "the speculative philosophy" that was then taking shape as Transcendentalism, he had made pilgrimages to Emerson's home, and was in the student audience for the Divinity School address, which he called "very singular."[21] When he eventually took up his appointment at the First Church, it was "at a time of prevailing unrest and excitement" over reform issues, notably slavery.

Believing, though, that his relatively conservative parishioners "prefer not to be shaken," and suspicious even of the word "reform," in the end Ellis chose not to join either the Transcendentalists or the social agitators. The Transcendentalists' diminished view of Christ was unacceptably patronizing, he thought, while abolitionism struck him as impractical: "Railing at [slavery] would not uproot it."[22] He disagreed about this "vehemently" with Theodore Parker, though he also professed his respect for his famous abolitionist colleague, who lived just across the street from him in Boston.[23] In his own estimation, Ellis remained in the difficult position of "a conservative among the Liberals."[24] Even so, when he came to look back on a career spent "witnessing for my liberal Christianity," he could see that the two movements—the one seeking the unseen but vital higher realities, the other calling a favored but erring nation to righteousness—had been its two great shaping influences.[25]

Within liberal Christianity, these two prophetic paths had various names. Where Lyman Abbott would call them "piety" and "sympathy," earlier writers often spoke of the "spiritual" and the "practical." Margaret Fuller preferred the terms "mystics" and "radicals." Both groups, Fuller believed, had recognized that America's post-revolutionary prosperity and freedom tended to "vulgarize" people by focusing them on worldly matters, making them "superficial, irreverent, and more anxious to get a living than to live mentally and morally." Seeing that the needed changes "cannot be wrought from without inwards," her fellow liberals were

> trying to quicken the soul, that they may work from within outwards. Disgusted with the vulgarity of a commercial aristocracy, they become radicals; disgusted with the materialistic working of "rational" religion, they become mystics. They quarrel with all that is, because it is not spiritual enough.[26]

Radicals and mystics were therefore speaking to the same set of spiritual deficits. What distinguished them, for Fuller, was which expression of vulgarity disgusted them most, the crassly economic or the philosophically mundane.

Emerson himself was alert to criticisms that his prophetic mode was one-dimensional and socially myopic, all mysticism and no radicalism. Although he began to speak on the slavery question as early as 1837, he distanced himself at first from the abolitionists, and in that same year he acknowledged in his journal the seeming inaction and "slightness of ... virtue" of those, like himself, who were not "active & zealous leaders" in that cause and others. His first instinct was to separate such ambitions from his own. Thus, he defended "quiet honor" over the activist's "proclaiming zeal," and compared himself to a householder who chooses to stick to basics, to build his house solidly and "weathertight" instead of spending his limited funds on fancy adornments. To challenge existing social forms requires being "critical," and that is an inward quality different from outward good character.[27] Five years later, Emerson took up the same problem at length in his essay "The Transcendentalist," acknowledging the antisocial nature of this group of "hermits": "They do not even like to vote." Philanthropists, those who cared for humankind's well-being, would prefer to hear that their friends were dead, he joked, than that they were Transcendentalists, hence "paralyzed" from doing anyone any good. But the charge was unfair; far from "sloth," genius was "the power to labor better and more availably." Out of "insatiable expectation," Transcendentalists made "exacting" demands on others. They proclaimed things, said Emerson, by silence and forbearance as much as by speech and action, and even "if they eat clouds, and drink wind, they have not been without service to the race of man."[28]

Furthermore, the "great and holy causes" to which the socially conscious demand attention "seem to them great abuses," just "paltry" when seen up close, and even a kind of quackery: "Each 'cause,' as it is called,—say Abolition, Temperance, say Calvinism, or Unitarianism,—becomes speedily a little shop, where the article, let it have been at first never so subtle and ethereal, is now made up into portable and convenient cakes, and retailed in small quantities to suit purchasers." Emerson employed lists and catalogs—something he and, even more so, Walt Whitman could use to great effect to suggest a wonderful profusion—to make society's many preoccupations sound trivial, random, and ephemeral in a bad way:

> Amidst the downward tendency and proneness of things, when every voice is raised for a new road or another statute or a subscription of stock; for an improvement in dress, or in dentistry; for a new house or a larger business; for a political party, or the division of an estate;—will you not tolerate one or two solitary voices in the land, speaking for thoughts and principles not marketable or perishable?[29]

In truth, though, "We are miserable with inaction," he admitted of his fellow hermits. They would happily have welcomed but were still awaiting the right call to act.[30] No such call came from either of the two national political parties; while "one has the best cause," Emerson wrote in another essay, "Politics," the other "contains the best men." The Democrats had the right social-reform agenda but unacceptable leaders and candidates, while the conservative Whig Party, though more cultivated, was merely a timid defender of property and "aspires to no real good" at all.[31]

As the full onset of the slavery crisis seemed to be bear out the warnings of the abolitionists, excuses like these became harder to sustain. In 1844 Emerson openly called for abolition. By 1845, when he wrote "Politics" and had come to the appreciation of Goethe that led him to say "We too must write Bibles," he added these reasons: "to unite again the heavens and the earthly world" and "to honor every truth by use."[32] New Bibles, then, would apparently be a means of social as well as spiritual edification. Following the Compromise of 1850, Emerson criticized its hugely controversial new Fugitive Slave Law in two lectures, finally attempting to explain in detail what Transcendentalism had to do with political and social reform.[33] Striking a different and markedly humbler tone than he had when criticizing social causes as "little shops," Emerson was no longer condescending toward reformers, and no longer spoke of having to choose between their causes and his higher concerns. True, he confessed, most of his previous work had been addressed to cerebral audiences of students and scholars:

> I do not often speak to public questions;—they are odious and hurtful, and it seems like meddling or leaving your work. I have my own spirits in prison;—spirits in deeper prisons, whom no man visits if I do not. And then I see what havoc it makes with any good mind, a dissipated philanthropy. The one thing not to be forgiven to intellectual persons is, not to know their own task, or to take their ideas from others.

Emerson, too, had been trying to free people, he insisted, but from the "deeper prisons" of the soul. These were within his proper sphere; people who speak up on matters outside their own experience—and he conceded that slavery had not personally affected him—"say what they would have you believe, but what they do not quite know."[34]

From there, however, the speech constructed an elegant critique of recent events based on Transcendentalist ideas, in effect placing these at the heart of abolitionism itself. Daniel Webster, Emerson's own Massachusetts Senator and a towering figure in American politics, had shocked his constituents four years earlier with his political capitulation to the Fugitive Slave Law at a moment when his leadership might have blocked it. (The law required all Americans to help return runaway slaves, in effect entrenching the property rights of slaveholders even in free states—an outrage to many in the North.) In Emerson's analysis, Webster compromised not for the vulgar reasons of most politicians, but because the qualities that made him so extraordinary did not include "that deep source of inspiration" that was needed to do what was right. It was a failure, in essence, of the soul. Among the rationales for it was a Whiggish conservatism that was skeptical of reformist ideals. Emerson generally shared this, but argued that respecting reality, as conservatives claimed to do, also meant recognizing the soul's realities—"the instinct of man to rise, and the instinct to love and help his brother." These demanded abolition. Webster's own brilliance at argument defeated him: "There are always texts and thoughts and arguments. But it is the genius and temper of the man which decides whether he will stand for right or for might."[35]

Expanding on this point, Emerson suggested that the whole slavery issue must be understood in terms of the weakness of textual authority. Because the law is only as good as the people who apply and are governed by it, "no forms, neither constitutions, nor laws, nor covenants, nor churches, nor bibles, are of any use in themselves. The Devil nestles comfortably into them all." Texts are circular routes back to what inspired them: "The teachings of the Spirit can be apprehended only by the same spirit that gave them forth." Hence, he told his listeners, they themselves, personally, must be "declarations of Independence, the charter, the battle and the victory." What counterbalances the world's falsehood and wrong is the soul, and therefore to qualify for society one must be able to stand alone—which means "there is no Church for him but his believing prayer; no Constitution but his dealing well and justly with his neighbor." A just person protects the state, not the other way around, and will find that "the constitution of the Universe is on his side." In this Transcendentalist reading, the American Declaration and Constitution are divinely inspired, not unlike the Bible but also not in the crude way some Americans would have it. They are not graven words of God, but the means of carrying into practical, worldly affairs the prophet's vertical inspiration from above. The radical depends on the mystical. Emerson's conclusion envisioned the antislavery cause sweeping the nation.

That development would amount to "the end of our unbelief," which is what Americans' social failures—their lack of "cooperation" with divine Providence—had essentially been.[36]

Viewing things in this light, we can also detect a telling shift in Emerson's terminology. For nearly twenty years he had been calling for a new religion, new and greater poets and worthy national epics. Now, at last, he had come to identify these goals with the concept that was front and center in the anti-slavery crusade—"liberty"—and also to endorse the notion of a social crusade itself: "Liberty is aggressive, Liberty is the Crusade of all brave and conscientious men, the Epic Poetry, the new religion, the chivalry of all gentlemen."[37] Although Emerson had called poets "liberating gods," the term *liberty* and its variants had barely registered in *Nature*, "Self-Reliance," "The Transcendentalist," or even "Politics," and did not appear at all in "The American Scholar," the Divinity School address, or "The Over-Soul." Here, finally, it appeared some twenty times. Emerson's implied message throughout this speech was that his program had always been that of the abolitionists, just operating at a deeper level—not apart from social activism, still less at odds with it, but fundamental to it and making it possible.

Theodore Parker's "Republic of Righteousness"

As artful as that formulation was, there were some large questions it did not answer. Even if it succeeded at enlisting the (mystical) Spirit on behalf of (radical) real-world action, it left unclear whether there was any role for textual authority at all. In Emerson's original call for a "new Teacher," this question had also been deferred: his hope had been for "the timely man ... whom all things await," that is, whose eventual answers had not yet been revealed.[38] Perhaps, in time, new bibles would be written, but it was hard to see how those would solve the original problem. A written text might convey merely the fleeting communication of a moment, but it might also be intended to fix a message in place enduringly, even perhaps for all time. Certainly the point of a law or a governing instrument, like the Constitution, was to set forth in language certain commands or common points of reference whereby people would reliably know what was supposed to be done. These qualities were central to the authority of such texts, and it was negated if they lacked fixity and did not deliver reliable meanings. Yet here was Emerson suggesting that even constitutions and covenants written recently, meant to define a particular nation in the present day and to state precise rules for it, had no such power: The people themselves must be their own declarations of independence, must safeguard the law—not the other way around—and should do so by appeal to a "constitution of the universe" that was nowhere written down. The texts as such neither govern, instill, nor enforce morality. Nor would new bibles be "of any use in themselves."

In what sense, then, would any text that claimed authority be worth even the paper it was printed on? Perhaps authority and written language simply had no bearing on each other, and the documents by which a society might hope to be governed were merely statements of the will of whatever power enforced them. In later chapters we will examine some of ways these questions were struggled over politically, with respect to the Declaration and Constitution—struggles that would become especially fraught in the great political crisis leading to the Civil War. Meanwhile two prominent figures, Theodore Parker and Horace Bushnell, had been struggling with them theologically. From different directions, Parker and Bushnell converged on similar solutions, proposals for understanding Scripture and textual meaning in ways that help clarify the major literary developments of the years just ahead.

In his comprehensive history of liberal Christianity, Gary Dorrien calls Bushnell the key figure and "theological father" of that movement, "a figure of singular historical importance" and "the most profound and spiritually uplifting American religious thinker of the nineteenth century."[39] Parker was important as well, "the pivotal figure of the Unitarian tradition" who pointed the way to its humanistic future.[40] Outside of Unitarian circles, he is mainly remembered today for his stalwart abolitionism. Both Parker and Bushnell were dissident and partly estranged members of their church bodies who provoked considerable controversy, not least because their theological work dwelt on the problem of what to make of Christian faith given that the Bible was, as each of them put it, "absurd."

Parker had detailed this indictment by the early 1840s in occasional sermons as well as a lecture series, *A Discourse of Matters Pertaining to Religion*, whose publication as a 500-page opus earned him the role of defendant in the odd spectacle of a Unitarian heresy trial—a seeming impossibility for this anti-creedal sect.[41] For someone who had not, however, like Emerson, formally left Unitarianism, Parker's position was indeed radical. He considered it bizarre that the Bible had long been the final appeal for infallible answers to questions of all kinds, including even foretellings of events that had not yet happened. A former student in Germany and early translator of the German scholars' new historical criticism, he had little patience for the long tradition of deference to Scripture:

> On the authority of the written word man was taught to believe impossible legends, conflicting assertions; to take fiction for fact, a dream for a miraculous revelation of God, an oriental poem for a grave history of miraculous events, a collection of amatory idyls for a serious discourse "touching the mutual love of Christ and the church;" they have been taught to accept a picture sketched by some glowing eastern imagination, never intended to be taken for a reality, as a proof that the Infinite God spoke in human words, appeared in the shape of a cloud, a flaming bush, or a man who ate, and drank, and vanished into smoke; that he

gave counsels to-day, and the opposite to-morrow; that he violated his own laws, was angry, and was only dissuaded by a mortal man from destroying at once a whole nation—millions of men who rebelled against their leader in a moment of anguish.[42]

Dispassionately viewed, the Bible was full of such "absurdities"—contradictions, obvious errors, and "the most awful imprecations human fancy ever clothed in speech."[43] For early Christians it had been less defined and more fluid: a servant rather than a master, inspirational writings to be called upon as needed or left aside. When "at last the present collection was fixed by authority," yet "by no certain criterion," and the faithful were compelled to affirm equally the undivided whole, then both testaments became millstones.[44] "All the books which caprice or accident had brought together between the lids of the Bible were declared to be the infallible word of God, the only certain rule of religious faith and practice," Parker complained. This "idolatrous regard for the imperfect scripture of God's word" would have "confounded" the Bible's own authors, who themselves had limited understandings, never claimed infallibility, and did not idolize books.[45]

Even without the support of mainstream Unitarians, Parker had no trouble drawing crowds to his independent ministry in a large rented hall in Boston. His popularity probably owed much to his biting, ironic wit; he had a skill like Abraham Lincoln's for leavening moral fervor with jokes and canny turns of phrase. In his retelling, the struggles over biblical authority become wryly comical. Protestants were given to "clinging like dying men to the letter of the Bible," but at least they partly "neutralized" this central flaw by allowing very wide freedom for individual interpretation. Churches, being churches, then had to rein in such freedom, which they did with various catechisms and confessions of faith—which, however, turned out to be as difficult to interpret as the Bible itself. In medieval Catholicism, although "the schoolmen doubted whether two similar spirits could occupy at once the same point of space, it is put beyond a doubt that two very dissimilar doctrines may occupy the same words, at the same time." By encouraging close study of the Bible, the Reformation made matters worse, promoting creative new ways to extract from Scriptural passages whatever meaning official doctrine required them to have.[46]

Thus the Bible became clay for the making of "ecclesiastical pottery." With the help of tricks like the chronologies in which "a day" meant a thousand years, it was remarkably easy to locate

> all the great events as they take place, and even the end of the world, in the day some fanatical interpreter happens to live. Is the Bible the Protestant standard of faith? Then it is more uncertain than the things to be measured. The cloud in Hamlet is not more variable than the "infallible rule" in the hands of the interpreters.[47]

It may be that "Job went through some troubles in his life," but "Professors and critics have handled him more sorely than Satan ... his greatest calamity was his exposition," Parker joked. Similarly, "Moses, says the Hebrew Scripture, was the most *tormented* of all the earth, but his trials in the wilderness were nothing to his sufferings on the rack of exegesis."[48]

Instead of resolving matters, Unitarianism's promise of escaping creeds created confusions of its own. Having started well—"an attempt to apply Good Sense to theology"—it "oscillates" between orthodox and liberal positions, denying traditional doctrines while still speaking in traditional language. Unitarians were masters at explaining things away, and would not be fazed even at the clearest disproof of their teachings. The result is that "Scripture is a piece of wax in the Unitarian hand, and takes any shape ... The Unitarian doctrine of inspiration—can anyone tell what it is?"[49]

Amid this sorry picture, Parker sardonically claimed to find a few bits of good news. Belief in the irreplaceable importance of the written text drove Christians' great efforts to spread it worldwide via missionaries—who may "do little good where they go," but "the very purpose and effort are good. A man is always warmed by the smoke of his own generous sacrifice."[50] Nor did the churches' many "ineptitudes" ultimately choke off the truth: "There is something so divine in Religion," he quipped, that it "lets light even into theology."[51]

Like many other observers down through the ages, Parker lamented the meager state of what he saw passing for Christian practice. Day to day, Christians acted out of custom, calculation, and convention. They valued Christianity insofar as it "serves a purpose," but too many saw that purpose mainly as salving their consciences while keeping order on behalf of elites—what Parker called the "great property establishment." People were Christian as a matter of mere respectability. The typical "semi-somnous" preacher "pours forth weekly his impotent drone," proving with his "anointed dullness" that the truly talented were choosing professions other than the ministry.[52] Beyond the churches, the situation was even grimmer. "Our Christianity is talk; it is not in the heart, nor the hand, nor the head, but only in the tongue ... No doubt the Christianity of the Pulpit is a poor thing," Parker charged, "But the Christianity of daily life, of the street, that is still worse, the whole Bible could not save it."[53]

These problems, however, did not reflect too weak an attachment to the Bible. Just the opposite: there had "always been too much belief" in the killing letter, and what it helped to kill was the active social engagement that would mark a truer faith, the quest to bring the kingdom of God into the world. For most people, that goal was just about the last of their concerns in life.[54] Far from solving this, worries about Scriptural orthodoxy were an obstacle. Churches got these priorities backwards. On their tolerance of "popular sin"—slavery, intemperance, "the butchery of Indians"—Parker was characteristically vivid:

> The Christianity of the church stands at the corner of the street, and bellows till all rings again from Cape Sable to the Lake of the Woods [i.e. from one end of the country to the other], if a single "heretic" lifts up his voice, though never so weak, in the obscurest corner of the earth; but Giant Sin may go through the land with his hideous rout; may ride over the poor rough-shod, and burn the standing corn and poison the waters of the nation, and shake the very church till the steeple rock—and there shall not a dog wag his tongue.[55]

Slavery, which became Parker's signature issue, was just part of "the baseness, political, commercial, social baseness daily done in the world," but churches that excused such an obvious evil were not merely falling short. As Emerson would also imply and as Harriet Beecher Stowe would explicitly charge, they were purveying a kind of unbelief. In that sense, a merely "*theological* religion" was, itself, "Infidelity."[56]

On the possibilities for reinvigorating the faith through conventional revivals, Parker was withering. Revivals were just more talk, which would do nothing for a Christianity that was already mere talk. By the late 1850s, nearing an untimely death from tuberculosis, Parker had seen "the revival machinery in motion" for decades. It claimed to be the answer to rote ritualism and "the dull death of our churches," but had itself become a kind of rote exercise, as easy to put up as a cattle show, with archetypal guest preachers like "The Rev. Mr. Great-talk" who could boast of scores or hundreds of converts at a time when churches put considerable stock in such numbers.[57] Worst of all was the sorry weakness of Unitarian revivals: "Strike two flints together and you get sparks of fire; from lumps of ice you get nothing but cold splinters."[58] In a country whose people longed to escape "this old winter cowyard of the church," Parker found it unsurprising that two of the fastest-growing religious enterprises were Spiritualism, the popular craze for séances and the like, and Mormonism. As easy as it was to ridicule the Spiritualists' follies—"rapping on coffin lids, listening for ghosts"—they were alone, he said, in their forward-looking willingness to "emancipate themselves from the Bible and the theology of the church."[59]

At any rate, revivals seemed to presume their own failure, since their organizers never seemed to think that reviving the faith would require changes in either doctrines or church structures. "The people mean a revival of religion," said Parker, "but the ministers will turn it to a revival of the ecclesiastic theology." A successful revival would even be counterproductive: "It will not open a school for black people south of Mason and Dixon's line. It will not break a chain, or alter a vote … not one."[60] In fact, if orthodox Protestant hopes for mass conversions were answered, the world would actually be worse off—less rather than more concerned to fight corruption, war, and other systemic evils, and perhaps even inclined to imagine them scripturally blessed.[61]

What, then, would be a revival *of religion*, a "true revival," as Parker called it? It would be one that sought to revive the kind of religion that Parker defended, which he called "Absolute Religion," an all-encompassing expression of an inborn human religious "Sentiment," the greater religion toward which traditional biblical faith merely gestured.[62] To activate this Sentiment would be a reviving in the sense of reaching back, and yet by the same token progressive:

> Jesus fell back on God, on absolute Religion, absolute Morality; the truth its own authority, his works his witness. The early Christians fell back on the authority of Jesus; their successors, on the Bible, the work of the apostles and prophets; the next generation on the church, the work of apostles and fathers. The world retreads this ground. Protestantism delivers us from the tyranny of the church, and carries us back to the Bible. Biblical criticism frees us from the thraldom of the Scripture, and brings us to the authority of Jesus. Philosophical spiritualism liberates us from all personal and finite authority, and restores us to GOD, the primeval fountain, whence the church, the Scriptures, and Jesus, have drawn all the water of life, wherewith they filled their urns. Thence, and thence only, shall mankind obtain absolute Religion and spiritual well-being. Is this a *retreat* for mankind? No, it is progress without end.[63]

Parker wrote this in 1842; in 1858 he was still waiting. "We want a revival of religion in the American church which shall be to the church what the religion of Jesus was to heathenism and Judaism," he said. "Such a revival of religion—it is possible; one day it will be actual."[64]

Absolute Religion, as Parker saw it, had large implications for both politics and literature. Politically, it pointed to parallels between churches and governments, prophets and patriots, God's kingdom and the political commonwealth. Churches could not truly minister to people only as individuals, said Parker; the minister's job is "also to diffuse the ideas which shall mold society."[65] That meant addressing the great social injustices, including slavery but also the mistreatment of women, Indians, laborers, and other classes of the oppressed. True religion *was* social reform. "We want a religion democratically organized, generating great political, social, domestic institutions," said Parker—or to put it another way: "Religion that thinks and works."[66] Parker framed the church's failures the same way the Declaration of Independence had framed the British colonial governments', as a catalogue of grievances that proved it illegitimately at odds with its reason for existing: "a church must protest against all wrong which it knows to be wrong; promote all right which it knows to be right. It is a church for that very purpose, and nothing less."[67] The work of the prophets, whose pronouncements became the Bible, was meant to serve that same purpose: "If these men are set up as masters of the soul, Justice must break her staff over their heads. But view them as patriots whom danger aroused from the repose of life,—as pious men awakened by concern for the public virtue, and nobler men never spoke speech."[68] Scripture itself, in its origins, was not merely words, not private counsel, but public action.

Parker's vision of the kingdom of God as something achievable in this world, his insistence that a practical faith "that thinks and works" could, in fact, work, had a distinctly American inflection. This is especially clear in his 1852 sermon "Of Justice and the Conscience," the source of one of his most famous quotations. Venturing further than usual into abstract philosophy, Parker here outlined a theory of moral laws that analogized them to the laws of physics. Justice is a force of nature, like gravity, and hence cannot long be defied. It will prevail in human affairs because it is "the constitution or fundamental law of the moral universe"—a phrase anticipating Emerson's— as well as God's own mode of action and an irrepressible human instinct.[69] People might be lulled into forgetting it, the powerful will ignore or deny it and the "leaders of modern civilization" treat it with scorn, but there is an "absolute" justice that ultimately inspires hatred of the wrong, driving the secular quests for justice that produce political revolutions and constitution-writing.[70] "Things refuse to be mismanaged long," Parker insisted, and so the "facts of the world" showed "a continual and progressive triumph of the right," following a long "arc" that "bends toward justice"—phrases that would reappear in the twentieth-century Civil Rights Movement.[71]

In making this argument, Parker deployed some especially noteworthy metaphors. He compared the fact of eternal, absolute justice to written text: "A sentence is written against all that is unjust, written by God in the nature of man and the nature of the universe, because it is in the nature of the Infinite God." Human beings are the essential "means" for realizing God's justice, and individuals in their everyday lives contribute their little bits to the "common store." Justice is thus "writ" in a way that is cumulative over time:

> Justice is the idea of God, the ideal of man, the rule of conduct writ in the nature of mankind. The ideal must become actual, God's thought a human thing, made real in a reign of righteousness, and a kingdom—no, a Commonwealth—of justice on the earth.

The conversion of kingdom to Commonwealth, of a "reign" to "the republic of righteousness, the democracy of justice" that relies on all (including the "obscurely faithful"), was of course not the afterthought that Parker's phrasing pretended. His listeners would have heard in it the intentional echo of America's own revolutionary transformation.[72]

As further evidence of the universal urge to "bear witness to the right," Parker pointed to literature, with its perennial quest for "poetical justice"—stories in which the good is affirmed and rewarded.[73] He noted this phenomenon only in passing, but it accords with the more ambitious arguments through which, in his religious treatises, Parker claimed to defend and vindicate the Bible. Paradoxically, he suggested, the best defense of the text depends on undercutting it. The great problem is distinguishing what is "transient" in Christianity from what is "permanent," and the Bible was typically placed on the wrong side of that divide. In an era when "modern criticism is fast breaking to pieces this idol which men have made out of the scriptures," it was possible to see that even they might prove transient—an important conduit for spiritual truth for a time, but not that truth in itself, only its contingent, corrupted, and now disintegrating means of expression, one passing "historical form" among many. Like any teacher, they would finally be outgrown.[74] Recognizing this, however, did not destroy the biblical books' true value but at last made it clear:

> They contradict one another, and some relate what no testimony can render less than absurd; but yet all taken together, [in] spite of their imperfections and positive faults, form such a collection of religious writings as the world never saw, so deep, so rich, so divine.[75]

The biblical writings must be taken for what they are worth, not made "masters of the soul."

Yet to do this does not lower the books' value but raises it. Christians were apt to put the Bible on the same ground as the holy books of other faiths, to "glory in believing whatever is prefaced with a Thus-saith-the-Lord; but then all superiority of the Bible over these books disappears forever."[76] Its true excellence appears only when we reject its untruths and its "theology," set aside claims for its special authority, and read its component writings as exemplars of their various literary genres: Genesis is "a grand hymn of creation"; the psalms are the world's greatest devotional hymns; the writings of the prophets and apostles—if rescued from the "monstrous prodigies" that the texts also preserve—are as powerful, deep, and noble as any ever set down. The Bible surpasses the world's other scriptures, but only when it is *not* idolatrously ranked as one of them but received as the literary product it essentially is. Compared to mere "Scripture" as Christians have traditionally construed the term, literature is superior: "The word of God—no Scripture will hold that."[77]

Horace Bushnell: The Gospel as a "Magnificent Work of Art"

These hints in Parker's works at the limits of words and writing are developed much more comprehensively in Horace Bushnell's. More than Parker, Bushnell was a close student and philosopher of language. He had studied at seminary with a philologist who was then developing a theory called "semasiology," which emphasized the ways in which most words were originally metaphorical. Like the Transcendentalists but not under their influence, Bushnell was also a disciple of Samuel Taylor Coleridge, leading him toward views that in some ways paralleled those that Emerson was developing at about the same time. A major preoccupation for Coleridge had been the figurative nature of language and its relationship to the divine.[78]

Bushnell's studies brought him to a simple conclusion: "the letter cannot teach" Christianity, and "words cannot tell us what it is."[79] Prefacing the book that made that statement, *God in Christ,* Bushnell presented a "Preliminary Dissertation on Language" explaining that words, and therefore the propositions built from them, do not function in the way that readers of Scripture commonly supposed. Rather than defining some fixed set of ideas, they work through internal states, inducing a state resembling the speaker's mind in the listener's. They do not "literally convey" thoughts, but are just "hints," creating "social understanding" in much the same way as gestures and facial expressions, from which in part they arise. A word might name something in the world, but even in doing so it offers a sign or image that "shadows forth" a thought into the receiving mind.[80] What led to Christians' endless sectarian strife was theologians' failure to understand this, and instead to take words "as absolute measures and equivalents of truth"—an error that made one "a mere uninspired, unfructifying logicker."[81]

On this view, inconsistencies and self-contradictions in language were not an obstacle to seeing truth but arguably a means to it, much as one might get a better idea of a landscape by walking around and taking it in from several standpoints.[82] No book, Bushnell conceded, contained more contradictions and "repugnances" than the Bible, so "if any man please to play off his constructive logic upon it, he can easily show it up as the absurdest book in the world." The better approach, however, was to think of its many authors as a "company" one was invited to join, with their differing views and their various idioms doing the reader the favor of shining "cross lights" on their common subject.[83] More than any other book, the Bible created harmony from the apparent lack of it:

> How, then, are we to receive it and come into its truth? Only in the comprehensive manner just now suggested; not by destroying the repugnances, but by allowing them to stand, offering our mind to their impressions, and allowing it to gravitate inwardly, towards that whole of truth, in which they coalesce.[84]

This "Christian comprehensiveness," as he later called it, reflected what Bushnell believed should be obvious: that "religion has a natural and profound alliance with poetry." As daunting a task as it would be for "some great universal poet of humanity" like Shakespeare "to express man," it is doubtless somewhat more for a book to be constructed that will express God, and open His eternity to man. And if it would be somewhat difficult to put the poet of humanity into a few short formulas, that will communicate all he expresses, with his manifold, wondrous art, will it probably be easier to transfer the grand poem of salvation, that which expresses God, even the feeling of God, into a few dull propositions; which, when they are produced, we may call the sum total of the Christian truth?[85]

Bushnell's rhetoric leaned heavily on this kind of contrast between the poetry of Scripture and matters of science or formal logic. The problem with "a few dull propositions" was not mainly that they were few or dull, but that they were propositions—a matter of "dialectics," part of a theological enterprise he disparaged as "this immense engineering process." Paradoxically, a statement of doctrine that people can assent to must in some sense be false: It will necessarily be a formulaic, literalizing reduction of what was originally a figurative truth, and "the letter is never true."[86]

It was a good thing, then, if there were many creeds, and even good if these were in conflict—a fact that, again paradoxically, might actually work to lower the temperature of Christian disputes. Differing creeds resembled the differing books of the Bible, which could become "a mere jingle of sounds" but, because "they act as complementary forces," instead lead to "the fullest, liveliest, and most many-sided apprehension of the Christian truth."[87] The greatest authors and teachers are always subjects of controversy and differing interpretations; this is a virtue, not a problem, reflecting the breadth and "piercing vigor" that make them great. True theology likewise called for this "more esthetic character." If Christians come to understand properly the workings of language,

> The scriptures will be more studied than they have been, and in a different manner—not as a magazine of propositions and mere dialectic entities, but as inspirations and poetic forms of life; requiring, also, divine inbreathings and exaltations in us, that we may ascend into their meaning. ... We shall seem to understand less, and shall actually receive more.

Moreover, Bushnell argued with remarkable optimism, reading in this "organic" way, instead of treating theology like "inorganic chemistry and atomic theory," will make opinions less definite and therefore easier to reconcile. Christians will then conduct their disagreements in a spirit of love, humility, and charitable patience.[88]

Of course, there was an obvious objection: some would be "apprehensive," Bushnell acknowledged, "that the views here offered may bring in an age of mysticism, and so of interminable confusion." Bushnell's answer, in effect, was no, it won't; but yes, in part it will; but, what's wrong with that? Mysticism involved looking for secret meanings, "some agency of LIFE, or LIVING THOUGHT" behind words, institutions, or events in their outward forms. Any living religion that was not "one-sided intellectualism" must do something of that kind:

> Man is designed, in his very nature, to be a partially mystic being; the world to be looked upon as a mystic world. Christ himself revealed a decidedly mystic element in his teachings. There is something of a mystic quality in almost every writing of the New Testament.

Yes, recognizing "the insufficiency and the partially repugnant character of words" might bring a "trace" of mysticism to "the stern, iron-limbed speculative logic of our New England theology," but that would not overturn it, merely give it spirit and life.[89] Most urgently, the right understanding of language could resolve persistently "contrarious" and "logically insoluble" problems like the Trinity, Incarnation, and Atonement—the three great questions of the nature and saving role of Christ that were sharply dividing Reformed Protestants, particularly Unitarians from the traditionally orthodox. These doctrines, too, must be viewed in terms of imagination and "the esthetic apprehension of faith"; they "belong to the sphere of expression, not to the sphere of logic." Bushnell pointed the "abstractionists and system-mongers" to Bunyan's *Pilgrim's Progress*, which both defends metaphorical speech and demonstrates the "solidity" of religious truths when presented to the imagination.[90] Christ himself, Bushnell would later write, was "the metaphor of God; God's last metaphor!"[91]

Having thus redefined religious language, Bushnell went on in *God in Christ* to deliver his thoughts on those contested doctrines and other matters high on the American Protestant agenda, including the question of revivals. As a law student, Bushnell himself had been caught up "the Great Yale Revival of 1831," which prompted his change to a career in ministry. Revivals, however, emphasized the sudden, individual conversion of adults, not gradual, family-based cultivation of the faith throughout childhood—the anti-revivalist philosophy of *Christian Nurture* that Bushnell had promoted in his 1847 book of that title (and for which he is most widely remembered today, given its large influence on Christian education).[92] Though less acerbically than Theodore Parker, and with more respect for institutional practices, Bushnell took a stance like Parker's that claimed to favor revival as a concept, "true" revival, while criticizing the actual revivals of the day as dim shadows or counterfeits. What people really longed for was "some true renovation of the religious spirit," or "THE TRUE REVIVING OF RELIGION," as he called it (in his capitals).[93] Existing revivals, too bound to established dogmas, aimed to revive churches rather than religion itself. Their "force is spent," but it was no good hoping for a "mere reviving of revivals."

The revival era's "sharp alternations between vitality and utter deadness" were themselves signs of spiritual disease, but also preparation for "a new Christian era"—"a grand inaugural of the Spirit throughout Christendom," superseding the "sporadic manifestations of the Spirit here and there, now in one village or town, now in another" that merely relapsed into deadness.[94]

How this vision differed from what conventional revivalists claimed to be seeking was not entirely clear, but Bushnell linked it to his idea that the Gospel was "a magnificent work of art." If the Spirit moved and changed the world, it did so through its recipients' "sensibility" and "esthetic talent."[95] Even long after the closing of the biblical canon, inspiration was still at work, Bushnell insisted (as had Emerson and Parker), and it reached even into the practical matters of life. There was hope, then, for a movement that would prove to be more than a "casual flame," that in fact would revive the "power of religion itself." With its disentanglement of religion from the civil order, moreover, America might well be the nation best positioned to lead this true reviving.[96]

Bushnell's ideas had drawn criticism for their "evil notoriety," as he put it, even before he published them in *God in Christ*.[97] His fellow Congregationalists looked askance not just at his views on the major doctrinal disputes, but at his rejection of the syllogistic methods on which the official doctrines relied. Like Parker, therefore, Bushnell was compelled to explain to a panel of fellow clergy why his alleged heresies should not see him expelled from their fellowship. In a book-length sequel and defense, *Christ in Theology*, he tried to demonstrate his language theory again, this time with examples especially chosen to impress his orthodox Protestant inquisitors. How did Catholics, for instance, arrive at scandalous ideas like "Mary is the Mother of God"? Or Unitarians reach the "revolting conclusion" that if Christ was God, then God must have died? Through "a misuse of the material offered us": Words present in Scripture for their expressive power "clash, as symbols, with each other, and then we take them all as so many centers of logical systems, piling up, age upon age, our Babels of wisdom." Statements in language are not calculus problems, but that's how theologians wrongly tried to read them.[98]

Similar fallacies, Bushnell argued, drove the kinds of errors that the orthodox encountered closer to home and spent their days combatting. Even the Nicene Creed, that ancient, core statement of shared Christian belief, had fallen victim to this "falsity" of method. Its framers had "laid hold of the Scripture phrases, 'Son,' 'begotten,' 'only begotten'—figures of rhetoric, even transcendently poetical—and squared them down into a solid block of science." Thus arose the paradoxes that had launched so many disputes, and thus did once-living ideas, reduced to "dead timber," eventually fall "out of the world's faith. Even where they are professed, they seem to be only timidly held, or half believed." Here, for Bushnell, was the pattern behind "all the wars of theology." What these had left in their wake, he repeatedly charged, was "feeble," a "notional, academic, professorial faith"—the lamentable Christianity of "bibliolators" who were not just uninspired, but who assumed that inspiration belonged only to authors long past.[99]

Much like Theodore Parker a few years earlier, Bushnell narrowly managed to fend off formal charges of heresy, but nonetheless found himself shunned among fellow ministers and leading a church that stood on its own, outside the usual denominational fellowship. In their chilliness toward received authorities and doctrines, both Parker and Bushnell were bound to disconcert other churchmen—and their efforts to excuse, even extol, the Bible's "absurdities" through ingenious comparisons to literature and art would likely strike most believers as conceding too much to modern skepticism, even if they pointed the way toward liberal theology's future. Parker's "Absolute Religion" conceded too much even for Bushnell, who took the position of a friendly critic, granting that Parker had important insights but concerned that this "new infidelity" denied the supernatural, and therefore tended toward atheism. Though less "crude-minded and malignant" than the angry old deism, critiques of Christianity like Parker's that came wrapped in professed admiration for it were perhaps that much more dangerous.[100] Emerson's philosophy was even more flawed: beautifully expressed, Bushnell granted, but with its emphasis on nature, not the supernatural, it was somehow both inspiring and disempowering at the same time. Without the impulse that comes from God, duty, and the objects of faith, it was "brilliant inanity"—the "beautiful thoughts" of a "reflective egoism," producing "the unreadiness, the almost aching incapacity felt to undertake any thing or become any thing, by one who has taken lessons at this school."[101]

Criticisms like those revealed that Bushnell, too, saw a need for action in the world, even if he was far less insistent on that point than Parker. While urging abolition, he scorned the "ill manners" and "battering-ram" approach of the anti-slavery societies; a better and fairer approach, he proposed, was appealing to southerners like Christian gentlemen and leaders of sovereign states. To issue demands in the "style and tone" of the Declaration of Independence—from a convention in Philadelphia, no less, as the American Anti-Slavery Society had done—was ludicrous and boorish, a tactic that could only alienate, not persuade. Other reform associations, in his view, similarly tended to undercut their own moral force.[102] In that guarded spirit, Bushnell differed with Parker over women's suffrage, which Parker supported but Bushnell called *The Reform against Nature*.[103]

What we see in comparing them, then, are two different but closely related orientations that match the two dimensions of prophecy: horizontal and vertical. Bushnell put the vertical first; by his own account he was a mystic, not a radical, preoccupied more with intuitions than institutions, the Spirit rather than the Kingdom. His focus was on how the divine could be received in the world and made intelligible. Parker's was essentially the reverse: His listeners were to go forth on the horizontal plane, carrying divine energies into worldly affairs and spreading a Kingdom of God on earth. The first-order goal was combatting Giant Sin, which meant social and political radicalism.

Yet each mode of prophetic renewal entailed the other. To receive the divine is to see how the world needs transforming, and to hope to transform it rightly it is an excellent reason to seek guidance from above. Hence the true revival, for Bushnell, would also produce something like Parker's Christian commonwealth, while for Parker it would not just radically improve society but resemble Bushnell's "grand inaugural of the Spirit."

Noble Schemes and Poetic Manifestations

As clever as they might be, these liberal defenses of Scripture—audaciously comparing its contradictions to the subtleties and polyphonic variety of great art, and suggesting that this resemblance to other literatures ennobled rather than diminished it—could achieve only so much. They could not restore the Bible's traditional authority, nor the assumptions about it held by most ordinary Christians: that here, in one large book, was a coherent collection of the oldest and best knowledge, nothing less than a comprehensive and reliable record of God's own thoughts. In fact, for liberals like Parker and Bushnell, the literary way of vindicating the Bible took its failures of coherence as a starting point. That was one key problem they were hoping to answer. Compared to the approaches of ultra-protestants like Miller, Campbell, and Smith, the liberals' answers reflected real historical awareness and were not logically self-canceling.[104] Yet they were all the more certain to dissatisfy conservative biblicists. The idea that all language was suggestive, the Bible's included—that words were inherently the stuff of poetry, not precision—might come across less as reassurance than as a counsel of despair. It could call into doubt one's hope of ever grasping not just religious truths but any truths at all.

That problem would continue to provoke bitter arguments among Christians well into the twentieth century. The continued development of historical biblical criticism, and even more so the theory of evolution—with its unbiblical picture of humankind as mere higher animals, an unusual species of ape that emerged only gradually over millions of years—would further inflame these arguments, leading to the Fundamentalist reaction, "Creationism," and many stepped-up efforts to prove the Bible true in every detail. Meanwhile, though, the liberal perception of the Bible itself as another evolved species, a close kin to literature and art, conversely suggested that other literatures, too, could be "scriptural" in some important sense. Emerson's call to write new Bibles might not produce Bibles of the old type, and from his viewpoint really should not, since that would just be reinstituting the "dead letter" of textual dogmatism. Nonetheless, the energies that of old had originally produced religion might somehow be reanimated, reappearing in other forms and in works yet to be written, and thus bring new inspiration to a desponding modern world.

As literary historians have noted, the Romantic movement and other developments had done much to fuse religion with literature, transferring assumptions about and modes of reading Scripture to secular works and suggesting a similar transfer of social roles. Stephen Prickett has argued that modern conceptions of literature could not exist without Scripture's "aesthetic lead." This, he says, was "the great paradox of the Bible in the nineteenth century: that at the very moment when it was seemingly losing both historical and even moral authority with biblical scholars and philosophers, it was permeating as never before the literature and imaginative thought of the time."[105] If the naïve scriptural faith of old was succumbing to the higher criticism and in other ways eclipsed, says Lawrence Buell, "At least partially offsetting the disillusioning sense that prophets were no more than poets was the exciting dream that poets might be prophets." Emerson had shown the way, continually linking "prophecy and poesis"; in his work, "Literature and scripture become interchangeable categories."[106]

From a Marxist perspective, Terry Eagleton has linked the elevation of literature as quasi-religion to the alarm of the Victorian elite, for which religion had failed to contain rising class and labor rebellion. Literature "was admirably well-fitted to carry through the ideological task which religion left off"; it could promote social pacification in a wide variety of ways, not least by filling the minds of the restive lower orders with a spiritualized vision of "great" works and writers in place of concern for their real material interests. Instruction in English literature at the nineteenth-century "working men's colleges"—its first institutional hosts—would be a solvent for class struggle, training erstwhile malcontents to join with their betters in a single, "'organic' national tradition and identity."[107]

In America, a less cynical analysis of these developments might foreground the theological liberals' program, which took a literary turn for additional reasons. The Transcendentalists and others were certainly very interested in the great question of how America's political and economic revolutions might be completed with a cultural revolution, an original and suitably American expressiveness that would break with the borrowed forms of the past. For all its material successes, the new nation still needed an "intellectual Declaration of Independence." That was what Oliver Wendell Holmes, Sr., father of the great jurist, called Emerson's "American Scholar" address, an inspirational statement whose young audience received it "as if a prophet had been proclaiming to them 'Thus saith the Lord.'"[108] The comment neatly suggests the confluence of the literary, political, and religious: Declarations of Independence were works of prophecy too, and all the more so when they announced not just a new political order but the liberation of a national spirit, a new and distinctive "genius" of the kind that could inform and generate a new national literature.

Expressiveness, however, can take the form of actions as well as words. Of all nations, America in particular might have a genius for doing, not just speaking (or writing). Far from cynically assisting in efforts at social control, a literary extension of religion's historic mission might involve advancing the Kingdom of God on earth. Parker's and Bushnell's visions of the "true revival" suggested as much, with Parker's focused especially intently on social activism aimed at bettering the lot of the disadvantaged—the leading example of which, of course, was a large group allegedly bearing the "mark of Cain" and living literally in captivity, a situation at least as dire as that which had once called forth as great a biblical figure as Moses. A religious quest carried on outside the four corners of traditional biblical belief might mean producing new literature, works in a modern idiom but with something like the Bible's old moral authority, but it might also mean trying to activate whatever powers there were in America that could make it a republic of righteousness. Both were projects in nation-building. Literature could give the nation a distinctive voice but also help make it Parker's modified Kingdom, the "Commonwealth of justice."

Margaret Fuller saw especially clearly how these features of the liberal enterprise were intertwined. The two prophetic groups—"radicals" and "mystics," in her terms—were pursuing goals that were dialectically related. Though oriented toward the facts of society, the radicals were also responding to a problem of the soul; they were aware, Fuller said, that a person is not just "a subscriber to the social contract." Social reform is also soul-work: "No institution can be good which does not tend to improve the individual." Conversely, the mystics were making contact with the core of humanity that inspired hope—and thereby enabled social reform. Fuller conceded that her friends in "the Transcendental party" might carry their efforts to utopian, impractical extremes, that they raised protests at times without knowing what they wanted done, and that they were still feeling their way toward "the work this country needs." Nonetheless, the reformer's "noble scheme" and the artist's "poetic manifestation" each "prophesies to man his eventual destiny." Hence, far from being unworldly, the Transcendentalists "are, in my view, the true utilitarians."[109]

That Fuller defined the field of activity as "the work this country needs" is interestingly counterintuitive. The belief that addressing either type of need, spiritual or social, also meant addressing the other was an obvious basis for shared projects among liberal Christians—but why would those projects be localized to America? Troubled societies and suffering souls were everywhere; true revivals and righteous commonwealths seemed to be called for across the globe. Liberal solicitude did at times widen its scope to that larger world, and even more often it focused in, magnifying for special concern something less than the whole nation: the slaveholding South, or particular oppressed and disenfranchised groups, or the crowded new industrial cities with their chronic poverty and growing labor troubles. Yet it was common for liberal efforts flowing from the crisis of textual authority to attempt to speak to America as such. "Practical" Christians, Fuller's radicals, were inclined to think in national terms for the obvious reason that they dealt with problems like those at the center of national political movements and policy debates, the same problems aired every day in Congress and the newspapers. For other reasons the mystics, too, while enthusing over nature, souls and "oversouls"—spiritualizing abstractions seemingly far removed from the news of the day—were often in practice also cultural nationalists. The new literature they spoke of was usually seen as a national one, part of a broader spiritual and cultural transformation of the kind that Walt Whitman would call "Religious Democracy" and would present as part of America's historic promise, a great but still unrealized national project specific to the United States.[110]

Meanwhile, textual culture in America was changing rapidly quite apart from what any Transcendentalists or liberal Christians had to say about it. Even with the nation's own times and circumstances still not "chanted" as Emerson was hoping, with his new Teacher still being looked for and his new Bibles yet to be written, America was leading the world in two key respects. A dynamic new publishing industry was producing printed matter in huge quantities at unprecedented speeds; the "penny press" in particular, and then in short order the telegraph, was revolutionizing information, turning it into a commodity as plentiful, cheap, and easily reproduced as the grains that were newly being farmed on the Western prairies. At the same time, America's origins in revolutionary manifestos and written governing instruments, especially the Declaration of Independence and the Constitution, created new sources of textual authority and, indeed, textual reverence—but a reverence which, like Christian reliance on the Bible, was as likely to provoke contentious debates as to settle them.

These developments stand, in a sense, at opposite poles, the one producing text of seemingly no lasting value at all—news one day, fishwrap the next—while the other accredited a certain select group of texts as a kind of national political scripture, words of inestimable and even, some claimed, timeless value, perhaps divinely inspired in themselves and, at any rate, sacred to the nation in their own way, bearing an authority similar to the Bible's and intertwined with it. The writers who would produce whatever new national literature might soon emerge would necessarily be working within this new framework, their own writings almost inevitably having reference to, or borrowing from, or perhaps even trying to synthesize these two "high" and "low" poles of textual culture. They would be writing for a national readership that was awash in cheaply produced information of the most ephemeral kind, but also seeking answers to great public questions through authoritative interpretations of sacred and near-sacred texts. Those interpretations, inevitably, would borrow from Protestant Christianity's long history of Bible-reading. All this, as we will see, had large implications for American literature and culture.

PART TWO

The Quest for New Scriptures

5

American Parascriptures: The Making of a National Political Canon

> [Chap. LX. The Independence of the thirteen United States, acknowledged in Europe. Peace is declared.] 4. And the Provinces in the land of Columbia, were called by a new name [United States of North America], and they became one people, and the great Sanhedrim ruled over them.
> 5. And on the twentieth day of the ſecond month, in the one thouſand ſeven hundred and eighty-ſecond year of the Chriſtian Hegira, was peace proclaimed: and the men of Britain, departed from the land of Columbia.
> 6. And each man of the hoſt of the people of the Provinces, went to his own houſe; and there was joy and gladneſs throughout the whole land.
>
> RICHARD SNOWDEN, *THE AMERICAN REVOLUTION: WRITTEN IN SCRIPTURAL, OR, ANCIENT HISTORICAL STYLE*[1]

This hard-won happy ending closes a long and very unusual history of the American Revolution. First published in 1793 and reissued in three further editions over the next thirty years, Richard Snowden's retelling of the epic events, still a matter of living memory in his time, narrates them in a sustained mimicry of Jacobean English, the increasingly non-colloquial diction that American readers nonetheless experienced as "biblical" after two centuries of saturation in the Authorized Version of 1611. In this deliberately unusual diction, Snowden describes the gathering political crisis from the Boston Tea

Party onwards. As war looms, "the great Sanhedrim of the people," who "bore the burthen in the heat of the day," need a captain for their "host," so they choose "*George*, whos[e] surname was *Washington*, he was from the south country, and had a goodly inheritance on Mount Vernon, and flocks and herds in abundance."[2] George then goes to meet the troops: "And lo! when he arrived at the camp, he found them, as sheep having no shepherd, every man doing that which was right in his own eyes."

The same affectation continues for hundreds of pages, with the text divided into Bible-styled chapters and verses. Words known from Scripture freely replace normal colloquial English, so the Continental Congress becomes the "Sanhedrim," a farmer becomes a "husbandman," cannons are "destroying engines," a forge is a "fiery furnace," a hill or bridge is a "high place." Some modern place names are given ancient equivalents, and archaic usages and spellings, like "goodly" and "burthen," are deliberately retained, as is (in early editions) the rapidly disappearing formality of the old elongated "s": "And the captains of the ſhips of the land of Columbia [America], took the engines [cannon] into the ſhips, and made all ſpeed to war with the ſea captains of the iſland of Britain."[3] Over the course of many episodes that often start with the biblical phrase "it came to pass," the story charts the setbacks, vicissitudes, and famous victories of "the valiant men of Columbia" until, finally, chief captain George leads them to victory at Yorktown.[4]

Though clearly reverencing biblical idioms, Snowden seems curiously indifferent to what the words actually meant. The Sanhedrim was an ancient religious court, not a republican Congress, and the Old Testament phrase "high place" normally meant a site of worship, or even of pagan idolatry. It is not needed to replace "hill," which itself is a perfectly common biblical word. Of course, anachronism would seem to be the point: Snowden aimed to make recent events echo with the sounds of the distant past, and especially with the ancient epic that Americans of the time knew best and revered most highly. Surprisingly, though, this exercise in what has since been called "pseudo-biblicism" was promoted at the time in quite different terms.[5] Reissuing the book thirty years after its first appearance, publisher Matthias Bartgis praised it as an attempt to tell the great story with "energy" and "elegance," while also making it "impartial," "intelligible," "concise," purely factual, and not least democratic—its "simplicity of style," he claimed, "renders it perfectly familiar to every capacity."[6] To modern ears, a labored imitation of the literary English of Shakespeare's day, with many repetitions and purely decorative phrases, sounds like unwitting parody—the very opposite of the simple, factual, impartial, intelligible, and concise. Yet "clear and concise" was also Gilbert J. Hunt's claim for his 1816 Snowden-inspired sequel, *The Late War, between the United States and Great Britain,* which brought a similar treatment to the War of 1812. Clarity and simplicity were features that supposedly commended these books to students, and it seems that both were highly successful in editions aimed at schools.[7]

In the same years that Snowden was producing his history, another American patriot was appropriating the Bible in a different way. Convinced that Jesus Christ, "this first of human sages," needed "to be put into human dress," this editor literally took a razor to the Gospels, cutting out lines and rearranging passages to "omit the question of his divinity." Like Snowden's, this exercise sometimes yielded awkward results. Determined to stay "within the physical laws of nature," the redactor, an Enlightenment skeptic, sliced out reports of miracles:

[Matthew 12:]

[10] And, behold, there was a man which had his hand withered. And they asked him, saying, Is it lawful to heal on the sabbath-days? that they might accuse him.

[11] And he said unto them, What man shall there be among you, that shall have one sheep, and if it fall into a pit on the sabbath day, will he not lay hold on it, and lift it out?

[12] How much then is a man better than a sheep? Wherefore it is lawful to do well on the sabbath days.

[Mark 2, inserted:]

[27] And he said unto them, The sabbath was made for man, and not man for the sabbath:

[28] ~~Therefore the Son of man is Lord also of the sabbath.~~

[13] ~~Then saith he to the man, Stretch forth thine hand. And he stretched it forth; and it was restored whole, like as the other.~~

[14] Then the Pharisees went out, and held a council against him, how they might destroy him.[8]

The redactor's method was less than perfect. Here, he apparently failed to notice that Jesus argues for healing the man but then never provides the actual healing. The redactor wanted the humanitarian teaching but not the supernatural act. In his defense, Gospel-cutting was an after-hours pastime for this unlikely Bible scholar, Thomas Jefferson; his days, he said, were "overwhelmed with other business," like serving as President of the United States.[9]

Each of these projects did leave at least an indirect mark on American religious history. The repurposed "biblical" style seems to have impressed a young schoolboy, Joseph Smith, who probably read Hunt's *Late War* in its classroom edition, *The Historical Reader*, and later applied the same technique in his "translation" of the Book of Mormon.[10] Jefferson never publicized his bible and, having long suffered political opponents berating him as an "infidel" and "heretic," he was anxious to keep his critiques of Scripture to himself. When the book eventually surfaced, though, and was published in 1904, it was generally taken as evidence against those charges. Jefferson's views were essentially Unitarian, and his bible was enthusiastically received as scripture within that church.[11]

If Snowden's and Jefferson's work had some further reach, then, it was at the margins of Christianity, among groups that many Christians would deny are Christian at all. In any case, both projects have had very few imitators. Each seems at cross-purposes to the requirements of its genre. To later readers, a history written in "scriptural, or ancient historical style" would seem not only needlessly dense but inauthentic, an obvious departure from the factual and accurate, marking it as unhistorical from the first line. Likewise, if the point of a "Bible" is to reveal God in sacred writing, Jefferson's edition would seem not to qualify: It treats the writing as partly disposable, specifically the parts that speak of God.

Nonetheless, the two projects are interestingly contrasting attempts to honor and appropriate the Bible's high authority. Snowden's approach was additive, extending the reach of the great biblical epics to include the American Founding, which now becomes another group of "Bible stories." What the "scriptural style" aimed to capture was the phenomenology of Bible-reading itself, the feel and resonance of specific words, and even the way they looked on the page. Jefferson's subtractive effort aimed at retrieval: pushing past what was on the page to recover something it obscured. In the Gospels was "the most sublime edifice of morality which had ever been exhibited to man," Jefferson explained, but this had been buried like "diamonds in a dunghill." Not only were the great teachings hidden under "heathen mysteries" and "the artificial vestments in which they have been muffled by priests," but they had sometimes been lost even on the master's own followers, the "*unlettered* apostles" who misremembered and conveyed them "unintelligibly" and "in very paradoxical shapes." Long before Jefferson cut out a single line, in fact before they were even written down, the Gospels had already been "disfigured" and "mutilated." The "sophisticating & perverting" that had then followed, the "frittering" of the simple doctrines into "subtleties" and "jargon," had "caused good men to reject the whole in disgust, & to view Jesus himself as an impostor."[12]

Proving himself "a *real Christian*," then, as he put it with his own emphasis, Jefferson saw his project as rescuing the Bible, certainly from its misinterpreters and "jugglers" but even to some extent from itself. His stated goal was the "restoration" of true, original Christianity in its "primitive simplicity."[13] In that sense it was a kind of ultra-protestant project, albeit one that broke entirely with traditional reverence for the Bible as divine revelation. Early on he summed up the Gospels' teachings, as he saw them, in an outline or "syllabus," and from there, a writer of

Jefferson's caliber could easily have retold them in his own famously elegant prose.[14] Instead he chose to keep what was left of his cut-up text intact, pasting the original Greek verses in parallel with English, Latin, and French. Interestingly, too, he had this unpolished and clearly preliminary product bound in the finest Moroccan leather, embossing and titling it in gold, and even including fold-out maps—as if roughing out the prototype for a new, replacement Bible, a book still of very high value but better suited, he may have hoped, to a new and enlightened nation like the United States. Like Tocqueville a few years later, Jefferson expected that Americans would rebel against religious confusion, or what he called the "*deliria* of crazy imaginations." Tocqueville thought the country might therefore resubmit to a creed-enforcing Catholicism, Jefferson that it would soon convert to an anti-creedal Unitarianism.[15] In its detached reasonableness, his Bible seems to have been designed to promote that soothing development.

As the ultra-protestants would show, some attempts at retrieving biblical truth focus on the text's meaning, others on its power and the sources thereof. Jefferson's and Snowden's projects marked out these same two paths: Jefferson's sought what Scripture essentially says, Snowden's what it essentially does—the qualities that make it compelling to readers. These twin goals would also drive other projects. Literary artists creating new texts would try to infuse them with Bible-like authority, usually not via Snowden's obvious mimicry but, to the contrary, in pursuit of the long-sought original expression of America's native "genius." As to unveiling the core truth and purpose of Scripture, we have seen that efforts of that kind ranged across the theological spectrum during the 1820s–40s, involving not just stalwart biblicists like Miller and Campbell but freewheeling sophisticates like Emerson and Parker.

Also in the offing, though, was an analogous and even more distinctively American project. It is noteworthy that both Snowden's and Jefferson's "bibles" emerged from America's Founding, with the one focused on the great events and the other coming from the hand of one of the leading Founders. Both patriots imagined they were marshaling sacred text to national purposes, distilling from it some essence that would meet the new country's needs. The Founding itself, however, had been achieved to an important degree through writing, and the texts that were central to it—the Declaration of Independence, and the U.S. Constitution—would eventually achieve a cultural importance that would make them bibles of a kind as well, with all that such a status implies. Americans would argue endlessly over both, attempting to excavate their core meanings and debating these as they debated the Christian Scriptures; and they would seek ways to appropriate and re-purpose them, with the result that a great many other texts would bear the founding charters' imprints or palimpsests. Like the Bible, the Declaration and Constitution would become infra-texts for the works of a wide range of American authors, who in various ways would aim to capture their power and prestige for use in still further texts.[16]

Toward Parascripture: The "Awkward and Uncouth" Declaration

On their face, the Declaration and Constitution were obvious candidates for an American patriotic canon. As the formative documents of the national compact, they "served to create and define Americans as a people," as Donald S. Lutz puts it, and provided them with the secularized equivalent of a biblical covenant.[17] Today it is common for Americans to rank them with the Bible. "The Constitution is sacred scripture," said one congressman in 1998, expressing a view that he apparently assumed his colleagues would not think to question.[18] Its creation was a "miracle," as George Washington put it and as one popular history claims in its title.[19] Even its critics recognize that Americans have long been taught to take its preternatural wisdom as an article of faith.[20] As one of them points out:

> Academic paint balls have splattered the parchment with some regularity. But in the public square the Constitution is beyond criticism. The American civic religion affords it Biblical or Koranic status, even to the point of seeing it as divinely inspired. It's the flag in prose. It's something to be venerated.[21]

Much the same can be said about the Declaration, which has likewise been called "the most sacred of all American political scriptures" and "something akin to holy writ."[22] Borrowing a term from scholars of the world's sacred literatures, we might call it a kind of secular "parascripture."

Assumptions like these, though, took surprisingly long to develop. Though Jefferson, its principal drafter, would later say the Declaration aimed to express "the American mind" in general by merely "harmonizing sentiments of the day" that were already widespread, it was very much a political statement, as was the Constitution.[23] That either one would come to be "venerated" was far from obvious at the time they were written (as is also likely true of many biblical books, for that matter). Both were the written output of controversial political projects that many Americans either opposed or supported only reluctantly. Produced in particular, time-bound circumstances, they were constructed to address or avoid certain problems of the moment. Both, therefore, were compromises, reflecting revisions and committee input that made them unsatisfactory in parts even to their own authors.

Ascending from these workaday origins to parascriptural prestige, to become the centerpieces of a new national canon, took time—and the time period in question was, not coincidentally, the same antebellum period in which the ultra-protestants and Transcendentalists were looking for ways to vindicate, renovate, or if need be replace the Bible's faded authority. Only in those decades, a generation or more after the Founding, did Americans come to treat its written products almost as addenda to holy writ. Once they were accepted, though, not merely as legal instruments but as inspiring statements of timeless principle, as guides to America's life and destiny, the Declaration and Constitution would become, like the Bible, objects of endless parsing. Supreme importance, and therefore sharp disagreements, would attach to crucial passages and sometimes even to single words.

In *American Scripture*, her history of the Declaration, Pauline Maier traces the developments that led a document that "was at first forgotten almost entirely" to end up on display at the U.S. National Archives in Washington in a kind of shrine, one that "resembles the awesome, gilded, pre-Vatican II altars of my Catholic girlhood."[24] Compared to this reverential treatment, the original "disregard" for the Declaration "verges on the incredible."[25] Granted, the Declaration's anniversary, the Fourth of July, was widely celebrated, not only as a national holiday but as an auspicious day for launching big projects. Maier points to construction commencing on some canals and railroads on the Fourth, Henry David Thoreau moving to Walden Pond on that day (in 1846) and Walt Whitman choosing it to publish both the first edition of *Leaves of Grass* (in 1855) and a later edition on the 1876 Centennial. It was an obvious day on which to strike some further blow for freedom: As Maier notes, some states made it the day on which slavery was officially abolished, and Nat Turner's slave uprising was planned for that day in 1831.[26] To these examples, we might add the attempted flight to freedom of a large group of escaping slaves in Maryland over the Fourth of July weekend in 1845; the Massachusetts Anti-Slavery Society rally in 1854 that became the occasion for William Lloyd Garrison's ceremonial burning of the Constitution and Fugitive Slave Act; and the National Woman Suffrage Association protest during an 1876 Centennial celebration at Independence Hall, where Susan B. Anthony and her colleagues demanded a platform for their Declaration of the Rights of Women.[27]

Nonetheless, the eventually famous phrases of the Declaration itself—"self-evident" truths, "all men are created equal," "certain inalienable rights," "life, liberty, and the pursuit of happiness," "our lives, our fortunes, and our sacred honor"—were surprisingly absent at first even from other American statements of rights that one might have expected to quote them.[28] In fact the text as such was dismissed either as unremarkable, a mere catalogue of anti-British grievances, or even as "awkward and uncouth," lacking the "grace, ease, and elegance of a beautiful diction." That was the opinion even of one of the Declaration's British friends, John Wilkes, who believed he was defending it against an even worse criticism—that it was "a wretched composition, very ill written"—by noting with some condescension that Americans were less interested in "harmonious, happy expressions" than in "nervous sense."[29]

Still controversial amid the vicious partisan squabbling of the new republic, when its association with Jefferson tended to identify it with one faction, the Declaration acquired its "quasi-religious attributes" and its new status as a national testament only after 1815, when the second war with Britain ended. As late as 1817, John Adams said that America "lacked any interest in its past," including the Revolution.[30] He himself had earlier objected to the "hypocritical Pageantry" deployed to celebrate Washington and other Founders: "It is as corrupt a System as that by which Saints were canonized and Cardinals Popes and whole hierarchical Systems created."[31] Jefferson, too, saw the problem that American liberty countered as "monkish ignorance and superstition," but he was more warmly disposed toward the growing reverence for the Declaration, even though he saw this as superstitious in its own way. In a materialist age, objects like his own writing desk, where he had worked on the Declaration's draft, could serve a "holy purpose" like "the relics of saints," fostering affection for "this holy bond of Union."[32]

By 1826, the fiftieth anniversary of independence, it was possible for a congressman to report that everything connected with the Declaration "excites deep and acute interest."[33] The anniversary itself helped bring that interest to a peak. Political disputes of the past were passing into history, as were the Founders themselves, a fact that was dramatically underscored when Adams and Jefferson, who had once been fierce political opponents, both died on the same Fourth of July, exactly fifty years after signing the Declaration. This startling coincidence drew comparisons with the "chariot of fire" which, according to the Old Testament, had carried the prophet Elijah directly to heaven.[34] American public rhetoric had long featured Scriptural analogies like that one; they can be found in previous eulogies—notably Washington's in 1800—and in any number of speeches and sermons of the Founding era itself. Venerating saints and relics, however, was widely seen as a Catholic practice, one that America's generally "low-church" Protestants, and especially evangelicals, prided themselves on having left far behind. Maier therefore sees the growing reverence for the Founding as "reconstructing a secular, eighteenth-century political tradition into a functional Catholicism for a Protestant country."[35]

It should be noted, though, that while there might have been something Catholic-like in the new cult of sacred objects, the same does not hold for the veneration of sacred words. Finding special power in the particular phrases of an ancient, mysterious, yet very familiar text, in the belief that it was divinely inspired, was already a central feature of Protestantism. In that light, what was new in the early nineteenth century was that Americans acquired and consecrated a new source of inspired verbal authority. In addition to drawing on actual Scripture to explain and glorify the Founding and other events, retelling the American story through biblical tropes and comparisons, they could now seek similar power in a stock of sacred phrases of their own. If not literally ancient, these were primordial to the nation in the same way that Scripture was primordial to Christendom, and they were rapidly becoming as familiar to Americans as the King James Bible's most famous phrases—and hence available for the same kinds of use. As Richard Snowden had done with Scripture itself, Americans would repeatedly seek textual authority through mimicry of the language, styles, and structures of their national parascriptures.

The National Compact and America's "Political Bible"

Besides discussing its post-1776 reputation, Maier's *American Scripture* also draws attention to the Declaration's forerunners, the various models and inspirations for it in similar declarations that came out of many American communities and states. Donald S. Lutz has done similar work on the Constitution, looking closely into the nation's archives to examine the Constitution's many predecessors. Both investigations make clear that the writings that Americans typically regard as points of origin had origins of their own, literary pre-histories in earlier textual traditions that in some ways were specific to America.[36] Lutz suggests that the ultimate origins were biblical: Early settlers began to constitute themselves as distinctive peoples through their various seventeenth-century chartering and governing instruments, which often relied in turn on the Old Testament model of a Chosen People's covenant—a solemn agreement with each other and with God. Covenants became compacts, and eventually, America's national compact came to include the federal Constitution and Bill of Rights together with the Declaration and the constitutions of the states. (Later, arguably, it would come to include famous restatements of national purpose like Abraham Lincoln's, in his Gettysburg and Second Inaugural Addresses.) It was these documents in combination that did what a compact does: create a "people," define its shared values and goals, and lay out the "civil body politic's" rules and institutions for governing and decision-making. This compact, says Lutz, clearly evolved from Judeo-Christian models, but also represented a distinctively "American form of constitutionalism."[37] Americans, then, were already primed from the very start to see their foundational documents as somehow resembling and enacting holy writ.

Even so, the Constitution's route of ascent to the status of "political bible," as it would soon be called, was also only gradual, as well as somewhat different from the Declaration's.[38] For obvious reasons, the Constitution was never neglected: Its ratification had involved close scrutiny and prolonged public debate, and unlike the Declaration it was enforceable law, hence the subject of ongoing dispute and interpretation in American courts. "Looking back from the late nineteenth century," says Michael Kammen, "it appeared that Constitution worship had begun immediately in 1789." On closer analysis, however, both Kammen and Mark A. Noll find that the Constitution's cult took a while to emerge.[39] Thomas Jefferson, who was not involved in the Constitution's drafting, urged skepticism toward constitutions in general. A key virtue for any constitution, he said, was "changeableness."[40] In 1816 he argued that every generation should frame its own government; otherwise, the dead would rule the living. Borrowing an image from the Exodus story and other Old Testament passages, he suggested that it was an error to treat constitutions "with sanctimonious reverence, and deem them like the ark of the covenant, too sacred to be touched."[41]

Over the course of the next quarter-century, Americans' reverence for the Constitution was muted and mixed. Constitution-writing was a common activity in this era, called for as corporations and associations of all kinds were formed, local governments chartered and new states proposed or organized. On the one hand, that fact made the practice widely familiar and relatively fluid, perhaps demystifying it in something like the way Jefferson had suggested. On the other, it repeatedly called attention to the U.S. Constitution as an overarching example or *ur*-text, the prototypical instance to which other such documents would normally have reference—legally, most likely, but perhaps also culturally and intertextually. In the "well-established political ritual" of constitution-writing, says one historian, American constitutional models exerted a kind of "gravitational force."[42]

As they became widely familiar, both the Declaration and the Constitution became available alongside the Bible to cite or allude to in the course of public argument. Anyone challenging established laws, institutions or hierarchies could claim to find a higher authority in the original charters, as Protestants had claimed to find in the Bible a higher authority than that of the Catholic Church.[43] Particular phrasings and verbal constructions from the Founding charters could also be deployed very much like the best-known Bible verses and quotes. To incorporate them into one's own text, and still more to write a declaration or constitution of one's own, was to lay claim to the Founding's ideals—or, perhaps, contest its meaning—in much the way that biblical references and allusions laid claim to Christianity's (or God's), even when that claim was not explicitly spelled out. As Maier explains it, from the 1820s on, "workers, farmers, women's rights advocates, and other groups" would attempt to seize the moral high ground by setting the Declaration against "the 'tyranny' of factory owners or railroads or great corporations or the male power structure," sometimes dramatizing the point by composing "alternative" declarations of their own.[44] These were typically assertions of rights and statements of political aims, often tracking more or less closely the original Declaration's structure, verbal formulas, argumentative logic, or some combination of these.[45] Perhaps the most famous instance, the Seneca Falls "Declaration of Sentiments and Resolution" of 1848, constructs an important early feminist manifesto from an especially close paraphrase of the Declaration of Independence:

> The history of mankind is a history of repeated injuries and usurpations on the part of man toward woman, having in direct object the establishment of an absolute tyranny over her. To prove this, let facts be submitted to a candid world.[46]

The rewordings are few, though obviously significant, placing "woman" and an anthropomorphized "her" in the position of America's aggrieved colonists. In doing so, the Declaration of Sentiments carried out one of the functions that Lutz identifies in founding compacts: defining and announcing the presence of a "people" newly understood to have a shared history, purpose, common life, and position in the world.[47]

Likewise, framing a constitution was often an exercise in fulfilling the further goals of stating a group's shared identity and values—shared not only among its members, perhaps, but with other groups or the larger whole. A particularly important example of textual appropriation for this purpose is the 1828 constitution of the Cherokee Nation. Beginning with "WE THE REPRESENTATIVES of the people of the CHEROKEE NATION," the document mimics the U.S. Constitution's preamble (and echoes the Declaration's final paragraph), then goes on to inaugurate a government for the Cherokee nation with three branches and other features borrowed from the American government's. In later arguments before the U.S. Supreme Court, when the Cherokee were seeking federal protection against dispossession in Georgia—the notorious event that would become known as the "Trail of Tears"—they would cite this constitution along with other evidence of their loyalty to the principles of America and "the white man."[48]

In a case like the Cherokees', imitating the Founding texts could serve a group suffering disfavor as a claim to legitimacy, a signal of its eagerness to join itself to the larger American experiment. In similar fashion, an early congress of trade unions was described in 1836 as "a system of our *National Government in miniature*."[49] In other cases, constitution-writing could be a way of looking beyond current arrangements, not simply imitating or miniaturizing them. In a constitution, groups or activists could model the ideal society of their imagining.[50]

In all, it appeared that Americans found Thomas Jefferson's advice unsatisfactory. Rather than keeping the Constitution in perspective and allowing that it should regularly change, as he had urged, many were doing just the opposite:

> One American woman, while travelling abroad in 1840, heaped lavish praise upon "our own glorious *Constitution* (whose every article should be held as sacred and unchangeable as were the laws of the Persian and the

Medes)." Schoolbooks of that era often stated that the Constitution had been divinely inspired. Their authors could not refer to the Constitution without a choral vocabulary of "revered," "glorious," and "sacred."[51]

A striking instance of the idea of constitutions as sacred comes from Mormonism. Among the less-noted distinctions of Joseph Smith's career is the fact that he not only ran for President of the United States, he was the first presidential candidate in U.S. history to be assassinated. His death at the hands of rioters in June 1844 occurred while hundreds of newly appointed "electioneer missionaries" were abroad in the land, promoting his candidacy and spreading a Mormon political gospel of "theodemocracy" as a basis for reforming American government. Opponents of the LDS church took this initiative seriously enough to mobilize against it, and fears over Smith's larger political aims appear to have been one factor leading to the mob attack in which he was killed. A curious feature of this campaign, though, is that if we take Smith's own claims seriously, the Presidency of the United States would have been a demotion. Already he had assumed the much grander titles of "Prophet, Priest and King" of the "Kingdom of God."

Since the first Christian generation, Christians had been looking forward to the Kingdom of God, the eschatological hope that often figured in the teachings of Jesus as reported in the gospels. Many had assumed that the Kingdom's arrival was imminent, and that the world as we know it is therefore in its "latter days." (Hence the Mormons' name for themselves, the "Latter-day Saints.") Nowhere in the New Testament, however, is the Kingdom of God described or specified in any detail. It is not even clear whether it would be experienced on earth. Smith took this ambiguity as a blank canvas on which to paint with his usual bold strokes, inviting his followers to literalize and enact a promise they otherwise knew only from parables in an ancient book. To that end, in the same months as his presidential campaign, he inaugurated a new Mormon organization that he called the "Council of the Kingdom of God" and, later, the "Council of Fifty." This council was meant to be separate from the Mormon Church proper and oriented toward civil matters, even if drawing on spiritual authority. It would, Smith and his associates hoped, make decisions not merely for the Mormon community but for the Kingdom of God as a whole—which ultimately would mean becoming, in effect, nothing less than a worldwide government for the impending new age.[52]

As it turned out, the council never really ruled anything. In the few years during which it was seriously active, its main achievement was helping to scout locations for a Mormon commonwealth and to organize the community's migration west to the Great Salt Lake. Its larger effort to constitute the Kingdom of God as a political entity ran into early difficulties. Smith at first appointed a committee of the Council to amend the U.S. Constitution to become "the voice of Jehovah," and "to draft a constitution which should be perfect, and embrace those principles of which [sic] the constitution of the United States lacked."[53] When the committee struggled to do this, Smith announced a new "revelation" essentially withdrawing the assignment.

In 2016, though, the secret minutes of the Council of Fifty were finally published, and today the committee's abandoned draft constitution is sold to Mormons as a frameable print designed to visually mimic the first parchment copies of the U.S. Constitution, with an image of the earth wrapped in an unofficial Mormon "flag of God's Kingdom" based on the Betsy Ross flag from the American Revolution. Much of the constitution's draft is a long preamble which, again mimicking the U.S. Constitution, begins "We the People of the Kingdom of God," and which also borrows from—and on the whole, more closely resembles—the Declaration of Independence: Governments, it says, exist in order "to grant that protection to the persons and rights of man, viz. life, liberty, possession of property, and pursuit of happiness, which was designed by their creator to all men," and their current rule was illegitimate inasmuch as this purpose was being widely ignored.[54]

On might suppose that the Kingdom of God would neither need nor be bound by the mere words of a constitution, with its designated powers and prescribed procedures, but Smith held constitutions in unusually high regard. Even in claiming his own prophetic power to "perfect" it, he was identifying the U.S. Constitution as inspired text on a par with the Bible, which his "Inspired Version" had likewise set out to perfect. Indeed, Smith had "revealed" years earlier that the Constitution was divinely given, a claim that Mormons have been teaching ever since.[55] One current Mormon artist pictures its advent in a 2009 painting in which the glorified Jesus Christ delivers the Constitution to the Founders and other assembled Americans, each symbolizing some particular type of patriot, hero, sinner, or traitor.[56] Mormons have sometimes described the government's misdeeds as "apostasies," that is, departures from constitutional principles that should be obeyed like religious doctrines.[57]

Other exceptionally ambitious attempts to model new founding charters on the Declaration and Constitution came and went in the middle of the nineteenth century. A spiritualist, Andrew Jackson Davis, attempted to organize what he called a "Harmonial Brotherhood" and wrote a declaration and constitution for it in 1851, claiming he had received their peculiar contents from the spirit world and "the science of human magnetism."[58] John Brown, the anti-slavery agitator, preceded his famous raid on the arsenal at Harper's Ferry with a constitutional "convention" at which he adopted a declaration and constitution for the new free republic he hoped to establish through a slave uprising.[59] Victoria Claflin Woodhull, the first-ever female candidate for president, ran on the "Woman's, Negro and Workingman's" ticket of the "Equal Rights Party" in 1872, with a platform framed as a proposed "Constitution for the United States of the

World." This incorporated its own declarations of independence and rights, all borrowing heavily from the U.S. Declaration, Constitution, and Bill of Rights, but expanding on them in ways meant to reflect the new and more "advanced" state that civilization had achieved in the nineteenth century.[60]

On its centennial in the late 1880s, it would be possible to hear the Constitution hailed as America's ark of the covenant—the complete inverse of Jefferson's hope. One prominent observer spoke with qualified approval of the Constitution as a "peculiarly sacred" object of "fetish worship," while others noted that Independence Hall in Philadelphia, where both the Declaration and Constitution had been debated and signed, had become "the holiest spot of American earth," with visitors compared to "pilgrims" and "worshippers before a shrine."[61] By then, however, it had become clear to some observers what problems could arise from sacralizing declarations and constitutions. To do so could lead to the "superstition" that they were "literally infallible" and an uncritical faith in certain political ideas, disabling critical scrutiny of inherited political arrangements.[62] "Like a text of Scripture," said the president of the Centennial Commission, the Constitution could become "overloaded with commentaries" and the subject of "disputatious theories," while at the same time becoming "a sort of dead letter, an ancient document," at some point needing a "revival" like those in the churches.[63] Comments like these, of course, followed the Civil War, which had made all too obvious that no matter how supposedly sacred, a constitution could also simply fail.

A *"Political Religion* of the Nation"

The specific issues and debates leading to that failure will be further discussed in chapter 8 below. They had already been foreseen, however, almost before the ink on the old parchments was even dry. James Madison, a key organizer and leader of the 1787 Constitutional Convention and popularly acclaimed "Father of the Constitution," had himself stated the fundamental problem clearly: The Constitution was written in language, and language required interpretation—which clearly would not be easy because, he explicitly noted, it had never been easy in the case of the Bible:

> Besides the obscurity arising from the complexity of objects, and the imperfection of the human faculties, the medium through which the conceptions of men are conveyed to each other adds a fresh embarrassment. The use of words is to express ideas. Perspicuity, therefore, requires not only that the ideas should be distinctly formed, but that they should be expressed by words distinctly and exclusively appropriate to them. But no language is so copious as to supply words

and phrases for every complex idea, or so correct as not to include many equivocally denoting different ideas.

It followed that even a very accurate definition of objects "may be rendered inaccurate by the inaccuracy of the terms in which it is delivered." If the objects were complex or novel, the difficulties were even greater. As the Bible's puzzlements suggested, said Madison, this problem challenged even God: "When the Almighty himself condescends to address mankind in their own language, his meaning, luminous as it must be, is rendered dim and doubtful by the cloudy medium through which it is communicated."[64]

Coming to grips with the problem would be the aim of several important figures in the early years of the new republic. In his landmark 1819 "Baltimore Sermon" explaining Unitarianism, William Ellery Channing echoed Madison's concerns, but with respect to biblical rather than constitutional interpretation. The Bible is written in ordinary language, in words with multiple meanings, not "in a language and style of its own" or in words "which admit but a single sense, and of sentences wholly detached from each other." That's why people can reason about it; a book of any other kind "would be of little worth." The complexity this produces, though, the "infinite" links and dependences among the words and propositions, calls for careful parsing. Therefore, "We reason about the Bible precisely as civilians do about the constitution under which we live." The same methods must apply to both: inquiring into the authors' original intentions, considering the writing's historical context, limiting the meaning of any given provision so it accords with the meaning of others, and so forth. "Without these principles of interpretation, we frankly acknowledge, that we cannot defend the divine authority of the Scriptures. Deny us this latitude, and we must abandon this book to its enemies," said Channing.[65] A text whose meanings were fixed apart from interpretation would not really be Scripture at all.

A related and further problem was that interpretations were bound to accumulate over time. Reformed Protestantism in general, and Unitarianism in particular, had been revolts against ancient dogmas that compiled past interpretations into what seemed like fossilized layers. These transferred power away from ordinary believers, elevating clerics, hierarchs, and professional theologians as a purported class of experts whose readings of those layers everyone else just had to accept. With regard to the Constitution, a similarly dismaying development seemed well underway. Already by 1833, less than fifty years after the federal government and courts had begun operating, attempts to deal with what Madison had called "the complexity and novelty of the objects defined" had proliferated to the point that Joseph Story's standard commentary on the Constitution ran to 1,700 pages in three volumes. This elaborate attempt to map the forest amid all the trees was not, Story hastened to say, a compendium of his own mere opinions, though he himself was no ordinary citizen but a Harvard law professor and Supreme

Court Justice. It reflected, rather, the views of "authorities," which meant the Founders, the courts, and the people involved "in the actual practice of the government."[66] Even in abridged and simplified editions, Story's work was aimed at advanced students and those "who have arrived at maturer years," but still he apologized for the "abstract" quality of some of the contents.[67] Constitutions, Story granted, might be "addressed to the common sense of the people," but he clearly assumed that reading them capably still called for effort, erudition, guidance, and a great many footnotes.[68]

One fairly new and largely self-taught lawyer and legislator, only recently arrived at maturer years, had no doubt read Story and was worried over the people's common sense.[69] In one of his first important public addresses, Illinois State Representative Abraham Lincoln, not yet twenty-nine, argued in 1838 that a reasoned constitutional politics was urgent because internal dissensus had already reached alarming levels. True, the heroic history of the Founding would continue to be read "so long as the Bible shall be read," but it was fading from living memory as the Bible's history had long since done, and thus there was a rising danger that a fractious republic would dissolve into mob rule. Political vices—ambition, unreasoning passion, jealousy, envy, avarice, savagery, hate, and revenge—that had once been harnessed to noble tasks, like achieving independence and launching a great experiment in self-government, might now be turned inward and directed against fellow citizens. Some shocking recent incidents of "ill-omen" were signaling just such an "increasing disregard for law."[70]

Against this evil, what Lincoln called for was a *"political religion of the nation"* (his emphasis). His argument resembled Channing's both in appealing to reason as a primary value, and in seeing it as the nexus that joined received religion and the Founding. The new pillar against internal strife, for Lincoln, would be "cold, calculating, unimpassioned reason," from which would come *"general intelligence, sound morality*, and in particular, *a reverence for the Constitution and laws"*—and freedom, in turn, would rest upon these "as the rock of its basis; and as truly as has been said of the only greater institution, *'the gates of hell shall not prevail against it.'"*[71] The greater institution to which Lincoln alluded was the Christian church; his closing quote invoked Jesus' words in Matthew 16:18: "upon this rock I will build my church; and the gates of hell shall not prevail against it." (Six years after Lincoln's speech, Joseph Smith's presidential campaign would take the Latin phrase for "I will build on this rock" as one of its slogans.) Where Channing had cited constitutional reasoning as a model for reading the Bible, Lincoln in effect proposed the converse, citing the Bible in defense of his political religion of constitutionalist reason.

In their different ways, both Channing and Lincoln were voicing the plausible fear that reason would prove too weak, that the value of an authoritative text would be lost in either the overgrown weeds of dogmatism or the uncontained passions of the mob. Christians might believe that the gates of hell would not prevail, but they had never agreed over what counted as hell or who, at any given time, was operating its gates. Not infrequently, they had claimed to see hell's own minions in each other—with each group equally certain that its own position was clearly the one better founded on Scripture. This danger had itself not diminished, and now Americans could add to it the parallel danger that efforts to apply the Declaration and Constitution and their principles would likewise melt down in the heat of unreasoning mutual hostility.

The most optimistic response to this worry was, in effect, to dismiss it—to simply ignore Madison's caveat about words and their inevitable ambiguities. That answer went hand-in-hand with a much simpler, more pious view of textual authority and how it made itself felt. "The Constitution in its words is plain and intelligible, and it is meant for the homebred, unsophisticated understandings of our fellow-citizens," wrote Vice President George Dallas in the late 1840s.[72] Citing the "sacred stability" and "purity of its text"—basically the opposite of how Madison had seen it—Dallas recommended that the Constitution "should be found wherever there is a capacity to read: not alone in legislative halls, judicial councils, libraries, and colleges, but also in the cabins and steerages of our mariners, at every common-school, log-hut, factory, or fireside."[73] This endorsement, printed to look like a handwritten letter, introduced a popular annotated edition whose editor, William Hickey, argued that "[e]*very good citizen*" was "bound by duty" to own a copy of the Constitution, and promised to supply these if the government would help fund the project. Hickey's vision was to place copies "in each village or neighborhood, which would introduce it to the knowledge of the people, who would then seek by their own means to possess it; and thus as a mustard seed would it multiply, and its salutary principles be extended."[74] The mustard seed, as American readers of the time well knew, was one of Jesus' images for the Kingdom of God: "the least of all seeds: but when it is grown, it is the greatest among herbs, and becometh a tree, so that the birds of the air come and lodge in the branches thereof" (Matthew 13:32).

The flaw in his analogy, which Hickey seemed not to notice, was that Jesus spoke of the Kingdom of God in parables because it was essentially a mystery, a counterintuitive concept that called for explanation. Like Lincoln, Hickey wanted to inspire in Americans a "reverential attachment" to the Constitution. The way he imagined doing this was by making it, "in its simplicity and purity," the "fireside companion" of ordinary citizens, trusting them in their "sovereign power" to judge its right uses. Like many others, he seemed to assume that its meaning would be obvious, and that reverence for it would make people of one mind. In fact, Americans had long revered the Bibles that were also sitting at their firesides, but that scarcely settled their disagreements about it. To the contrary, it sharpened them by raising the stakes. Yet Hickey believed that simply absorbing the text, guided at most by his modest annotations, would enable readers "to separate the wheat from the tares"—another Gospel parable (Matthew 13:24-30)—thereby securing political "orthodoxy" and safeguarding them against the "vituperative" arguments they might yield to if they relied on the opinions of others.[75]

This optimistic and democratic premise, one modern commentator bluntly says, "could not have been more mistaken." It assumed "that, unlike sacred texts, [the Constitution] can be read and understood by anyone," when in fact it "is elusive, ambiguous, murky, and sometimes quite opaque," and therefore was bound to "come to be just like a sacred text, its meaning knowable only through some human, and fallible, means of interpretation."[76] That criticism itself, though, even if correct exegetically, is mistaken historically, assuming as it does that a heavily Protestant public imagined sacred texts to be hard to interpret. In fact, Americans were inclined to suppose that the Bible too would make its simple meanings known to all. James Madison had set the ideal of "perspicuity" against the "unavoidable inaccuracy" of the Constitution's actual English phrases, but Protestants had long explicitly argued that Scripture was perspicuous—that any reader could understand the biblical text if guided by faith, with help from at most a few brief commentaries or marginal notes or the occasional decent sermon. Complicated, abstract theological doctrines and arguments, and dependence on the credentialed authorities that produced them, not only were not helpful, they were the diseases that reading the Bible for oneself was meant to cure.

Taking a similarly pious view of the Constitution, and lacking young Lincoln's tragic vision, Hickey, Dallas, and others of the time extended that assumption from Scripture to parascripture. As the Founding's ultimate outcome, the Constitution could be viewed as expressing the special genius of America, both in its elegant design and in its native-bred purity and plainness. Proposals to make it every household's fireside companion resembled what organizations like the American Bible Society were attempting in these same years through their mass distribution of Bibles and free religious literature, a phenomenally large publishing and logistical enterprise. Just give readers the unembellished text, "without note or comment" as the ABS put it, and a single true faith would spread throughout the land.[77]

Inevitably, hopes like these would be disappointed. As one newspaper lamented in 1856, the Constitution was already by then "a subject of infinite sects, like the Bible."[78] Along with sectarian strife came similar levels of partisan hostility. It was difficult to see how Lincoln's "political" religion would avoid conflict and stay grounded in reason any better than religion *per se*. Indeed, a quarter-century after his precocious attempt to link religion to freedom, Lincoln himself would preside over the most violent of those conflicts, a war in which each side justified massive death and destruction by claiming to fight for freedom—all while charging the other with betraying the Declaration's, the Constitution's, *and* the Bible's true meanings. A government of the book, it turned out, was as tightly chained to the problems of textuality as a religion of the book. As in Christian history, some of the resulting disputes could not be settled except by sheer force.

6

Sacred Ephemera: News, Literature, and *Uncle Tom's Cabin*

Even while the Founding charters were acquiring a kind of canonical status, an entirely different kind of text was also assuming a culturally central role. Rapid developments in printing and communications technology gave rise to mass-circulation newspapers and news reporting, expanding "the press" into the industrial-scale enterprise we know today. Far from sacred or timeless, the voluminous written matter that poured from the new high-speed, high-capacity printing plants was timely, disposable, and made for obsolescence. Even more than the printed ephemera of the past, much of it was presumed to be worth reading only that day or that hour, after which it would be discarded in favor of the next edition. As writing created for and by the moment, however, it would also address the circumstances of the moment with a specificity previously unknown, and impossible for any text passed down from generations or centuries earlier. A worried exegete like William Miller might have hoped that ancient Scriptures could deliver news of the present and coming days, if the code could be cracked through prolonged and arduous close reading; but readers of the newspapers emerging in his time would find masses of information on present events—including Miller's own movement—ready at hand in a form designed to reward even a half-attentive quick skimming.

"A Great Deal More News Nowadays"

Newspapers had existed since the seventeenth century, and other means of delivering the latest tidings long before that, but in the early nineteenth century the production and distribution of news were both profoundly transformed. As Matthew Rubery sums it up, "From the province to the metropolis, the newspaper went in a remarkably short span of time from being an item few could afford to an item few could afford to be without."[1] He is speaking of Great Britain, but in America the change was even more dramatic. Already, "The American Revolution made newspaper reading a way of life for many," according to Nathan O. Hatch, and in the early years of the new and expanding republic, between 1790 and 1810, newspapers were being founded rapidly, at a rate of about ten per year. The real "explosion of popular print," however, was still ahead.[2] According to one recent count, by the 1830s America had twice as many newspapers as Britain, and by 1850 it had more than 2,500, with an annual circulation totaling half a billion.[3] The industrial revolution had reached the news business, bringing with it cheaper paper, new and faster methods of setting type, giant steam-driven cylinder presses, the receipt of news via telegraph, and the rapid production of photo-based illustrations for print.

These developments enabled the new "penny press," beginning with Benjamin Day's *New York Sun* and James Gordon Bennett's *New York Herald,* to discover and nurture a mass audience for published news, a new and wider readership than the older, more expensive papers' audience of business elites. Reaching this audience meant delivering large volumes of material that was competitively gathered, developed specifically for the paper, chosen and framed for its popular appeal, and, of course, constantly updated, certainly by the day and sometimes by the hour. News became another mass-produced industrial product, distributed like other products to a national market through agencies like the newly founded Associated Press.

As these innovations took hold, they worked a fundamental change in how "news" was acquired and understood. In previous times news might be a rarity, and treated as such—a condition that Washington Irving satirized in his famous 1819 tall tale "Rip Van Winkle." In the years before the American Revolution and his long sleep, Rip was given to whiling away his days on a bench outside the local tavern. There, "a kind of perpetual club of the sages, philosophers, and other idle personages of the village" would normally be found "talking listlessly over village gossip, or telling endless sleepy stories about nothing":

> But it would have been worth any statesman's money to have heard the profound discussions which sometimes took place, when by chance an old newspaper fell into their hands from some passing traveler. How solemnly they would listen to the contents, as drawled out by Derrick Van Bummel, the schoolmaster, a dapper learned little man, who was not to be daunted by the most gigantic word in the dictionary; and how sagely they would deliberate upon public events some months after they had taken place.[4]

One might suppose this was just Irving's comic exaggeration, but others looking back in all seriousness gave remarkably similar accounts. Samuel

Bowles, a prominent New England editor, wrote in 1851 that "there is a great deal more news nowadays than there used to be," recalling that "publishers of country weeklies used to fish with considerable anxiety in a shallow sea, for matter sufficient to fill their sheets."[5] In 1854, New York judge James Kent remembered his local paper in the century's early years as "quiet as the times, and gentle as the manners were of yore." That old paper, the *Albany Gazette,* was not, like the later papers, "crowded with intelligence from all Christendom," laboring to monitor distant affairs "by the hour" and "examining everything, disturbing everything, and controlling everything." Yet it gave readers "all we wanted to know," including "advices [sic] from Europe two or three months old, and all the simple annals of a primitive and quiet neighborhood." At the humble bookstore where it was published, "under the old elm tree," the paper inspired lively, Van Winkle-like discussions among the locals "which, if they reached the ears of the Arch-Duke Charles and the Emperor Napoleon, might have had an important influence on the conduct of their campaigns. But I believe they never reached so far." Unlike the "hardier and more skilful journals" that came along afterwards, with their "dexterous argument," "brilliant repartee," and incessant focus on crises, the *Gazette* was "a sensible and useful paper" for a more placid and sensible time.[6]

A third writer, Samuel Goodrich, likewise looked back from 1856 to the world of his childhood, noting that many "amusements" had not changed much. However:

> Books and newspapers—which are now diffused even among the country towns, so as to be in the hands of all, young and old—were then scarce, and were read respectfully, and as if they were grave matters, demanding thought and attention. They were not toys and pastimes, taken up every day, and by everybody, in the short intervals of labor, and then hastily dismissed, like waste paper. The aged sat down when they read, and drew forth their spectacles, and put them deliberately and reverently upon the nose. ... Even the young approached a book with reverence, and a newspaper with awe. How the world has changed![7]

All these observers were recalling what a modern media historian sees as the prevailing condition of the early nineteenth century: a world of "informational constraints" that "are scarcely imaginable today." In an earlier era, when "news" meant not what happened but what happened to be available, when bad weather on the postal roads might prompt a paper to apologize for having no news, readers had a "sense of the scarcity and preciousness of information."[8] Accordingly, even a newspaper might be considered a thing of gravity, solemnity, and awe.

Then, over the course of a mere two or three decades, all that changed. By mid-century the newsgathering revolution had produced a very different informational culture, one that was variously frivolous or alarmist but, in any case, both ubiquitous and strikingly ephemeral. Massive quantities of print were generated in the expectation that they would be read quickly and just as quickly tossed aside, "like waste paper."

While that revolution depended on new technologies, as well as new business models and organizational styles, it was also both an effect and a further cause of a new definition of news—of what was worth knowing, and what pains were worth taking to make it known. Loath to serve as political party organs like the older papers, and unwilling to wait back and see what the post or packet ship happened to bring, the new penny papers competed ruthlessly to offer the most interesting content, which necessarily meant both the freshest and the most attention-grabbing. Occasionally that meant making things up, as in the case of the notorious "Great Moon Hoax," the 1835 series in the *New York Sun* claiming that a secret new telescope had found an alien civilization on the moon. More typical, though, were what we would now call "pro-active" measures to get real information first. To this end, the New York papers were already experimenting before the telegraph with new gimmicks for fast transmission: relay networks, optical signaling systems, even fleets of carrier pigeons. A key innovation was sending fast boats to meet ships from Europe as they neared the American coast, thus acquiring foreign papers and correspondence before the ships even reached harbor.[9] Suddenly there was commercial value in advantages of speed measurable in hours, or even minutes.

To succeed as a journalist in this emerging news culture meant internalizing this new value of speed for its own sake, to act as if by instinct to be fast and first, getting facts to readers even before there was any chance of analyzing or making sense of them. A later history of the *Brooklyn Daily Eagle,* one of the papers that Walt Whitman had edited as a young unknown, took pride not in having once hosted a literary great but in the exploits of other early editors who made their mark, or even became journalists in the first place, through feats of reportorial derring-do. One had been a worker at a fireworks factory who, on narrowly escaping an explosion there, had the presence of mind to run straight to the newspaper office with his eyewitness report. Another of these intrepid souls, injured in the New York draft riots of 1863, wrote up the story that same day with his head wrapped in a bandage. The *Daily Eagle*'s historian proudly linked this compulsive urge to report, at whatever risk to life and limb, with the paper's role as "defender of the people," its dedication to putting the interests of "the public" first.[10] On this view, party politics was subtly demoted, ceasing to be either the reason for a newspaper's existence or a worthy means in its own right for defending the people and advancing their interests. Instead it became just more news, another in the endless succession of spectacles to be chronicled, not different in kind from a fireworks factory blowing up.

Feeding the new ubiquity of news, in other words, was a new set of values and a new view of the world: an assumption that news of some kind is always there. The world is always in motion—the "objects of the universe perpetually flow," as Whitman would poetically put it—so every day offers vivid scenes worthy of drawing to a reader's attention.[11] This view displaced an older and more static assumption, according to which there is a limited index of subjects or focal points of interest, and these may or may not be in motion at any given time. One of the first issues of the New York *Times*, in 1851, began a front-page digest of the foreign press by noting that "no startling event has occurred in any part of Europe." It then dutifully listed the routine items available from European papers that had just arrived by steamer, starting with the fact that the Royal Family was still in Scotland, just as at last report, and that the Crystal Palace Exhibition "continues to be crowded."[12] These were items on the list of recognized worthy subjects, and therefore their current status was to be checked off even if there had been no recent change. By modern definitions, of course, the status quo—unless for some reason it comes as a surprise—is not news at all but the lack of it. One does not report that no startling event has occurred; one scans the horizon for whatever *is* startling and ignores what isn't.

Reports like the *Times*', however, were rapidly becoming anachronisms. The transatlantic telegraph cable would soon end the scarcity of European news, much as the old scarcity had already come to an end within the United States. More importantly, it would come to be assumed that Henry David Thoreau was wrong. In a well-known passage of *Walden* disparaging modern innovations generally as distractions and "pretty toys," Thoreau wrote:

> We are in great haste to construct a magnetic telegraph from Maine to Texas; but Maine and Texas, it may be, have nothing important to communicate. Either is in such a predicament as the man who was earnest to be introduced to a distinguished deaf woman, but when he was presented, and one end of her ear trumpet was put into his hand, had nothing to say. As if the main object were to talk fast and not to talk sensibly. We are eager to tunnel under the Atlantic and bring the Old World some weeks nearer to the New; but perchance the first news that will leak through into the broad, flapping American ear will be that the Princess Adelaide has the whooping cough.

"After all," he added, "the man whose horse trots a mile in a minute does not carry the most important messages."[13] Thoreau lampooned those who demanded the latest news immediately upon waking ("Pray tell me anything new that has happened to a man anywhere on this globe"), insisted that he himself had little interest even in receiving personal letters, and declared:

> I am sure that I never read any memorable news in a newspaper. If we read of one man robbed, or murdered, or killed by accident, or one house burned, or one vessel wrecked, or one steamboat blown up, or

one cow run over on the Western Railroad, or one mad dog killed, or one lot of grasshoppers in the winter—we never need read of another. One is enough. If you are acquainted with the principle, what do you care for a myriad instances and applications? To a philosopher all *news*, as it is called, is gossip, and they who edit and read it are old women over their tea.[14]

By the time Thoreau published these thoughts, in 1854, they had already been widely contradicted. Samuel Bowles believed that the telegraph, along with faster transport, has "made neighborhood among widely dissevered states." That is, Maine and Texas by definition had something to communicate, because the very possibility of easy, fast communication made them neighbors, joined them in effect in a single community.[15] However pointless it may have seemed to Thoreau, Texans would want to know what was happening in Maine and vice versa; and since Maine and Texas were at opposite reaches of the then-contiguous states, the same was implicitly true of the whole nation as a single "neighborhood." The new media cabined the news within a vessel at least the size of the nation, and were poised to exert a national influence that the old papers had not.[16] For the same reasons, once it became feasible, Americans would want their papers "crowded with intelligence from all Christendom" and updated "by the hour," in James Kent's words, even when there had been no particular "startling event"—which, according to the new standards, would simply never be the case: Somewhere or other in all Christendom, something startling was sure to have happened.

"We Do Not Care for the Bible, but We Do Care for the Newspaper"

As some analysts see it, the definition of news was simultaneously expanding along other dimensions as well. Even as they were bringing Maine closer to Texas and Europe closer to America, the speedily produced newspapers of the mid-nineteenth century were putting a new emphasis on "the nearby and the everyday," reporting local events and "human interest stories" in an entirely new way. "The penny papers saw news in ordinary events where no one had seen anything noteworthy before," says Michael Schudson in his influential social history of newspapers. Schudson quotes the *New York Herald* declaring in 1837 that the "greatest everlasting" matters of "eternity" are found in the slightest and most insignificant events. The new approach to newspapering, says Schudson, "invented a genre which acknowledged, and so enhanced, the importance of everyday life."[17] Hans Bergmann, similarly, sees the penny papers as inventing both the news and the "disposable culture" we know today by making their subject "the quotidian, the perfectly astonishing ordinary."[18] This in turn, Bergmann argues, was part of a distinctive New York writing style based on "narratives of urban encounter" that informed the work of both Whitman and Herman Melville, and that marked a shift in cultural power toward the working classes.[19] Catering to a mass public not mainly interested in the elevated or edifying, the penny press disdained older, snobbishly moralistic standards of tastefulness and bourgeois respectability to serve up tales of crime, sensation and scandal, often by snooping into private affairs ("keyhole reporting") like a devil who could peer into every corrupted soul.[20] The papers would claim to leave nothing unnoticed: "All there is is there, and all there is is New York *now*."[21] This "panoramic attention" to "the whole quotidian city," says Bergmann, the idea that it could all be taken in at once, made their contents "verbal equivalents of the New York panoramic illustrations very popular in the antebellum period."[22] (Whitman's poetry, then, would marry this new "panoramic aesthetic" to Transcendentalism.[23])

Together these developments made the old scarcity inconceivable; there would never be a day without plenty of news. In effect, Thoreau was also judged to be wrong on the question of whether reading of "one man robbed, or murdered, or killed by accident, or one house burned, or one vessel wrecked" was the same as reading of every similar event. The myriad repetitive instances he disparaged were of interest in themselves, and Thoreau's dismissal of news as gossip over tea was at odds with an emerging cultural consensus. Anything that happened might be "newsworthy," and conversely, newspapers could claim to cover everything that happened. As Walter J. Ong has noted, this claim was already implicit the moment the reader laid eyes on the paper, whose pages were always filled to the margins.[24] Ambitious publishers were hardly subtle about it, promising to cover "EVERY HAPPENING OF IMPORTANCE," as the later founders of *Time* magazine would put it.[25] A newspaper would be its readers' single point of access to whatever the daily or weekly "news cycle" had produced that was worth knowing—in effect, a complete history of the city, nation, or world since the last edition. It would come with the tacit promise that a similar instant history, superseding the one before, would always be manufactured the next day, and the next.

In a culture as intensely Protestant as that of antebellum America, these developments in the print media, as one might expect, also reflected Protestant and sometimes even ultra-protestant assumptions. (William Miller's, Alexander Campbell's, and Joseph Smith's movements all had associated newspapers and publishers.) Religious publications alone, says Nathan O. Hatch, were a major part of the "explosion of popular printed material," rapidly becoming "the grand engine of a burgeoning religious culture."[26] Horace Bushnell, in 1844, expressed his doubts that "God would offer man a mechanical engine for converting the world," but in saying this he acknowledged that many Protestants of the time saw the printing press as exactly that.[27] Of course, religious papers did not exist to cover news as such; their goal was Christian ministry and mission work by other means. Still, what Hatch calls "the devotion to print resulting from a Protestant commitment to the written word" was bound to influence the way a Protestant culture like America's received the new styles of secular news reporting as well.[28] In covering seemingly any subject from great to minor and from highest to lowest, in bringing together a myriad of very different "stories" whose import varied among the personal, local, national, and world-historical as one turned the pages, the newspaper's claim to comprehensiveness resembled the Bible's. Both offered to give readers everything they needed to know in a single printed text. The difference was that the Bible claimed to do this for all time, but the newspaper only in day-to-day fragments. The one defined the permanent and sacred, while the other epitomized the secular—bound to worldly time—and the profane: that is, uncouth, but also, in its original and technical sense, "unholy."

Comparisons to the Bible certainly suggested themselves to those describing newspapers' cultural authority. One reporter for Horace Greeley's New York *Weekly Tribune* bragged, it seems accurately, that the paper "comes next to the Bible all through the West." Clarence Darrow later remembered it as "the political and social Bible of our home" during his mid-century Ohio childhood.[29] Such comments perhaps used the term "Bible" loosely, but Henry David Thoreau would make a similar point quite heatedly during the great public debates over the Fugitive Slave Act. Outraged at the "corrupt" acquiescence of the press to that hated law, Thoreau likened its output to "the gurgling of the sewer" and the newspaper reader to "the dog that returns to his vomit." The press "exerts a greater and a more pernicious influence than the Church did in its worst period," he charged. Americans were not "a religious people" and "do not care for the Bible, but we do care for the newspaper." Politicians who found it "impertinent" to quote the Bible would readily quote the newspaper, which is

> a Bible which we read every morning and every afternoon, standing and sitting, riding and walking. It is a Bible which every man carries in his pocket, which lies on every table and counter, and which the mail, and thousands of missionaries, are continually dispensing. It is, in short, the only book which America has printed, and which America reads. So wide is its influence.[30]

Less acidly, Emerson made a similar point during the same debates. Thanks to "the silent revolution which the newspaper has wrought," all classes were now readers and thinkers:

> Look into the morning trains which, from every suburb, carry the business men into the city to their shops, counting-rooms, work-yards and warehouses. With them enters the car—the newsboy, that humble priest of politics, finance, philosophy, and religion. He unfolds his magical sheets,—twopence a head his bread of knowledge costs—and instantly the entire rectangular assembly, fresh from their breakfast, are bending as one man to their second breakfast.

"There is, no doubt, chaff enough in what he brings," Emerson added, "but there is fact, thought, and wisdom in the crude mass, from all regions of the world."[31]

Obviously Americans of the 1850s were still religious and cared for the Bible, but Thoreau's angry hyperbole was nonetheless telling. It showed that by mid-century, observers could see a basic shift: the newspaper—along with the Constitution, said Thoreau—had come to loom exceptionally large in people's thinking, not merely ranging alongside the Bible but seeming to take over what had once been its place in public discussion. Thoreau also captured in a few words both the ubiquity and the casualness of newspapers in daily life. It was not just that they were read and discarded quickly, with nothing like reverence or devotional attention; they were read in the middle of and without even pausing other activities—"standing and sitting, riding and walking"—as if readers were mentally half-discarding the paper already at the moment of reading it.

"Story"-telling and Literary Scripturism

By the middle years of the century the revolution in news reporting was making its effects felt among American literary artists. One exemplary case was that of Edgar Allan Poe, still a largely unknown writer and journalist in his mid-twenties when his exposé of "the Turk," published in 1836, was widely quoted and reprinted in newspapers throughout the country. The Turk was an international sensation, a machine that was advertised as playing chess well enough to beat nearly all comers, as it had been doing on tours of Europe and America over the course of the previous half-century. As Poe correctly surmised, the alleged "Automaton" was actually an elaborate stage trick involving a small human chess player hidden inside an intricately designed cabinet. Methodically sorting through clues, Poe showed how to solve the mystery in a series of logical steps, a kind of suspenseful unfolding that he would then turn into narrative structures in "The Murders in the Rue Morgue" and his other "tales of ratiocination," as he called them. This method then became the template for detective stories generally, influencing later writers like Sir Arthur Conan Doyle.[32] A journalistic exercise, together with the rise of crime reporting and of professional police work—also favorite newspaper subjects—thus laid the basis for one of the leading genres of modern popular fiction.

Developments like these were steps in a long co-evolution of news and fiction, two kinds of writing that both go by the name "stories." Matthew Rubery charts the influence of news on Victorian literature in general, noting that "the age of the novel" was known in its time as the age of newspapers, and that the two forms were rival practices of "realistic representation."[33] Barbara J. Shapiro identifies both newspapers and the novel as products of a "culture of fact" that she traces to seventeenth-century England, where it shares common origins with new forms in law, science, and other fields. Once "the genres associated with 'news' adopted 'matter of fact' as their reason for being," Shapiro writes, the conventions that developed for reporting facts and "the ubiquitous methods of proving them provided a mechanism for the creation of a new kind of fiction." Based as it was on "fictional facts," the novel was already by the early eighteenth century beginning "to appropriate many of the forms and locutions associated with 'matter of fact'."[34] One early review of *Moby-Dick* targeted exactly that feature, complaining that Herman Melville's 1851 *magnum opus* was "an ill-compounded mixture of romance and matter-of-fact."[35] D.H. Lawrence, whose praise for Melville in 1920 contributed to the so-called "Melville revival," also noted of *Moby-Dick,* "At first you are put off by the style," which "reads like journalism."[36]

Melville, however, had high aspirations. Americans, he insisted, could not forever accept a reputation for deficient literary production: "it will never do for us who in most other things out-do as well as out-brag the world, it will not do for us to fold our hands and say, In the highest department advance there is none." Even if, as he doubted, the antique Shakespeare was an appropriate model for a republican nation, Melville assured his readers "that Shakespeares are this day being born on the banks of the Ohio." Nathaniel Hawthorne, he said, already came close, but by 1850 Melville was envisioning an attempt of his own, a great Shakespearean tragedy set amid the businesslike operations of an American whaling ship.[37] The "ill-compounded mixture" referred to *Moby-Dick*'s striking effort to root lofty speculations on cosmic truth in a variety of genres that included not just an adventure story at sea, but such pedestrian repositories of fact as legal affidavits, encyclopedia entries, and "how-to"-like accounts of whale-butchering. Some critics were baffled, but many responded with varying degrees of admiration. Melville's epic, said *New York Tribune* editor Horace Greeley, found "subtle mysticism" in "odorous realities" and minute and "homely" descriptions, while one London reviewer similarly praised it for "investing objects apparently the most unattractive with an absorbing fascination." Though perhaps too irreverent toward "sacred subjects," said this anonymous critic, Melville had confounded those who would never have thought that "materials seemingly so uncouth" could yield profundity. "Who would have looked for philosophy in whales, or for poetry in blubber," the critic wondered, yet there they were.[38]

Melville's experiment was one example of the merging of secular and sacred literary impulses that literary historian Lawrence Buell labels "literary scripturism" and sees as characteristic of the period.[39] Buell recounts Emerson's experiments with "polyglossia," or the mixing of high and low styles, then credits several other writers, including Harriet Beecher Stowe, Melville, Walt Whitman, and Emily Dickinson, with pursuing an idea "of the writer as prophet commissioned to write the ultimate scripture-poem of the universe."[40] Melville was looking for a way to speak with "prophetic authority," and so produced a novel that "is a sort of scripture," a "modern Book of Revelation" with language "drenched in sacramentalism." For Buell, "*Moby-Dick,* along with *Leaves of Grass,* stands as a great pioneering work of comparative religion and as one of the most ambitious products of the religious imagination that American literature is likely to produce."[41] The truth of this observation, however, depends on the presence of the low along with the high. Religious imagination and language can also produce the self-conscious mimicry of Richard Snowden, Gilbert Hunt, and Joseph Smith, whose works read like burlesques on the Bible.[42] The experiments that looked to transform American literature in the 1850s involved authors scouting trails upward to the elevated and sacred through mountains of the newly mass-produced and perishable. Melville's last novel, *The Confidence-Man,* six years after *Moby-Dick,* subtly compared itself to the Bible; it sought to uncover "an original character," an extreme rarity that Melville saw as "almost as much of a prodigy" in fiction "as in real history is a new lawgiver, a revolutionizing philosopher, or the founder of a new religion." While tied to things "local, or of the age," such characters were like the products of Creation itself in Genesis.[43] For some reviewers, though, Melville's "eccentric" way of packaging his higher metaphysical philosophizing was incomprehensible, "a sad jumble" that one critic acidly compared to reading police reports.[44]

The Parascripture(s) of Harriet Beecher Stowe

Unlike *Moby-Dick,* Harriet Beecher Stowe's venture into literary scripturism, *Uncle Tom's Cabin,* was an immediate sensation, making Stowe the bestselling author of the nineteenth century not just in America but worldwide. For some British critics it settled the question of America's literary delinquency: one linked it to Shakespeare and called it "the greatest novel ever written," another praised it as "free from all that hapless second & third-hand

Germanism, & Italianism, & all other unreal-isms which make me sigh over almost every American book I open," and a third acknowledged Britain's long-held mixture of contempt and "patronizing wonder" toward American letters but said, "Let us hear no more of the poverty of American brains, or the barrenness of American literature," which *Cabin* had made "forever illustrious."[45] Its heavy reliance on religious elements drew immediate attention—it was featured in Sunday schools, and one unimpressed reviewer in France dismissed it as "a long and boring Methodist declamation"—but a recent and more common judgment rates *Cabin* as the "religious novel *par excellence*" of the American literary canon.[46]

Stowe was raised from childhood on religious literature and preaching, a tradition for which her family was famous. ("This country is inhabited by saints, sinners and Beechers," one of their friends wisecracked.[47]) Daughter of a seminary president, sister of several ministers and theologians, and wife of a professor of sacred literature, she believed she was "made for a preacher" herself.[48] Many of *Cabin's* debts to Beecher/Stowe Reformed faith and its practices are obvious; they include dozens of biblical quotes and allusions, many hymns and references to spiritual music, and plot elements based on the Bible, notably Uncle Tom's role as a Christ figure. Overall, the story is "manifestly organized according to what one religious historian has termed the 'Christian plot' but that, in Stowe's work, could be more accurately described as the 'Protestant plot': the expectation that human history will inevitably result in redemption and restoration."[49] A "distinctively Protestant liturgy" has been observed behind famous episodes like the death of Little Eva, and Stowe has also been credited with "the skillful blending of Puritan genres," including tracts, jeremiads, spiritual autobiographies, and captivity and conversion narratives, while rigorously fitting the whole into the same structure as a sermon.[50] For one modern critic, the essence of her project is to transform this "sermonic mode" through a radical reimagining of preaching in a woman's voice,[51] while for another it is to "make the sanctification of a black man the clinching argument for the full humanity and Christian potential of the African race."[52]

From its first appearance until well into the twentieth century, many popular stage adaptations, musicals, and "Tom shows" brought this Protestant plot to countless additional viewers, making it probably the most widely seen American stage production of all time.[53] These events were also overtly Christian spectacles, and because they are usually discussed in the context of theater history, not religious history, it is not often recognized how essentially liturgical they often were. Stowe reported having had the idea for the story in the first place in church, while partaking of a Communion liturgy—she was "overcome" by a "tangible vision" of the death of Uncle Tom, "like the unrolling of a picture"—and then writing the rest as it came to her "in visions, one after another."[54] Like most Christians at a church service or mass, audiences for *Uncle Tom's Cabin* on stage typically did not attend to learn the well-known underlying story, but to be guided through a kind of ritual, with each of the familiar moments vividly memorialized like the "stations of the cross." Sometimes they were living still pictures, or "tableaux," with actors striking the requisite poses. Favorite episodes like Eliza's desperate escape from slavecatchers across a frozen river, and Little Eva's death and ascension to heaven, were achieved in better-funded productions through clever stage mechanics, and sometimes much more elaborately than the relatively spare narration in the novel.[55] Bandanas, wallpaper, and commemorative plates and cups featuring similar episodic images were among the many items available in the novel's huge aftermarket of souvenirs. Edwin S. Porter's 1903 film adaptation, one of the earliest story films and the first of the nine film versions that made *Cabin* the most often adapted literary work of the silent-movie era, does not even attempt to narrate the story but is just nineteen minutes of tableaux in motion—brief mini-scenes that would be incomprehensible if not for the fact that the events they referred to were already well known and much-loved and needed merely to be evoked.[56]

If the stage shows did not quite replace churchgoing, they were sometimes credited with providing the religious edification that viewers inclined to skip actual church were otherwise missing. They reportedly drew big emotional reactions from diverse audiences that included many religious people, a remarkable development given the longstanding suspicions of many Reformed Protestants toward theater and its dangers to the soul.[57] One theater impresario, billing his early New York production's venue the "Temple of the Moral Drama," adorned the lobby "with Scriptural texts and commissioned a painter to portray him with a Bible in one hand and *Uncle Tom's Cabin* in the other."[58] An abolitionist, Parker Pillsbury, who saw the play in Boston in its earliest months, reported

> one of the largest and best looking audiences I ever saw in any theatre. And five hundred people bought tickets in the forenoon for *secured seats, at double price,*—and excepting those seats, the house was almost literally crammed nearly an hour before the rising of the curtain. And the most radical sentiments, together with the shooting dead of the kidnappers in pursuit of 'George and Eliza,' were most loudly applauded ...

For Pillsbury, the play's obvious success was more than just great news for the abolitionist cause. With one of its characters declaring that "*Slavery is of the Devil*," the Theater was finally opposing the Church, an older "theater" that largely said "*it is of God*." So, "The question is before a jury composed of the civilized world."[59] Further events seemed to vindicate Pillsbury's hopes, leading to the famous if possibly apocryphal moment when President Lincoln greeted Stowe as "the little lady who made this great war."[60]

The question would not have been so squarely put before the civilized world, however, either by the story alone or by its heavy reliance on religion, without the addition of a further element. Also crucial, but very easy to overlook, is the extent to which Stowe herself thought of *Uncle Tom's Cabin* in terms that were also, essentially, journalistic. Like other literary scripturists, Stowe was not merely trying to create a text with high spiritual value, but was merging that aspiration with a deep concern with present facts and a feeling of responsibility for seeing them reported.

Two years before writing the novel, Stowe had contributed the introductory essay to a book by one of her minister brothers, Charles Beecher: *The Incarnation; or, Pictures of the Virgin and Her Son,* an extended narrative gloss on Scripture that filled out some of the spare Gospel passages with novelistic detail. As Stowe acknowledged,

> There may be some who at first would feel a prejudice against this species of composition, as so blending together the outlines of truth and fiction as to spread a doubtful hue of romance over the whole. They wish to know that what they are reading is true. They dislike to have their sympathies enlisted and their feelings carried away by what, after all, may never have happened.

Stowe defended her brother's interpolations on factual grounds: they were well-informed, well-sourced, and "probable" enough to make the narrative "precise and authentic." What called for them in the first place was a problem we have seen others observe in this era—that Scripture itself suffered from being too well known. Even for the most spiritually sincere readers, "early and long-continued familiarity with its language" could give it a disappointing "want of freshness and reality," and hence

> they deeply lament when they find that its reading is to them but a wearisome task. In vain they ponder its pages; nothing is suggested; and while words known by heart from childhood pass under their eye, their mind wanders in dreamy vacancy. They start at the end of a chapter, and rise from it sighing and discouraged.

Novelistic yet fact-based embellishment would help "unimaginative" and un-poetical readers who might otherwise struggle to give the story "wing and fire" on their own. Facts, that is, were prompts to the imagination—a faculty wrongly underrated "as of no practical value," but all the more needed in this "hard and utilitarian age" if suitably "combined" with "critical ingenuity."[61]

If brother Charles' project involved adding details defended as factual, and designed to move readers, to a Christian biblical narrative already considered supremely important, sister Harriet's great aim would be the converse: to move readers and impress them with her subject's importance by constructing a Christian narrative which, on every point, could be defended as factual. Stowe brought to this effort her awareness that even readers willing to give over their feelings and sympathies "wish to know that what they are reading is true." In her explanations of *Uncle Tom's Cabin,* therefore, the emotional, spiritual, and reportorial purposes are completely intertwined. If anything, the latter seem to take priority. As news of the reality of slavery came to her from eyewitness reports and her own observations, Stowe said she came to believe that even good Christians were closing "their eyes, ears, and hearts to the harrowing details." So she "said to herself, these people cannot know what slavery is; they do not see what they are defending; and hence arose a purpose to write some sketches which should show to the world slavery as she had herself seen it." Taking inspiration from a courageous antislavery newspaper editor, Gamaliel Bailey, who would go on to publish the novel in its original serial installments, Stowe set out to acquire the facts and to give them to readers. Her "one purpose," she said, was "to show the institution of slavery truly, just as it existed."[62] This was a purpose "entirely transcending the artistic one"[63] At pains to get the details right, she not only researched written sources on slavery but sought informational interviews, soliciting Frederick Douglass' help in getting answers to questions directly from slaves themselves.

Uncle Tom's Cabin first appeared as a weekly serial in Bailey's paper, *The National Era,* in 1851–2. Some recent analysts have suggested that its initial existence as a newspaper feature, with letters arriving in response while the novel was still being written, gave Stowe a vivid sense of her community of readers and shaped both the language and other elements of the work in progress.[64] Contemporaries linked *Uncle Tom's* literary and religious virtues to its journalistic achievement; it had attracted even readers who would normally "frown with holy horror upon novels," said one, but Stowe's ability to break through the usual abstract arguments against slavery depended both on "intense sympathy" and her focus on "concrete reality":

> She does not *tell,* but *shows* us what it is. She does not analyze, or demonstrate, or describe, but, by a skilful manner of indirection, takes us over the plantation, into the fields,—through the whole Southern country in fact,—and shows us not only the worst but the best phases of the slavery system, and allows us to see it as it really is.[65]

Reporting the reality meant including slavery's "best phases" because, in Stowe's own words, "justice required" giving slaveholders their due, recognizing how they, too, were entrapped in the system's evils.[66]

Here she was voicing another set of emerging journalistic ideals: objectivity and balance. In *A Key to Uncle Tom's Cabin,* her book-length 1853 gloss on the novel, Stowe went to the trouble of reprinting the opinions of critics at length, explaining that she "endeavored to lay before the world, in the fullest manner, all that can be objected to her work, that both sides may have an opportunity of impartial hearing." The *Key*, she said, "aimed, as far as possible, to say what is true, and only that, without regard to the effect which it may have upon any person or party."[67] Here Stowe anticipated *The Atlantic Monthly's* founding motto, "Of no party or clique," by four years, and the famous *New York Times* credo—"to give the news impartially, without fear or favor, regardless of party, sect, or interests involved"—by more than forty. Like the novel, *A Key to Uncle Tom's Cabin* also sold extremely well: 40,000 advance copies and 100,000 in the first year.[68]

If it was not clear enough from the novel itself, the *Key* shows how much of the ambition driving Stowe's work was journalistic. Modern critics have largely neglected this companion volume, partly because the issue it was addressed to has long been settled—on whether slavery was evil or not, Stowe's position won—but also in the mistaken belief that compared to the novel itself, it "was, obviously, an afterthought."[69] It is true that the *Key* responds to criticisms that arose in the novel's wake, especially in the South, and that it includes materials that had not directly informed the novel at first but that Stowe gathered after the fact. But it was clearly a forethought, and Stowe's grand literary project is not complete without it. It was both implicitly promised in the novel's original preface—"What personal knowledge the author has had, of the truth of incidents such as are here related, will appear in its time"—and previewed in its final chapter, which directly addressed readers who had already been asking "whether this narrative is a true one."[70] It was separately published only because it outgrew the lengthy appendix that Stowe had originally envisioned. The novel itself, moreover, included footnotes, one of which provoked a public dispute that led to an exchange of attacks and defenses later incorporated into the *Key*.[71] Within the story itself are also authenticating asides, with Stowe briefly pausing the narrative to reference real-world conditions.[72]

On the question of factuality, Stowe was unrelenting. Introducing the novel to European readers, she took the opportunity to reply to claims "that the representations of this book are exaggerations! and oh would that this were true! would that this book were indeed a fiction, and not a close wrought mosaic of facts!"[73] Its truth, she said, was attested and confirmed by thousands of witnesses. Repeating that same phrase, "a mosaic of facts," the *Key* made clear that it meant to be the examination of those witnesses in print—a massive compilation meant to "authenticate" the novel in great depth and detail, to show that it was not only true but could withstand the harshest scrutiny.[74] The *Key*, that is, was the rest of the package, the second phase of a single publishing venture. Its importance to Stowe is clear from a statement that anticipated Lincoln's "little lady" joke, which assumed it was the novel that had generated the strong feelings leading to war. Years earlier, though, Stowe herself had jokingly suggested that the book that would actually dissolve the Union was the *Key*.[75]

The *Key* exists because Stowe resolved from the start to defend the novel as accurate and well-reported. She was determined not only to vindicate her disputed footnote rather than withdraw and apologize for it, but to forego other possible *apologia* that might be made for fictional works in general—that they speak for themselves, that they need no defense, that they should not be judged in strictly factual terms. Even while conceding that she had made artistic choices, which were necessarily contestable and meant to appeal to the heart as well as the head, she insisted there was real-world factual support for every detail in *Uncle Tom's Cabin*. For example, while agreeing that paragons of virtue like Uncle Tom were rare, she nonetheless sought to document that they did exist and that Tom was not merely a fanciful caricature. Among other proofs, the *Key* reprints in full one former owner's glowing testimonial to a Tom-like manumitted slave.[76]

All this was part of Stowe's broader rhetorical and political strategy, in which *Uncle Tom's Cabin* was the central but not the only element. For Stowe and her admirers, the novel wielded whatever power it did based on its factuality, the belief that behind its seemingly sentimental episodes stood "a mountain of materials," as Stowe put it, which themselves were only a sampling of the whole appalling truth.[77] Something like the *Key*, in other words, was already contained within the novel by implication, even before the *Key* itself was in print. At the same time, the actual *Key* was needed because the story's effects depended on its power to shock. The facts might be true and verifiable, but the closing of eyes, ears, and hearts to them also made them literally "novel," that is, not the subject of a ready public consensus. It was to help forge such a consensus that Stowe had written *Uncle Tom's Cabin,* but choosing to do this through fiction created a potentially self-canceling dilemma: the same invented elements that aimed to move readers emotionally might also cast doubt on the story's claim to truth, and thus its claim on the readers' emotions—which depended on their shocked awareness that even if Uncle Tom, Eliza, and Little Eva were products of Stowe's imagination, real people, too, were suffering all the same vividly dramatized wrongs.

Stowe grappled with this dilemma in the *Key's* introductory pages. No mere *apologia* for the novel, these were something more complex: a capsule philosophical critique of fiction-writing itself, which is all the more remarkable for having come from the world's suddenly most popular fiction writer.[78] Fiction, said Stowe, traffics in the "picturesque and beautiful," categories that she contrasts with "the hard and the terrible." A fiction writer can "find refuge" from a terrible reality by inventing pleasing scenes. This possibility had perversely served slavery's cause, allowing its advocates to confuse people by enfolding it in a generally benign portrait of the South.

In fact, Stowe countered, slavery and the South's charms were independent variables; slavery was purely an evil, "not the element which forms the picturesque and beautiful of Southern life."[79] Fiction, therefore, could not redeem it.

Normally, "to disentangle the glittering web of fiction" and expose an underlying reality is "unartistic." Given, though, that it had a purpose "entirely transcending the artistic one," *Uncle Tom's Cabin* was different. To a greater degree than other fictions, it was "a collection and arrangement of real incidents,— of actions really performed, of words and expressions really uttered." What made it like a mosaic was that the picture it created emerged from an artful grouping of fragments, and in this case the fragments were provable facts. Such a book "encounters, at the hands of the public, demands not usually made on fictitious works. It is *treated* as a reality,— sifted, tried and tested, as a reality; and therefore as a reality it may be proper that it should be defended." The one basic inaccuracy that Stowe would concede was that slavery ultimately defied fictionalizing; its true features were "too dreadful for the purposes of art." In a novel, she added later, they would seem a "a plot of monstrous improbability," by comparison to which her fiction was "tame." Fictional works aim to give pleasure, and a story that tried to convey slavery in full would be impossible to read.[80]

Stowe's promise to defend her work "as a reality" included the narrow question of whether she got her facts right. Importantly, though, it also went further. For pious Americans, the highest realities were known through Christian revelation. *Uncle Tom's Cabin* could make no claim to truth unless it accorded with these; it must be biblically correct, not just to be suitably inspirational in religious terms but even to be truly factual. In meeting this imperative, then, Stowe's religious and journalistic impulses were one and the same. As the wife of a professor who was one of America's authorities on the higher criticism, she was well aware of the disturbing critical questions that had been raised in her time about the Bible. The novel refers to these directly. In one episode, a virtuous soul who briefly harbors the fleeing Eliza and Harry explains why he had long refused to join a church: "'cause the ministers round in our parts used to preach that the Bible went in for these ere cuttings up,— and I couldn't be up to 'em with their Greek and Hebrew." He relented, he says, when he "found a minister that was up to 'em all in Greek and all that, and he said right the contrary."[81] Ancient texts and critical analysis, "these ere cuttings up," are an obstacle to faith, but one that even a lay person cannot just easily dismiss; the man first needed reassurance from a minister whom he could take to be the critics' equal.

Several other scenes in *Uncle Tom's Cabin* also involve characters reading or discussing the Bible. At one point the slaveholder Augustine St. Clare, Tom's temporary owner, suggests that "religious talk" and "all this sanctified stuff" regarding slavery are not really "intelligible." He is then asked about the Bible, which he dismisses as "my *mother's* book," liable to complete and cynical reversals of interpretation in light of real-world interests like the price of cotton. He acknowledges, though, that Tom "isn't a bad hand, now, at explaining Scripture, I'll dare swear." Tom even prays for St. Clare "with a zeal that was quite apostolic."[82] His method of Bible-reading had been detailed earlier:

> Having learned late in life, Tom was but a slow reader, and passed on laboriously from verse to verse. Fortunate for him was it that the book he was intent on was one which slow reading cannot injure,— nay, one whose words, like ingots of gold, seem often to need to be weighed separately, that the mind may take in their priceless value. ... Tom's Bible, though it had no annotations and helps in margin from learned commentators, still it had been embellished with certain way-marks and guide-boards of Tom's own invention, and which helped him more than the most learned expositions could have done.[83]

Guilelessly receptive to the "sublime words of hope," a struggling reader like Tom was better off than a Cicero, who "must fill his head first with a thousand questions of authenticity of manuscript, and correctness of translation. But, to poor Tom, there it lay, just what he needed, so evidently true and divine that the possibility of a question never entered his simple head. It must be true; for, if not true, how could he live?"[84] By the standards of the higher critics to whom Stowe alludes, Tom's method of reading is naïve and precritical, but he has what St. Clare admires as "a natural genius for religion."[85] His self-devised "way-marks and guide-boards" are another, more natural and practical approach to textual analysis, one free of the burdens of higher learning and instead guided by spiritual need.

Here Stowe was illustrating her own general theory of the Bible. In another pre-*Uncle Tom* essay, she had contrasted philosophical correctness, "definitions or distinct outlines," and "the harsh hands of metaphysical analysis" with what the Bible actually provides, which are "images" that are "inexpressibly affecting to the unlettered human heart." The "idea of the Bible," she wrote, is to leave the reader personally implicated, not merely a "spectator" or "uninterested judge."[86] Providing images of a similar kind would be the purpose of *Uncle Tom's Cabin*, which she described as follows in first proposing it:

> My vocation is simply that of a *painter*, and my object will be to hold up in the most lifelike and graphic manner possible slavery, its reverses, changes, and the negro character, which I have had ample opportunities for studying. There is no arguing with *pictures*, and everybody is impressed by them, whether they mean to be or not.[87]

Those pictures would likewise resemble the Bible's in aiming to move readers to participation and action. In a letter written while she was working on the *Key*, Stowe lamented "a terrible deadness of moral sense" that kept people from acting on the appalling facts they already knew. Even in the free states, citizens were inclined instead "to *get used to them*, to discuss them coolly, to dismiss them coolly."[88] If the Bible, as Stowe explained in the *Key*, presents God's revelations in the "fervent language and with the glowing imagery of the more susceptible and passionate oriental races" (like "the Hebrews of old"), this was perhaps for the greater good of the "cool, logical and practical" Anglo-Saxons. Black Americans already grasped it; against the "deadening of sensibility," the "numbness" and "deadness of public sentiment" that defenses of slavery relied on and reinforced, they were both the victims to be rescued and a counter-ideal—a "more simple, docile, child-like and affectionate" people, according to Stowe, whose lively imaginations naturally inclined them to pictorial appeals, as the simple but visionary Uncle Tom was meant to illustrate.[89]

For both Stowe and many of her critics, what was at issue in the debate over *Uncle Tom's Cabin* was not just slavery, but the right uses of the Bible and the meaning of Christianity itself. Slavery was not merely a legal and political wrong, Stowe insisted, but "practical infidelity," a "sacrilegious system" and a "heresy," among the worst of affronts to Christian truth.[90] Her critics returned the charges in kind, denouncing both *Uncle Tom's Cabin* and the *Key* as "anti-christian," and charging Stowe's "irreligious" work with promoting "infidelity and open atheism." (Other religious terms that thus proliferated into politics were "impiety" and "idolatry.") In this regard, wrote one hostile clergyman, her books were akin to much of the press, especially Greeley's New York *Tribune*, as well as supposed "moral reform" movements in general and the atheistic preachings of Theodore Parker, with his claims that people in the present day could be inspired in the same way as biblical prophets.[91] A substantial part of the *Key* was devoted to airing and answering these charges—which in turn meant that many pages dwelt on Scriptural interpretation, with Stowe maintaining her defense by going on offense against churches and clerics whose sophistries she saw as turning the Bible's meaning on its head.[92] Indeed the *Key* not only reads at times like a biblical commentary, with close parsings of disputed Scriptural passages, but was titled like one: "Keys" to many important subjects were common at the time, and Stowe would have been well aware that the word often appeared in titles of handbooks to the Bible or parts of it: *A Key to the New Testament, A Key to the Gospels, A Key to the Book of Revelation,* and so on.

The project of establishing *Uncle Tom's Cabin* as "true," then, was twofold. At one level, it required Stowe to vindicate her reporting and prove the book factually correct; but at another level, it meant making the case that reading the novel conduced to the same result as reading the Bible, that she had merely reprised the Bible's own pictorial methods in the further mission of fighting the most dangerous heresy of her time. In later years Stowe came close to likening the novel to the Bible even more explicitly.

Besides recalling the overwhelming vision that inspired it one Sunday during Communion, she claimed to have brought it into being under something like divine inspiration: "The Lord himself wrote it, and I was but the humblest of instruments in his hand."[93] (She produced the *Key*, too, as God's "unwilling agent."[94]) Modern critics have noted that Stowe's was not the only example of "sentimental" fiction that readers in this era "vested with visionary, scriptural authority" like that of a sacred text.[95] With its "typological" and "eschatological" features and reliance on a "spiritual map," says Jane Tompkins, *Uncle Tom's Cabin* is difficult to fit into the classical tradition of the English novel: "what seem from a modernist point of view to be gross stereotypes in characterization and a needless proliferation of incident, are essential properties of a narrative aimed at demonstrating that human history is a continual reenactment of the sacred drama of redemption." In essence, the book "rewrites the Bible as the story of a Negro slave," retelling "the culture's central religious myth ... in terms of the nation's greatest political conflict."[96]

In the critical terminology of today, such a work is difficult to classify: not merely imaginative literature, not merely a novelized political appeal, it was intended and, in its time, widely received as something grander, another example of American parascripture. Describing it in a way that Stowe evidently approved of and may have voiced herself, her son and authorized biographer called it

> a work of religion; the fundamental principles of the gospel applied to the burning question of negro slavery. It sets forth those principles of the Declaration of Independence that made Jefferson, Hamilton, Washington, and Patrick Henry anti-slavery men; not in the language of the philosopher, but in a series of pictures. Mrs. Stowe spoke to the understanding and moral sense through the imagination.[97]

It is interesting to see this defense of the work as morally vivifying "pictures" used to link it to both Scripture and the Declaration—and in the same breath, as if the two comparisons were essentially the same. According to Michael T. Gilmore, Stowe was one of a number of writers of the American Renaissance era who were preoccupied with the question of writing's authority, and whose response to the slavery crisis was to try to recover the Founding ideal of language as action capable of transforming the world. While the Bible was Stowe's "template," as well as "western civilization's clearest illustration of the inseparability of language and events," it was only one of two influential models of "literary efficacy" of this kind. Besides the religious tradition, there was a "revolutionary" or "republican" tradition, and the leading model in that line was the Declaration.[98] That document, as we have seen, was also parascripture by the time Stowe began her great project.

7

Walt Whitman's "New Bible" and the Spiritual Vitalizing of Facts

Walt Whitman's early departure from newspaper journalism was not something the newspapers he worked for saw much cause to regret. During his brief stint as editor of the New York *Aurora* in 1842, the long daily strolls he was known for led one of the owners to call him "the laziest fellow who ever undertook to edit a city paper."[1] His better-known work as editor of the *Brooklyn Daily Eagle* a few years later gets remarkably little notice in that paper's official history. Looking back from 1893, finding no journalistic achievements worth mentioning, and quoting Whitman's own recollection of his "easy work and hours," the historian writes that the paper's most famous alumnus "occupied the editorial chair principally on stormy days; for nothing could keep him out of the sunshine, and in pleasant weather his editorial duties received scant attention."[2] As newsmen go, Whitman apparently had the soul of poet.

Thanks to a recent discovery, we have new information about what Whitman was probably doing while out in the sunshine—and with it, the chance for a deeper insight into how the poet and the newsman, the young and the mature Whitman, were related. The discovery is a lost Whitman novel, *Life and Adventures of Jack Engle: An Auto-Biography,* serialized in New York's *Sunday Dispatch* in 1852, ignored by Whitman and his readers thereafter, and forgotten until Zachary Turpin identified it as Whitman's in 2016. One chapter of this novel is an odd little vignette, a set piece in which its hero, a young legal apprentice unenthused with his usual work, takes time to wander through a cemetery. That this is something Whitman liked to do in real life was already known from his newspaper essays: On days when the weather was exactly right, he wrote in 1846, the destination he would "choose, of all the world" was a cemetery like Greenwood in Brooklyn, where he would contemplate the lives referred to in the tombstone inscriptions. *Jack Engle* gives us what appears to be a more detailed account of these cemetery visits, and with it, new clues to one of the more baffling questions in Whitman scholarship: How did the unremarkable journalist and author of forgettable novels make such a leap, over the course of a few mostly unchronicled years, to a new, hybrid form of writing that was nothing less than a "radical reconception of the art of poetry," in the words of recent critics?[3] For Whitman scholars, the drastic change from the one to the other, the "sudden outburst of poetic genius"[4] whose steps cannot be traced, has generated various theories.[5] One is that Whitman the poet represents a sharp break from Whitman the newsman, or at least expresses a very different side of the writer who would later famously say that he contained multitudes. Perhaps there was an intervening event, like a mystical experience or an unreported love affair.[6] Or, perhaps journalism was the chrysalis from which the poet emerged, with covering Brooklyn news somehow essential preparation for "Crossing Brooklyn Ferry." In *Leaves of Grass,* Ralph Waldo Emerson claimed to detect "a remarkable mixture of the Bhagvat Ghita and the *New York Herald.*"[7] More recently, Jorge Luis Borges suggested that Whitman somehow found a way to make "the editor of the Brooklyn *Daily Eagle* into Walt Whitman, into America, into all of us."[8] Whitman, say modern commentators, found an "uncanny" combination of high and low modes, as if he had "touched the gods with ink-smudged fingers."[9]

The current if hazy consensus, as one critic sums it up, is that Whitman's newspapering was important in some undefined way, "a literary forum in which he rehearsed" his later themes in "inchoate versions."[10] Whitman's earlier writings were *Leaves of Grass* in embryo, but still mired in convention and without the later incandescent brilliance. Others note that this answer is unsatisfying but struggle to find a better one.[11] In *Jack Engle,* however, we have the hint of a missing link. Neatly situated as it is between Whitman's *Daily Eagle* days and *Leaves of Grass,* Whitman's lost novel gives us a vivid picture of a young writer training himself to see the world in ways newly relevant to newsmen and poets alike.

"I Must Get What the Writing Means"

Jack Engle is for the most part a conventional tale of a young woman's inheritance, the lawyer scheming to cheat her out of it, and the friend, Jack Engle, who comes to her rescue and also narrates the story. The cemetery idyll occurs near the end, in chapter 19 of 22: *"Some hours in an old New-York church-yard; where I am led to investigations and meditations."* Fitted into Whitman's career, this chapter is a striking transitional text—a colorful and more complete development of Whitman's Greenwood Cemetery musings, which read now like its rough draft, as well as a further rough draft itself, prefiguring passages of *Leaves* on which Whitman was just then beginning work.

The narrator, Jack, is twenty-two, or about the same age Whitman was when he edited the *Aurora* and gained his reputation for footloose wandering about the city. As the scene opens, he has just been attending the burial of an older man in the graveyard of Manhattan's Trinity Church. Lingering afterwards, he spends the morning in a solitary "ramble," browsing at random among the graves. "I felt in the humor, serious without deep sadness, and I went from spot to spot, and sometimes copied the inscriptions," he says. "Long, rank grass covered my face." The tombstones he examines in his "researches," as he calls them, belong to an assortment of people otherwise unknown—but also to two casualties of America's early wars, as well as one of the nation's founding statesmen, Alexander Hamilton. A grave from 1704 reminds him that the churchyard, in a sense, embraces all of America's history, with all its great events and "grandeur."[12]

Prompted by the tomb inscriptions, Jack tries to envision the deceased, their family relationships, and the events of their deaths and burials. He describes a few of these imaginings, and at one point directly addresses a few lines in the second person to one of the deceased, just as the later poet would. When he finally leaves the graveyard and steps back into "the broad, bright current," Jack is struck by "how bustling was life, and how jauntily it wandered close along the side of those warnings of its inevitable end." Watching the gaily dressed "throng," he offers the last of his "sentimental meditations": "Could it be that coffins, six feet below where I stood, enclosed the ashes of like young men, whose vestments, during life, had engrossed the same anxious care—and schoolboys and beautiful women; for they too were buried here, as well as the aged and infirm."[13]

It is impossible to read this little sketch today without seeing premonitions of *Leaves of Grass*. It even mentions grass, notably describing it as covering the writer's face when the meaning seems to be that it obscured the tombstones. Comparing the chapter to *Leaves'* famous image of grass as "the beautiful uncut hair of graves" and other such passages, Turpin, the novel's rediscoverer, writes: "In its moments in the Trinity Churchyard, *Jack Engle* strikes similar notes, and perhaps hints at the geographic origins of some of *Leaves'* meditations on mortality."[14] This is true, but it is interesting in addition that Jack's reflections do not just mediate between life and death or among America's various historic eras. Because Jack *copies* the inscriptions—with a pencil and "slip of paper," he mentions—they also mediate between reading and writing.[15] It is a strangely gratuitous detail, otherwise unmotivated except perhaps as Whitman's device for explaining how Jack's "auto-biography" managed to reproduce the inscriptions verbatim. Regardless, through this fictional avatar Whitman is almost certainly describing his own actual practice. He would himself, after all, have had to copy the words he quotes, apparently taken from real graves, in order to reproduce them in the novel.

Thus what we have here is a curious bit of journalism, one that merges two very different kinds of text: copies scribbled in pencil, by a casual passerby, of words chiseled in stone by people who felt them supremely important. Tomb inscriptions are not in themselves sacred texts, but they often quote these, and they belong to a set of practices meant to acknowledge the sacred and lift the memory of individuals onto that higher plane—to preserve an "eternal" or "perpetual memory," as the conventional phrases put it. To copy and carry, or "re-port," these gestures of permanence from granite to paper is to blur the distinction between the sanctified on the one hand, and the casual or disposable on the other. In this it foreshadows the poet whose work would borrow from both Scripture and the New York *Herald*, who would describe events and impressions of the moment in a style imitating the Old Testament psalms, and who would call for a "divine literatus," proposing to celebrate the everyday life and business of America in a project he described as "the Great Construction of the New Bible."[16] It calls to mind that poet's assurance that "All sculpture and monuments and anything inscribed anywhere are tallied in you," and also lines like these:

I know I am solid and sound,
To me the converging objects of the universe perpetually flow,
All are written to me, and I must get what the writing means.[17]

Jack seems to feel that the tomb inscriptions—hence the lives they reference—are all written to him, and in tallying them on paper he makes them his, literally something to carry away in his pocket. Whitman, of course, further intended that Jack's copies, along with the rest of the novel, would appear in a newspaper. This would give them a reach well beyond visitors to the churchyard. As it happens, it also extended that reach into the future: A few of these inscriptions may have outlived their original grave sites thanks to *Jack Engle* and Whitman's later fame. The pencil jottings, not the stones, were their true bulwark against time and forgetting.

In addition to and perhaps with the help of his copying, Jack also tries to "get what the writing means." The inscriptions themselves are evocative but inert; to give them meaning, Jack must conjure up the stories they suggest in his mind's eye. Thus, for Jack, the tomb of Captain James Lawrence, a young sailor famous for his dying words, "Don't give up the ship!", becomes an imagined battle scene, with Jack filling in the noise, the smoke, and the idealism of the struggle.[18] As the hours of Jack's ramble wear on, it becomes clear that equally vivid stories are everywhere in the churchyard, living dramas imaginatively present even in this quiet setting separated from the busy world. Each story is different; each is unconnected to the others, apart from their common enclosure in a churchyard emblematic of the nation; and the paths that take Jack from story to story are purely serendipitous, following no logic beyond the accident of placement. Jack's readings are therefore active but uncontrolled, governed only by an ingenuous interest in receiving whatever story happens to come next. The stories operate on different scales, with some touching only private toils and others the historical and public. Finally, as grim as many of the stories are, the whole exercise is nonetheless a pleasant way to spend the morning. For Jack, life is pleasurable, "matter of fact as it was and is in reality."[19] The facts and realities of other lives and deaths may be horrifying, and one might not wish for the experience of suffering itself, but the *mediated* experience as one finds it in a churchyard is just another invigorating revelation of the great panoply of life.

In all these ways, getting what the writing means—"reading" the churchyard—is like reading the news. The newspaper is another medium devoted to delivering, in writing, assortments of factually based stories, laid out mostly at random and therefore serendipitously encountered, some concerning great public figures and some the otherwise obscure. It too presents "converging objects" that are "perpetually flowing," written to readers at a point of access where they are all assembled in one place. It is not limited to, but does foreground, stories of suffering and death, while making these over as vicarious experience meant to be stimulating, or in the favored term of the era's papers, "thrilling." (There is evidence that the words *thrilling* and *fact* both became significantly more common in print during the 1840s.[20]) In actually telling the stories, moreover, often with melodramatic flourishes—and before long, literally picturing them in the new illustrated papers—newspapers spared readers some of the work of vivid imagining, thereby democratizing the kind of reading experience that might otherwise be available only to talented visionaries like Jack Engle, or Walt Whitman.

The news business was a combination of emerging industrial and literary forms that depended on readers who could receive this jumble of inputs without confusion, and in the right spirit: "in the humor, serious without deep sadness." With *Jack Engle* in view, it becomes easier to see how Whitman, as a product and proprietor of newspapers, was primed to become the leading poet of a culture that was learning to receive and value information in ways that were new and characteristic of the industrial age. He was, himself, a consumer of information and stories of exactly the kind that the news business of the time presumed and was busy constructing. His achievement lay in part in seeing literary value in these new forms and appropriating it for his new poetic hybrid. That effort, in turn, was part of a larger project, a program of spiritual and national upbuilding that would entail what modern critics have recognized as "a new democratic act of reading."[21] The irony of Whitman's willing reputation for "loaferism" is that for this task, loafing was essential.[22] Rather than breaking from the newsman at work, the proto-poet rambling away from the office on sunny days was engaged in a variant of the same pursuit.

"Our Current Copious Fields of Print"

Having served at various times and papers not just as writer, editor, founder, and publisher but as typesetter, compositor, printer, and even traveling sales agent, Whitman was about as well-positioned as any American could be to witness the industrial transformation of print culture in what has aptly been called the age of "accelerating print."[23] He was greatly impressed with its imposing scale, noting in 1856, "Of the twenty-four modern mammoth two-double, three-double, and four-double cylinder presses now in the world, printing by steam, twenty-one of them are in These States." Piling on the statistics, he counts twelve thousand public libraries, twelve thousand book and newspaper shops, thousands of editors, and three thousand newspapers of a great many varieties. He goes on to catalogue all this in characteristically Whitmanian fashion, concluding, "What a progress popular reading and writing has made in fifty years! What a progress fifty years hence!" The sheer volume of popular publishing gave him hope that "inherent literature" would shortly be a leading American commodity, "as general and real as steam-power, iron, corn, beef, fish."[24] The first national telegraph network began supplying news while Whitman was editing the *Daily Eagle,* and he was impressed with this technology too, marveling on a later visit to the western frontier at "a canvas office where you could send a message by electricity anywhere around the world!"[25] Still another new object of fascination was photography; daguerreotype portraits, which he liked to admire in a local gallery, were an "electric chain" joining the viewer across time and space to "the thousand human histories" they implied, and vibrating with all the *"life"* and *"fact"* and *"realities"* that Whitman could call down by putting those words in italics.[26]

As the years went on, Whitman's enthusiasm never flagged: "There is something impressive about the huge editions of the dailies and weeklies, the mountain stacks of white paper piled in the press-vaults, and the proud, crashing, ten-cylinder presses, which I can stand and watch any time by the half hour."[27] America circa 1870, he wrote in *Democratic Vistas,* was "busily using, working, more printer's type, more presses, than any other country" and "uttering and absorbing more publications than any other" to produce "our current copious fields of print." His worry at that point, though, like that of so many of his contemporaries, was that there was still no true national or "New World literature."[28] Even the "rivers and oceans of very readable print," the "countless shelves" and "swarms" of nominally literary works, if they settled for the merely "erudite or elegant," did not add up to one.[29] As long as "America has yet morally and artistically originated nothing," the remarkable profusion of published writing was mere "glibness."[30]

In Whitman's view, America had arrived, but possibly stalled, at a second stage of cultural development. The first stage had been its political founding; the second was the current period of expansion, improved communication and material prosperity.[31] Newspapers, for Whitman, were part of this culture of abundance and "oceanic practical grandeur."[32] In welcoming the "intense practical energy, the demand for facts, even the business materialism of the current age," he differed from other Romantic-influenced critics who viewed the new industrial era with alarm.[33] Still, he shared some of the usual concerns. At a time when the "solely materialistic bearings" on their lives "now seem, with steam-engine speed, to be everywhere turning out the generations of humanity like uniform iron castings," people were in danger of becoming industrial products themselves.[34] Whitman feared that Americans failed to see this—that they mistook the sheer impressiveness of the nation they were busy building, its "surfeit of prosperity," for the condition to be achieved.[35] In fact it was at best a transition to a necessary third stage, a "deeper, higher progress" that Whitman called "Religious Democracy."[36] This third stage would arrive through literature; the "spiritualization" and the "native, first-class formulation" that Whitman called for would create "a new and greater literatus order."[37] That would then be the base on which all other cultural achievements would stand.

Even the literature of this new order, however, would also be a kind of reportage. Whitman repeatedly insists that it would need to deal in "facts": the "hardest basic fact, and only entrance to all facts"; "the facts of farms and jack-planes and engineers"; "real mental and physical facts"; "our own unquestion'd facts."[38] This stress on the ordinary and observable echoed that of Emerson, who had argued that the everyday goings-on of America in a commercial age—the same topics that Americans encountered when reading the news—were, if properly appreciated, the stuff of great literature.[39] The "poem" that is America but was yet unsung, Emerson had said, included ordinary, seemingly "flat and dull" events that rested nonetheless "on the same foundations of wonder" as the grandest classical epics. Noting that the poet who would eventually sing them, "the timely man," would be "present and privy to the appearance which he describes," Emerson had declared him "the only teller of news."[40]

Like Emerson, Whitman believed that the lingering dominance of "creeds, conventions," and mimicry of European models was causing Americans to fail to see these wonders in their own surroundings.[41] To reach the third cultural stage, they needed to recognize as readers of literature what they had already been learning as readers of newspapers. There are vivid stories everywhere; the events of any given moment are never flat and dull but always worthy of attention—and moreover, of response: one reads about what is happening partly to join in, to determine where and when to intervene as a citizen in the ever-rushing stream of events. Emerson's famous portrait of "The American Scholar" had demanded "creative reading" and condemned mere studious inaction as cowardice. To read properly, for Emerson, was to "run eagerly into this resounding tumult. I grasp the hands of those next me, and take my place in the ring to suffer and to work."[42] Whitman, likewise, insisted that American democracy would flourish only on the basis of "a new theory of literary composition" that was really a theory of active reading:

> Books are to be call'd for, and supplied, on the assumption that the process of reading is not a half sleep, but, in highest sense, an exercise, a gymnast's struggle; that the reader is to do something for himself, must be on the alert, must himself or herself construct indeed the poem, argument, history, metaphysical essay—the text furnishing the hints, the clue, the start or frame-work. Not the book needs so much to be the complete thing, but the reader of the book does.[43]

The "democratic literature of the future," as Whitman saw it, would be a co-creation of poets and alert readers, who would turn the hints and clues into living stories in much the same way as the churchyard rambler with his scribbling survey of tomb inscriptions. This new literature would respond to the same social and political realities featured in the news, but "vitalized" through the poet's efforts.[44]

"Whatever Interests the Rest Interests Me"

Before unveiling his own attempt at that kind of transformational poetry in *Leaves of Grass*, Whitman had made notes on several ideas for poems or stories revolving around the phrase "every day": "A man appears in public every day," "a child went forth every day," a philosopher "sits every day" at his door, a "variety of characters" comes forth every day. There were "things appearing," he noted, every day.[45] The first edition of *Leaves* appeared soon afterwards with a long preface devoted, in part, to the central importance of "today." Today is the "direct trial of him who would be the greatest poet," Whitman asserts, and such a poet must "flood himself with the immediate age as with vast oceanic tides." From the point of view of eternity, there is a "similitude to all periods and locations," an "inconceivable vagueness" that emerges concretely in "the swimming shape of to-day."[46] In lines which, we can now see, restate Jack Engle's churchyard activities as an artist's manifesto, Whitman writes:

> Past and present and future are not disjoined but joined. The greatest poet forms the consistence of what is to be from what has been and is.

> He drags the dead out of their coffins and stands them again on their feet ... he says to the past, Rise and walk before me that I may realize you. He learns the lesson ... he places himself where the future becomes present.

The greatest poet not only makes the past live again, but "sees the solid and beautiful forms of the future where there are now no solid forms" (iv). This need to synthesize past and future puts enormous emphasis on "the present spot," which is "the passage from what was to what shall be"—not in the banal sense that time just mechanically passes, but because the poet's work actively "makes" it so (xi). As Whitman puts it in the first of *Leaves'* poems, the one later titled "Song of Myself":

> There was never any more inception than there is now,
> Nor any more youth or age than there is now;
> And will never be any more perfection than there is now,
> Nor any more heaven or hell than there is now.
>
> (14)

There was never, and will never be, any more for the poet to respond to than there is now, because "now" is where the dead past and the unrealized future are both made real. The central importance of now and "the immediate age" makes the great poet Emerson's timely man, focusing him or her on "the representation of this wave of an hour" and even the minute (xi). The poet's task, in other words, is essentially journalistic. Accordingly, like a good reporter, Whitman pledges "with perfect candor" to produce an "unintermitted" investigation of all things "as they are" (viii): "What I tell I tell for precisely what it is" (vii).

In the early passages of that first long poem, the *ur*-"Song of Myself," the speaker presents himself as leaning and loafing on grass, a vantage point from which he can contemplate and, he suggests, perhaps in some sense experience the whole universe. He casts this experience as a kind of reading: the grass itself is "a uniform hieroglyphic," and it carries "hints" about the buried dead that "I wish I could translate" (16). What he intends to read, it seems, is the whole human story; in further long sections (notably those later numbered 8 and 15), he lists what seem to be disconnected impressions or imagined scenes, variously drawn from and mixing private lives and occupations with events of the kind that might be reported as news:

> The little one sleeps in its cradle,
> I lift the gauze and look a long time, and silently brush away flies
>   with my hand.
> The youngster and the redfaced girl turn aside up the bushy hill,
> I peeringly view them from the top.

> The suicide sprawls on the bloody floor of the bedroom.
> It is so ... I witnessed the corpse ... there the pistol had fallen.
> * * * * *
> The camera and plate are prepared, the lady must sit for her daguerreotype,
> The bride unrumples her white dress, the minutehand of the clock moves slowly,
> The opium eater reclines with rigid head and just-opened lips,
> The prostitute draggles her shawl, her bonnet bobs on her tipsy and pimpled neck,
> The crowd laugh at her blackguard oaths, the men jeer and wink to each other,
> (Miserable! I do not laugh at your oaths nor jeer you,)
> The President holds a cabinet council, he is surrounded by the great secretaries,
> On the piazza walk five friendly matrons with twined arms;
>   (17-18, 22-23)

One can quote at almost any length and still understate the sheer plenitude of these glimpsed moments, which go on for pages. The commas and semicolons that end most lines suggest that the list as a whole could continue indefinitely—much as each of these events, however significant or not, will continue even as attention turns from one to the next. "None shall escape me," the speaker vows (59), and the overall impression is that he is determined to see everything at once and report as much of it as he can.

At first, the speaker identifies his point of view: leaning over the cradle, standing at the top of the hill. Mostly, though, he omits this and leaves his own position unstated. He is "not contained between my hat and boots," he says (17), and therefore can range freely, identifying with all those he sees: "In all people I see myself" (26). We would conventionally assume that this mystical panoptic vision is unfolding in the poet's mind's eye, and that may well be how Whitman imagined it too. One could, however, compile very similar lists by loafing on the grass while paging (or "leafing") through a newspaper, especially an illustrated weekly of the kind that began appearing in New York as Whitman was writing *Leaves'* first edition. The little one- and two-line narratives that make up Whitman's lists are captured moments—not quite still images, since each points to something happening, but similar even in this to photographs, which are also normally experienced not as frozen instants but as triggers for describing actions that occur over time ("Here we are hiking through the Grand Canyon"; "This is me when I was living in New York"). The actions are abbreviated and removed from their original contexts, but they then reappear in the new context of the poet's imagining, where their particular order does not matter because they are all simultaneous expressions of the superabundance of existence.

In those respects, too, they resemble both the images and the random assortment of brief reports in a newspaper. One can find visual analogues to every kind of item in Whitman's lists in the pages of *Frank Leslie's Illustrated Weekly* and *Harper's Weekly*, publications which—by way of illustrating not just news, but travelogues, extended anecdotes, commentaries on manners and mores, and much else—placed ordinary scenes of daily life side-by-side with pictures of public events; of crimes, fires and other disasters; of workers at work doing their usual jobs; and even of private domestic moments as if glimpsed through a keyhole. As one turned the page, almost anything might appear next, from a baby in its cradle to holidaymakers skating on a frozen pond to high officers of state like the president. A suitably sensitive reader, coming across a report of what the paper would tout as "thrilling and heartrending scenes" from an event like a mill explosion, might project himself there, feel himself joined as if by Whitman's electric chain to the people pictured:

> I am the mashed fireman with breastbone broken ... tumbling walls buried me in their debris,
> Heat and smoke I inspired ... I heard the yelling shouts of my comrades,
> I heard the distant click of their picks and shovels;
> They have cleared the beams away ... they tenderly lift me forth.
>
> (39)

A vivid little narrative like this so closely resembles those of the illustrated papers, which would likewise parse larger disasters for individual tales of peril, rescue, and heartbreak, that it would be surprising if Whitman had *not* taken inspiration from them.[47] Like the reader of news, he cannot actually speak to the victims, and therefore "I do not ask the wounded person how he feels"—but he can leap right past that to something grander: "I myself become the wounded person."[48]

Newspapers of Whitman's day did editorialize, take positions on public affairs, critique the era's life and times, and treat some reports of events as moral fables. Yet in rejecting bourgeois respectability in favor of new criteria of selection, a standard of news judgment that seemed scandalously willing to cater to voyeurism and vulgar taste, the penny press anticipated Whitman's principle that the "greatest poet does not moralize or make applications of morals" (vi)—a principle which, he says, makes him "not the poet of goodness only" but "the poet of wickedness also": "Evil propels me, and reform of evil propels me ... I stand indifferent" between virtue and vice (27-28). Newspapers were happy to inveigh against what they called evil, yet they did still let it "propel" them, as well as propel their calls for reform. It was the ceaseless existence of the one and need for the other that kept them in business. Their willingness, while not endorsing immorality, to traffic in it for profit was a corollary of another and larger principle, one that Whitman also borrowed:

> This is the city ... and I am one of the citizens;
> Whatever interests the rest interests me ... politics, churches, newspapers, schools,
> Benevolent societies, improvements, banks, tariffs, steamships, factories, markets,
> Stocks and stores and real estate and personal estate.
>
> (47)

These lines could be the newspaper reader's credo. The items in the list are almost identical to the "slugs" or keywords that would appear as column headers in the papers of this pre-headline era.

Lithographing the Ancient Gods

Of course, what distinguishes Whitman the poet from most readers is his insistence on seeing ordinary events not merely as interesting, but as revelations—points of access to the spiritual and ideal. This was the further requirement if a commodified print culture was to be saved from mere glibness and made worthy of a nation aspiring to "Religious Democracy." The practical grandeur of such a nation cried to be seen and reported, but also spiritualized. Whitman's poetry aims to do both. Its panoptical vantage point could be that of an imaginative news reader, but equally well that of a god. Whitman captures these twin possibilities in print-culture metaphors: He claims to be "lithographing" the ancient gods in his own person (45), and he compares the countless epiphanies he finds in everyday city life to "letters from God dropped in the street," with more such letters certain to "punctually come forever and ever" (54). ("Punctually" implies a set schedule. Letters from God, then, have at least that much in common with newspapers, which are also dropped in the street.) Emerson's "only teller of news" would be a supreme figure, the messianic "reconciler" of a "new religion," and it seems that Whitman, having heard such calls from Emerson and Thomas Carlyle, intended to be that figure himself.[49]

He may also have hearkened to Emerson's demand, "We too must write Bibles."[50] Raised like most Americans on the biblical texts, which he says he went over "thoroughly" in his youth, Whitman literalized his proposed new Bible with a number of features borrowed from the old one.[51] The future "Song of Myself" was at one point titled just "Walt Whitman," as if it were a biblical book like Isaiah or Luke.[52] One early critic described *Leaves* as "a number of prose sentences printed somewhat after a biblical fashion."⁵³ That puts it a bit reductively, but Whitman, connecting his own poetic advent with "the great psalm of the republic,"⁵⁴ clearly did model some of his verses on the biblical psalms—for instance, Psalm 23, whose beloved King James rendering innumerable readers have learned by heart:

1. The Lord is my shepherd; I shall not want.
2. He maketh me to lie down in green pastures:
    he leadeth me beside the still waters.
3. He restoreth my soul:
    he leadeth me in the paths of righteousness for his name's sake.
5. Yea, though I walk through the valley of the shadow of death,
    I will fear no evil:
    for thou art with me;
    thy rod and thy staff they comfort me.

When we turn to a work like "Crossing Brooklyn Ferry," the borrowing of biblical rhythms, repetitions, Jacobean locutions, and even versification is plain:

10. I loved well those cities,
    I loved well the stately and rapid river,
    The men and women I saw were all near to me,
    Others the same—others who look back on me,
        because I looked forward to them,
    (The time will come, though I stop here to-day and to-night.)
11. What is it, then, between us?
    What is the count of the scores or hundreds of years between us?
12. Whatever it is, it avails not—distance avails not, and
        place avails not.
13. I too lived, (I was of old Brooklyn,)
    I too walked the streets of Manhattan Island, and
        bathed in the waters around it,
    I too felt the curious abrupt questionings stir within
        me,
    In the day, among crowds of people, sometimes they
        came upon me,
    In my walks home late at night, or as I lay in my
        bed, they came upon me.⁵⁵

The juxtaposing of levels is also present in "Crossing's" message and tone. Like Jack Engle in the churchyard, the poet acknowledges a great shared experience with others not present, including people living in different epochs. He seems to look back on his own world as bygone, with something like the wistfulness of the exiled Psalmist "by the rivers of Babylon" recalling Jerusalem.[56] Yet what prompts all this is nothing more elevated than the humdrum daily chore of a New York commute.

In his early notebook entries, Whitman floated the possibility of writing a play in which the stage directions would "be also in poetry, carefully finished as the dialogue."[57] We might say that even before he had firmly chosen poetry as his *métier*, he was looking for ways to "interrogate" the conventional boundary between high and low. "Purposely in his poems," says David S. Reynolds, "Whitman shuttled back and forth between the grimy and the spiritual."[58] Whitman himself agreed, describing *Leaves of Grass* as an "incongruous hash of mud and gold."[59] *Drum-Taps*, the cycle of Civil War poems that include "psalms of the dead," as the text itself calls them, were partly drafted in the same notebooks in which Whitman logged his activities as an army hospital nurse.[60] Mixing factual description with poetic meditation, they give us closely observed details similar to a modern combat reporter's, but on the premise (as the poet asserts) that the scenes he witnessed were transcendently meaningful, "a sight beyond all the pictures and poems ever made."[61] Likewise in his popular lecture on the death of Abraham Lincoln, which looked for the epochal meaning of that event in journalistic details taken from eyewitness reports.[62]

Though less often celebrated for his jokes, Whitman knew that juxtaposing the high and mundane could also be done for comic effect. In his "Song of the Exposition," written in the 1870s for industrial fairs, he begins as in classical odes by invoking the Muse, only to summon her away from the sites associated with the well-known but bygone epics— Troy, Parnassus, Jerusalem, the ancient temples and medieval castles of the traditional heroes and gods—to "a better, fresher, busier sphere, a wide, untried domain." Standing in the vast gallery, surrounded by the new, noisy mechanical wonders, the poet claims to see her arriving in answer to his call,

> Making directly for this rendezvous, vigorously clearing a path
>   for herself, striding through the confusion,
> By thud of machinery and shrill steam-whistle undismay'd,
> Bluff'd not a bit by drain-pipe, gasometers, artificial fertilizers,
> Smiling and pleas'd with palpable intent to stay,
> She's here, install'd amid the kitchen ware![63]

The Muse not only makes her presence felt but is "install'd" within the vast new industrial machine, although among its humblest components. To continue its historic work, the inspiration that once moved the prophets and the greatest storytellers will now help to power an America whose manufactured achievements are simultaneously both trivial and utterly stupendous.

"The Continuousness of It All"

In 1922 a legendary newspaper editor and literary patron, Henry Justin Smith, wrote a short sketch, "The Day," describing a typical day in a newsroom like that of his own Chicago *Daily News*. There is much in Smith's description that is "Whitmanesque," as he may well have known: sensually felt descriptions of workers at their mundane tasks, a Whitman-like newsroom poet based on the real-life *Daily News* reporter Carl Sandburg, "a resistless movement of the commonplace" as "the symphony of the city" waits to deliver news, and the wires over which one "can fancy that he hears the shrill and terrible voices of a hundred other cities where life seethes."[64, 65]

After an otherwise dull morning, a shocking event—a coordinated attack of terrorist bombings—suddenly turns the whole building into a "delirium" of "gorgeous" activity, as all hands race to tell "this tale of tales" in print.[66] The result of their hours of frantic effort is a "structure nevertheless built to last but a day, to outlast scarcely even our pride in it." By quitting time, the product is already wastepaper being swept into garbage bags, with the whole routine due to start over again the next day. Watching the newsroom empty out, a copyreader reflects on the "continuousness of it all," wondering "what the fascination of news is. I wonder what news really is."[67]

As Whitman did in poetry, Smith emphasizes the juxtaposition of everyday tedium with the sudden and shocking; the gorgeousness and "joy" even of pain and tragedy; and the sense of timely timelessness, of occurrences unbounded by any start or finish but plucked at random from a stream that perpetually flows and repeats.[68] What the little sketch suggests is that the news business, as it further developed, followed a kind of Whitmanian logic, institutionalizing and routinizing a distinctly modern outlook that Whitman seems to have co-developed with that enterprise in its early stages but carried into a different genre. The great play of busy randomness that is the life of the city and nation has an immanent if unstructured coherence; to a suitably sensitive observer, it becomes its own kind of "symphony" in which one can, "if one puts his ear to the wires," hear America singing. The question is: Who is that observer? For the symphony to be heard, it must be conducted to us. The newspaper does this in one way, structuring events through the operations that Smith describes—the well-worn routines that make up what we now call the "news cycle." In a different but parallel way, a poet or "divine literatus" might "chant" the varied carols as cycles of poetry, as Whitman held himself to be doing in *Leaves*.

Looking back from late in life, Whitman explained his career in terms of two basic goals: to observe and report, putting what he experienced "unerringly on record"; and "to give ultimate vivification" to what was otherwise static, old, or dead—a project we can now see him engaged in as far back as *Jack Engle*, when he conjured living stories from tombstones.[69] America was at the forefront of the new "material facts" and "concrete realities" that the spread of science and democracy had been delivering as never before. Poetry in general, and an American national literature in particular, must reveal the "glows and glories" of the "new genius and environments," the "unprecedented stimulants of to-day and here" that made the modern era the first in history in which the "limitlessness" of the human soul could be fully expressed.[70]

The problem was that the unprecedented stimulants did not automatically stimulate. In fact, "The educated world seems to have been growing more and more ennuyed for ages, leaving to our time the inheritance of it all."[71] This was an old worry for Whitman, and as we have seen, an even older one for others: Transcendentalism had been founded on texts like Emerson's Divinity School address of 1838, a long lament over the spiritual coldness and decay that pervaded "these desponding days."[72] Whitman presents his work as an answer to this incipient cultural failure. When he speaks of making "a faithful and doubtless self-will'd record" of contemporary facts, he is not talking about preserving their memory but about overcoming *ennui*. Vivification depends on reportage; a record is needed to give the facts "illustration"—a term in which Whitman combines the dual meanings of making pictures of things and revealing their true value, their "final illustriousness."[73] The "genesis and ensemble of to-day" must be mediated through a recording and picturing intelligence, or what Whitman—in a phrase he repeats, italicizes, and even footnotes to Immanuel Kant—calls a "*point of view.*"[74]

One might suppose that a point of view, by definition, must be limited, but Whitman suggests otherwise. Recalling Milton's grand ambition to "justify the ways of God to man," he describes a desire to ground the record he spent his life compiling on "an implicit belief in the wisdom, health, mystery, beauty of every process, every concrete object, every human or other existence, not only consider'd from the point of view of all, but of each." Beyond even this, the record would extend to the "invisible spiritual results" that "eventuate all concrete life and all materialism, through Time." Such a totality of vision, with everything seen from every vantage, is best compared to God's. Yet even so, it is highly specific. The poet illustrates the larger ensemble by recording "*a Person*, a human being," with a definite position in ephemeral history: "myself, in the latter half of the Nineteenth Century, in America."[75] He is one man, set apart from "other faiths or other identities," though with a faith in the nation that leads him to choose what to say (or "sing") "quite solely with reference to America and to-day."

America and today, however, are in a sense inexhaustible, the closest thing yet to revelations of ultimate reality, furnishing "area and points of view" unavailable to poets of the past.[76]

Returning for a moment to Henry Justin Smith's newsroom, it is striking what Smith never mentions: any general view of things, any editorial stance the newspaper is propounding, or any other larger goal besides beating the competition. Nothing unifies the events that the paper covers apart from happening on the same day and being "news," a condition that everyone in the newsroom instantly recognizes but never explains. Smith gives us the copyreader's question, "I wonder what news really is," but never tries to answer it. Those who have done so in recent years have found it a philosophical challenge, one that calls for help from as far afield as the writings of Wittgenstein and Clifford Geertz.[77] By the early twentieth century, an increasingly nonpartisan and professionalized journalism was claiming "objectivity," which meant that "publishers no longer upheld their sheets' right to purvey an explicit point of view." Positioning themselves outside "the swirl of opinions and partisan biases," journalists "claimed to be neutrally speaking for the commonweal."[78] This disavowal of points of view, still largely prevailing in today's so-called mainstream media, is often criticized as a "godlike" pretense, a "view from nowhere."[79] What seems to substitute for a point of view, in Smith's newsroom as in thousands since, is the delirium of activity itself—an inarticulate but deeply internalized concept of newsworthiness, the aggressive responses this generates to certain facts, and the industrialized processes, the "finely-timed engine" as Smith calls it, forever at work to mass-assemble those responses into a single printed product.[80]

To speak neutrally for the commonweal, though, does suggest a more definite frame of reference. Smith's choice of dramatic event is telling: terror attacks both on the local streets and in the nation's capital. For most American journalists—as for Whitman, the city journalist and poet who strove to be America's bard—city and nation are the principal fields of operation, the two communities whose weal they would most likely claim to be serving. In his often-cited account of the rise of nations as *Imagined Communities,* Benedict Anderson argues that the forming of nations actually depended in part on the modern production of news: Newspapers inevitably do imply a point of view, not by imposing an editorial slant but as an emergent property of the news format itself. Readers faced with the newspaper's daily jumble of events assume an "imagined linkage," a view from somewhere.[81] They also know that innumerable others are reading the same news at the same time. This leads them to project behind the paper's contents a reality in which they must all be participants, "a deep, horizontal comradeship," and it is this which helps engender the nation, overriding older ties of religion and tribe.[82]

Whitman, who saw one of the purposes of his life's work as "the forming of a great aggregate Nation," also spoke often of national bonding as "comradeship."[83] What united the United States was "a chain of comrades," a condition that his art both celebrated and was meant to encourage.[84] Given this, it is not surprising that Anderson's linking of news and nation also seems anticipated in Whitman—for instance, in his recollection of reading the first reports of the Civil War alongside unknown other New Yorkers, all gathered near streetlamps with copies of the evening "extras."[85] If, for Whitman, "Whatever interests the rest interests me," Anderson's modern newsreader assumes the converse: Whatever interests me interests the rest. Therefore, we all must have a society and identity in common; a nation must exist of which we are all fellow citizens. The journalistic view "from nowhere" actually comes from the standpoint of this imagined community, and seems to come from nowhere only because projecting the view is inseparable from the act of imagining that creates that standpoint in the first place.

Anderson describes comradeship as a spontaneous inference, a result of readers' efforts to make sense of the newspaper's onrush of facts.[86] Whitman's comradeship is a deliberate and more far-reaching construction. As he saw it, the danger for his readers was not just disorientation or puzzlement, but *ennui*: the facts also needed vivifying. The nation, moreover, was still struggling to emerge. Its community had not yet been fully imagined, and there was a chance that American nationality might remain "defective"—an especially large problem if, as Whitman often said, America was not just any nation but the key to the world's spiritual and creative renewal.[87] Even as late as 1871, with Whitman himself and other home-grown authors fixed in an emerging national canon, America was still "ignorant of its genius, not yet inaugurating the native, the universal, and the near, still importing the distant, the partial, and the dead."[88] Americans had "myriad audible and visible worldly interests," but American democracy remained "materialistic and vulgar." Those interests—the kinds of things that Americans were reading about in their newspapers—still needed "spiritualization." This would come from comradeship, which would run like "threads" through the visible facts, binding them "like a half-hid warp."[89] Weaving those threads into the American fabric had been one of Whitman's principal goals, but he closed his career with this cultural mission incomplete, still looking forward to a distinctively American "race of singers and poems" that would carry it through.[90]

When Whitman wrote early on of lithographing old gods, of taking pages and "rough deific sketches" from the old sacred books, he apparently envisioned his new Bible absorbing the best of bibles past while assuming their function for the epoch now at hand.[91] At one point he even wrote down a list of word counts, literally sizing up *Leaves of Grass* against the Old Testament, the New Testament, the whole Bible, the *Iliad,* the *Aeneid,* the *Inferno,* and *Paradise Lost*.⁹² Culture-making power flowed from the written word, but those old monuments would not suffice for a new and modern nation. A fresher effort was needed, but perhaps something else was already moving into the void, as Thoreau, Emerson, and others suggested in observing the growing cultural authority of newspapers.⁹³ Whitman, who had once called newspapers "mighty engines of truth," was better disposed toward them than Thoreau.⁹⁴ They appear in the list of dozens of "great" things that closes the first edition of *Leaves of Grass*.⁹⁵ But there was still a need for a genuine American bible of that kind that he might hope to supply.

What that effort would reveal is that such a bible, if it were to serve the times and the nation, would need to do many of the same things that newspapers did—would need the immediacy, vitality, and specific yet all-embracing factuality of news. It follows that a onetime journalist who sets out to write the great psalm of the republic will not really have left journalism behind. He will, rather, have carried it to a higher plane. This may be why, after all his grand ambitions and many years of constant revising, Whitman seems surprisingly modest about his final poetic result. It should not even be thought of as literature, he says.⁹⁶ Instead it was arguably something greater: just good reporting.

PART THREE

The Quest for National Salvation

8

Slavery, Liberty, and the Three Great Charters

Slavery, of course, was not the era's only source of contention, but it was a great moral problem that had been left unsolved at the Founding, and it had a remarkable power to generate arguments over all the nation's canonical texts. Questions at issue in the slavery debates could be seen as turning on exactly how one read the Bible, with its varied moral codes and *exempla* and its grand schemes of human origins and history; the Declaration of Independence, with its philosophical syllogisms linking equality, rights, and consent; and the Constitution's statements of rights as well as its intricate plan for multilayered government in an uneasy union of states. The question was how particular national policies should be measured, and the complicating factor was that America's instrument for measuring—the original meaning of the word "canon"—now included two new scriptures.

Political arguments therefore entailed arguments over textual origins, authority, and meaning that closely resembled, and sometimes incorporated, the kinds of theological arguments that had long both marked and marred the Christian world. In a recent history, Jordan T. Watkins has detailed how the biblical and constitutional debates over slavery tracked each other and heavily overlapped, with many of the same people and same methods involved in both.[1] In search of "favored pasts," Americans gradually settled on two particular favorites, the biblical past and the Founding era. Watkins explains the ensuing struggle as setting "sacralization," the casting of sacred texts and favored pasts as fonts of timeless wisdom, still perfectly applicable in one's own day, with "historicization," a growing sense that they were distant and different, periods whose values (and the writings that conveyed them) were unlike those of the present.[2] Even finding timeless truths, if they were mixed in with the "historical chaff" of earlier eras, could heighten this impression of historical distance.[3]

It is worth emphasizing, moreover, that each favored past had produced *two* canonical texts, each of which could be interpreted differently and perhaps set against the other. The Bible's Old Testament—the origin story of Creation, Exodus, the Children of Israel, and the Promised Land—and its New, the story of the "primitive" Christian church, might converge in meaning or might point in different directions. Likewise the Declaration of Independence and the Constitution. The great debates of the era, then, concerned not just the meaning of each text in itself, but how the meaning of each bore on that of the others. Further, both pro- and anti-slavery factions might variously find support for their positions in what Watkins calls the sacralized or the historicized views. Both in defense of slavery and in opposition to it, Americans could invoke sacred texts, or disparage and reject them as outmoded, or attempt to reinterpret them as marking out useful paths toward moral improvement which, sadly, the texts' own authors had followed only partway.

In these overlapping, cross-cutting debates, the same canonical writing might come to mean quite different things even to political allies or, in some cases, to the same individual at different times. For slavery's opponents, the problem was especially acute. Slavery had continued long past the American Founding; it had coexisted with the Constitution for decades, and with the Bible for centuries, without being seen as obviously violating either one—an easy, happy conclusion for the slaveocrats. Abolitionists, by contrast, had to choose between continued reverence, strained apologies, or simply contempt. They had to decide whether the different authorities could somehow be disentangled, lest evil results issuing from one of them discredited the others. As William Lloyd Garrison would put it at a moment of particularly high tension, a commissioner acting under law to send back an escaped slave, under the escort of federal troops, was in effect "pronouncing the Declaration of Independence to be a lie, George Washington and his associates traitors and cut-throats, the golden Rule an absurdity, and Jesus of Nazareth an impostor."[4] The Constitution, that is, authorized procedures that arguably traduced not only the principles of the Founding, but even the most inspirational teachings of the New Testament.

Perhaps, in fact, according to this logic, the Founding itself should not even have happened: rather than an act of national genius it had been a great moral error. The British Empire had outlawed slavery, which raised the galling possibility that independence, by taking America out of that empire, had perversely given it a safe haven. In that case America's foundational writings would be instruments of a kind of national anti-covenant, a demonic deception *masquerading* as scripture. Garrison implied such a reading when, quoting the Bible (Isaiah 28:15), he denounced the Constitution and the compact it created between North and South, declaring them "a covenant with death and an agreement with hell."[5]

"The Bible Is an Unintelligible Book"

Though Garrison found a cudgel against the Constitution in the words of the biblical prophet, in general it was hard for the anti-slavery forces to extract authority for their cause from the Bible. One might hope that an immoral institution like slavery would be clearly condemned in the Word of a God of righteousness, but in fact, on any casual reading, the dispiriting question seemed to be not whether slavery was biblical, but whether Scripture merely permitted it, or expected and perhaps even commanded it—whether it was even "ordained of God," as one of many treatises on the subject claimed in its title.[6] The Bible describes ancient slave societies with seeming approval and prescribes laws for them, certainly in the Old Testament but even in the New, where Jesus never speaks against Roman-era slavery and Paul instructs slaves to obey their masters, at one point writing a letter urging the return of a runaway slave. Racial oppression, moreover, had biblical warrants—or so it was claimed—in early stories about a "mark of Cain" in Genesis 4 and a "curse of Ham" in Genesis 9. The curse of Ham, in turn, was part of a larger scheme of Christian history that prevailed for many centuries, a story that explained human variety in terms of continents—the "three soils," Europe, Asia, and Africa, that each of Noah's three sons went forth and "seeded" after the Great Flood. In this scheme, according to Genesis 9, Africans were rightly enslaved by divine edict to Europe's white descendants. (Also, though, in this scheme, there was no America. As noted earlier, the unexpected existence of this "fourth soil" and its native inhabitants would puzzle Western investigators for centuries, but also inspire such imaginative explanations as the Book of Mormon's.)

Some abolitionists insisted nonetheless that American slavery had no biblical justification whatever. Theodore Weld, for instance, tried to prove as much through close textual analysis, distinguishing different meanings of words like *slavery*, *property*, and *master*.[7] More typically, condemning slavery on biblical grounds meant either making the "liberal" argument, less amenable to proof-texting, that Scripture was aimed at an earlier level of human moral understanding—which might seem to suggest that modern critics knew God's mind better than the biblical writers did—or contrasting the "letter" of Scripture with its "spirit," the troublesome literal statements as against some broader general import. To that end, other features of the Bible could be noted: a heroic Exodus from bondage, under the ringing phrase "Let my people go"; several books in which Old Testament prophets demanded justice for the downtrodden; and of course the fact that the later revelation, or "New" Testament, spoke of liberation from the old law, described a Son of God who preached mercy and the Golden Rule, and had apostles like Paul radically proclaiming a new dispensation: "There is neither Jew nor Greek, there is neither bond nor free, there is neither male nor female" (Galatians 3:28).

Of course, to set one testament against the other in this way came close to suggesting that, in practice, there were two Bibles with quite different messages. One Catholic commentator, impressed with how Americans were forever quoting both testaments in political argument, wrote in 1861 that "suddenly both parties have become theologians, the one side quoting the Pentateuch to justify slavery, the other side quoting the gospel to condemn it."[8] How exactly Christianity was related to its predecessor faith was a very old question, never entirely settled since the early, contested decision to retain the old Hebrew writings as Christian Scripture. Was biblical authority uniformly the same throughout the text, or did the Old Testament have a different and perhaps lesser status? One frustrated abolitionist, Charles B. Stearns, called for simply discarding it.[9] Or was it partly valid, with some of its directives still meant to be followed but others not, and if so, how could we determine which? Harriet Beecher Stowe, Frederick Douglass, and others would argue that even the Old Testament, properly read, revealed a "Mosaic" aim—i.e., attributable to Moses, reputed author of the Bible's first five books—to limit and perhaps ultimately end slavery. A "Thou shalt not" command in Deuteronomy 23 against returning escaped slaves could perhaps reconcile the testaments by suggesting a kinder interpretation of Paul's notoriously contrary New Testament advice to Philemon.[10] The leading but moderately conservative theologian and biblical scholar Moses Stuart had proposed that the truest reading, fully historicized, would show that Moses and the New Testament apostles alike had been moving toward abolition, but by degrees, within the cultural realities and limitations of their times. In other words, their equivocal view of slavery was very much like that of Stuart himself, who opposed slavery in principle but favored following the biblical writers in accommodating it for the time being. This more nuanced conclusion about the ancient world was not accessible to the ordinary reader, but that fact merely demonstrated why trained historical scholarship like Stuart's was needed.[11] At any rate, on that theory the testaments did have a shared import, albeit one that was unsatisfyingly complex.

Arguments like these based on subtle exegesis, however, were thin reeds to hold up against the many passages in which God quite plainly approves of slavery and dictates laws for it as if it were a normal practice. Answers to the abolitionists' arguments therefore just seemed too easy to find. Paul's remark in Galatians, for instance, about the abolition of human distinctions "in Christ" could hardly be taken as a description of present reality: the Christian revelation had not literally erased the categories "male and female," so if the same verse said there was "neither bond nor free," that too must have reference to something other than the everyday world of laws and policies. Presumably Paul had meant to invoke some future eschatological ideal.

In short, the simplest readings seemed to put Scripture on the slaveholders' side. In obscuring this fact, the abolitionists' critics charged, they were in effect saying "the Bible is an unintelligible book."[12] To make their case, wrote *Slavery Ordained of God* author Fred A. Ross, an Alabama minister, abolitionists had been "torturing" both the Bible and the English language, but their efforts had backfired. They had succeeded only in provoking Southerners' close attention to the Bible while promoting Northerners' alienation from it, leading to "infidelity" in the North even among ministers. The most consistent of the abolitionists, he jeered, "have now turned away from the word, in despondency; and are seeking, somewhere, an abolition Bible, an abolition Constitution for the United States, and an abolition God."[13]

Ross was not wrong in describing abolitionists as despondent. For some of them, contending with the Bible's apparent support for slavery had been a serious trial; one, Henry C. Wright, described struggling for ten years to marshal biblical authority against oppression and injustice and finally giving up, at least on questions related to slavery and war. Theodore Parker was pithy, as usual: "If the Bible defends slavery, it is not so much the better for slavery, but so much the worse for the Bible." That was the "short and easy method" for reading it, and the same held for Calvinism, Catholicism, the Apostle Paul, and Christianity itself: so much the worse for them all.[14]

Garrison's own hostility to biblical teachings developed by stages between the 1830s and 1850s. At first "a pillar of rectitude in religious matters," according to one modern review of his career, he assumed, like most evangelicals, that the Bible would be essential in awakening the public's conscience. That view changed as he encountered "indifference and hostility" from "a large segment of the American religious establishment." The "doctrinal dogmatism of his hoped-for allies" freed Garrison to "investigate the foundations on which his personal beliefs were based," and he found himself drawn to the non-dogmatic, "practical righteousness" of figures like Wright and Parker.[15] He also discovered and, to his surprise, found congenial the old "infidel" writings of Thomas Paine. His thinking thereupon underwent a further evolution, from reading the Bible discriminatingly while still, on the whole, assuming its authority, to speaking of it as mere "parchment" that might as likely be false as true on any given point, as reason might best determine.[16]

By June 1853, when he attended the Hartford Bible Convention, Garrison had publicly abandoned anything resembling traditional scriptural reverence. The convention's participants were mainly abolitionists, along with spiritualists like the key organizer Andrew Jackson Davis, brought together to confront the problem of the Bible directly and collectively—or as the official description put it, "for the purpose of freely and fully canvassing the ORIGIN, AUTHORITY, AND INFLUENCE OF THE JEWISH AND CHRISTIAN SCRIPTURES."[17] Referencing what convention president Joseph Barker called the "common view" of these matters, Garrison urged the assembly to declare it "self-evidently absurd" that the Bible was the divinely inspired Word of God, an assumption "exceedingly injurious both to the intellect and soul, highly pernicious in its application, and a stumbling-block in the way of human redemption." Virtually quoting Parker, Garrison said the Word was not bound "within the lids of any book," and the Scriptures must be judged as freely "as any other books" to determine what was "worthless or valuable." Some passages were "soul-sustaining and glorious," but centuries of history had shown that approved interpretations of the Bible would always be those that served a given era's despotic powers. Given that "all forms of government—autocratic, monarchical, military, and republican—have alike found their sanction and support in its pages," belief in biblical authority was "simply to be with the majority and to take the side of the strongest."[18]

According to the convention record, comments like these were met with "stamping and hissing." As biblical claims and passages were picked apart in long speeches over the meeting's four days, some serious debate was heard on the floor, but much of the opposition was voiced through "ribald" heckling from the audience, including some local divinity students and one unnamed audience member who denounced what he was hearing as a "tirade of hellish stuff." When some mischief-maker shut off the gaslights, "for some minutes a continual hissing, shrieking, stamping, drumming of canes, and whistling was kept up [in darkness] by the rioters, mainly occupying the gallery."[19] With the mayor having called in his "constabulary," a scuffle ensued, "blows were freely interchanged, knives were drawn, and sword-canes were menacingly flourished."[20] At the close of the "Infidel Convention," as hostile newspapers called it, Garrison and others needed bodyguards to escort them safely past an angry crowd, and the Connecticut state legislature was urged to outlaw any further meetings of the kind.[21] But looking back years later, after the end of slavery, Garrison wryly took the condemnations as praise, judging it "a good thing to be a heretic."[22]

William Lloyd Garrison's "Lutheran Incendiarism"

Fred A. Ross's charge that abolitionists "have now turned away from the word" was also correct in identifying that "word" as including both the Bible and the Constitution. Controversy over the spread of slavery further west led to the Compromise of 1850, which created a new flashpoint—a redoubled Fugitive Slave Act that ordered citizens in the free states to help return runaway slaves. Opponents denounced the requirement as compelled kidnapping, effectively the legalization of slavery nationwide. Martin R. Delany warned that Black freemen would never be safe; their fellow citizens would not protect them, precisely because Americans considered "their Laws their Scriptures" and obeyed magistrates' decrees like "the fiat of God."[23] Theodore Parker, again, was blunt. In attacking accommodationists like Moses Stuart and Daniel Webster—moderates who opposed slavery in principle, but nonetheless seemed to confirm Delany's warning (Webster had helped pass the Compromise in the Senate)—Parker said of the Constitution, as he had said of the Bible, so much the worse for it. If it would not allow an end to slavery, then "there is another Constitution that will. Then the title, Defender and expounder of the Constitution of the United States, will give way to this,—'Defender and expounder of the Constitution of the Universe,' and we shall reaffirm the ordinance of nature, and reënact the will of God."[24]

In effect, radicals like Parker saw slavery as a kind of *reductio ad absurdum,* a logical disproof of any claim to moral authority. If slavery was a valid conclusion, then the premise must be wrong, so any document that produced arguments supporting it must be morally invalid—even if historically it had been received as either religious or secular scripture. Stowe would make a similar point, citing the case of a skeptic whose "minister had constructed a scriptural argument in defence of slavery which he was unable to answer." So shocked was the man with "the idea that the Bible defended such an atrocious system, that he became an entire unbeliever," at least until a different minister corrected the misreading.[25]

What the Founders had done in the 1780s—perhaps, some argued, in the hope that slavery was already nearing extinction—had created an acute crisis by the 1850s. Certain facts were all too obvious: Not only had members of the "slaveocracy" itself been instrumental in the Constitution's drafting, some even with the conscious aim of protecting the slave system, but the Constitution's existence had not freed any slaves. In that sense, a proslavery interpretation had been well established decades before the Supreme Court, in its 1857 *Dred Scott* ruling, made shockingly explicit that Black Americans constitutionally "had no rights which the white man was bound to respect." Yet if such was really the Constitution's plain meaning, and if its meanings, as Vice President George Dallas and others claimed, were available to any reader—which would normally be a moral good—then, from the anti-slavery viewpoint, the Constitution was likely doing actual evil, not just permitting slavery but teaching Americans to tolerate it, and maybe worse, undercutting the high moral claims of the Founding itself.[26]

As they had done somewhat more reluctantly with the Bible, some abolitionists responded by conceding large parts of the slaveholders' case. Wendell Phillips wrote an entire short book trying to prove *The Constitution a Pro-Slavery Compact*, extensively quoting the statements and debates of its original framers.[27] Garrison enshrined the denunciation he had borrowed from Old Testament prophecy, "a 'covenant with death, and an agreement with hell'," at the top of the front page in of his influential newspaper, *The Liberator*, right next to the newspaper's nameplate. He and his colleagues also debated whether the best or only right course of action might simply be to withdraw from the covenant, as in fact the southern rebels would later attempt. Another Garrisonian slogan was "No Union with Slavery," though this had variants, like "No Union with Slaveholders," that might suggest a different political strategy. Abolitionists divided, in part, over how best to move public opinion—whether it was better to placate southern slaveholders or confront them, and whether presenting the Constitution as hopelessly pro-slavery was more or less likely to increase support for abolition in the North and the border states.[28] For some, though, including Garrison, "The call for disunion was precisely analogous to the call for immediate emancipation and the call for Christlike perfection; it was the statement of a moral imperative, a reveille to the conscience," regardless of its tactical wisdom.[29]

Garrison staged a vivid public demonstration of his "reveille to the conscience" over the Anthony Burns case in 1854. Weeks earlier, federal courts in Boston had outraged northern opinion by enforcing the Fugitive Slave Act against Burns, a captured runaway, ordering him returned to slaveholders under the guard of federal troops—a legalized kidnapping, in the view of many in the North. An armed attempt to break him out of jail led to a guard being killed, and several leaders of a "Boston Vigilance Committee," including Parker and Phillips, were charged with inciting a riot (though trial juries repeatedly refused to convict). In response, the Massachusetts Anti-Slavery Society declared that year's Fourth of July a day of public mourning. Garrison's famous act of protest on that occasion is conventionally referred to as "burning the Constitution," but such a description fails to capture it in full. In their memoir of Garrison, his children called it "this Lutheran incendiarism," apparently by way of comparison with Martin Luther's public burning of the pope's decree of 1520 demanding he recant his teachings on pain of excommunication. Garrison framed his imitation of this act in classically Protestant terms, as "the testimony of his own soul to all present," staged it on the Fourth, and opened it with Scripture readings and a lament over the contrast between the sorry state of the slaveholding republic and the Declaration of Independence. He then burned, first, a copy of the Fugitive Slave Act—after which:

> Using an old and well-known phrase, he said, "And let all the people say *Amen*;" and a unanimous cheer and shout of "Amen" burst from the vast audience. In like manner, Mr. Garrison burned the decision of [Judge] Edward G. Loring in the case of Anthony Burns, and the late charge of Judge Benjamin R. Curtis to the United States Grand Jury in reference

to the "treasonable" assault upon the Court House for the rescue of the fugitive—the multitude ratifying the fiery immolation with shouts of applause.

Only then did Garrison produce the Constitution, branding it "the source and parent of all the other atrocities" and repeating his "covenant with death" formula,

> and consumed it to ashes on the spot, exclaiming, "So perish all compromises with tyranny! And let all the people say, Amen!" A tremendous shout of "Amen!" went up to heaven in ratification of the deed, mingled with a few hisses and wrathful exclamations from some who were evidently in a rowdyish state of mind, but who were at once cowed by the popular feeling.[30]

The burning of the Constitution, then, for Garrison and presumably his crowd of witnesses, was in fact a quasi-religious ritual, drawing on images from both Protestant and biblical history. Like Luther, Garrison burned several documents—both the general charter of authority and the specific but illegitimate orders it authorized. (Luther's burning had included a copy of the Catholic Church's canon law, a "godless book" as he called it, and some works of church theology along with the papal bull itself.)

This protest was one Christian soul's public "testimony," but more than that, it was "ratified," as Garrison called forth responses from the crowd like a minister leading a congregation. The specific call, "And let all the people say Amen!", is a liturgical phrase, evoking several Old Testament passages in which the people of Israel affirm their covenant with God and repent for worshiping false gods. As an ancient Christian formula it had entered the Anglican Book of Common Prayer, which gave it a complicated historical role in early New England's religious politics, including a certain power to shock.[31] Garrison also responded to critics by pointing out that he had merely performed what he had long been saying, "in order to make my position palpable to the dullest vision," and that of course he had not burned anything of value:

> If they have discovered an anti-slavery Constitution, they know I did not burn that (why should I?) on the occasion referred to. ... I burnt a PRO-SLAVERY Constitution, in my judgment, *in the judgment of the nation ever since its adoption*, and therefore was faithful to the slave in so doing.[32]

The Constitution, as he had put it earlier, was merely "a rope of sand—a fanciful nonentity—a mere piece of parchment—a rhetorical flourish and splendid absurdity."[33] Garrison claimed to have no quarrel with a legitimate national compact, but only with "a mere piece of parchment."

The Constitution and "Plain, Common-sense Rules"

Hostility to the Constitution like Garrison's would obviously deal a serious blow to any hope for the kind of national "political religion" that many hoped for and that young Abe Lincoln had once urged. If such a religion depended on respect for the Constitution and laws, as Lincoln had argued, then consigning these to the flames as absurdities on parchment raised the question of whether a national compact really existed at all—and therefore, whether the nation itself can or should endure. This would be the great question facing Lincoln a few years later.[34] Meanwhile, the need to interpret a Constitution that remained in effect raised a number of daunting questions. Where should one seek the authority of such a text: in its framers' intentions, in its actual words, or in the spirit of the words applied at a historical distance and, perhaps, adapted to historical circumstances that did not exist when they were written? Were the original aims that prompted the text wrong in themselves, or correct but later put aside or betrayed? Could they even really be known? If not—or even if so—whose views on these matters should be taken as controlling? If the answer was "the people's," how was that controlling interpretation discovered?

As with biblical interpretation, questions like these cut across other dividing lines, generating disagreements even among like-minded advocates of similar goals. Frederick Douglass was thinking them through as events unfolded. Like Garrison, Douglass is a complicated figure whose views and tactical approaches evolved over time. At first he had taken his lead from Garrison, even recalling that "Mr. Garrison, and his paper [*The Liberator*] took a place in my heart second only to the Bible," and for close to a decade Douglass's views tracked Garrison's closely.[35] But beginning in the late 1840s they underwent a significant revision, and by the early 1850s he had arrived at a counter-position that at least partly answered Garrison's. Refounding his anti-slavery position on the Constitution, Douglass tried to marshal the popular reverence for it to his cause.[36] In the best-known part of his lacerating July Fourth address of 1852, Douglass asks, "What, to the American slave, is your 4th of July?" and answers with a series of invectives, calling it a revelation of injustice and cruelty, and condemning patriotic displays as "a sham," "swelling vanity," "brass fronted impudence," and "hollow mockery."[37] Even the associated prayers, hymns, sermons, and religious parade were

> mere bombast, fraud, deception, impiety, and hypocrisy—a thin veil to cover up crimes which would disgrace a nation of savages.
>
> There is not a nation on the earth guilty of practices, more shocking and bloody, than are the people of these United States, at this very hour. Go

where you may, search where you will, roam through all the monarchies and despotisms of the old world, travel through South America, search out every abuse, and when you have found the last, lay your facts by the side of the everyday practices of this nation, and you will say with me, that, for revolting barbarity and shameless hypocrisy, America reigns without a rival.
(20–21)

The slave power, said Douglass, had become "co-extensive with the star-spangled banner and American Christianity. Where these go, may also go the merciless slave-hunter" (25). He was outraged at those who claimed religious and scriptural sanction for the slave system; if they were right, he thundered, then "welcome infidelity! welcome atheism! welcome anything! in preference to the gospel, as preached by those Divines!" (29).

On the other hand, although slavery may have corrupted America's religious and political institutions, its courts, its patriotic celebrations, public opinion and in some sense the nation itself, Douglass no longer followed his radical colleagues in rejecting the national *ethos* of high regard for America's foundational writings. Instead the problem was their misuse. He pronounced his jeremiad "in the name of the Constitution and the Bible, which are disregarded and trampled upon." If "interpreted as it *ought* to be interpreted," Douglass insisted, "the Constitution is a GLORIOUS LIBERTY DOCUMENT" (36). It proclaimed a message of freedom.

Moreover, it did so clearly. For Douglass, the glory was twofold: not just the proclamation itself, but—as more naïve patriots liked to argue—the fact that any ordinary reader could see this, that the Constitution's meaning was accessible to all. After all, said Douglass, it was absurd to suppose that the basic issues were complicated or required any kind of subtle reasoning:

> Must I argue the wrongfulness of slavery? Is that a question for Republicans? Is it to be settled by the rules of logic and argumentation, as a matter beset with great difficulty, involving a doubtful application of the principle of justice, hard to be understood? How should I look to-day, in the presence of Americans, dividing, and subdividing a discourse, to show that men have a natural right to freedom? speaking of it relatively, and positively, negatively, and affirmatively. To do so, would be to make myself ridiculous, and [to] offer an insult to your understanding.
> (19)

On this premise that the underlying issues were in no way complex, Douglass declared his scorn for "the idea that the question of the constitutionality or unconstitutionality of slavery is not a question for the people. I hold that every American citizen has a right to form an opinion of the constitution, and to propagate that opinion, and to use all honorable means to make his opinion the prevailing one" (36). He directly quoted Vice President

Dallas's praise for the Constitution's "plain and intelligible" suitability for "home-bred, unsophisticated understandings," and he cited other political luminaries, all of them "sound lawyers," on every citizen's "personal interest in understanding [it] thoroughly" (37). As Douglass's audience would have recognized, the figures he named had all, like Dallas, been friendly to slavery to varying degrees; one had even called it the Constitution's "foundation."[38] Slyly, Douglass was reappropriating the complacent constitutional pieties of slavery's own apologists, converting them into a plank in his angry, unyielding abolitionist platform.

Granted, for all its plainness, the Constitution still needed interpreting: "there are certain rules of interpretation, for the proper understanding of all legal instruments." Even these, though, Douglass held to be "well-established"—not anything that should really be controversial. They were "plain, common-sense rules, such as you and I, and all of us, can understand and apply, without having passed years in the study of law" (36). Pressed for time, he did not spell out the rules, but he did favorably cite the work of Lysander Spooner, who had likewise read the Constitution as anti-slavery in a book-length exposition (35). Spooner, however, was a lawyer, and the views he set forth in *The Unconstitutionality of Slavery* depended not on a plain reading but on a detailed, heavily researched, and somewhat idiosyncratic analysis, one that involved carefully parsing key terms and their relationships in light of legal history and sophisticated theories of ratification, consent, and natural law. It was precisely the fact that words did not have single, indisputable meanings but could mean many things, Spooner explained, that called for "some rule of interpretation for determining which of these various meanings are the true ones."[39] Douglass may have welcomed Spooner's conclusion, but his "plain, common-sense rules" that anyone could apply without studying law are difficult to identify with Spooner's rules, whose learned application to the slavery issue eventually ran to nearly 300 pages—more than a quarter of which were needed just for the chapter describing the rules. Other abolitionists, moreover, had disputed Spooner's entire system of rules.[40]

On his own premise of textual clarity, though, Douglass pressed his startling point: "Now, take the constitution according to its plain reading, and I defy the presentation of a single pro-slavery clause in it. On the other hand it will be found to contain principles and purposes, entirely hostile to the existence of slavery" (37). Consciously or not, this phrasing recalled one of the legendary founding statements of Protestantism, "Here I stand," Martin Luther's 1521 defense of his reformist theses, which he similarly threw down in defiance of critics who, he said, would have to prove him wrong by reference to Scripture. The learned doctors may preach the opposite, the great weight of official judgment may all go the other way, but the sacred writing remains, its authority actually superseding that of the institutions it had chartered and those who ruled through them. Those agencies, this position implied, had issued words on paper that escaped the rulers' own intentions and channeled the intentions of a power superior to theirs.

Though Douglass was taking his stand on the written word, it would be inaccurate to call his reading either literal or nonliteral. Like anti-slavery biblical exegesis, it was both, inviting attention first to what the words actually said and then, beyond this, to the seeming spirit of the whole. Slavery's defenders had often seized on silences and ambiguities in the Bible, noting that it had emerged from ancient slaveholding societies yet did not explicitly condemn slavery as such—implying, they claimed, tolerance for the practice or even approval. This principle, however, could be turned the other way around, as Theodore Weld had pointed out: "Is that *silent entry* God's *endorsement?* Because the Bible in its catalogue of human actions, does not stamp on every crime its name and number, and write against it, *this is a crime*—does that wash out its guilt, and bleach it into a virtue?"[41] Douglass brought a similar reading to the silences in the Constitution; to read a text carefully, in this view, is to notice not just what it says but what it does not. There was meaning in the fact that the Founders, like God, had passed up the chance to write slavery more explicitly into their great text—leaving blanks to be filled with infusions of its spirit, or in Douglass's words, its larger "principles and purposes" (36–37).[42]

These Douglass found in "the Declaration of Independence, the great principles it contains, and the genius of American Institutions," which were converging with certain "obvious tendencies of the age"—rising levels of knowledge, a shrinking and more interdependent world—to "inevitably work the downfall of slavery" (37–38). Meanwhile, Douglass was happy if his own contribution was "biting ridicule, blasting reproach, withering sarcasm, and stern rebuke. For it is not light that is needed, but fire; it is not the gentle shower, but thunder. We need the storm, the whirlwind, and the earthquake" (20). This, too, recalled Luther, who had claimed to welcome "the parties and dissensions excited in the world by means of my doctrine" and to "rejoice exceedingly to see the Gospel this day, as of old, a cause of disturbance and disagreement."[43] Correct interpretation would not just illuminate the sacred words but activate them. It would pour their meaning, as Douglass put it, into "the nation's ear" (20).

"An *Excrescence* on the Tree of Our Liberty"

With its bold assertion of "self-evident" equality and rights for "all men," the Declaration was easier than the Constitution to enlist in the anti-slavery cause, and Frederick Douglass was far from alone in so doing. As early as 1791, Benjamin Banneker had invoked the Declaration in defense of slaves and African Americans in a letter to Thomas Jefferson, and David Walker's 1830 *Appeal* to "the Coloured Citizens of the World" quoted the Declaration while in effect overwriting the Constitution with a "Preamble" and "Articles" of Walker's own.[44] For all their fury at the Constitution, Garrison and his National Anti-Slavery Convention had claimed to "plant ourselves upon the Declaration of Independence, and upon the truths of Divine Revelation, as upon EVERLASTING ROCK."[45]

Unlike the Constitution, the Declaration was a manifesto, an explicit statement of principles, and these could well be viewed as inconsistent with slavery even if signed by slaveholders. Though lacking the formal legal force of the Constitution, it was also historically prior, and thus arguably the superior statement of what the Founding had meant to found. These facts made it potentially as great a stumbling-block for slavery's advocates as the Constitution was for slavery's opponents. In the words of Gerrit Smith, the abolitionist, women's suffrage advocate and 1848 presidential candidate of the anti-slavery Liberty Party, the Declaration could not be superseded: "You might as well talk of supplanting the Bible with the farthing Tract written to expound it, as talk of supplanting the Declaration of Independence with any subsequent paper," including even the Constitution. For Smith, American independence would have been impossible without it; the Declaration was like the cross of Constantine, the "sign" under which "our fathers conquered."[46]

The ironic result of praise like this was that even as—and because—the Declaration's great affirmations of liberty were becoming the center of the patriotic canon, they also came under vitriolic attack. Because of slavery, said Smith, they had "fallen into disrepute" and "ridicule." The dismissals were both contemptuous and colorful: Jefferson's words were "a fanfaranode of nonsense," said one Senator; at best, "glittering and sounding generalities," said another; not self-evident truths but "a self-evident lie," said a third.[47] A leading pro-slavery writer, George Fitzhugh, called them "exhuberantly false [sic], and arborescently fallacious," i.e., given to branching and spreading the error like a tree. (Fitzhugh claimed to borrow these "tumid yet appropriate epithets" from one of Jefferson's Revolutionary colleagues.[48]) For Senator and former Vice President John C. Calhoun, the popular "axiom" that "all men are born free and equal" was a "hypothetical truism" based on a "hypothetical and misnamed state of nature." It was "the most false and dangerous of all political errors" with "not a word of truth in it," and the Declaration's slightly different wording, "though less dangerous, is not less erroneous." Not needed in the first place to achieve the Declaration's purpose, it had yet gained "the authority of a document put forth on so great an occasion," and therefore had "spread far and wide, and fixed itself deeply in the public mind." By the time Calhoun was speaking, in 1848, it was "disorganizing" government both at home and abroad, causing anarchy in Europe and threatening soon to "ingulf" America's political institutions: "We now begin to experience the danger of admitting so great an error to have a place in the declaration of our independence. For a long time it lay dormant; but in the process of time it began to germinate, and produce its poisonous fruits."[49]

Another line of criticism suggested that even if the Declaration was not nonsense on its face, there was no straightforward way of reading its ideals into either the Constitution or American governance. Reviewing the new Republican Party's 1856 anti-slavery platform, former Massachusetts Senator and Attorney General Rufus Choate mockingly compared claims to find principles of constitutional interpretation in the Declaration to an imaginary new party vaguely claiming the sanction of the Bible. What "principles"? he demanded to know.[50] The following year, in a likewise religious vein, Fred A. Ross lambasted the Declaration's most famous paragraph as "an *excrescence* on the tree of our liberty," one that God will curse "as long as time" no matter how prominent its defenders or how people pretended to "worship" it. The "notion of created equality and unalienable right," he said, was both "falsehood and infidelity," an "infidel theory of human government foisted" into America's founding text. In his own close reading, Ross claimed to expose the Declaration's entire structure of rights, consent, and the social compact as "unscriptural dogmas" based on "imaginary maxims."[51]

The reason that Ross invoked terms like "infidel" and "unscriptural" was not just that he was a clergyman determined to prove *Slavery Ordained of God*. He was also intent on refuting one of the key textual arguments of slavery's opponents. The debates of the time, as we have seen, involved the Bible, the Declaration, and the Constitution all at once. Any of the three might be questioned, critiqued, or even rejected in favor of one or both of the others. A comprehensive textual grounding, whether for slavery or its abolition, would require interpretations of all three texts—four, if Old and New Testaments were read separately—as well a sense of their relative moral weighting and a theory of how moral authority flowed from one to the other. Slavery's opponents, Ross remarked with his usual scorn, seemed to imagine that ancient Scripture had foretold the doctrines of Thomas Jefferson. Discovering otherwise, they treated the Declaration as the superior text, elevating it "above the ordinance of God."[52] Ross was criticizing what he saw as an effort to read modern theories of natural rights back into the Bible—to let America's Declaration define what the Bible must have meant. Those he criticized put it the other way around: For many abolitionists, the Declaration was the vector through which biblical principles had informed America's Founding.

In making this point, anti-slavery writers claimed to find the Bible and the Declaration in accord on one of the great contested questions of nineteenth-century ethnography. Citing Acts 17:26, they appealed to "one-bloodism," or what would be known scientifically as "monogenesis"—the view that the various human races or types all had a common descent, as opposed to having been created separately. In one public debate, Jonathan Blanchard said in 1845 that he and his fellow abolitionists "take their stand" on one-bloodism and, with it, the biblical doctrine of "the natural equity of man," which in turn informed "those great principles of human rights, drawn from the New Testament, and announced in the American Declaration of Independence, declaring that all men have natural and inalienable rights to person, property and the pursuit of happiness."[53] Moses Stuart likewise insisted on one-bloodism (against the "polygenist" views of the great naturalist Louis Agassiz), similarly asserting it as a "first and fundamental principle, not only of the Bible which declares that all are of *one blood,* but of our Declaration of Independence, which avers, that all men are born with an *inherent and inalienable right to life, liberty and property.*"[54]

Of course, one could argue that the Constitution had simply backpedaled from this, betraying the sacred principles that had "made us once the admiration of the world"—that it had "shipwrecked" the Declaration's great experiment, as Phillips and Garrison put it.[55] For Stuart, though, the Founders' purposes ruled this out:

> After such a declaration before heaven and earth, without one dissenting voice, how could the immortal men, whose names are appended to that Declaration, publish to the world in their Constitution of government, that they fully admitted in practice what they had solemnly denied in principle? How could they say: We authorize the practical denial of equality and liberty, and hold, that the right to them of a part of the community is *not* inalienable? How would the despotisms of the old world have pointed the finger of scorn, at the palpable disagreement between the Declaration of Independence, and the Constitution of the United States![56]

What an argument like this did was attempt to settle the question of whether the Bible was pro- or anti-slavery by treating the Declaration itself as a kind of biblical commentary or gloss. Scripture might seem friendly to slavery in this or that passage, but its premise was equal creation—and as far as America was concerned, the Declaration's embrace of this doctrine had made the anti-slavery reading canonical. This in turn entailed reading the Constitution, too, as anti-slavery, lest the Founding as a whole dissolve into hypocrisy and incoherence. It would further follow that the Declaration was a kind of epitome of the Constitution, the essential meaning that emerged from behind the proslavery laws and constitutional doctrines—much as Jefferson, Theodore Parker, and others claimed to find in Scripture a sublime core message buried beneath layers of textual and doctrinal distortions. This Declaration-centric view of the Founding would be central to the thinking of Abraham Lincoln, whose arguments along these lines will be examined in the next chapter.

John Brown's Compact for a New Republic

The case of John Brown, the radical abolitionist, is particularly interesting, not only because he authored both a declaration and a constitution of his own, but because he envisioned these as actual governing documents, sought legitimacy for them through a "convention" as the Founders had done, and came to the whole effort in the first place as a pious Reformed Protestant textualist deeply immersed in Bible-reading. Brown owned many copies of the Bible, tried to memorize the entire thing, and could adduce biblical quotes by the dozens in long strings that went on for pages.[57] Yet he was painfully aware of the doubts that were destabilizing scriptural authority in his time. His own children, as young adults, appeared to be losing the faith, in part because they shared his disgust at the churches' complicity in slavery. Brown was alarmed, though, that they were taking things too far:

> In choosing my texts, and in quoting from the Bible, I perhaps select the very portions which "another portion" of my family hold are not to be wholly received as *true*. I forgot to say that my younger sons (as is common in this "progressive age") appear to be a *little in advance* of my older, and have thrown off the *old shackles* entirely; after THOROUGH AND CANDID investigation they have discovered the Bible to be ALL a fiction!

Surprisingly, he went on to reply to his son John on this point in what sounds like an idiom borrowed from the higher critics, speaking of "so-called prophets" and the unknown "motives of the different writers" who "made" the various characters, including God himself, say this or that. For a man of faith, Brown seems to have had an unusually accurate sense of the skeptical currents of his "progressive age," but he nonetheless urged "steadfastness" in responding to what he still maintained was the Bible's consistent message.[58]

Early on, even before he swore himself to a career aimed at destroying slavery, Brown hoped to "do something in a practical way for my poor fellow-men who are in bondage."[59] The action that would make his name a Civil War rallying cry, his failed guerilla raid on the Harpers Ferry federal arsenal in October 1859, was not very "practical" in the sense of effective; on the day he was hanged for it, Brown himself seemed to put it down to idealistic miscalculation.[60] Part of his error may have been mistaking what it means to be "practical." In the same months that he was making what turned out to be inadequate tactical plans for the massive slave revolt he envisioned, Brown had taken time to write both a "Provisional Constitution" for the new free republic he hoped to found, and a "Declaration of Liberty," dated the Fourth of July, that reprised arguments from the original Declaration in the name of "the Representatives of the circumscribed citizens of the United States, of America [sic] in General Congress assembled." Since it carried no signatures, the text of this declaration was not clear on who that included.[61] Brown's constitution, however, was nominally the product of a "convention" of a few dozen associates, most of them African American, that he summoned to "ordain and establish" it and to appoint officers to its provisional government—although this very brief gathering in Chatham, Ontario, received a finished draft that Brown himself had borrowed and adapted from the U.S. Constitution, a method more like the Constitution's state ratification conventions than the lengthy debates of the 1787 Constitutional Convention.[62]

At any rate, Brown seemed to believe that legitimizing his intended new order was part of conjuring it into being, that it required supplying the right kind of textual basis, and that he could do this on his own initiative, in advance of the action he hoped to prompt—instead of, as in the case of the Founding, in response to pressures already arising among constituents and future citizens and with armed conflict already in progress. On that basis, and perhaps fatally, he spent time formally constituting his putative republic when he still lacked a clear military plan to bring it about.

Brown's constitution became a key piece of evidence at his trial, momentarily putting Brown, or at least his attorneys, in the peculiar position of belittling his own handiwork. Brown's provisional government was not operational, his legal team argued, but merely "imaginary," more a kind of debating society, and his constitution was just a "pamphlet," similar to the charters and bylaws of any number of "harmless organizations."[63] It was Virginia's prosecutors who insisted on taking it seriously, arguing that the provisional government "was a real thing," and that the title and office of commander in chief it gave Brown was therefore an act of treason. Unlike debating societies, which bandy words about largely for the pleasure of doing so, Brown's paper-made title and the words behind it were accorded the power of an overt and hostile act.

Though it helped get him condemned, in the end that may be what Brown actually preferred to hear, for the same reason he had refused advice to try pleading insanity. In an editorial titled "John Brown Not Insane," Frederick Douglass, a key supporter, explained Brown's actions on the "natural and simple" principle that Brown believed "the Declaration of Independence to be true, and the Bible to be a guide to human conduct ... This age is too gross and sensual to appreciate his deeds, and so calls him mad."[64] Ralph Waldo Emerson likewise credited Brown with an idealistic faith that made the Gospel's Golden Rule, the Declaration, and constitutional "strict construction" all of a piece, with Brown as a walking embodiment of all three. Like God's law and alongside it, Emerson suggested, the American Founding can be written into a person's heart and mind.[65] For Brown, denying that his new constitution actually constituted something—that it was meant not just to read like the U.S. Constitution but to do the same thing—would have been akin to calling himself mad. It would have drained his efforts of intentionality, which among other things would have denied him his emerging role as the nation's most celebrated anti-slavery martyr and, soon, a wartime rallying cry.

The problem, of course, was that at least in the short term, Brown's idealism had led to failure for all concerned: a number of men had been killed or condemned, no slaves had been freed, and as Emerson put it, "the governor of Virginia is forced to hang a man whom he declares to be a man of the most integrity, truthfulness and courage he has ever met."[66] Embracing martyrdom, Brown rejected his allies' offer to break him out of jail, and then spent his last days there going back to the text: he immersed himself again in Scripture, painstakingly marking up passages in a jailhouse Bible to compose "a kind of spiritual autobiography and apologetic," as one modern analyst describes it.[67] Brown seems to have been trying to reconstruct the textual readings that had inspired and, he seemed determined to show, legitimized his efforts.

In his last letter to his family, Brown surprisingly devoted significant space to a kind of farewell sermon on Bible-reading. Apparently still worried that his closest kin did not share his view, he insisted again on his "conviction" concerning Scripture's "truth and genuineness," urging them to "see whether you cannot discover such evidence yourselves."[68] Not only did he want his family to study the Bible night and day, but he asked them to hand down a "carefully preserved" heirloom copy "in remembrance of me," borrowing that liturgical phrase from the King James New Testament, where Jesus pronounces it while instituting the Lord's Supper on the eve of his own martyrdom.

Brown's last acts were thus attempts to inscribe himself in the Bible's text and see its authority perpetuated, at least within his own line. This effort seems to have been his way of vindicating that authority while also, he may have hoped, achieving a kind of immortality. He was frequently compared to an Old Testament prophet, but most prophets did not lead armed revolts, still less work up point-by-point plans of government.[69] Brown took his cues from the biblical prophets and the teachings they had handed down, but when he then acted, it was in imitation of the American Founding—a quest to become, in effect, a new Founding Father.

Martin Delany: Secret Agency and the "Nation within a Nation"

One of the delegates at Brown's Chatham "convention" was Martin Delany, longtime associate and sometime rival of Frederick Douglass and a prominent African American leader in his own right: "the Patrick Henry of his race" in a "revolution for the rights of the colored man," in one contemporary's estimation.[70] As an organizer, essayist, and pamphleteer,

Delany played a key role in the nineteenth century's ongoing debates about a Black nation—whether one already exists or could be created, whether doing so was the best way forward, whether it could be done in America or would require removal or "colonization" abroad, and whether it was principally an American or an international project.[71]

Delany's 1852 treatise, *The Condition, Elevation, Emigration, and Destiny of the Colored People of the United States*, published in the same weeks as *Uncle Tom's Cabin*, was ahead of its time in describing race as what today would be called a "social construction." Racial disadvantage reflects a "policy of political degradation" that does not arise from racial differences, Delany argued, but instead constitutes them. Subordinate groups are chosen because they are politically vulnerable, and only then are racist claims about them—"their inferiority by nature as distinct races"—concocted as rationalizing libels. White groups have sometimes been treated this way too; natural features like skin color and hair are not needed, though conveniently visible markers will be seized upon where available. But racist claims are a pretext for what is in fact "mere policy, with nature having nothing to do with it."[72]

To maintain the oppression, the degraded group must be denied a political identity of its own. This discourages other groups and nations from coming to its defense.[73] Defined by its alleged "incapacity for self-government," the oppressed are de-constituted, cast in the role of "excrescences on the body politic"—"nonentities" having "no part nor lot in the government of the country."[74] On these premises, slaves and free Black Americans alike had been reduced to "a *broken people*." The harsh irony was that African Americans had come to be "singled out" as "a distinct nation," but only on conditions and for purposes determined by those who meant them ill.[75]

All this also means, however, that African America was a "nation within a nation." That phrase, along with "state within a state," has long been part of political debate, applied at various times to such disparate entities as the Dutch East India Company, Protestants in France, Freemasons, the Catholic Church, the Prussian army, labor unions, the industrial proletariat, European settlers in Africa, the Québécois, and various other ethnic minorities including, most ominously, Jews: "*einen Staat innerhalb der Staaten*," as Hitler would put it in *Mein Kampf*.[76] The rise of modern nation-states involved both centripetal forces—the fitful, ongoing effort to subsume the claims of various sub-national groups under a single rule of law—and centrifugal: to identify the "peoples" entitled to nationhood and assert their claims to self-rule within bounded territories of their own. A nation within a nation existed where these processes were incomplete or mismatched. It could be a group that was not yet fully assimilated, but also, perhaps, a people still unformed and struggling for self-awareness but present in embryo, an incipient rebuke to the larger nation's failure to enfold all its constituents in a single, shared citizenship and cultural identity. Such half-realized nations existed "in all ages, in almost every nation," Delany noted, citing many examples spread across Europe.[77]

This political analysis also suggested a political solution: The mechanism of degradation could be turned around and run in reverse. If racist oppression arises from political vulnerability, it would best be fought by asserting political agency. As Delany put it, "Every people should be the originators of their own designs, the projectors of their own schemes, and creators of the events that lead to their destiny—the consummation of their desires."[78] The oppressed group must assert this right, demonstrating its ability to make a history for itself on the same terms as other peoples. By showing itself capable of self-government, it would win the right to appeal for help to other nations: "The claims of no people ... are respected by any nation, until they are presented in a national capacity."[79] That African Americans were a nation within the nation, a nation "enveloped by the United States," must be turned from disability to advantage.[80] A nation not admitted to the larger body politic should become a body politic of its own. As Delany put it, "We must MAKE an ISSUE, CREATE an EVENT, and ESTABLISH a NATIONAL POSITION for OURSELVES."[81]

Possibly this would require relocating outside the United States. Delany was critical of some white-sponsored colonization schemes and condemned Liberia's constitution as a "burlesque," creating a "mockery" and "parody" of a puppet government controlled by enslavers.[82] But he also joined in constitution-writing for various organizations, eventually including John Brown's imagined republic, and as a young man he had sketched a proposal for a project to found a new Black nation in East Africa. Updating this plan, Delany's 1852 report laid out what amounted to a draft constitution for African America. Its central feature was a "National Confidential Council," a "great representative gathering of the colored people of the United States" that could speak with their authority. This council would appoint boards of directors and commissioners with an eye to founding an East African nation, building a great trans-African railway, and thereby taking control of much of the trade between Asia and the Americas. As a duly constituted body, the National Confidential Council—"confidential" because composed of freemen who had their people's confidence—would be able to appeal for support from England and France "in a national capacity," and would eventually seed a powerful nation "to whom all the world must pay commercial tribute." This at last would make the "colored race," which was two-thirds of the world's people, "*lords* of terrestrial creation."[83] The global Black majority carried "the highest traits of civilization," and must develop these "in their purity" so as to "instruct the world."[84]

Delany's council did not take shape as he imagined it, but many "colored conventions" over the decades did seek to give Black America a collective voice.[85] In 1854 Delany helped organize a "National Emigration Convention," keynoting it with a call to resist the "Anglo-Saxon" and, even more, "Anglo-American" campaign "to crush the colored races wherever found" and deny them control of any territory on earth.[86] In 1859 he would travel to Africa himself to scout possible sites for a Black republic. By then, however, he had also launched another experiment, an attempt to dramatize his ideas through literature: his only work of fiction, the two-part serialized novel *Blake: or, the Huts of America*.

The hero of *Blake* is a sophisticated, suave, and brilliant former Black freeman, Henry Blake, who had been tricked and sold into slavery in Mississippi, but escapes when his wife is sold away from him to a slaveholder who takes her to Cuba. In Part 1 of the novel, serialized in 1859, Blake travels around the American South, variously on foot, horseback, or riverboat, aiming to rescue her but also laying the groundwork for a broader slave revolt. Eventually he guides a party of escaped slaves on a dangerous trek to freedom in Canada, then sails from New York to Havana, where he locates and frees his wife. In Part 2, serialized in 1862 after the Civil War had begun, Blake oversees a secret underground of "colored" Cubans who are preparing for race war. An expert seaman, he also infiltrates the slave trade by signing on as sailing-master on an illegal slave transport, the aptly named *Vulture*, which takes him to one of the "slave factories" on the West African coast. Narrowly managing to make it back to Havana under hot pursuit from British warships, Blake arranges for the slaves in the *Vulture's* cargo to be purchased and freed in Cuba, while recruiting the leaders of a shipboard revolt into his underground. Eventually, in response to continuing local outrages, his compatriots vote to attack the ruling white community in a general uprising.[87]

Largely ignored, *Blake* was not published as a book until 1970, when the modern civil-rights movement revived interest in older African American fiction. Modern critics have recognized the story's significance as a document of early Black nationalism, but otherwise have not been sure what to make of it. Borrowing quotations from *Uncle Tom's Cabin* as epigraphs, it seems at least partly a response to that novel, which Delany had criticized.[88] It has been variously assigned to many different genres, including even seafaring stories, "proto-science fiction," and alternate history, none of which it fits very neatly.[89] Its final chapters were apparently lost, so it is not certain what becomes of the uprising or what ending Delany intended. (The last extant line has one of Blake's associates vowing, "Woe be unto those devils of whites, I say!"[90]) The work is seldom admired for its literary qualities; its first modern editor politely called it "the creative offering of an activist rather than the political expression of an artist," and a more recent editor, while appreciating what he sees as a "startlingly innovative" aesthetic in this "prophecy of black liberation," sees it as a "highly unusual," even "unique" work and grants the common—and "not mistaken"—view that Delany "was a very bad novelist."[91]

We can make better sense of *Blake*, however, if we read it with specific reference to Delany's earlier writings. In outlining their woeful condition, Delany had criticized the "slothfulness" of his fellow Black citizens, urging them to stop relying on prayer, the patronage of "philanthropists," or the "futile hope" that people with no national identity of their own could rely on others to serve as their "agent." They should not be content to remain "sparsely interspersed among our white fellow-countrymen," nor to "stand still and continue inactive."[92] Henry Blake's goal in Part 1 of the novel is to set these conditions right. As he travels among the scattered huts, meeting with slaves in private "seclusions," he combats the ignorance and "want of general information" that Delany had diagnosed as a key problem, joining Black Americans into a common fellowship and giving them the promise of becoming "a people," as one of them exults.[93] He also prepares them for action while modeling it himself. To do this, he must correct an ironic scriptural error. The King James translation of Exodus 14:13 has Moses telling the Israelites newly escaped from Egypt to "stand still, and see the salvation of the Lord." America's slaves, raised on the Bible but under the cynical ministrations of whites, have misunderstood "stand still" and "salvation" as a counsel of passivity, an offer of hope only in the next life. But as other translations make clear, Moses is actually urging courage— stand "firm," take a stand—and promising imminent freedom, as the Red Sea is about to part.

Despite her title character's long-suffering mildness, which eventually made the name "Uncle Tom" a disparaging catchphrase, Harriet Beecher Stowe had sharply criticized the "system of religion" taught to slaves as a falsification of the gospel.[94] Henry Blake takes the same view and carries it to its conclusion. His work among the slaves as in part exegetical, a matter of textual reinterpretation: "They use the Scriptures to make you submit," he tells them, but "we must now begin to understand the Bible so as to make it of interest to us."[95] "Salvation," he instructs, is their forthcoming release from slavery, and "standing still" merely patience in awaiting the right moment to strike. A man of action, ranging widely across the country, Blake himself does the opposite of standing still.

Delany seems to consider, but reject, comparisons between Blake and both Moses and Nat Turner, two other legendary leaders of slave revolts who were hailed as religious visionaries and prophets. Though Christian, Blake sees religion as by and large an obstacle, and explicitly rejects the role of spiritual leader.[96] Nonetheless, in spreading among slaves a new gospel of resistance, he resembles a missionary. But his efforts are also a "mission" of another kind: that of a secret agent. In fact, if *Blake* is difficult to fit into the existing genres of its time, that may be because the better comparison is to a later genre, one that would fully emerge only in the twentieth century. Henry Blake is a "superspy," a character of the kind that would later be familiar to readers and filmgoers from the tales of John Buchan's Richard Hannay, Ian Fleming's James Bond, Tom Clancy's Jack Ryan, and their countless imitators in popular fiction and film. Though not the first spy in American fiction—Delany may have drawn inspiration from James Fenimore Cooper's long-selling, very popular Revolutionary War tale *The Spy*—he seems to be the first instance of the secret agent as international, free-ranging, omni-capable adventurer and man of action.

Blake includes a number of references to spying and espionage, and while sailing on the *Vulture* Blake is suspected of being a spy (for England, though, incorrectly).[97] If he has not been recognized as a superspy of the literary type, it might be because his exploits in slave country are unglamorous compared to those of his later successors. Blake must make do without their high-tech gadgetry, and he is a pillar of virtue, not a Bond-style ladies' man with a taste for Scotch and sardonic *badinage*. Even so, like other superspies he cuts a finer, more cultured figure than those around him, especially the villains. Born to wealth and "of good literary attainments," he is multi-lingual, and his elegant, cosmopolitan English contrasts with other characters' thick local dialects. Though a terror to opponents, he is "always mild, gentle and courteous," yet fully capable of the "bold and adventurous deeds of manly daring" that Delany had long been calling for.[98] He can work incognito, is adept with disguises, aliases, and cover stories, is an expert with vehicles and weapons, and is in constant motion—forever infiltrating, impersonating, improvising, and making narrow escapes, sometimes relying "adroitly" on skill and subtlety and sometimes on agility and strength.[99] His ability to move about with what one modern critic calls "a speed that defies plausibility" produces the loose plotting for which *Blake* is sometimes faulted, but is typical of superspy adventures, whose whirlwind of shifting scenes and credulity-stretching perils are offered not for their narrative logic but to showcase the hero's astonishing range of talents.[100] Also like modern superspy stories, the novel inflects these adventures with occasional bits of comic relief, humorous moments in which the quick-witted hero gets the better of various greedy or ignorant blunderers.

In Part 2, except for his undercover voyage to West Africa, Blake stops traveling and settles in Havana. There, his "seclusions" develop into a secret "Grand Council," whose clandestine "Army of Emancipation" he takes command of while it prepares for a "war upon the whites."[101] Havana, presumably, is Delany's chosen locale because, in some Confederate schemes, it was the prospective capital of a hemispheric slave empire to be built once the Southern rebellion succeeded. Delany therefore presents it as the center of revolutionary resistance.[102] It is also the home of a "colored" population that is not solely Black or American, but resembles the polyglot worldwide body of the oppressed that Delany's earlier proposals were meant to defend. The program that Blake mounts in Cuba is similar to John Brown's in some ways but more carefully developed, as if Delany had taken lessons from Brown's recent failure and was trying to correct his mistakes.

Compared to Part 1's man of action, Blake is a relatively diminished figure in Part 2, unseen for stretches of the narrative while other characters come to the fore. But this modulating of his role may be the novel's most important political message. To act "in a national capacity" and therefore effectively, Delany had earlier argued, the nonwhite population had to be properly constituted. Hence his earlier call for a "National Confidential Council" with a body of rules and a fairly elaborate structure. Blake's fictional Grand Council likewise apportions roles and appoints agents, including ministers of state like a provisional government's and the "generals" of its nascent guerilla army. As General-in-Chief, however, Blake is not a romantic or swashbuckling figure, a nineteenth-century Che Guevara. The office is a duty and a constraint, a new "bondage" in which he must "submit entirely to others," as he concedes. It limits his previous freedom of action and subordinates him to an emerging political entity, one whose confidence he needs in order to act.[103] From then on, his voice is just one voice among many. Remarkably—although, granted, the climactic chapters may be lost—we never see General Blake actually lead anything except meetings.

In *Blake,* then, Delany dramatizes a theory of how nations are made. As he had previously argued, they are the means of giving a people agency— of enabling them to establish and protect themselves, formulate their intentions, win support from other nations, and become "projectors" to carry their intentions into the world. A "broken people" like his own had yet to define its own national existence. It was standing still, inactive, and to foster an effective politics thus required, first, activating the people, and second, constituting them as a body that could authorize ongoing action on their behalf.

These are Blake's dual roles. Later superspies, freewheeling though they are, have at least nominally served established powers—the British Empire, the West, the "Free World"—but Secret Agent Blake serves a nation that has not yet been realized, that is a secret even to itself.[104] Its only agency, at first, is that which he supplies as his own "projector," with an original mission not to defend the nation from outside threats but to bring it into being in the first place. A mission in two senses, this effort is also missionary work, a bringing of light to those living in darkness, like the spreading of the gospel, and promising their "deliverance."[105] In this case the gospel is the good news that the nation exists. The original Old English translation of *evangelion* was GŌDSPEL, which also meant "good *story*," and a crucial feature of the national gospel is the recognition that a scattered and degraded people *has* a story, a shared narrative unfolding coherently over time, one that is capable of being "spelled." Blake's effort to instill this awareness through his sharing of information, the "seclusions" that join the slaves together into a larger whole, is spiritually transforming, redeeming the slaves from the stupor of their isolated huts and giving them a new existence as a people. The imagining of a shared community replaces what Hannah Arendt called the "dark background of mere givenness," an inchoate existence of households and tiny clans just struggling to survive.[106] Thus is Delany's lamented "political degradation" overcome, and a broken people made an unbroken polity.[107]

In the second stage, however, the project broadens, giving General Blake a position in a developing organization, a proto-government, that is able to commission and coordinate its agents, including him. (Intriguingly, the text refers to Blake as "Henry" throughout Part 1, when he is acting on his personal initiative, and "Blake" throughout Part 2, as he settles into a formal role.) It seems that at the moment the novel's text breaks off, the emerging nation is about to rise up and declare itself.[108] This would be the final step. Gospels must be proclaimed, and a nation must be "brought forth," enabled to act in public and in the same arena as other nations. John Brown, too, may have had such goals in mind, but Delany seems to have thought the problem through more thoroughly, though he opted for radical action only as a literary experiment.

Nonetheless, both Brown's failed effort, and the possibilities for larger slave uprisings like Henry Blake's, are generally thought to have frightened Southern slaveholders enough to have helped bring on their rebellion.[109] It is another notable irony, therefore, that the South's ordinances of secession are among the many American texts that mimicked the Declaration and Constitution; Florida's, for instance, opens with phrases conspicuously borrowed from both.[110] Even rebels against the United States recognized its foundational writings as models for legitimating political authority in words. On the other side, Abraham Lincoln spoke for an American nation that had already been "brought forth," but whose meaning and even continued existence, as he saw it, called not just for invoking those original charters but for a profound reengagement with them. That effort is the subject of the next chapter.

9

Lincoln's Miniature Bible: Salvation History in the Gettysburg Address

One recurring joke in the 1957 Broadway musical *The Music Man* involves the hapless mayor of River City, Iowa, the iconic but fictional small town where the story is set in 1912. Called to preside at various civic events and to address the townspeople on the Fourth of July, Mayor Shinn makes a show each time of gathering himself for a great burst of oratory, pauses portentously, then begins, "Four score ..." In each case, some interruption cuts him off, but of course, in just those two words, everyone has already recognized the famous opening of Abraham Lincoln's Gettysburg Address. For Lincoln the words "Four score and seven years ago" referred to a specific date, but Mayor Shinn absurdly imagines that just by themselves, no matter in what year they're spoken, they lend any politician's ceremonial remarks extra weight and profundity.

The joke, however, in a sense goes even further, for Lincoln himself chose the phrasing with an obviously similar if more defensible aim. "Fore score" is recognizable—where a mere "eighty" would not be—because it is archaic, a manner of numbering borrowed from King James' English. ("The days of our years are threescore years and ten": Psalm 90:10.) That it resonated with the Bible, Lincoln apparently thought, made it appropriate to the somber moment at the Gettysburg cemetery, which called for a suitable gravity of speech. Mayor Shinn's quote would not feed his hopes of reaching Lincolnian levels of *gravitas* if Lincoln had not, himself, likewise been reaching for words in a higher key of sacredness.

This rhetorical heightening was important to Lincoln's project, but was only part of it. As Mayor Shinn fails to grasp, the number itself is important because 1776, the year it refers to, was when America declared independence. The pre-Civil War slavery debates, we have previously seen, were partly arguments about how the Founding texts related to each other and to the Bible. In those debates, Lincoln had been a key participant, gaining his national reputation by marking out a distinctive and, in the end, politically successful position. When, at Gettysburg, he cast back fourscore and seven years from a moment of supreme crisis, and in so doing deliberately chose an idiom that incorporated and resembled Scripture, he was both recalling his earlier views and constructing a text that would carry them to their grandest possible conclusion.

"An Interesting Memorial of the Dead Past?"

Building on his youthful hope for an American "political religion," Lincoln spent the years leading up to his presidency defending the Founding texts and their biblical correctness in various public statements. He was aghast at the "pro-slavery theology" of someone like the Rev. Fred A. Ross, whose cynical argument that God "ordained" slavery he privately mocked. Apologists like Ross, he charged, took the difficulty of applying God's will to particular cases in the real world as permission for slaveholders to substitute their own voice for God's.[1] In fact, Lincoln argued in one speech, Scripture had already anticipated this problem:

> The Savior, I suppose, did not expect that any human creature could be perfect as the Father in Heaven; but He said, "As your Father in Heaven is perfect, be ye also perfect." He set that up as a standard, and he who did most towards reaching that standard, attained the highest degree of moral perfection. So I say in relation to the principle that all men are created equal, let it be as nearly reached as we can.[2]

Rather than discredit the Declaration, the fact of real-world inequality aligned it all the better with God's Word, which set many standards that humankind fell short of and always would.

In other arguments, too, Lincoln ranged himself with those opponents of slavery who viewed the Founding as a single, coherent, and biblically correct project, and who refused to undercut it—as some of the more radical abolitionists were willing to do—by supposing its core texts to be either hypocritical or somehow at odds. We find many examples in the celebrated Lincoln-Douglas debates, whose real subject, said one close observer, was "above all the meaning of the Declaration" and its claims about rights.[3] At times, Lincoln's artful strategy was to acknowledge what was said to be wrong with the text, but then recast the alleged faults as virtues. For instance, the Declaration's "all men are created equal" not only did not describe a visible reality, but, as some critics noted, was not needed for the immediate purpose: one could arrive at the conclusion that America should be independent simply from the colonists' long list of grievances.

For Lincoln, however, this criticism understated what the Revolution was about. Its aim had been to establish not just self-government, but better government. The Declaration cannot have been promising Americans merely "that we should be *equal* to [British subjects] in their own oppressed and *unequal* condition," still "saddled with a King and Lords of our own." It must have promised a better political condition. It also cannot have been limited just to its original audience. Lincoln mockingly paraphrased his arch-rival Senator Stephen Douglas' narrow reading of it: "We hold these truths to be self-evident that all British subjects who were on this continent eighty-one years ago, were created equal to all British subjects born and *then* residing in Great Britain." If that was the whole message, what were Americans in the present day even bothering to celebrate on the Fourth of July? What meaning could the Declaration still have for them, let alone for Black citizens? The Declaration's promise extends either to everyone or to no one.[4]

Here Lincoln was being politically savvy, recognizing that his Illinois audiences included many German-Americans and others whose forebears had arrived post-Revolution, and who might feel or have heard themselves belittled for that reason—treated as foreigners, essentially, with no pride of place in the making of America. The Declaration, he argued, answered this concern by marking out a larger aspiration than mere independence. The higher principles it invoked were "an electric cord" that bound Americans together across the generations. Their very generality made them inclusive, which allowed Lincoln to flatter his non-Anglo constituents as joined to the Founding genetically: "blood of the blood, and flesh of the flesh of the men who wrote that Declaration," and therefore second to none as participants in the great American project.[5] The fact that the principles obviously had not been immediately and fully enacted was also, in its way, a good thing: It had the happy effect of making the electric cord even longer, extending it into the future by ensuring that the project would be dynamic and ongoing. With its lofty language, the Declaration drove that forward motion in two ways, setting a goal that demanded continual striving—"the progressive improvement in the condition of all men everywhere"—and at the same time blocking retreat, creating "a stumbling block to those who in after times might seek to turn a free people back into the hateful paths of despotism."[6]

Far from worthless, let alone harmful, then, it was the aspirational language, the appeal to universal rights and not just the narrow rights of British colonists, that provided the "vitality" without which something once glorious was "a mere wreck—mangled ruin." Appealing across parties, Lincoln asked, "Are you really willing that the Declaration shall be thus frittered away?—thus left no more at most, than an interesting memorial of the dead past?" In a striking anticipation of his famous future post-battle address, he suggested that doing so would make it "of no practical use now—mere rubbish—old wadding left to rot on the battle-field after the victory is won."[7]

What the Bible and the Declaration actually did, according to Lincoln, was chart a general direction or "channel." Into this, the Constitution had then placed the government. The three American scriptures were therefore all of a piece; each took on its full meaning only from its interplay with the others. Lincoln called on his listeners to join in seeing to it that America continued forward in that original channel, however imperfectly, rather than "turning in the contrary direction" in which political leaders like Douglas were threatening to take it.[8] It is a mark of this argument's success that certain biblical phrases—notably, "a house divided"—are probably better known among Americans today from Lincoln's borrowed use of them than from the original Bible passages he was quoting.

The Legendary "Back of the Envelope"

In the Gettysburg Address, of course, we have not only famous phrases, but a text that would come to stand alongside the few most famous lines from the Declaration and Constitution, and perhaps a handful of quotations and song lyrics, as one of the best-remembered political utterances in the American patriotic canon. This is due in no small part to the fact that generations of children were expected to memorize this short speech in school. It has been cast in bronze, inscribed in marble, framed and hung on thousands of walls, set to grand orchestral music, and printed in full on commemorative knicknacks ranging from pendants and collectors' plates to sofa pillows, shot glasses, and pandemic face masks. (In an interesting gesture, during a visit to Independence Hall in 2015, Pope Francis chose to defend immigrants in a speech delivered from Lincoln's Gettysburg podium.[9])

The address has even been sold as an imitation illuminated manuscript modeled on medieval Bibles (Figure 9.1),[10] an homage to which it is especially suited not only because of its enormous prestige but because, as one book-length study has carefully documented, its language and cadences throughout, not just the memorable beginning, owe a great deal to the King James Bible and the Anglican Book of Common Prayer.[11] That study, moreover, is just one of many books and innumerable articles devoted to this brief text of just 272 words. Indeed, in America, *The Gettysburg Gospel*, as another of those books calls it, is among the most closely studied and frequently recited short messages apart from sacred Scripture itself: the Lord's Prayer, the Sermon on the Mount, the Nativity story in Luke, and that popular choice for weddings, the thirteenth chapter of First Corinthians.

FIGURE 9.1 *The Gettysburg Address as illuminated manuscript, 1919. Public Domain. Courtesy of HathiTrust.*

Whether the speech was "the voice of God speaking through the lips of Abraham Lincoln," as Lincoln's Secretary of War, Edwin M. Stanton, would put it, it was obviously consciously cast in an idiom that could be perceived as sacred, or as Lincoln said, "hallowed."[12] At the same time, the text itself famously asserts its own ephemerality: "The world will little note, nor long remember what we say here." It is not only very short, but written in an economical style that has been called "telegraphic," perhaps reflecting Lincoln's admiration for telegraphy and his long experience at that point with dispatching military orders by telegraph.[13] Those messages were, necessarily, concise and unembellished to the point of bluntness, and the sentences of the Gettysburg Address likewise contrast in striking ways with conventional nineteenth-century oratory—for instance, Edward Everett's much longer address at the same event, which sounded some of the same themes as Lincoln's but in a far more leisurely style:

> Standing beneath this serene sky, overlooking these broad fields now reposing from the labors of the waning year, the mighty Alleghenies dimly towering before us, the graves of our brethren beneath our feet, it is with hesitation that I raise my poor voice to break the eloquent silence of God and Nature.

That is Everett's opening sentence, and within his 58 paragraphs are individual sentences which, at their longest, are more than half the length of Lincoln's entire address.[14]

Though it had its admirers from the start, among them Ralph Waldo Emerson,[15] Lincoln's prediction that the address would not long be remembered seemed at first likely to come true. Despite Stanton's dramatic readings of it as an "altar call" at Republican campaign rallies, the speech took a generation or so to enter the secular canon, and until it did, the Lincoln texts that were framed and hung on walls were the Emancipation Proclamation—technically a military directive, short on literary flourishes—and his proclamation of the first official Thanksgiving Day, sometimes recast as the words of a hymn.[16] Historian Gabor Boritt notes the irony:

> The Proclamation and the Hymn were probably the most reproduced Lincoln documents of the war. ... Indeed, compared to [these], his remarks at Gettysburg shrank to modest significance. On the very day Lincoln spoke at the cemetery, newspapers around the country that would ignore those words printed his Proclamation, or his Hymn, or both.

Eventually, "his half dozen words of consecration," as his own secretary casually called them[17]—words described in the Gettysburg ceremony's official program merely as "Dedicatory Remarks" (as opposed to Edward Everett's headline "Oration"[18])—would hang beside or even supplant these grand public acts. Perhaps this would have pleased Lincoln; it almost surely would have surprised him.

Contrary to a legend that developed early, the address appears to have been carefully prepared, not scrawled on the back of an envelope aboard the train to Gettysburg.[19] That legend nonetheless is highly revealing: It associates the enduring value of the address with the supposedly haphazard circumstances of its composition, grounding its sacralized qualities in its allegedly rude origins. It also analogizes the address to Lincoln himself, projecting a similarly paradoxical mix of traits onto his own person. "His remarks at Gettysburg, which have been compared to the Sermon on the Mount, were written in the [train] car on his way from Washington to the battlefield, upon a piece of pasteboard held on his knee, with persons talking all around him," journalist Benjamin Perley Poore wrote in the 1880s, though without specifying his source.[20] Hearing some version of this account, Mary Raymond Shipman Andrews developed it into a 1906 novella, *The Perfect Tribute*. This popular tale, like the address itself, reached generations of twentieth-century schoolchildren as well as the audiences for the story's two film and television adaptations.

In Andrews' fictionalized telling, Lincoln struggles to write the address with a gloomy sense that he is unequal to the task. Sitting on the train, he notes the contrast between Everett, the scholarly, well-bred "finished gentleman" who would deliver the event's keynote, and his own "rough-hewn" self: "of what use was it for such a one to try to fashion a speech fit to take a place by the side of Everett's silver sentences? He sighed."[21] Resigning himself to do his modest best, he looks about the train car for writing materials and notices that Secretary of State Seward has just unwrapped some books. On a bit of the brown wrapping paper, "torn carelessly in a zig-zag," and with "the untidy stump of a pencil," Lincoln labors to chisel the speech "from the rock of his sincerity." He continues this painful toil all too aware that he lacks Everett's artistry with words, which seems to him like a brilliant musician's skill at a keyboard.[22]

As the story continues, the party arrives at Gettysburg, Lincoln delivers the speech, receives no applause or "sound of approval" (another disputed legend), and concludes with further shaken confidence that it "must have been pretty poor stuff."[23] Only later, on a chance visit to a Washington military hospital, does he learn from a dying Confederate soldier what a profound impact it has apparently had across the whole divided nation. The crowd's silence, it turns out, was awe: "One might as well applaud the Lord's Prayer—it would have been sacrilege," the young officer explains to him.[24]

An envelope is paper designed to contain other paper, the text on it normally not the message itself but instructions for delivering one. That the "envelope" in Andrews' story was merely wrapping paper both heightens the point and makes it more ironic. Wrapping paper might not carry any text at all, and if it wrapped books, then its intended use was to protect works that do. The books were valuable enough to be wrapped, yet thanks to Lincoln, what gets written on the temporary wrapping, after it has been tossed aside, will far exceed in value anything contained in the books. The scrap of brown paper is obviously meant to resemble Lincoln himself: a "rough-hewn," seemingly inadequate, yet ready medium for an expression of transcendent meaning.

Central to the popular myth of the Gettysburg Address, in other words, is a dialectical relationship between the utterly disposable and the profoundly important, a relationship in which material of the most minor and temporary value, having already been used up and discarded, mediates the drafting of a text on a par with the Lord's Prayer—and to the author's own surprise, as one might expect if he was operating under something like divine inspiration. That this is apparently not what really happened makes this account all the more revealing of the role the address plays in the popular imagination. Yet at the same time, the "back of the envelope" legend does reflect something that is genuinely there in the text. The structure of the address presents us with essentially that same dialectic: a remarkably intricate scheme in which the enduring and sacred give meaning to a transitory moment, which in turn provides the occasion on which the sacred is performed and given life.

The basic movement within the text is a simple one-cycle oscillation, beginning and ending with a panoramic view of all human history, and descending from this through ever-narrower levels to alight, briefly, on the address itself and the moment of its delivery, before then re-achieving the grand vision. Those intermediate levels identify a sacred trust, one that America's history delivers to Americans of the present and calls on them to carry into the future on behalf of all humankind. The address and its immediate occasion are mere, momentary, passing reminders, the plain brown wrapper through which the sacred trust is conveyed. That, however, is not Lincoln's own metaphor. His controlling image is ground or territory, with each step forward in time taking us first towards ever narrower ground and then, in the second half of the cycle, towards ever wider, until we finish, in the final two words, on the widest territory of all: "the earth."

Type and Antitype: The Biblical "U-shape"

These movements and relationships readily become apparent from a close look at the way the address is structured. Analysts have already shown that the logic of the argument follows a pattern of birth and baptism, death, and rebirth, a schema that Lincoln would have known well from Christian teachings and especially the Anglican liturgy.[25] This accounts for its basic shape. In fact, though, the plan is more intricate than that. It develops almost line-by-line in such a way that each individual element in the second half of the cycle mirrors and matches one in the first (Figure 9.2).[26]

Implicit in Lincoln's famous opening is the view that the world at large, presumably for all its previous history, had been under the dominion of governments that were *not* conceived in liberty or equality—tyrannies, that

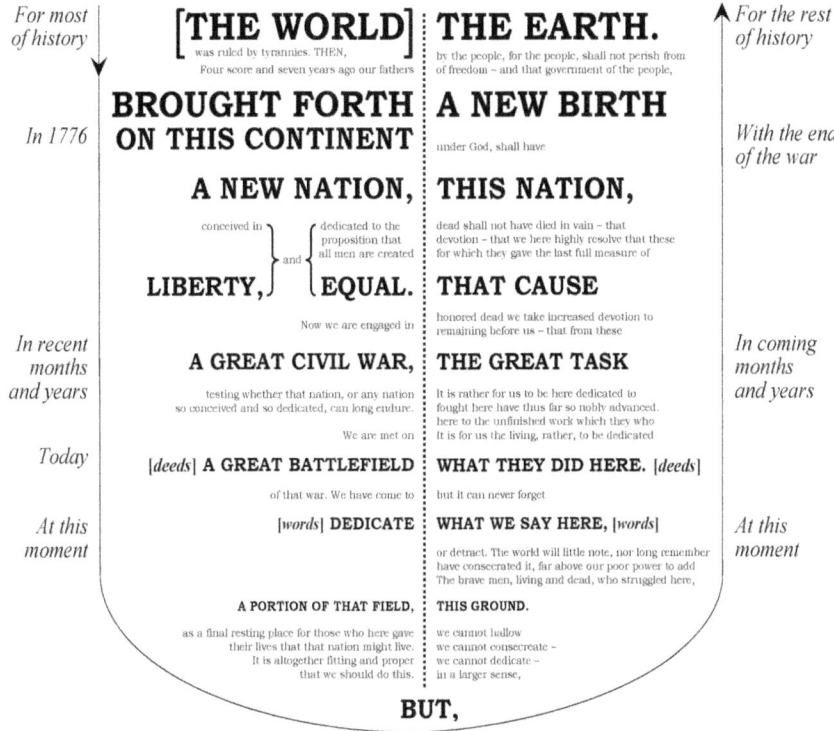

FIGURE 9.2 *The U-shaped structure of the Gettysburg Address. Image credit to the author.*

is, of one sort or another, or what he had previously called "king-craft."[27] Then, "four score and seven years ago," in one part of the world ("on this continent"), something happened that changed the course of that history: a new nation was born, "brought forth," dedicated to exactly those values. We then jump to the present, "now," when that nation and its values are undergoing their severest test. That "now" refers generally to the current situation; Lincoln was speaking in the war's thirty-second month. The next step, however, takes us to a narrower now, the day of the address itself, when "we are met" on a narrower plot of ground: one of the war's most important battlefields. A still narrower "portion" of that field is to be dedicated to the memory of those men. That is the immediate task of the moment, the act that Lincoln and his audience are actually present to perform.

Then, beginning with the word "But," the movement reverses. (The right side of the diagram now reads "upwards.") Having just affirmed that gathering to dedicate the field is "fitting and proper," Lincoln now declares that "in a larger sense" it is beside the point. Explaining this, he unfolds that larger sense through the same levels but in the opposite order. First, he recalls what happened on this ground: the battle and the sacrifice it involved. The consecration was already achieved on those recent days. Hence what really remains for "us, the living," occupying that ground at this moment, is not just to speak these commemorative words but to re-commit to the broader, near-term effort of which the battle was one part—that is, the great Civil War, finishing which is now "the great task" of coming months or years. As Lincoln had said moments earlier, the war represents a broader "testing," and he and his listeners are the ones being tested; on them depends the survival of those historically special values of liberty and equality. Since these were the founding values of the nation, vindicating them will mean giving that nation "a new birth of freedom," mirroring its formal birth four score and seven years earlier. This new birth, finally, will not just restore or even improve the nation itself, but will secure the founding values, the viability of government "of the people, by the people, for the people," for humankind as such, and for the rest of foreseeable time.

In Lincoln's telling, then, one tiny plot of ground, and the momentary task of speaking some words over it—passing words of "poor power," words that the world will little note nor long remember—is the fulcrum of all human history, the decisive moment at which, following the fallen soldiers' inspiring example, listeners can take the step whose ultimate outcome will be saving the world from tyranny. The official act, in itself, is effectively useless: these mere words cannot dedicate, consecrate, or hallow. What they might do is spur Americans on to their greater duty, which is to win the war, allowing the nation to carry on the still greater duty for which it was founded.

Thus the widest possible meaning unfurls from the meager effort of a moment. Lincoln aligns these differently weighted events with the different shades of meaning in the word *dedicate,* on which he essentially puns: The inert and backward-looking act of dedicating a memorial to the dead is an occasion for us, the living, to (re-)dedicate ourselves actively to the greater cause of a nation which was, itself, founded in dedication to the highest causes in political life.

Lincoln may not have known that his brief "Remarks" would become secular scripture, but the scriptural design of the address is evident in ways that go beyond its biblically resonant phrasings. Its two parts imitate the biblical Old and New Testaments as Christians were accustomed to reading them, as an earlier story of promise matched point-by-point to a later story of fulfillment. As Northrop Frye has demonstrated at length, this structure of "type" and "antitype," which he calls "U-shaped," is the Bible's "overall containing form" as well as the shape of many of its individual stories.[28] Within it, the movement that Lincoln rhetorically traces—a descent from the highest plane to the humblest plot of earth, where suffering and death are experienced but vindicated, prompting a re-ascent to a future, more permanent victory—follows a sequence that his Christian listeners would recognize from familiar episodes in the life of Christ: Incarnation, Passion, Resurrection, and Ascension. These in turn are key moments in salvation history, also called "sacred" or "providential" history, the God-ordained, gradually unscrolling plan or pattern into which earthly events were expected to fit. Christians had long taken God's guiding hand in history as a given, but the mostly Reformed Protestants who settled and founded America, and whose theology held the Bible's authority especially high, were more eager than most to situate their own experience in relation to sacred history's grand overarching drama. As Mark A. Noll puts it,

> the Bible was not so much the truth above all truth as it was the story above all stories. On public occasions Scripture appeared regularly as a typical narrative imparting significance to the antitypical events, people, and situations of United States history. That is, ministers preached as if the stories of Scripture were being repeated, or could be repeated, in the unfolding life of the United States. ... In the years between the American Revolution and the Civil War, the Bible offered to many Americans a key for understanding not only private religious reality but the public life of the country.[29]

As a storehouse of paradigms, archetypes, and "the controlling myth for American experience," says Noll, "the Bible was woven into the warp and woof of American culture" and "had worked itself into the foundation of national consciousness," albeit at times to sharply opposed political purposes.[30]

Christian sacred history held that the world's direction was ultimately progressive, although with episodes of rising and falling action all along the way. Humankind's story begins with a perfect Creation and original Fall from Grace, and it culminates in a final, climactic end, an Apocalypse that is also the passage into a newly perfected and eternal state. In between, God's "Chosen People"—bearers of his special promise or "Covenant," and claimants to a divinely appointed home, a "Promised Land"—experience various ordeals (temptation, testing, bondage, exile, and wanderings in the wilderness) and moments of rescue (the Flood and the ark, the Exodus from Egypt, the return from Babylonian Captivity, and the rebuilding of the Temple). These are all types or prefigurations of the ultimate rescue: God's own Son becoming human, suffering, and dying as redemption for the sins of the world, then rising again in a final victory over sin and death. That decisive moment is the hinge on which the fate of the whole cosmos turns.

Yet, very importantly, most of the players in this immense drama are common people, mere humble sinners, often from society's lowest ranks. Its events take place in our own historical time, the most crucial of them some ninescore decades before Lincoln, in such unremarkable settings as a manger, an upper room, a road, a hill, and a garden on a particular Sunday morning. Christianity sees salvation as "new birth" and predicates it on a great but historically specific act of sacrifice. It promises this new birth to the faithful—no longer just the children of Israel, the "Chosen" of the Old Covenant, but literally anyone—if, in their own moment of decision, they too highly resolve to take the saving message they receive locally and deliver it to the rest of the world.

That Lincoln evidently had all this mind in writing the address does not, by itself, explain its rise to the first rank of the patriotic canon. Obviously the context was vastly important: Gettysburg was the decisive battle in a war whose outcome, in turn, was decisive for the nation's future. Given a high view of America's mission, analogizing that battle and the sacrifices it entailed to the saving sacrifice at the center of Christian history would have struck Lincoln's hearers as plausible, even expected. They had long been accustomed to speeches and sermons on great national occasions quoting or alluding to the Bible, presenting biblical characters and tales as *exempla*, and drawing parallels between contemporary events and those recorded in Scripture. Everett's Gettysburg oration, for instance, recalled the battle's aftermath, and the plight of the wounded and dying, in ways that paralleled Lincoln's but much more long-windedly.[31] The same audience that would register the "biblicality" of Lincoln's address would certainly have recognized the many biblical phrases and tropes in Everett's as well. Both speakers were drawing on long-established ways of infusing words with what Americans of the time felt to be the greatest possible depth and power.

What makes Lincoln's address different is partly how short it is: the entire speech is substantially shorter than some single paragraphs of Everett's. This was not because Lincoln was simply a man of fewer words; he too was capable of speaking in public for hours at a time, as he had done during the Lincoln-Douglas debates. It seems, rather, to be a case of Lincoln turning the brevity suggested by the genre—"Remarks," not "Oration"—to deliberate strategic effect. In its extreme structural compression, the address presents the biblical message as a whole in microcosm. Copying the point-by-point symmetry of the two Testaments and their mirroring of type with antitype, it rapidly recapitulates each of the key elements of sacred history: a moment of creation at the start, and a promise of ultimate fulfillment in a fully achieved state at the end; a chosen nation struggling in a fallen world, in danger of failure but pressing on; a redemptive sacrifice, with a local setting and an instant in time on which a great destiny depends; and a call to take up that spirit of sacrifice in one's own life, thereby carrying the mission to completion. Transposing the Christian cosmic drama into the present, and recasting America, its soldiers and its citizens in the leading roles, Lincoln does not merely draw parallels; he elevates American events to a world-saving significance that resembles that of Scripture.

To "scripturalize" a war in which the nation is tested and on which its future depends was also Richard Snowden's project in retelling the American Revolution "in Scriptural Style."[32] Yet Lincoln's way of doing this is obviously much subtler and less labored than Snowden's—not to mention much briefer: the length of the whole is no greater than that of a typical biblical parable or psalm. The address is a kind of Scripture writ small, like one of the miniature or "thumb" Bibles that were in vogue at the time. Its very brevity allows the whole biblical scheme to be taken in at once, as if it were an urgent dispatch just received by telegraph. These are qualities that a leisurely two-hour exposition like Everett's, whatever its other virtues, is bound to lack.

They also highlight the fact that this message is not meant just to be passively absorbed. It must be acted upon. In the Christian vision, everything depends on performance. Logically, a God of the whole universe could save the world without taking human form or relying on people's own agency, and there are "Gnostic" and other officially heretical variants of Christianity that ignore the biblical stories, deny the role of mundane events or the human personhood of Christ, and place little emphasis on the actions of individuals, apart perhaps from a secretly instructed spiritual elite. The Christianity that Lincoln and his listeners knew, by contrast, lends supreme importance to those elements of the everyday. The cosmic drama it claims to reveal depends on individuals who, like Lincoln but even more so, are "rough-hewn": fishermen, tax collectors, shepherds, servants, publicans, and prostitutes. Though the passing thoughts and actions of these humble folks happen in ephemeral time, they have consequences on which even God pauses and waits.[33] Fundamentally, Christian faith is about what ordinary people choose to do, and it makes urgent demands on them to choose rightly.

So it was with Lincoln's often noted and long-remembered words. His reference to the poor power of these resembles a standard speechmaker's *faux*-modest apology, the kind that Everett makes too in referring to his own "poor voice." For Everett, though, the speaker's inadequacy contrasts with his duty to rise to the occasion and speak nonetheless. The contrast that Lincoln draws is between words and performance. Ephemeral speech—his own, Everett's, that of "us, the living" in general—is inadequate to the great sacrifices made on the battlefield. Further great deeds, however, will now be required to win the war and vindicate the great cause. The words are a summons to these, a challenge to the nation like a biblical prophet's. They sit at the "bottom" of the U-shape, the junction point of the two-part structure, the moment where past gives way to future. Receiving the words positions Lincoln's listeners on the same moral continuum as the fallen soldiers—and back of that, the Founders and the America they intended to make. In one of his first public statements as president-elect, Lincoln had told well-wishers that the Union's "salvation" was more their business than his: "not with politicians, not with Presidents, not with office-seekers, but with you, is the question: shall the Union and shall the liberties of this country be preserved to the latest generations?"[34] The challenge he gave them in the Gettysburg Address was similar but larger, a reminder that the radical new potential for liberty and equality that America modeled for the world would not succeed, or even survive, unless ordinary Americans now took up the parts assigned to them in the grand scheme. On battlefields like Gettysburg, the way had now been shown. As in Christian thought, with its saints and martyrs as well as Christ himself, there were exemplary lives and deaths to look to, and it behooved the faithful to take the further actions that would give those sacrifices meaning in the present.

Sacred History and the Ephemeral Moment

Although, again, there is nothing unusual in a public speaker hoping to inspire people to act, Lincoln's way of connecting words and deeds extends into a further dimension. It expresses a large theme, a view of political effectuality that was a key premise of much of his public career. Lincoln's lifelong political project, as many historians have seen it, was reading (and helping make) American history as the gradual effort to bring the abstract higher principles announced at the Founding, and specifically a certain high interpretation of them, into practical effect in the America that lay at hand. Garry Wills, for instance, sees in the address a "dialectic of ideals struggling for their realization in history." This in turn, he says, reflected Lincoln's debt to "the primary intellectual fashion of his period, Transcendentalism," which reached Lincoln through the historian George Bancroft as well as his own law partner, William Herndon, a "disciple" of Theodore Parker's:

> Bancroft, who had imbibed the elements of Transcendentalism from [theologian] Friedrich Schleiermacher in Berlin, expressed his political creed in the 1854 lecture: "In public life, by the side of the actual state of the world, there exists this ideal state toward which it should tend." The historian's task, he felt, is to follow "the clashing between the fact and the higher law." In the case of the United States, this meant tracing the fulfillment of the great American idea enunciated in the Declaration of Independence.[35]

Similarly, says Wills, Theodore Parker

> saw the world progressing toward the realization of the supreme value, human freedom. For him there were four great leaps forward toward the realization of that ideal—the birth of Jesus, the Protestant Reformation, the puritan societies of New England, and the Declaration

of Independence. In each case, mere fact is made to express, at last, transcendent aspirations and ideals.[36]

Analogizing this view to the Christian idea of the Kingdom of God, "Parker drew his all-important theological-political analogy: as Jesus is to the Bible (the ideal to the limited reality), so is the Declaration to the Constitution," which was the means to the Declaration's end, albeit a badly compromised one insofar as it permitted slavery.[37]

It may be that Wills is assigning a bit too much importance to Parker. As a young state legislator, Lincoln was already celebrating the Declaration when Parker's preaching career was just beginning.[38] There were many roads, as it were, to Gettysburg. Motivating action in service of larger principles or goals is hardly unique to the Gettysburg Address; it is the point of much lesser political speeches ("Vote for me so we can make America great again"), as is the task of rallying citizens to persevere through wars and other great struggles.

Further, even without any influence from Transcendentalists, Lincoln might well have arrived at his political philosophy just from the pressure of events. Speaking for an upper Midwestern constituency that had material reasons for wanting slavery restricted, he re-entered politics in 1854 amid the great national debate over the Kansas-Nebraska Act, a debate that turned in part on clashing readings of the Declaration and its "self-evident" premise that "all men are created equal." Was that statement simply wrong, as John C. Calhoun and other slavery advocates claimed? Was it meant to refer only to whites or to Englishmen, a reading consistent with the Founders' own continued slaveholding? Was it a rhetorical flourish gratuitously added to a document more narrowly intended as a legal notice and press release? Was it cynical posturing, as some angry abolitionists saw it? Or was it a ringing assertion of the values underlying and justifying the constitutional order in the first place, the key to the Founding itself and to America's continuing revolutionary purpose?[39] In coming to the latter conclusion—and helping turn it from contested point into today's received wisdom—Lincoln encamped with the likes of Parker, the abolitionist preacher and pronouncer of jeremiads, even if, as a practical politician, he carried on more circumspectly. In this, though, he may not have been following Parker so much as drawing from the same, very old reservoirs of American idealism. Visions of a higher perfection, calls to have faith in it and to act on it in the here and now, and the resulting idea of one special people's messianic mission to the rest of the world were all readily available to Lincoln even without being decanted through the special enthusiasms of the Transcendentalists. To the contrary, the outlook expressed in his rhetoric had been shaping Americans' vision of their country and its historic role since long before Lincoln was born.

There is another sense, however, in which the Transcendentalists can help us understand the address. In carefully patterning the ephemeral message of a moment on sacred history, even to the point of creating a simulacrum of the Bible itself, Lincoln obviously was attempting to borrow authority for his message from the most revered of his culture's texts and traditions. At the same time, a secularized performance like this lends the texts and traditions something in return, lifting the cosmic drama they describe out of the pages of a very old book and giving it the practical urgency of real and deeply felt present events. Lincoln makes his words a kind of prism, a means of diffracting the undifferentiated white light of ethereal truth into the recognizable colors of the real world, where they can and must be acted upon in the specific historical circumstances of the moment. In borrowing from but applying scriptural tropes, he demonstrates another means of replacing a dead letter with a perpetual Scripture, as Ralph Waldo Emerson had urged. In this he is doing the work of the new Teacher that Emerson had called for, the "divine literatus" that Walt Whitman saw arriving.[40] The power to vivify the inert and antique literary expressions of ages past was for Whitman the difference between great poets, the "orbic bards" whom America now awaited and who would be more important than presidents, and the conventional writers of the "old track" who mimicked other poets in service of the mass public's urge "to rhyme and to read rhyme." As an excellent example of such derivative work, we have the versified revision that one non-divine literatus gave the Gettysburg Address in 1869:

> Let us, the Living, rather dedicate
> Ourselves to the unfinished work, which they
> Thus far advanced so nobly on its way,
> And save the perilled State!
> Let us, upon this field where they, the brave,
> Their last full measure of devotion gave,
> Highly resolve they have not died in vain!—
> That, under God, the Nation's later birth
> Of freedom, and the people's gain
> Of their own Sovereignty, shall never wane
> And perish from the circle of the earth![41]

Embedded within a longer poem, this "Gettysburg Ode" copies Lincoln's phrases but scrambles their order. This allows for facially poetic structuring—meter and rhyme—but at the cost of the deeper, more forcefully expressive structure of type and antitype that was Lincoln's key to the meaning of events.

A different lyric that makes for a more worthy comparison is "The Battle Hymn of the Republic," which would enter the American musical canon as one of its best-known patriotic songs. Julia Ward Howe's lyrical borrowings from Scripture are even denser than Lincoln's, with virtually every phrase a quote or allusion: "trampling out the vintage" and "grapes of wrath" from Jeremiah 25 and Revelation 14 and 19; a "terrible, swift sword" from Isaiah 27; "crush the serpent with his heel" from Genesis 3, and so on. This parade of warlike images, chosen from the Bible's most combative texts and pounded home with the borrowed tune's relentless cannon-fire stresses— what one admirer called "Thor-Hammer lines"—is charged with a stridency that the Gettysburg Address seemingly lacks.[42] For Garry Wills, "Nothing could be farther from the crusading righteousness" of Howe's lyrics than Lincoln's seemingly gentler mode. His "submission to Providence is made in a spirit of humility, reflected in the series of Fast Day and Thanksgiving Day proclamations issued throughout the war, where the people as a whole are called on to repent the sins that led to violence."[43] Lincoln's tone at Gettysburg is somber, not aggressive, as befitted the occasion: He was dedicating a cemetery.

These differences in tone, however, are misleading. In terms of what they call for, the works are fundamentally similar. Howe's patchwork pastiche of biblical quotes would not be intelligible at all without context—if not that of the Civil War itself, then more broadly that of a militant, religiously styled political mission to the world, which is how Americans seem to receive the "Battle Hymn" today.[44] Indeed the lyrics make the most sense as what originally inspired Howe: words accompanying soldiers literally on the march, already in motion en route to enacting in the present and visible world the metaphors drawn from the prophets of old.[45] That performative situation, or the imagining of it, gives the scriptural allusions their meaning. Similarly, in context, Lincoln's quieter words are also a kind of battle hymn. It is true that at times he presented the war as recompense for the sin of slavery, most famously so in his Second Inaugural Address. Yet even there, this "mighty scourge" was not one that Americans just passively underwent, like a natural disaster. It was something that Lincoln believed they were summoned to enact, a great task that "all sought to avert" but must now "strive on to finish."[46] By the Second Inaugural, moreover, the war's destruction was nearly complete; when Lincoln was speaking at Gettysburg, a significant fraction of it was still to come. Though he phrased it obliquely, what the high resolve and "unfinished work" he referred to meant in practice was ruthless military force—operations like General Sherman's "March to the Sea," a scorched-earth and distinctly wrathful campaign in which wide swaths of southern territory would quite literally be "trampled out." Unlike Edward Everett, who closed his address on a sentimental vision of eventual reunion, Lincoln was steeling his listeners for the harsh and dangerous fighting ahead. Softer phrasings aside, his words are closer in their tacit militancy to Howe's.

The "Fourth Soil" and the Great Reversal

Its tacit militancy is just one of the ways in which Lincoln's account of the national mission also resembles Martin Delany's. As we saw in the previous chapter, Delany's political theory, and its dramatization in his novel *Blake*, focused on the essential tasks of defining a people and spurring it into action. Only through acting, exercising agency, could it lay claim to nationhood. For Lincoln the problem was not creating a nation in the first place but saving one that had already been "brought forth." It resembled Delany's incipient nation, though, in standing at a crossroads, facing a decisive moment in which it would either fulfill its promise or, perhaps, fail its great test and be dissolved again.

That promise, in both cases, was a kind of gospel. For Delany, the good news was the recognition that a people was emerging out of what had previously been only isolated huts. This new nation would then, perhaps, lead a collective uprising to overthrow the world's unjust white rule, or—in Delany's nonfiction writings—take a commanding position among nations through its pivotal role in the world economy. As grand as that vision was, Lincoln's gospel reached even further: Perhaps the nation would not "long endure," but if it could, there was a hope of securing not just America's freedom, but the world's—of delivering all nations from earth's long history of tyranny, and into a worldwide, never-perishing future of government of, by, and for the people. History itself hinged on the outcome of his nation's great struggle, which would signal whether or not free self-governing nations were possible to constitute at all.

To achieve this, Lincoln did as various prophets and kings had done at key moments in biblical history: He summoned the people to renew and rededicate themselves to their original covenant. For America, this covenant had been set down in the Founding parascriptures—documents which, as Donald S. Lutz has carefully demonstrated, developed in a particular American line of descent from the biblical covenants of ancient times.[47] The nation-forming "compact," in Lutz's terms, is even more essential than its constitution or plan of government, since it is the basis for a nation's action as a people, the text where it defines its identity in terms of "the moral values, major principles, and definition of justice."[48] Lincoln had recognized as much in the many statements in which he staked the Founding's meaning on the Declaration. At Gettysburg he universalized that meaning, offering it as a hoped-for covenant for the entire world. By taking an epitome of the national political compact, extending it in this way and charting its progress through time as an analogue of Christian salvation history, Lincoln managed, apparently without intending to, to create a canonical American parascripture of his own.

For all its overt scripturism, however, what the address conveyed was ultimately a political hope of a secular kind. In this respect it also reflected a basic modern transformation in historical consciousness, the "great reversal" described in chapter 1. As noted there, in that "epochal moment" for the West—already achieved among many intellectuals, but just beginning to make its way into popular thinking in the nineteenth century—an older outlook, which assumed that the Bible was the normative framework for all knowledge, and therefore that it overarched all other histories, gave way to a new view in which secular history and science were the framework, the normative picture of the world. Biblical claims and histories, then, had to be incorporated into secular history, not the other way around.[49] Lincoln's succinct little sketch of America's origins and destiny was a modern one, and in that regard markedly different from comparable surveys of America in earlier eras—for example, the seventeenth century, when settlement from Europe was in its early stages. As soon as it was clear to European explorers that America was its own gigantic landmass and not, as Columbus had thought, the outer islands of East Asia, the problem had been how to explain this "fourth soil"—two entire continents and their many tribes and nations, all previously unknown in Europe. The biblically correct number of continents had been three, corresponding to the three sons of Noah who had populated each of them after the Flood (with one carrying Noah's curse to Africa, from which it would in time re-emerge to become a rationalization for American slavery).

Since the Bible contained no apparent account of either the existence of this unknown land, or the origins and identity of its inhabitants, efforts to fit the new facts into the biblical scheme generated a number of creative but conflicting efforts. Perhaps America was the devil's hideout and the aborigines his minions, refugees from the spread of the Gospel in Christian Europe, said a Bible scholar in England, Joseph Mede, in 1634.[50] More optimistically, Cotton Mather suggested in 1709 that a fourth soil was called for to make up for the spiritual failures of the first three. Copiously quoting Scripture's promises of a "**GODLY CITY**" and a "*Glorious Holy Mountain,*" Mather insisted that "America is Legible in these Promises."[51]

Against that old way of thinking, Lincoln presented America's own history and future as the framing story, a U-shaped salvation history unto itself. He was not concerned, as biblicists like William Miller or Joseph Smith might have been, to identify America or the war as fulfillments of particular Old Testament prophecies, or to show where they fit within the grand sweep of historical events and empires like those in the Book of Daniel. In his telling, America's origin and destiny were the grand historical sweep in themselves. The establishment of the United States, its struggles, its eventual new birth, the hoped-for success of its originating mission, and the hinge point—the ephemeral moment in present time, in mundane local reality, when a recent martyrdom has called the faithful to decision and action: that ancient sacred narrative was now America's, not by incorporation or analogy to the Bible's but in the first instance. America itself was the messianic presence transforming the world, or would be if the present war came out as Lincoln foresaw.

Of course, a history like this was not purely secular. It was a secular repurposing of the old sacred schematics. In the Christian understanding, history was not a mere succession of happenstance events, but a grand plan with a particular shape, culmination, and final purpose. Lincoln was at pains to give Americans a story of their nation that would resonate, would accord with their sense of what history was all about. Strictly speaking, then, the Gettysburg Address did not completely reverse the frameworks. It did, though, very decidedly set the secular story in the foreground. The Founding had been a great act of liberation, one that Americans of the time often analogized to the biblical Exodus. Hence, like the covenant and laws that followed the Exodus at Mount Sinai, its key texts were holy writ, the original testament of the national political religion for which Lincoln had called since the start of his career.

The Gettysburg Address, by further analogy, was like one of Paul's letters, an admonition to the faithful on a particular, perilous occasion. It was a new(er) testament, unfolding what the earlier prophets had meant while also promising that the day of fulfillment and a transfigured world were at hand. As Walt Whitman had done in poetry, Lincoln borrowed structures from Scripture and refilled them with American contents. His was the equivalent in political rhetoric of a Whitman poem replacing the Psalmist's "Thou," a God of manifold great works, with an America lauded as "Thou envy of the globe! thou miracle!"—an America of "Thy countless saviours, latent within thyself, thy bibles incessant/within thyself, equal to any, divine as any."[52]

"The Greatest Actor in All the Drama"

Of course, the historical reputation of the Gettysburg Address cannot be separated from Lincoln's own. The address is deeply embedded within the vast Lincoln mythography, the immense weight of cultural meanings that Americans came to assign to Lincoln himself.[53] As we can see in stories like *The Perfect Tribute* and many others, the sacralization of the address and the sacralization of Lincoln were joint and mutually reinforcing developments. Lincoln, said many eulogists, was the symbolic "last casualty" of the war, an "American Christ," assassinated on Good Friday—another day of dedication, hallowed in Christian understanding by Christ's saving sacrifice, a central event of salvation history.[54] At the least, as one early commentator put it, Lincoln's listeners at Gettysburg must have been "fully conscious that he was the greatest actor in all the drama."[55]

Whitman, who greatly admired Lincoln, was an enthusiastic participant in the making of the Lincoln legend. In a popular public lecture, which he delivered on anniversaries of the assassination and other occasions between 1879 and 1890, he too drew on metaphors from acting and drama.[56] It was ironic, said Whitman, that Lincoln was shot while watching actors in a conventional and forgettable play, when he himself was "in some respects the leading actor in the stormiest drama known to real history's stage through centuries"[57]:

Why, if the old Greeks had had this man, what trilogies of plays—what epics—would have been made out of him! How the rhapsodes would have recited him! How quickly that quaint tall form would have enter'd into the region where men vitalize gods, and gods divinify men!

John Wilkes Booth, the actor-assassin, with his melodramatic (though clumsy) leap from the presidential box onto the stage, had designed the act as a moment of high drama. Whitman observes that he had obviously even rehearsed it, though its true meaning was lost on him (312).

Strikingly, Whitman's own route to that meaning runs through journalism. Before proceeding with interpretations that spare no superlatives, Whitman devotes a long section of his lecture to a matter-of-fact account, based on eyewitness reports, of the "facts" and "visible incidents" at Ford's Theater, "as they really occurred" (310, 313). These include such otherwise trivial, newspaper-like details as Booth making his escape by crossing the stage diagonally. We find the momentous in the seemingly minor, Whitman suggests—like the fact that lilacs were then blooming, a memory on which he had based one of his most famous poems (310).[58] Even the fatal shot itself, for all its tremendous importance, was oddly ordinary, marked by "the quiet and simplicity of any commonest occurrence—the bursting of a bud or pod in the growth of vegetation, for instance" (311). What impresses Whitman is the enormous quantity of meaning that emerges from one "simple, fierce deed," and how much of history can turn upon it: a "long and varied series of contradictory events," the many "bloody and angry problems" of the whole, prolonged secession period, "arrives at last at its highest poetic, single, central, pictorial denouement," one of the "climax-moments" that ring down the curtain "on the stage of universal Time" (313–14).

At least in one way, this great event was, for Whitman, ultimately a relief. While it was tragic, it was tragedy in the great classical sense, one of those "dramatic deaths" on which the creation of "a Nationality" depends (314). Because "the immeasurable value and meaning of that whole tragedy lies, to me, in senses finally dearest to a nation, (and here all our own)—the imaginative and artistic senses—the literary and dramatic ones," a death like Lincoln's, which "outvies" even other great deaths like Socrates' and

Julius Caesar's, guaranteed that America's own stories would rank at least as highly as other nations' in the world's literary canon (313–14). Hence it was further assurance against the driving anxiety, which had burdened America's *literati* for a century and was still present to a leading poet's mind as late as the 1880s, that America might yet come up short in literary achievements. "How the imagination—how the student loves these things! America, too, is to have them" (314):

> A great literature will yet arise out of the era of those four years, those scenes—era compressing centuries of native passion, first-class pictures, tempests of life and death—an inexhaustible mine for the histories, drama, romance, and even philosophy, of peoples to come—indeed the verteber of poetry and art, (of personal character too,) for all future America—far more grand, in my opinion, to the hands capable of it, than Homer's siege of Troy, or the French wars to [Shakespeare].
>
> (309–10)[59]

For Lincoln himself, the drama of universal Time was staged on battlefields like Gettysburg; it was there that ideals entered history and human actions revealed the sacred—men vitalizing gods and gods divinifying men, as Whitman puts it (314). For Whitman this happened on an equally grand scale in Lincoln's own life and death.

Whitman, though, was a rhapsodist, not a biographer. Though he reported having glimpsed Lincoln in person on many occasions, the figure he describes is less a living man than a neoclassical abstraction. The "quaint tall form" he conjures in his lecture resembles the idealized, nearly godlike "Type of American Genius" that a much lesser poet dubbed Lincoln in a long epic poem of 1881 (314).[60] By contrast, William H. Herndon, the onetime law partner and biographer of Lincoln's who did know him well, and who also lectured on him frequently in the years after his death, emphasized the less elevated kinds of details that might be called "novelistic," in two senses: they read like, and at times possibly were, fiction. Among the tales Herndon collected and published that became favorite bits of the Lincoln legend, for instance, is the famous story of young Abe's doomed love for Ann Rutledge, an episode that remains undocumented apart from Herndon's own much later reconstruction.[61] Though prettified in twentieth-century retellings, the story as Herndon gave it grimly pictured a 26-year-old Lincoln "plunged in despair" over Ann's death almost to the point of insanity.[62]

Herndon was criticized for trafficking in stories like this, stories which, even (or especially) if true, might be thought unseemly or scandalous by Victorian standards, and in some cases might reveal Lincoln's faults. His defense against this charge was notably modern and, at the same time, old-fashioned, a window onto the era's changing views of where authority was to be found. In admitting to what might be "ghastly exposures," he insisted repeatedly on the importance of uncolored, unsuppressed facts, "the real data" about Lincoln the person. If Lincoln was truly to live in memory, "We must have all the facts—we must be prepared to take him as he was." According to Herndon, one of Lincoln's closest friends had urged on his project, suggesting that he model his Lincoln biography on the only "true history" ever written, the only one that presented "the whole truth—the inner life" of its subjects. "The heart and secret acts are brought to light and faithfully photographed" in this book alone, which Herndon agreed his volumes of "collected data" would do well to mimic. That book, too, was the Bible.[63]

Conclusion: The New American Testaments

The various debates and projects reviewed in the previous chapters did not all take the same form or come to a single common result. Americans' struggles over textual authority in the nineteenth century left imprints of several kinds on American culture and institutions. They were also, of course, not unique to America; other nations, too, struggled to define and develop national literatures in similar circumstances of rapid and industrial-scale changes in the culture of print. Nonetheless, the movements we have examined here did all have distinctively American features. These are worth noting by way of conclusion, along with the leading themes toward which these disparate projects broadly converged.

The ultra-protestant movements all had origins in America's unusually intense religious revivalism and its freewheeling, entrepreneurial culture of religious freedom and invention. In America, anyone with an idea could become a traveling salesman for it, as William Miller did once he decided to take his biblical prophecies public. There was nothing new about Miller's millenarianism as such; parsing Scripture, reading the signs of the times, and preaching that the end was nigh were centuries-old and probably inevitable features of Christianity.[1] Miller's movement flourished, however, as historians of it have noted, in an America whose Puritan heritage, national founding myths and evangelical culture made it a quintessentially millenarian nation. In America, the millennial hopes previously associated with dissenters and fringe groups were "bound so tightly to American culture" that they became a kind of orthodoxy.[2] Millerism also had a "natural" base in its home region, upstate New York, where it cut through and across existing churches with disruptive revivalist force.[3] Miller himself, moreover, was an American patriot and son of a Revolutionary War veteran; initially drawn to the deism and radical skepticism of other patriots like Colonel Ethan Allen, he found his childhood Christian faith reignited while serving in the War of 1812, where America, like the children of Israel, seemed to him to have had help from a Supreme Being in winning battles against mightier enemies.[4] That this ordinary farmer and self-taught scholar could then convince people that he had, through solitary study, solved the Bible's mysteries, unveiling a dramatic hidden meaning that had escaped all the religious leaders and trained experts, exemplified "the democratic art of persuasion" which, in America, bypassed organized church structures to speak to "the deepest hopes and aspirations of popular constituencies" directly, in the words of Nathan O. Hatch.[5]

Thomas and Alexander Campbell were immigrants, but their efforts also found fertile ground on an American frontier where self-help was called for and the policing of doctrinal fidelity was relatively weak. "Whatever Alexander Campbell may have brought to America of his Scottish and Presbyterian heritage," says Hatch, "he discarded much of it for an explicitly American theology."[6] The thin scattering of parishioners from various churches in remote and still-developing settlements furnished a laboratory for the Campbells' experiments in dissolving sects and ending the "partyism" that was the bane of Protestantism. Perhaps in these western reaches with their primitive conditions, the "Primitive Gospel" could emerge again as it once had in the eastern reaches of the Roman Empire. Casting off the burden of centuries of contentious and mystifying doctrines acquired in Europe, scattered communities of present-day American believers might best mimic the scattered congregations of first-century Asia Minor, re-founding the undivided, lowercase "christian" practice the original *ekklesia* had first received from the Apostle Paul.

Specifically American elements are most obvious in Mormonism, a movement that overtly meant to extend the Christian *mythos* to the New World. For Joseph Smith, America was the divinely appointed site of the restoration, the hiding place of a scripture that had preserved the lost "plain and precious things," and the place where the New Jerusalem would eventually descend to earth. It was in America that the Kingdom of God would not merely appear in its fullness but finally be "constituted," in a manner very similar to and overlapping that of the American nation, and from there expand to become the government of the whole earth. Joseph Smith not only published new American scriptures, he joined many others in recognizing scriptural elements in the textual products of America's Founding, and he set out to appropriate these for his own religious project. Taking a hint, it seems, from Richard Snowden and Gilbert L. Hunt, he discovered the grander possibilities that might come from fusing patriotic and biblical-style storytelling. While he might never even have heard of Novalis, Thomas Carlyle, Samuel Taylor Coleridge, Emmanuel Swedenborg, or William Blake, Smith aspired as they did to find ways of prophesying and writing new bibles, and he seemed to believe along with those high Romantics that such operations were the means of piercing through the dull, desultory nature of everyday experience, of rekindling deep feeling and reconnecting with the cosmic energies that make human life meaningful. Whether or not all those goals were met, the Book of Mormon has had enormous reach. Carried worldwide by missionaries, and with nearly 200 million copies published to date in some ninety languages, it has probably eclipsed even *Uncle Tom's Cabin* as the most widely circulated nineteenth-century work of American storytelling.

The Transcendentalist movement explicitly said from the start that "American Genius" was among its central concerns, and its members set out, along with other American intellectuals, to identify and vindicate this genius by way of ending the young nation's alleged literary and cultural delinquency. Ralph Waldo Emerson's exhortations to "self-reliance" and the like were usually addressed to all humankind, but as he made clear in "The American Scholar," they were especially urgent for America, which had yet to find its unique literary voice. Americans were not the only people living retrospectively and amid "the sepulchres of the fathers" in those "desponding days," but having cast off the European past in other respects, they were uniquely positioned to bring on the new renaissance and conduct the world into it. It seemed to Emerson and his colleagues that a failure of American Genius would be inexplicable; when Margaret Fuller said "an original idea must animate this nation," one could almost hear her putting unusual stress on the word "must"—meaning, such an idea needed to be found, but also, it simply *must* be out there somewhere. America, after all, was busily producing all sorts of new things, many quite common but some of them spectacular.

In doing so, Emerson pointed out, it was already unleashing the same productive and creative energies that had originally created the world of old, including the great cultures and their highest cultural productions: the grand verses and epics and, not least, the original religions and scriptures that had now become legacies (and therefore, also sepulchres). To "chant" the everyday, ephemeral, busy lives of Americans, then, turning them into poetry and perhaps even a new and "perpetual scripture," would be the best answer to the common complaint that all those material, mercantile, and mundane concerns that kept people so busy were suppressing the national genius. No, they were the germs of its new and greater religion, Walt Whitman would say. Taking up Emerson's suggestion, and rethinking poetic language as scriptural—the converse of Theodore Parker's and Horace Bushnell's arguments that scriptural language was poetic—Whitman would set out to prove that a growing body of verse, one that merged newspaper-like observations of the present and the ordinary with overt celebrations of

America, and with biblical phrasings and resonances more subtle and adept than Richard Snowden's or Joseph Smith's, could indeed provide a "new Bible" of a kind the country was longing for.

Harriet Beecher Stowe, similarly, was experimenting with new, hybrid ways of conveying American reality, especially the reality of slavery. Her variant of "literary scripturism" also sought to merge the highest things with the most mundane, the cosmic Christian story of salvation with facts and details clipped from newspapers and legal affidavits. The producers who adapted her story for the stage also seemed to recognize that they were servicing audiences like congregations, giving them a vivid new quasi-liturgy. Not every American author would pursue aims as ambitious as Stowe's, Whitman's, and Melville's, that is, the creation of literary works that rose above literature to become, in effect, parascriptures. Nor were American authors alone in aiming this high. Still, "biblicist" and parascriptural ambitions, *The Dream of the Great American Novel* that Lawrence Buell chronicles in his recent book of that title, have provided American literature with many of its landmarks—in recent years, for instance, novels like Toni Morrison's *Beloved* and Cormac McCarthy's *The Road*.[7]

In a sense, Emerson, Parker, Stowe, Whitman, the other creative authors whose works would help define the emerging American literary canon, and their successors in recent years, have been embarked on a great project similar to that of the writers of the New Testament. To read the New Testament is to experience the profound faith and hope of people who believed they had just received a great and perhaps final revelation from God—that in fact they themselves, or others they knew near at hand, had lately been in the presence of the incarnated God himself. But it is also to experience something else: a major effort at reinterpreting traditions and sacred writings handed down over the centuries. Innumerable passages in the New Testament are glosses on the Old, attempts to unfold the meaning of what were already, by the first century, ancient prophecies and exemplary tales from olden times. The idea that Christianity's founding events had transpired "that the scripture might be fulfilled" is pervasive and often explicitly stated, and the literary results were writings that then became scriptures themselves.

Likewise, America was founded on ancient promises and prophecies, not least the Bible's. Its foundational writings became new scriptures and the sources of new promises. Since the early era when they worried over "literary delinquency," America's authors have been struggling for ways to fulfill those promises, which required understanding just what they were—what Americans had really committed themselves to when they declared their nationhood and set out on what was already called, in its early years, "the American experiment." What would be a literature commensurate with this nation and its aspirations? What would it need to achieve, and how could this be done?

In one sense, answering these questions was bound to be frustrating. As powerfully as it has been wished for, "textual authority" strictly speaking does not, in the end, even really exist. Written texts do not "speak" in some voice of their own; they do not have any agency in themselves. They carry only the authority of whomever is thought to be speaking through them: God, a nation, a government, a church, a minority group newly claiming the rights of full citizenship, or dissidents confronting a corrupt or indifferent establishment with their superior moral witness. An American literature would speak for America only if "America," however defined, somehow spoke through that literature. American authors collectively, in the early years and since, have aimed to enable it to do so, in effect composing a new American national testament. This, too, has been a project not just of creation but of interpretation. How thoroughly it has succeeded, who and how much has still been left out, are questions that are themselves much debated today. This newer era of prophecy, however, has not closed.

NOTES

Introduction

1. Channing, "Reflections on the Literary Delinquency of America."
2. This wry judgment is Barbara L. Packer's in *The Transcendetalists*, 67.
3. William Clifton in 1799, quoted in Knapp, *Lectures on American Literature*, 189.
4. Edwards, "Thomas Jefferson's Secret Reason for Sending Lewis and Clark West."
5. Jefferson, *Notes on the State of Virginia*, Query 6, 40–71.
6. Buell, *Dream of the Great American Novel*, 2. For further details of the debate beyond the brief summary here, see Smith, "'Where Genius Dies'." Also see Spiller, *American Literary Revolution*.
7. Sarah Hall, correspondence of 1821, quoted in Harrison Hall, *Selections from the Writings of Mrs. Sarah Hall*, xxix; Reynolds, *American Literature*, 31, emphases in the original.
8. Tocqueville, "Some Observations of the Drama among Democratic Nations," *Democracy in America*, vol. 2, chapter 19. In chapter 14, "The Trade of Literature," Tocqueville also suggests that democratic readerships demand writing they like rather than admire, and tempt authors with the hope of making fortunes: "Democratic literature is always infested with a tribe of writers who look upon letters as a mere trade; and for some few great authors who adorn it, you may reckon thousands of idea-mongers."
9. Smith, "Art. III: America," 78–80, sic.
10. Hankins, *Second Great Awakening and the Transcendentalists*, 24. Also see Myerson, "A Calendar of Transcendental Club Meetings," 200.
11. Smith, "Where Genius Dies."
12. Martineau, *Society in America*, 303–4.
13. Martineau, 300–3.
14. Miller, *The Transcendentalists*, 9.
15. Emerson's views are further detailed in chapters 3 and 4 below.
16. Emerson, *Journals and Miscellaneous Notebooks*, vol. 4, 77, 93–4 (entries of July and October 1833). Emerson's proposals are further discussed in chapter 3 below.

Chapter 1

1. Hall, *Conversations on the Bible*, v, 13. The book appeared in five editions between 1818 and 1837.
2. "The Baptist Faith and Message," emphasis added; "On Biblical Scholarship and the Doctrine of Inerrancy," 95–6. The resolution was adopted in 2012

in response to "biblical scholars who identify themselves as evangelicals" but deny the Bible's historicity and "have called on other evangelical scholars to abandon the doctrine of inerrancy."
3   Hall, *Conversations on the Bible*, 29. As examples of current teaching, "Old Testament Orientation 1," a graduate survey course on the Old Testament at the conservative Baptist Liberty University, offers both a core text and a bibliography providing copious background on ancient literatures and cultures. Moody Publishers, an arm of the historically Fundamentalist Moody Bible Institute in Chicago, also publishes Bible introductions acknowledging complex histories of ancient Near Eastern forerunners and cognate writings.
4   Examples that will be discussed later include Matthias Bartgis' comments introducing Richard Snowden's "Scripture Style" retelling of the American Revolution (chapter 5), and William Herndon's defense of his biographical work on Lincoln (chapter 9).
5   McCalla, *Creationist Debate*, 1, 33.
6   Preus, *Spinoza and the Irrelevance of Biblical Authority*, 27.
7   Elliott, *Cambridge Introduction to Early American Literature*, 32.
8   Keel, *Divine Variations*, 41, emphasis in the original.
9   Frei, *Eclipse of Biblical Narrative*, 2–3.
10 Dodd, *Authority of the Bible*, 8.
11 Thuesen, *In Discordance with the Scriptures*, 11.
12 Examples often cited in biblical apologetics include 2 Timothy 3:16–17 and 2 Peter 1:20–21.
13 Calvin, *Institutes of the Christian Religion*, Book One, Chapter VII, sections 1–2.
14 Calvin, Book One, Chapter VIII, sections 1–3.
15 It should be noted that pre-Protestant medieval practice also included vernacular translations, but with the lesser status of "interpretations." See van Liere, *Introduction to the Medieval Bible*, 203–5 and chapter 7.
16 McCalla, *Creationist Debate*, 5.
17 McCalla, 6.
18 McCalla, 33.
19 Watts, "Prophecy and Discovery."
20 McCalla, *Creationist Debate*, 33 and chapters 3 and 4.
21 McCalla, 45, 119; see also Frei, *Eclipse of Biblical Narrative*, 130.
22 McCalla, *Creationist Debate*, 45.
23 McCalla, 106.
24 Legaspi, *Death of Scripture*, viii, 3, 4, 25 and chapter 1.
25 Lee, *Erosion of Biblical Certainty*, 3. Also see McCalla, *Creationist Debate*, chapter 7.
26 Driver, *Introduction to the Literature of the Old Testament*, vii–viii.
27 Thuesen, *In Discordance with the Scriptures*, 10.
28 This development will be discussed in the next chapter.
29 Jefferson to John Adams, October 12, 1813. The "Jefferson Bible" is further discussed in chapter 5 below.
30 Lee, *Erosion of Biblical Certainty*, 182.
31 McCalla, *Creationist Debate*, 177, 178.
32 Noll, *America's God*, 292, 370–6.
33 Noll, 376–82.

34 Noll, 383, quoting Thomas Campbell in 1809, John Holt Rice in 1832, and George Duffield in 1842.
35 Noll, 382–3, quoting Charles Finney in 1821 and Sarah Grimké in 1837.
36 Noll, 371–3.
37 Nord, *Faith in Reading*, 4, 11, quoting the publisher and frontier missionary Samuel Mills in 1815. Also see Noll, *America's God*, 371–2. For the broader history, see Nord, especially chapters 1, 2, 6, and 7; Cohen and Boyer, eds., *Religion and the Culture of Print*, especially Cohen's and Boyer's own essays; and Fea, *The Bible Cause*.
38 Baird, *Religion in America*, 270.
39 Baird, 264–5.
40 Paine, *Age of Reason*, 89, emphases in the original.
41 Paine, 89.
42 Lee, *Erosion of Biblical Certainty*, 7, 182.
43 Hatch, *Democratization of American Christianity*, 64.
44 Hatch, 81, quoting Richard McNemar (1807?).
45 Lee, *Erosion of Biblical Certainty*, 183.
46 Theophilus Armenius [Thomas S. Hinde], "Account of the Rise and Progress of the Work of God," 350–2; Noll, *America's God*, 402, emphasis in the original.
47 Sturtevant, ed., *Julian M. Sturtevant: An Autobiography*, 160–3; Hatch, 64.
48 Hatch, 81. Hatch is referring to the Campbellite movement, which will be discussed here in chapter 2, but he correctly suggests that the point applies more broadly.
49 Parker Pillsbury, quoted in *Proceedings of the Hartford Bible Convention*, 143.
50 Tocqueville, "The Progress of Roman Catholicism in The United States," *Democracy in America*, vol. 2, chapter 6.
51 Maffly-Kipp, *American Scriptures*, introduction.
52 Sawyer, *Elements of Biblical Interpretation*, 11.
53 Sawyer, 166.
54 Sawyer, 11, 12, 28, 166 and chapter IV.
55 Linton, *Healing of the Nations*, 15–19, spellings as in the original.
56 Linton, 17–18.
57 Dobie, *Key to the Bible*, 15, 21–2.

Chapter 2

1 Hatch, *Democratization of American Christianity*, 11, 56–8.
2 Dorrien, *The Making of American Liberal Theology*, 2; Chauncy, *Seasonable Thoughts*, 77, 94–5, 104–5, spellings and emphases in the original.
3 Theophilus Armenius [Thomas S. Hinde], "Rise and Progress of the Work of God," 350–3. Spellings and emphases in the original. On Hinde's broader efforts and importance, see Williams, *Religion and Violence*, 110–14.
4 Watson, *Methodist Error*, 17–18, 24–5, 28–33, emphases in the original.
5 Hankins, *Second Great Awakening and the Transcendentalists*, 187.
6 Finney, *Lectures on Revivals*, 9, 14, 260, 282.

7   Finney, 267, emphasis in the original.
8   Phelps, "Criticisms of Revivals," 135.
9   Theodore Parker, "False and True Revival of Religion" (4 April 1858), in *Transient and Permanent*, 385. Parker's views are further detailed in chapter 4 below.
10 Schaff, *Principle of Protestantism*, 116, 120, 156, and quoted in Graham, *Cosmos in the Chaos*, 9, 18, 19, 32.
11 See the discussion of Schaff, Nevin, and the "Mercersburg Theology" in Hatch, 162–7.
12 Schaff, *Principle of Protestantism*, 138–9, and quoted in Graham, *Cosmos in the Chaos*, 18–19. On the sharp controversy—including a trial for heresy—that Schaff's views provoked in America, where even a Lutheran's talk of the historical continuity of an "evangelical catholic" church ran up against ingrained anti-Catholicism, see Graham, 11–15.
13 Nevin, quoted in Hatch, 81, 166, 167, 183.
14 Schaff, *Principle of Protestantism*, 119–21, and quoted in Graham, *Cosmos in the Chaos*, 25–6, 32, emphasis and typography in the original.
15 Taylor, *Ancient Christianity*, 75–82, 49, 87. This book was Taylor's response to the "Oxford Movement" within the Church of England, the movement that led the celebrated theologian and poet John Henry Newman and others back toward Roman Catholicism or "Anglo-Catholicism." Taylor himself, as it happens, was also the brother of poets, including the author of the lullaby "Twinkle, Twinkle, Little Star."
16 Cross, *Burned-over District*, 173, 185–8.
17 This is a central argument of Taylor's book and the title of a long section; see pages 40–93.
18 See Hatch, 167–70. On the movements discussed in the sections that follow below, also see Hughes, *American Quest for the Primitive Church*, especially the introduction and chapters 12, 14, and 15; and Hughes and Allen, *Illusions of Innocence*, especially chapters 1, 6, 7, 8, and 10.
19 On "reactionary biblicism," see McCalla, *Creationist Debate*, xiii, 173, 186, 191, 217. McCalla, though, focuses on the reactionary movements of later in the century that gave rise to Fundamentalism. "Revivalist Protestantism" and the contrast with Unitarianism are Barry Hankins' formulas; see Hankins, *Second Great Awakening and the Transcendentalists*, 32. Unitarianism and "Liberal" Christianity are the subjects of chapter 3 below.
20 Miller, *Apology and Defence*, 4.
21 William Miller, quoted in Himes, *Views of the Prophecies and Prophetic Chronology*, 10–11.
22 Miller, *Apology and Defence*, 5.
23 Miller, 6, emphasis in the original. Proving that the prophecies harmonized was also the hope of Isaac Newton and other seventeenth-century interpreters for saving biblical authority, says Reiner Smolinski. Newton, though, criticized efforts to predict the world's end as the "folly of Interpreters" who tried to make themselves prophets, thus bringing the prophecies into contempt. Smolinski, "Threefold Paradise of Cotton Mather," 61.

24 Bliss, *Memoirs of William Miller*, 69, 70, 76–7. For the published lectures, see Miller, *Evidence from Scripture and History*.
25 Miller, *Apology and Defence*, 6.
26 Bliss, *Memoirs of William Miller*, 68–70; Himes, *Views of the Prophecies*, 11.
27 Bliss, 70, 76–7.
28 Miller and his followers actually proposed a few different dates, and after 1843 Miller made a major correction, so the final predicted date was October 22, 1844.
29 Himes, *Views of the Prophecies*, 71; Miller, *Apology and Defence*, 5, 15.
30 Crocombe, *Feast of Reason*, 22–3.
31 Arasola, *End of Historicism*, 169.
32 Rowe, *Thunder and Trumpets*, 47–8.
33 For recent examples, see Sarachik, "3 Doomsday Predictors."
34 Miller, *Voice of Warning*, 3.
35 For details and critiques of Miller's methods, see Crocombe, *Feast of Reason*, especially chapters 2 and 4, and Arasola, *End of Historicism*.
36 Miller, *Evidence from Scripture and History*, 206.
37 Miller, quoted in White, *Sketches of the Christian Life*, 49.
38 Richardson, *Memoirs of Alexander Campbell*, vol. 1, 39.
39 Richardson, 41–5.
40 Richardson, 224–34, 245.
41 Richardson, 234–9, citing Matthew 19:14.
42 Richardson, 245–6, emphasis in the original.
43 Richardson, *Memoirs of Alexander Campbell*, vol. 2, 13.
44 Richardson, 11–12.
45 Campbell, "Ancient Gospel," 296–8; Richardson, *Memoirs of Alexander Campbell*, vol. 1, 391–405, emphasis in the original.
46 Richardson, 391–405; also see Moritz, "The Landmark Controversy," 3–8.
47 Richardson, *Memoirs of Alexander Campbell*, vol. 2, 156.
48 Campbell, "Millennium—No. 1," 56–7.
49 Richardson, *Memoirs of Alexander Campbell*, vol. 2, 146, emphasis in the original; as noted below in chapter 6, Harriet Beecher Stowe would make a similar point some twenty years later about the problem of overly familiar words.
50 Richardson, 149–50.
51 Richardson, 121, quoting an associate of Campbell's.
52 Campbell, "Millennium—No. 1," 57.
53 Campbell, quoted in "Sketches of Religious History," 167, emphasis in the original.
54 On the different views of the "millennium" and Campbell's orientation toward them, see Danner, "Millennium in the Restoration Movement."
55 Richardson, *Memoirs of Alexander Campbell*, vol. 1, 257–8; Campbell, "Millennium—No. 1," 55.
56 Richardson, *Memoirs of Alexander Campbell*, vol. 2, 204, emphasis in the original.
57 Campbell "Anti-Campbellism," 118.
58 Campbell, "Millennium—No. 1," 57–8; *Memoirs 2*, 121, 123.

59 Richardson, *Memoirs of Alexander Campbell*, vol. 1, 257–8, 276–7, emphasis in the original.
60 Campbell, "Restoration of the Ancient Order," 170–1, 175.
61 Campbell, quoted in "Sketches of Religious History," 166, emphasis added.
62 Campbell, "Restoration of the Ancient Order," 175.
63 Cambell, 171, 175; "Sketches of Religious History," 166.
64 Campbell, "Conversion of the World," 155; "Reply" to R.B.S., 204.
65 Campbell, "General Preface," iii.
66 Campbell, xiii–xiv.
67 Richardson, *Memoirs of Alexander Campbell*, vol. 2, 149–50.
68 Gutjahr, "Evolution of the Culturally Relevant Bible," 328–9.
69 Richardson, *Memoirs of Alexander Campbell*, vol. 2, 121, 154, emphasis in the original.
70 Gutjahr, "Evolution of the Culturally Relevant Bible," 330.
71 Campbell, "General Preface," ix–x.
72 Campbell, xi.
73 Richardson, *Memoirs of Alexander Campbell*, vol. 1, 257–8.
74 Richardson, 125–8.
75 Campbell, *Sacred Writings*, 63, 103, emphasis added.
76 Richardson, *Memoirs of Alexander Campbell*, vol. 2, chapters 5–6; also see Moritz, "The Landmark Controversy."
77 Richardson, *Memoirs of Alexander Campbell*, vol. 2, 148–9.
78 Richardson, 147–8.
79 Moritz, "The Landmark Controversy," 8.
80 Moritz, 3–7.
81 Richardson, *Memoirs of Alexander Campbell*, vol. 2, 441.
82 Miller, "Apology and Defence," 5, 12; Campbell, "Restoration of the Ancient Order," 175.
83 Oliver Cowdery, "Letter IV [to W.W. Phelps]," *Latter Day Saints' Messenger and Advocate*, 78; Smith, "Extracts from the History of Joseph Smith," paragraphs 12, 5, 6, 8; "Comparison of 9 First Vision Accounts." As that comparison indicates, there is no single definitive account of Smith's visions, descriptions of which seem to have evolved over time.
84 Smith, "Extracts from the History of Joseph Smith," paragraph 9; Neibaur, "Journal, 24 May 1844," 23.
85 Smith, paragraphs 12–19; "Church History," 707.
86 Benson, "Fourteen Fundamentals."
87 Pratt, *Key to the Science of Theology*, 109; Smith, "Church History," 709.
88 Cowdery, *Latter Day Saints' Messenger and Advocate*, 78, emphases in the original.
89 Doctrine and Covenants 130:22 and 130:3.
90 See Bloom, *American Religion*, 99–103.
91 Smith, "Church History," 708.
92 Smith, "Extracts from the History of Joseph Smith," paragraph 8.
93 Marquardt and Walters, *Inventing Mormonism*, chapter 4. Also see "Treasure seeking, money digging and Joseph Smith, Jr."
94 Bloom, *The American Religion*, especially chapter 5.

95 Hunt, *The Late War*, in *An Historical Reader*, a schoolbook that seems to have been circulating in upstate New York when Smith was in school there; see Johnson, "Comparison of The Book of Mormon and The Late War," and the further discussion of Hunt, Richard Snowden and "scriptural style" in chapter 5 below.
96 Smith, *Book of Mormon*. The parenthetical quote is from 1 Nephi 18:25.
97 Smith's possible sources and influences have been subjects of extensive discussion. For instance, William L. Davis's "Hiding in Plain Sight" emphasizes parallels between the Book of Mormon and John Bunyan's writings; David Persuitte's *Joseph Smith and the Origins of the Book of Mormon* details Smith's possible borrowings from Ethan Smith's *View of the Hebrews*; and "Book of Mormon plagiarism accusations" includes entries discussing a number of authorship theories, including the possible influence of Hunt's *The Late War*.
98 Doctrine and Covenants 132.
99 Doxey, "New Jerusalem."
100 Smith, *Book of Mormon*, 30, now, 1 Nephi 13:28 with the capitalization of "Book" removed.
101 Pratt, "Questions and Answers on Doctrine," 213; Matthews, "Joseph Smith's Inspired Translation." The former Reorganized Church of Jesus Christ of Latter Day Saints (RLDS) has produced a convenient online side-by-side "Comparison of the Inspired Version to the King James Version."
102 Gee, "Joseph Smith and the Papyri"; Ritner, "'Translation and Historicity of the Book of Abraham'—A Response."
103 Compare the earlier "Introductory Note" to *The Pearl of Great Price* (1986) with the same note in the current edition online.
104 See George A. Horton Jr.'s comments in Matthews, "The JST," 299.
105 Matthews, "Major Doctrinal Contributions," 288; "The JST"; and "Joseph Smith's Inspired Translation."
106 Perkins, "The JST on the Second Coming," 237–8.
107 Matthews, "Major Doctrinal Contributions," 287, 289, emphasis in the original. Similarly, Robert L. Millet argues, "To doubt either the Prophet's intentions or abilities with regard to the Bible is to open the door unnecessarily to other questions relative to the books in the [Mormon] canon of scripture … to study and teach without [Smith's translation] … is tantamount to being choosy about what we will receive from the Lord and what we will not." Millet, "Joseph Smith's Translation," 44, 46.
108 See the further discussion of these events in chapter 5 below.
109 Persuitte, *Joseph Smith and the Origins of the Book of Mormon*, 220–31.
110 One scholar has described Campbell's 1831 *Millennial Harbinger* article "Delusions" as "the first serious, critical analysis" of the Book of Mormon: De Pillis, "The Quest for Religious Authority," 79.
111 Butler, "From Millerism to Seventh-Day Adventism," 50–64; "What Adventists Believe" (Belief 24).
112 See Acts 6 and 15, 2 Corinthians 11, and Galatians 1 and 2.
113 Lipscomb, *Christian Unity*, 34.
114 Book of Mormon Critical Text Project; Bittner, "Critical Text Project Evaluates Changes"; Skousen, "A Brief History of Critical Text Work," 233–48.

115 By some indications the Community of Christ, formerly the "Reorganized" LDS, has de-emphasized the Book of Mormon: "They haven't rejected it, but [some] have begun to discount its doctrinal and historical value." Matthews, "The JST," 303. Studies of textual anomalies and of parallels with existing sources reportedly also led B. H. Roberts, a prominent Mormon scholar, to doubts of his own about the Book of Mormon's authenticity. See Roberts, *Studies of the Book of Mormon*, and Tanner, "B.H. Roberts' Secret Manuscript" and "Book of Mormon: Ancient or Modern?."
116 Midgley, "Prophetic Messages or Dogmatic Theology?" 92–113, and "More Revisionist Legerdemain," 261–311.
117 Williams, "A House, 10 Wives."
118 Lee, *Erosion of Biblical Certainty*. Consistently with but somewhat differently from the argument presented here, Lee suggests that various efforts from the eighteenth century onward to forestall this erosion effectively backfired, conceding too much to the forces bringing it on. What the stories of Miller, Campbell, and Smith suggest is that the Bible's would-be defenders had little choice: concessions are both inevitable and bound to fail, because the problem is insoluble in principle—it arises from within the logic of biblical faith itself.
119 Hatch, 80–1. This is also where Hatch notes the ironic self-contradiction quoted in chapter 1 above: "a commitment to private judgment could drive people apart, even as it raised beyond measure their hopes for unity."
120 Barr, *Scope and Authority of the Bible*, 39.
121 Barr, 39.

Chapter 3

1 Dorrien, *Making of American Liberal Theology*, xiii–xvi, xviii, xxi.
2 Dorrien, xiii.
3 See the discussion of revivals in chapter 2 above.
4 Mayhew, "Sermon IV," emphases in the original.
5 Mayhew.
6 Mayhew, emphases in the original.
7 Dorrien, *Making of American Liberal Theology*, 4.
8 Channing, "Unitarian Christianity" (May 5, 1819).
9 Dorrien, *Making of American Liberal Theology*, 35–6.
10 Channing, "Unitarian Christianity."
11 Channing, "Letter on Creeds," 8, 7, 10.
12 Paine, *Age of Reason*, 22, 53–4, 102, 110, 113, emphasis in the original.
13 Paine, 46, 75.
14 Paine, 50.
15 Dorrien, *Making of American Liberal Theology*, 23; Joseph Priestley, *Comparison of the Institutions of Moses with Those of the Hindoos*, 135, 531–3. Theodore P. Letis argues that Priestley's method of "conjectural emendation," inspired in part by Isaac Newton's biblical researches, was an important bridge to the higher criticism; see Letis, "From Lower Criticism to Higher Criticism," 31–48.

16 Quoted in Letis, 40.
17 Stuart, *Letters to the Rev. Wm. E. Channing*, 149–50; also cited in Dorrien, *Making of American Liberal Theology*, 35.
18 Channing, "Letter on Creeds," 9; on the evolution of Channing's thought, see Dorrien, 48–50.
19 Channing, "Letter on Creeds," 8–14; "The Present Age," 161. In the 1820s, taking a turn toward literary criticism, Channing also followed his brother, Walter Channing, in taking up the (later) Emersonian theme of a national literature; see Dorrien, 47.
20 Innumerable studies have examined the intellectual context and impetus behind Transcendentalism. For notable examples, see Packer, "The Transcendentalists," chapters 1–3; Gura, *American Transcendentalism*, introduction and chapters 1–3; and Grusin, *Transcendentalist Hermeneutics*, introduction and chapters 1–2.
21 Marsh, Preliminary Essay, vii, and Notes, 308, in Coleridge, *Aids to Reflection*; also see Packer, "The Transcendentalists," 385, 406. For an account of Emerson's place in "the Romantic zeitgeist," see Keane, *Emerson, Romanticism, and Intuitive Reason*, 15 and chapter 1.
22 Dorrien, *Making of American Liberal Theology*, xvii.
23 Carafiol, "James Marsh's American Aids to Reflection," 31. Carafiol also enumerates various Transcendentalists' differing uses of Coleridge. Also see Packer, "The Transcendentalists," 344–9.
24 Emerson, *The Journals and Miscellaneous Notebooks of Ralph Waldo Emerson*, vol. 4, 77 (July 11, 1833); quoted in Dorrien, *Making of American Liberal Theology*, 62.
25 Packer, "The Transcendentalists," 376–7, quoting Frederic Henry Hedge.
26 Allen, *Our Liberal Movement in Theology*, 70.
27 Emerson, "The Lord's Supper" (September 9, 1832). On the circumstances of Emerson's resignation, see Gura, *American Transcendentalism*, 42–4.
28 Packer, "The Transcendentalists," 331, 376–7; Hankins, *Second Great Awakening and the Transcendentalists*, 24.
29 Myerson, "Calendar of Transcendental Club Meetings," 197–207.
30 Emerson, *Nature*, 3.
31 Emerson, 32–3, 40–3, 57–8.
32 Emerson, 25–7, 29–31, 44–5, 60.
33 Ripley, Review of Martineau's *The Rationale of Religious Enquiry*, November 5, 1836.
34 Norton, Letter to the *Boston Daily Advertiser*, November 5, 1836, emphasis in the original.
35 Norton, *The Evidences of the Genuineness of the Gospels*.
36 Ripley, Letter to the *Boston Daily Advertiser*, November 9, 1836. On the issues driving the Miracles Controversy, see Lee, *Erosion of Biblical Certainty*, prologue and chapter 5. Also see Keane, chapter 9, and Hurth, *Between Faith and Unbelief*, chapter 2.
37 Emerson, *Nature*, 74.
38 Emerson, "The American Scholar" (August 31, 1837), 81, 84, 89–90, 114.
39 Emerson, 88–90.
40 Emerson, 111–12.

41 Emerson, "An Address Delivered before the Senior Class in Divinity College," or Divinity School Address (July 15, 1838). Also see Grusin, *Transcendentalist Hermeneutics,* especially chapter 2.
42 See the Google "Ngram" analysis of the word's frequency over time at https://books.google.com/ngrams.
43 Emerson, Divinity School Address, 121–2, 126, 129–31, 134, 141.
44 Emerson, 127, 134–5, 143–5, 147, 151.
45 Emerson, 127–8, 144, 146, 150–1.
46 Emerson, 151.
47 Habich, "Emerson's Reluctant Foe," 209, 230; Norton, "The Latest Form of Infidelity" (July 19, 1839).
48 Ripley, *"The Latest Form of Infidelity" Examined* (September 5, 1839).
49 Emerson to Carlyle, October 17, 1838, *Correspondence of Thomas Carlyle and Ralph Waldo Emerson,* vol. 1, 183.
50 Norton, "The Latest Form of Infidelity."
51 Norton. This address followed by one year Emerson's Divinity School address, and seems to have been solicited by Harvard alumni specifically as an answer to it.
52 Norton; see especially the appended Note II, "On the objection to faith in Christianity, as resting on historical facts and critical learning." Also see Packer, "The Transcendenalists," 385, 406.
53 Ripley, *"The Latest Form of Infidelity" Examined*, capitalization in the original.
54 Paine, *Age of Reason*, 90. "Cultured despisers" was Friedrich Schleiermacher's phrase; see chapter 1 above.
55 Emerson, *Journals and Notebooks,* vol. 4 (July and October 1833), 77, 93–4.
56 Park, "Build, Therefore, Your Own World," 41–3. See also Brodhead, "Prophets in America circa 1830," chapter 2.
57 See the discussion of Smith and the "ultra-protestants" in chapter 2 above.
58 Criticisms of this kind from Theodore Parker and Horace Bushnell are reviewed in chapter 4 below.
59 Emerson, Divinity School Address, 135, 141, 144.
60 Cole, "Jones Very's 'Epistles to the Unborn'," 169–83.
61 William Ware, quoted in Clarence Gohdes, "Some Remarks on Emerson's Divinity School Address," 28.
62 Versluis, *Esoteric Origins of the American Renaisssance,* 68; Bentley, "A Swedenborgian Bible."
63 Emerson, Divinity School Address, 145; "Swedenborg; or, the Mystic," 120–2, 137, 143, 145–6.
64 Carlyle to Emerson, April 1, 1840, *Correspondence,* 303. "*Eine Bibel ist die höchste Aufgabe der Schriftstellerei*" (the "highest problem of authorship," in Carlyle's translation); "*toter, irdischer, zweideutiger Buchstabe*," and "*Wenn der Geist heiligt, so ist jedes echte Buch Bibel.*" Novalis, *Schriften,* 297, 310.
65 Emerson, July 21, 1836, *Journals and Miscellaneous Notebooks,* vol. 5, Journal B, 186. Editor's insertions omitted; spelling and punctuation as in the original.
66 Emerson, "Books," 218.

67 On "Transcendentalist Orientalism" see Versluis, *American Transcendentalism and Asian Religions*, especially 51–79 on Emerson.
68 Emerson, "Books," 219–20.
69 Emerson, "The Poet," 30, 32, 34, 35.
70 Emerson, 37–8. Emerson wrote "chaunt," an archaic form of "chant."
71 Emerson, July 16, 1843 (entry 168), *Journals and Miscellaneous Notebooks*, vol. 8, 438.
72 Emerson, "Goethe; or, The Writer," 290. See also Braun, "Goethe as Viewed by Emerson." Following an earlier memoirst, Braun dates the Goethe essay to 1845.
73 Emerson, "The Poet," 38.
74 Emerson, "Goethe; or, The Writer," 271–2, 289.
75 Emerson, Divinity School Address, 127.

Chapter 4

1 Lawrence, *Drawing-room Scrap Book*, 75.
2 Fuller, *Memoirs*, vol. 2, 26. Also see the introduction to Gura's *American Transcendentalism*.
3 Parker, "The Revival We Need" (April 11, 1858), in *Transient and Permanent*, 422–3.
4 Clancy, *Transcendentalism and the Crisis of Self*, 98–9.
5 Packer, *Transcendentalists*, 64–6.
6 Habich, "Emerson's Reluctant Foe," 220–1.
7 Emerson, "Self-Reliance," 49–50.
8 Emerson, 51, 52, emphasis in the original.
9 Emerson, "The Over-Soul," 268–9, 277, 278.
10 Quoted in Packer, "The Transcendentalists," 382–3.
11 Emerson to Carlyle, October 30, 1840, *Correspondence of Thomas Carlyle and Ralph Waldo Emerson*, vol. 1, 334–5.
12 Granted, Thoreau was at other times an engaged social critic and activist; apart from *Walden*, his best-known writings include his essay "On Civil Disobedience," arising from a protest over the Mexican War, and his outraged denunciation of the Fugitive Slave Act. On social reform, "Thoreau was indeed Emerson's man of action"; more than other Transcendentalists, he "acted on his views, albeit individualistically," says Barry Hankins in *The Second Great Awakening and the Transcendentalists*, 33. On Thoreau's growing radicalization, culminating in his support for John Brown's failed revolt, see Hankins, 103–5.
13 Peabody, "Egotheism, the Atheism of To-Day." Peabody may have borrowed the term from William Ellery Channing; for its context, see Irons, "Channing's Influence on Peabody," 121–35.
14 Habich, "Emerson's Reluctant Foe," 224, 229, 234, 237, emphasis in the original. Norton's earlier contretemps with George Ripley are discussed in chapter 3 above.
15 Carlyle to Emerson, November 3, 1844, *Correspondence of Thomas Carlyle and Ralph Waldo Emerson*, vol. 2, 81–2, emphases in the original.

16 Hankins, *Second Great Awakening and the Transcendentalists*, 100–6.
17 Emerson, October 1, 1837 (entry 151). *Journals and Miscellaneous Notebooks*, vol. 5, 382.
18 Hankins, *Second Great Awakening and the Transcendentalists*, 101–2.
19 Ellen Tucker Emerson, *Life of Lidian Jackson Emerson*, 81–3.
20 Abbott, "What Is a Prophet?," 3–7, 9, 11. The last sentence quotes Matthew 10:27 and Luke 12:3.
21 Ellis, *Memoir of Rufus Ellis*, 27–30.
22 Ellis, 107–11, 124–5.
23 Ellis, 168.
24 Ellis, 282.
25 Ellis, 183.
26 Fuller, writing in 1840, in *Memoirs of Margaret Fuller Ossoli*, vol. 2, 27–8.
27 Emerson, *Journals and Miscellaneous Notebooks*, October 1, 1837, 380–1. The excuse that attention is a scarce resource apparently also appeared in Emerson's lost anti-slavery statement of 1837: Hankins, *Second Great Awakening and the Transcendentalists*, 101.
28 Emerson, "The Transcendentalist" (January 1842), 346–8.
29 Emerson, 359.
30 Emerson, 349, 350.
31 Emerson, "Politics," 209–10.
32 Emerson, "Goethe; or, The Writer," 290.
33 Emerson, "The Fugitive Slave Law" (May 3, 1851), and "The Fugitive Slave Law" (March 7, 1854).
34 Emerson, "The Fugitive Slave Law" (March 7, 1854), 217 (unnumbered).
35 Emerson, 223–5, 230–2.
36 Emerson, 234–6, 244.
37 Emerson, 243–4.
38 See the discussion of these proposals in chapter 3 above. As noted there, the quoted phrases are from Emerson's Divinity School Address and his essay "The Poet."
39 Dorrien, *Making of American Liberal Theology*, xvii, xxv, 111. Harold Bloom also calls Bushnell the "subtlest of the American theologians": Bloom, *The Western Canon*, 286.
40 Dorrien, xvii, 102–7.
41 On the background and consequences of these writings, see Dorrien, 85–105.
42 Parker, "The Transient and Permanent in Christianity" (May 19, 1841), in *Transient and Permanent*, 13. On Parker and German criticism, see Dorrien, *Making of American Liberal Theology*, 83–5, 91–7.
43 Parker, "Transient and Permanent," 16, and *Discourse of Matters Pertaining to Religion*, 325–6.
44 Parker, *Discourse of Matters Pertaining to Religion*, 364–7.
45 Parker, "Transient and Permanent," 15–17.
46 Parker, *Discourse of Matters Pertaining to Religion*, 439, 440, 444–5.
47 Parker, 446, 447. In mocking the "fanatical," Parker does not name names, but these remarks were published when the Millerite movement was in the newspapers and building toward its predicted great day.
48 Parker, 446, emphasis in the original.

49 Parker, 474, 475.
50 Parker, 454.
51 Parker, 466.
52 Parker, "The Christianity of Christ, of the Church, and of Society" (June 28, 1840), in *Transient and Permanent*, 96–9, spelling modernized.
53 Parker, *Discourse of Matters Pertaining to Religion*, 496, 498
54 Parker, "The Christianity of Christ," 97, 99.
55 Parker, *Discourse of Matters Pertaining to Religion*, 502.
56 Parker, 494, 501–3, emphasis and capitalization in the original.
57 Parker, "A False and True Revival of Religion" (April 4, 1858) and "The Revival We Need" (April 11, 1858), in *Transient and Permanent*, 385, 399. On the importance of conversion numbers in measuring revivals, see Dorrien, *Making of American Liberal Theology*, 135.
58 Parker, "A False and True Revival," 384.
59 Parker, "The Revival We Need," 398, 413–14. Parker saw foolishness in Spiritualism but also virtue in its freedom from Bibles and churches. Mormonism he associated with the comfort he seemed to think it gave women.
60 Parker, "A False and True Revival," 389.
61 Parker, "The Revival We Need," 404–5.
62 Parker, *Discourse of Matters Pertaining to Religion*, 237–9, capitalizations in the original.
63 Parker, 483, emphases in the original.
64 Parker, "The Revival We Need," 413, 419.
65 Parker, 402.
66 Parker, 413; Parker, *Discourse of Matters Pertaining to Religion*, 500, emphases in the original.
67 Parker, "The Revival We Need," 403.
68 Parker, *Discourse of Matters Pertaining to Religion*, 373, capitalization in the original.
69 Parker, "Of Justice and the Conscience" (1852), in *Ten Sermons of Religion*, 71. Others in the Romantic era had put forward arguments like this; Packer, for instance, notes ideas like these in the writings of Emerson and, before him, Emanuel Swedenborg (Packer, "The Transcendentalists," 378). Emerson even draws a similar analogy, for instance in his Divinity School address, where he suggests that "the religious sentiment" comes from noticing the identity of natural and moral laws, including specifically the laws of gravitation. Characteristically, though, Emerson's emphasis is less on the social consequences of this than on the spiritual.
70 Parker, 82, 91, 95, 96.
71 Parker, 84–5. Martin Luther King Jr.'s famous 1967 rephrasing, "The arc of the moral universe is long, but it bends toward justice," was woven along with other inspirational quotes into the carpeting of the White House Oval Office during the presidency of Barack Obama.
72 Parker, 97, 100–1.
73 Parker, 82–3.
74 Parker, "Transient and Permanent," 15–17; "The Relation of the Bible to the Soul" (April 21, 1839), in *Transient and Permanent*, 60–1, 65, 67.

75 Parker, *Discourse of Matters Pertaining to Religion*, 365–6.
76 Parker, 368.
77 Parker, 370–5.
78 Dorrien, *Making of American Liberal Theology*, 122–7. Bushnell, who kept a toehold in orthodoxy, as it were, expressed concern about the German biblical criticism and the extremes to which it could lead: "rationalism," he wrote, is "filling the sky of Germany with darkness, and hiding the sun Luther once looked upon." Bushnell, "Discourse at Andover," in *God in Christ*, 293. Nonetheless, his work assumes the basic results of higher criticism. On Coleridge, Bushnell reported finding his landmark *Aids to Reflection* "foggy and unintelligible" at first, but then becoming deeply absorbed in it. According to his daughter, Mary Bushnell Cheney, he often said "that he was more indebted to Coleridge than to any extra-Scriptural author." Cheney, *Life and Letters of Horace Bushnell*, 208–9, 499.
79 Bushnell, God in Christ, 303.
80 Bushnell, "Preliminary Dissertation on Language," in *God in Christ*, 22–4.
81 Bushnell, 40, 46, 57.
82 Bushnell, 57, 67, 80.
83 Bushnell, 69–70.
84 Bushnell, 71.
85 Bushnell, 74.
86 Bushnell, 77, 80–1.
87 Bushnell, 83–4.
88 Bushnell, 90–4.
89 Bushnell, 94–6, capitalization in the original.
90 Bushnell, 102, 104–6.
91 Bushnell, "Our Gospel a Gift to the Imagination" (1869), in Bushnell, *Building Eras in Religion*, 259, exclamation in the original.
92 Dorrien, *Making of American Liberal Theology*, 112–14, 134–8; Smith, "Horace Bushnell: Advocate of Progressive Orthodoxy and Christian Nurture."
93 Bushnell, "Discourse at Andover," 279–80.
94 Bushnell, 293–8.
95 Bushnell, 302.
96 Bushnell, 350–5.
97 Bushnell, "Preliminary Dissertation," 97.
98 Bushnell, *Christ in Theology*, 15–19.
99 Bushnell, 20–2, 334, 338, spelling in the original.
100 Dorrien, *Making of American Liberal Theology*, 159–61.
101 Bushnell, *Nature and the Supernatural*, 68–9.
102 Bushnell, *Discourse on the Slavery Question* (January 10, 1839), 16–22. Bushnell was apparently referring to co-founder William Lloyd Garrison's "Declaration of Sentiments" at the Society's 1833 founding convention. Also see David Torbett, *Theology and Slavery*.
103 Parker, "Sermon on the Public Function of Woman" (March 27, 1853); Bushnell, *Women's Suffrage; The Reform against Nature* (New York: Charles Scribner and Co., 1869).
104 See the discussion of ultra-protestant approaches in chapter 2 above.

105 Prickett, "The Bible and Literary Interpretation," 405, 407.
106 Buell, "*Moby-Dick* as Sacred Text," 56, 57.
107 Eagleton, *Literary Theory: An Introduction*, 20–6. This view has been carried into the present through the efforts of various literary-critical schools, including some with less cynical motives for viewing "literature as a displaced version of religion." Eagleton, 81.
108 Holmes, *Ralph Waldo Emerson*, 115.
109 Fuller, writing in 1840, quoted *Memoirs of Margaret Fuller Ossoli*, vol. 2, 26–9.
110 Whitman's ideas about Religious Democracy and their relation to his own work are discussed further in chapter 7 below.

Chapter 5

1 Snowden, *American Revolution*, 1802 edn, 357–9. In this and subsequent quoted passages, emphases and spellings are as in the original.
2 Snowden, 38.
3 Snowden, 42–3. Snowden's "ancient fantasy," with its effort to present the Revolution as a "distant, revered, and mythic occurrence" from "a world of legendary happenings long gone by," is discussed in the context of the ideology of early American history-writing in Shalev, *Rome Reborn on Western Shores*, 202–5.
4 Snowden, 350–1.
5 On pseudo-biblicism in general, including other examples besides Snowden's, see Shalev, "Written in the Style of Antiquity," 800–26.
6 Bartgis, "To the Public," iii–iv.
7 Hunt, *An Historical Reader*, iv. Snowden, too, addressed schoolmasters directly at one point in a footnote, and some editions of *The American Revolution* bound Snowden's narrative with the Declaration of Independence, the Constitution and other patriotic texts, apparently for schoolroom use.
8 Jefferson, *Life and Morals*. The text here consists of the original King James Bible passages with Jefferson's edits noted, based on the Library of Congress online facsimile.
9 Jefferson to F. A. Van der Kemp, April 25, 1816, Jefferson Papers.
10 This possible influence on Joseph Smith is discussed in chapter 2 above.
11 Peterson, *Jefferson Image in the American Mind*, 300–4.
12 Jefferson's comments on his Bible project are from his letters to Dr. Joseph Priestley, April 9, 1803; to Benjamin Rush, April 21, 1803, with enclosure, "Doctrines of Jesus Compared with Others"; to James Fishback, September 27, 1809; to John Adams, October 12, 1813; to Charles Thomson, January 9, 1816; and to F. A. Van der Kemp, April 25, 1816. Jefferson Papers, emphasis in the original.
13 Jefferson to Thomson, January 9, 1816; to Van der Kemp, April 25, 1816; to Adams, October 12, 1813. Jefferson Papers, emphasis in the original.
14 Jefferson to Rush, with syllabus enclosed, April 21, 1803. Jefferson Papers.

15 Jefferson to Dr. Benjamin Waterhouse, June 26, 1822, 349–50, emphasis in the original. On the other hand, Jefferson also predicted, more or less correctly, that even Unitarianism's "votaries will fall into the fatal error of fabricating formulas of creed and confessions of faith," thus re-introducing the original problem. On Tocqeville's prediction, see chapter 1 above.
16 See the analyses in Harris, *E Pluribus Unum,* and McCann, *A Pinnacle of Feeling.*
17 Lutz, *Origins of American Constitutionalism,* 121.
18 Democratic Rep. Tim Roemer of Indiana, 144 Cong. Rec. 27915 (December 18, 1998). Roemer was speaking in opposition to the impeachment of President Bill Clinton.
19 Bowen, *Miracle at Philadelphia.*
20 Lind, "Let's Stop Pretending the Constitution Is Sacred."
21 Hertzberg, "Framed Up."
22 Detweiler, "Changing Reputation of the Declaration," 557; Maier, *American Scripture,* 154.
23 Jefferson to Henry Lee, May 8, 1825. Jefferson Papers.
24 Maier, xiv, 154.
25 Maier, 160.
26 Maier, 178, 198; Harris, *E Pluribus Unum,* 2.
27 On the Maryland events, see Clavin, "Slavery, Freedom, and the Fourth of July," and "'Disciples of the Declaration'," 239–66. On Garrison's public protest, see chapter 8 below. On the suffragists' protest, see David M. Dismore, "Today in Feminist History."
28 Maier, *American Scripture,* 163, 167.
29 Maier, 160, 162.
30 Maier, 175.
31 John Adams to Benjamin Rush, March 14, 1809. Punctuation and capitalizations are in the original.
32 Maier, *American Scripture,* 186-8.
33 Maier, 190, quoting Peleg Sprague of Maine.
34 Maier, 175, 189; also see 2 Kings 2:11–12.
35 Maier, 189–90. Although correct on this point, Maier overstates the novelty of religious rhetoric in American political speech in the 1820s. For many earlier examples, see Sandoz, *Political Sermons,* and Cope, "How General George Outlived His Own Funeral Orations."
36 Maier credits the Declaration and its predecessors "with a peculiar American twist," i.e., the way they mobilized the people at large, while Lutz describes traditions that "blended to produce a constitutional perspective uniquely American." Maier, 50, 58 and chapter 2; Lutz, "Introductory Essay," in Lutz, *Colonial Origins,* xxi. That essay summarizes the book-length analysis in Lutz's *Origins of American Constitutionalism.*
37 Lutz, *Colonial Origins,* xv–xvii, xxiii–xxiv, xxxv–xxxvi. Also see "United States Constitution as an Incomplete Text," 23–32; Lutz, "Declaration of Independence," 41–58; and Elazar, "Political Theory of Covenant," 3–30.
38 As one example, one eulogist called Andrew Jackson "a most thorough and constant reader of our great political bible, the constitution of the Union." Woodbury, "Life and Character of Andrew Jackson," 373.

39 Kammen, *Machine That Would Go of Itself*, 22, 46; Noll, *America's God*, 373.
40 Kammen, 15, quoting Jefferson in 1791.
41 Jefferson to Samuel Kercheval, July 12, 1816. The sentence quoted is on the letter's sixth page.
42 Oman, "'We the People of the Kingdom of God'," 3, 14. Also see Tsai, *America's Forgotten Constitutions*, 1–17.
43 McCalla links these parallel uses of Bible and Constitution to "Common Sense" philosophy, which challenged both theological and political authority on the basis of supposedly shared moral intuitions. *Creationist Debate*, 144.
44 Maier, *American Scripture*, 197.
45 For examples with commentary see Foner, *We the Other People*, especially 47–76.
46 Foner, 79; also see 78–83.
47 Lutz, *Colonial Origins*, xv, xxiv.
48 *Cherokee Nation v. Georgia*, 6, 18.
49 Foner, *We the Other People*, 51, emphasis in the original.
50 Tsai, *America's Forgotten Constitutions*, 2, 16.
51 Kammen, *Machine That Would Go of Itself*, 3, emphasis in the original.
52 Quoted in Stephen O. Smoot, "The Council of Fifty and Its Minutes: A Review," *Interpreter: A Journal of Mormon Scripture* 23 (2017), 51; Andrew F. Ehat, "'It Seems Like Heaven Began on Earth': Joseph Smith and the Constitution of the Kingdom of God," *Brigham Young University Studies* 20:3 (Spring 1980), 259–61, http://www.jstor.org/stable/43042360.
53 Oman, 1, 9, 20.
54 "The Constitution of the Kingdom of God" (April 18, 1844), *Latter-day Conservative*, https://www.latterdayconservative.com/joseph-smith/constitution-of-the-kingdom-of-god/. For an image of the frameable display copy, see "What Do You Know about the Political Kingdom of God?," May 10, 2018, *Mormon Chronicle,* https://www.mormonchronicle.com/what-do-you-know-about-the-political-kingdom-of-god/.
55 Doctrine and Covenants 101:80, *Scriptures,* Church of Jesus Christ of Latter-day Saints [hereafter "LDS"], https://www.churchofjesuschrist.org/study/scriptures/dc-testament/dc/101; Klaus J. Hansen, *Quest for Empire: The Political Kingdom of God and the Council of Fifty in Mormon History* (East Lansing, MI: Michigan State Univ. Press, 1967), 41–4, 117–20. For detailed statements and criticism of LDS claims about the US Constitution, see Reed D. Slack, "The Mormon Belief of [*sic*] an Inspired Constitution," *Journal of Church and State* 36:1 (Winter 1994), 35–56; Dallin H. Oaks "The Divinely Inspired Constitution," *Ensign* (February 1992), LDS, https://www.churchofjesuschrist.org/study/ensign/1992/02/the-divinely-inspired-constitution; and "Latter Day Saints, Idol Worship, and the U.S. Government," Mormon Chronicle, December 10, 2017, https://www.mormonchronicle.com/latter-day-saints-idol-worship-and-the-us-government/.
56 John McNaughton, "One Nation under God" (2009), McNaughton Fine Art Company, https://jonmcnaughton.com/one-nation-under-god/ and https://jonmcnaughton.com/one-nation-under-god-interactive/.
57 For instance, LDS President Ezra Taft Benson charged that the United States had "apostatized in various degrees from different Constitutional principles as proclaimed by the inspired founders." Benson, "Our Divine Constitution,"

General Conference (October 1987), LDS, https://www.churchofjesuschrist.org/study/general-conference/1987/10/our-divine-constitution.

58 Robert W. Delp, "A Spiritualist in Connecticut: Andrew Jackson Davis, the Hartford Years, 1850–1854," *The New England Quarterly* 53:3 (September 1980), 351–2.
59 See the discussion of Brown's efforts in chapter 8 below.
60 Foner, 177–201; "Our Platform," *Woodhull & Claflin's Weekly*, June 15, 1872, *Victoria Woodhull: The Spirit to Run the White House*, http://www.victoria-woodhull.com/wc061500.htm.
61 Kammen, *Machine That Would Go of Itself*, 22, 142.
62 Moncure D. Conway, Republican Superstitions: As Illustrated in the Political History of America (London: Henry S. King & Co., 1872), vi–vii, xi, 1–3, 5, 8, 15, 47, 102.
63 John A. Kasson, remarks at a banquet in Philadelphia, October 13, 1887, quoted in Hampton L. Carson, *History of the Celebration of the One Hundredth Anniversary of the Promulgation of the Constitution of the United States*, vol. 2 (Philadelphia: J.B. Lippincott, 1889), 422, 423.
64 "Publius" [James Madison], "Concerning the Difficulties of the Convention in Devising a Proper Form of Government," (*Federalist* 37), 11 January 1788. *The Avalon Project*, Yale Law School, http://avalon.law.yale.edu/18th_century/fed37.asp.
65 William Ellery Channing, "Unitarian Christianity" (May 5, 1819). *Classical American Unitarian Christian Sermons and Writings,* American Unitarian Conference, http://www.americanunitarian.org/unitarianchristianity.htm.
66 Joseph Story, *Commentaries on the Constitution of the United States*, vol. 1 (Boston: Hilliard, Gray, 1833), vi-vii.
67 Story, *A Familiar Exposition of the Constitution of the United States* (Boston: Thomas H. Webb, 1840), 5.
68 Story, *Commentaries*, vi.
69 On Lincoln's immersion in legal commentaries, including some of Joseph Story's, see Steiner, "Abraham Lincoln and the Rule of Law Books."
70 Lincoln, "Perpetuation of Our Political Institutions," emphases in the original, capitalizations modernized.
71 Lincoln, emphases in the original.
72 Hickey, *Constitution of the United States*, vi. For a general discussion of changing views of the Constitution in this era, see Kammen, *Machine That Would Go of Itself,* especially chapter 4.
73 Hickey, viii, reprinting a letter from George Dallas, February 18, 1845.
74 Hickey, xviii, emphasis in the original.
75 Hickey, v, xix, xxi. Hickey does grant the value of guidance from "the wise and the good," a handful of authorities that includes the Founders and the opinions of the Supreme Court. These must not be treated with "irreverence" (xxiv–xxv), an obvious danger of unleashing the people to judge constitutional questions for themselves. This is a brief concession, however; he spends more time quoting John Locke to the opposite effect, arguing that one can successfully read texts to form opinions of one's own and thus attain real knowledge (xxiii–xxiv).
76 Lieberman, *Practical Companion to the Constitution*, 7.

77 Nord, *Faith in Reading*, 43–5, 51–3, 66–7. As Nord points out, publishers like ABS were early to adopt the new high-speed printing techniques that were radically changing the entire media landscape—a topic further discussed in chapter 6 below.
78 Kammen, *Machine That Would Go of Itself*, 103.

Chapter 6

1 Rubery, *Novelty of Newspapers*, 3–4.
2 Hatch, *Democratization of American Christianity*, 24–5, 73.
3 "The Early Nineteenth-Century Newspaper Boom."
4 Irving, "Rip Van Winkle," 37.
5 Samuel Bowles, writing in the Springfield (MA) *Republican*, January 1851, quoted in Schwarzlose, *Nation's Newsbrokers*, 164.
6 James Kent, lecture before the Young Men's Association at Albany, February 1854, quoted in Hudson, *Journalism in the United States*, 280.
7 Goodrich, *Recollections of a Lifetime*, 86.
8 Bernstein, *Masters of the Word*, 202.
9 Pisani, "Plundered by Harpies," 22–3. Also see Bernstein, chapter 6.
10 Howard, ed., *Eagle and Brooklyn*, 97–8.
11 Whitman, *Leaves of Grass* (1855), 26.
12 New York *Daily Times* 1, no. 10, September 29, 1851, p. 1.
13 Thoreau, *Walden*, 34.
14 Thoreau, 61, emphasis in the original.
15 Bowles, quoted in Schwarzlose, 164.
16 Bernstein, 207.
17 Schudson, *Discovering the News*, 26–7.
18 Bergmann, *God in the Street*, 20, 45.
19 Bergmann, 10, and chapter 1, which focuses on the "penny press."
20 Bergmann, 24, 27.
21 Bergmann, 45, emphasis in the original.
22 Bergmann, 19, 23, 48.
23 Bergmann, 84, and chapter 3, which focuses on Walt Whitman. Also see the further discussion of Whitman in chapter 7 below.
24 Ong, *Orality and Literacy*, 130.
25 Alan Brinkley, *The Publisher*, 102, emphasis in the original. The phrase is from an advertising circular that Luce and his business partner, Brit Hadden, issued in preparation for the 1923 launch of *Time* magazine.
26 Hatch, *Democratization of American Christianity*, 125–6.
27 Hatch, 125–6, emphasis in the original.
28 Hatch, 142–3.
29 Darrow, *Story of My Life*, 40; Capper, *Margaret Fuller*, 196.
30 Thoreau, "Slavery in Massachusetts" (1854), paragraph 26.
31 Emerson, "Fugitive Slave Law" (March 7, 1854). Emerson's reference to breakfast recalls the philosopher Hegel's observation "that newspapers serve

modern man as a substitute for morning prayers." Quoted in Anderson, *Imagined Communities,* 35.
32 Standage, *The Turk,* 176–84; Eschner, "Without Edgar Allan Poe"; Helena Marković and Biljana Oklopčić, "Edgar Allan Poe's Chevalier Auguste Dupin."
33 Rubery, *Novelty of Newspapers,* 4. Benedict Anderson makes a similar, sustained comparison of novels to newspapers in *Imagined Communities* (22–36), suggesting that both print products promote the kind of consciousness essential to nationalism.
34 Barbara J. Shapiro, *Culture of Fact,* 3–4, 6, 206, 212.
35 Henry F. Chorley, *London Athenaeum,* October 25, 1851, in *Moby-Dick,* "Contemporary Criticism and Reviews."
36 Lawrence, *Studies in Classic American Literature,* 145.
37 Melville, "Hawthorne and His Mosses" (1850), 1161–2; Markels, "Melville's Markings in Shakespeare's Plays."
38 Horace Greeley, *New York Tribune,* November 22, 1851, and N.a., *The London John Bull,* October 25, 1851, in Moby-Dick, "Contemporary Criticism and Reviews."
39 Buell, *New England Literary Culture,* chapter 7.
40 Buell, *New England Literary Culture,* 157, 182 and chapters 6 and 7.
41 Buell, "*Moby-Dick* as Sacred Text," 53–7, 69. See also Herbert, "Calvinist Earthquake," in the same volume.
42 See the discussions of these figures in chapters 2 and 5 above.
43 Herman Melville, *The Confidence-Man* (1857), chapter 44.
44 Higgins and Parker, eds., *Herman Melville: The Contemporary Reviews,* 499, 500, 501, 504, 506.
45 Quoted in Joan D. Hedrick, *Harriet Beecher Stowe,* 233–4.
46 Gossett, *Uncle Tom's Cabin and American Culture,* 164; Furnas, *Goodbye to Uncle Tom,* 58, quoting the French critic; Coleman, "Unsentimental Woman Preacher," 266, emphasis in the original, citing what she sees as a widespread view.
47 Quoted in the foreword to Lyman Beecher Stowe, *Saints, Sinners and Beechers,* 7.
48 Quoted in Hedrick, *Harriet Beecher Stowe,* 64.
49 Root, "Music of *Uncle Tom's Cabin*"; Stokes, 106.
50 Hedrick, *Harriet Beecher Stowe,* 8; Lewis, *Message, Messenger, and Response,* 3, 15, 38–45.
51 Coleman, "Unsentimental Woman Preacher," 266, 271, 272.
52 Hill, "*Uncle Tom's Cabin* as a Religious Text."
53 Reynolds, *Mightier Than the Sword,* 142.
54 Stowe's accounts of her original inspirations are recorded in the Introduction to the New Edition (1879), xiii–xiv; Charles Edward Stowe, *Life of Harriet Beecher Stowe,* 148–9; and Fields, *Life and Letters,* 163. Also see Gossett, *Uncle Tom's Cabin and American Culture,* 95–6.
55 Reynolds, *Mightier Than the Sword,* 187–8; Frick, *Uncle Tom's Cabin on the American Stage and Screen,* 130–1. Frick's book is a comprehensive history of the stage and film adaptations. Also see Gossett, *Uncle Tom's Cabin and American Culture,* chapter XIX.
56 Railton, "Uncle Tom's Cabin on Film 1."

57 Reynolds, *Mightier Than the Sword*, 147–8; Meer, *Uncle Tom Mania*, 108–10, 113–15, 138–9, 185.
58 Frick, *Uncle Tom's Cabin on the American Stage and Screen*, 48; also see his article "Uncle Tom's Cabin on the Antebellum Stage."
59 Pillsbury, "'Uncle Tom's Cabin' at a Boston Theatre," emphases in the original.
60 Gossett, *Uncle Tom's Cabin and American Culture*, 315–16.
61 Stowe, Introductory Essay, iii–vi, viii. On the similar complaints from revivalists and ultra-protestants about Scripture having become rote and over-familiar, see chapter 2 above.
62 Stowe, Introduction to the New Edition (1879), xiii, xiv.
63 Stowe, *Key to Uncle Tom's Cabin*, 5.
64 Coleman, "Unsentimental Woman Preacher," 272; Parfait, "Nineteenth-Century Serial as a Collective Enterprise"; Smith, "Serialization and the Nature of *Uncle Tom's Cabin*."
65 Parker, "Harriet Beecher Stowe," 316–18, emphases in the original.
66 Parker, 318; Introduction to the New Edition (1879), xiv–xv.
67 Stowe, *Key to Uncle Tom's Cabin*, 70, iv. *The Key* was modeled in part on Theodore D. Weld's anthology of testimonies, *American Slavery As It Is*, published for the American Anti-Slavery Society in 1839. That book quoted and aimed to refute slaveholders' objections but without a similar promise to give them their "due."
68 Reynolds, *Mightier Than the Sword*, 148.
69 Charles Nichols, "Origins of *Uncle Tom's Cabin*," 329.
70 Stowe, preface to *Uncle Tom's Cabin; or, Life among the Lowly*, vol. 1, vii; and "Concluding Remarks," chapter XLV, vol. 2, 310–22.
71 Hedrick, *Harriet Beecher Stowe*, 225–30.
72 Concluding a conspiratorial meeting among slave-catchers, for instance, she writes: "If any of our refined and Christian readers object to the society into which this scene introduces them, let us beg them to begin and conquer their prejudices in time. The catching business, we beg to remind them, is rising to the dignity of a lawful and patriotic profession. ... the trader and catcher may yet be among our aristocracy." Stowe, *Uncle Tom's Cabin*, vol. 1, 109.
73 Stowe, "Preface to the European Edition," v.
74 Variants of *authenticate* appear repeatedly: Stowe, *Key to Uncle Tom's Cabin*, 47, 165, 194.
75 Vollaro, "Lincoln, Stowe," 18–34; Hedrick, *Harriet Beecher Stowe*, 230.
76 Stowe, *Key to Uncle Tom's Cabin*, 23–30.
77 Stowe, iii.
78 This is a different reading from that of Samuel Otter, who calls these opening comments "a defense of *Uncle Tom's Cabin* in particular and fiction in general." Otter does go on to say, though, that further along in the *Key* the distinction between fact and fiction collapses, and he credits the *Key* as "a complicated formal and intellectual work in its own right." Otter, "Stowe and Race," 25, 28.
79 Stowe, *Key to Uncle Tom's Cabin*, iii.
80 Stowe, 5, 61, 115, emphasis in the original.
81 Stowe, *Uncle Tom's Cabin*, vol. 1, 189.
82 Stowe, 264–7, emphasis in the original.

83 Stowe, 210.
84 Stowe, 210–11.
85 Stowe, 267.
86 Stowe, quoted in Smylie, "*Uncle Tom's Cabin* Revisited," 166–7.
87 Stowe to Gamaliel Bailey, March 9, 1851, emphases in the original. Also see Dinius, *Camera and the Press,* chapter 4, on Stowe's keen interest in the daguerreotype and her use of the term as a verb for describing characters like Uncle Tom.
88 Stowe to Lord Carlisle, in Charles Edward Stowe, *Life of Harriet Beecher Stowe,* 165–6, emphasis in the original.
89 Stowe, *Key to Uncle Tom's Cabin,* 203, 83, 204, 25, 27–8.
90 Stowe, 128, 151, 205–6; Preface to the European Edition, v.
91 Stearns, *Notes on Uncle Tom's Cabin,* 155–7, 187, chapter 18, 309 and Appendix P, typography as in the original. Writing to Lord Carlisle, Stowe reported, "Religious papers, notably the 'New York Observer,' came out and denounced the book as anti-Christian, anti-evangelical, resorting even to personal slander on the author as a means of diverting attention from the work." Charles Edward Stowe, *Life of Harriet Beecher Stowe,* 168.
92 For instance, 249–52 and Part IV, chapter 2.
93 Quoted in Charles Edward Stowe, *Life of Harriet Beecher Stowe,* 156; Introduction to the New Edition (1879), xi. Similarly, "I did not write it. God wrote it. I merely did his dictation." Fields, *Life and Letters,* 377.
94 Quoted in Charles Edward Stowe, *Life of Harriet Beecher Stowe,* 174.
95 Stokes, *Altar at Home,* 8, 32.
96 Tompkins, *Sensational Designs,* 134–5.
97 Charles Edward Stowe, *Life of Harriet Beecher Stowe,* 154.
98 See Gilmore, "*Uncle Tom's Cabin* and the American Renaissance," 58–76.

Chapter 7

1 Cauldwell, "Walt at the *Daily Aurora,*" 81, 82.
2 Howard, *The Eagle and Brooklyn,* 95. Whitman was editor from March 5, 1846, to January 18, 1848.
3 Folsom and Price, *Re-Scripting Walt Whitman,* 19.
4 Herrero Brasas, *Walt Whitman's Mystical Ethics of Comradeship,* 33.
5 Bergmann, *God in the Street,* 71.
6 For discussions of these proposals, see Eiselein, "Whitman's Life and Work," 15–16; Herrero Brasas, *Walt Whitman's Mystical Ethics of Comradeship,* 4–5, 33–4 and chapter 2; and Folsom and Price, *Re-Scripting Walt Whitman,* 21–5. Earlier, Jerome Loving, citing Richard Chase, acknowledged but criticized an additional theory: that the transformation had something to do with Whitman discovering his supposed homosexuality. Loving, *Emerson, Whitman, and the American Muse,* 67–8.
7 "Walt Whitman's Leaves of Grass," 37; Emerson is quoted in Sanborn, "Reminiscent of Whitman," 66. Spelling follows the original.
8 Quoted in Folsom and Price, *Re-Scripting Walt Whitman,* 47.

9   Folsom and Price, 25, 42–4.
10 Henderson, "'What Is the Grass?'," 98.
11 Folsom and Price, *Re-Scripting Walt Whitman*, 17. For further examples of the contrasting positions on this point, see Noverr, "Journalism," 38–40, and for other details, see Smith, "Things Appearing, Every Day," from which this chapter is condensed. It should be noted that neither Henderson's, Folsom and Price's, nor Noverr's canvasses of the critical literature includes Hans Bergmann's *God in the Street*, which explicitly sets Whitman's work in the context of New York journalism and the "penny press."
12 Whitman, *Life and Adventures of Jack Engle*, 332, 334, 336.
13 Whitman, 337.
14 Turpin, "Introduction to Walt Whitman's *Life and Adventures of Jack Engle*," 242–3.
15 Whitman, *Jack Engle*, 336.
16 Whitman, *Democratic Vistas*, 206; Whitman, *Notebooks and Unpublished Prose Manuscripts*, 353.
17 Whitman, *Leaves of Grass* (1855 edn), 60, 26.
18 Whitman, *Jack Engle*, 335–6.
19 Whitman, 333.
20 Based on search results for those terms on Google Ngrams, https://books.google.com/ngrams.
21 Folsom and Price, *Re-Scripting Walt Whitman*, 47.
22 Bergmann, *God in the Street*, 79; on "loaferism," see Reynolds, *Walt Whitman's America*, 64–74.
23 Folsom and Price, *Re-Scripting Walt Whitman*, xii and chapter 1. On the transformation of "news" and the rise of an industrial print culture in the 1830s–40s, see chapter 6 above.
24 Whitman, "Letter to Ralph Waldo Emerson" (August 1856), in *Leaves of Grass* (1856 edn), 349, 350. Typography as in the original.
25 Whitman, "Steam-Power, Telegraphs, &c.," in *Complete Prose Works*, 144.
26 Whitman, "Visit to Plumbe's Gallery" (July 2, 1846), in Published Works: Periodicals. Also see Orvell, *The Real Thing*, chapter 1.
27 Whitman, *Democratic Vistas*, 241. Whitman also celebrated printing and related technologies in his poems, at one point bidding readers to "mark in amazement the Hoe press whirling its cylinders, / shedding the printed leaves steady and fast." (In late nineteenth-century publishing, Richard March Hoe's cylinder presses were the state of the art.) Whitman, "Song of the Exposition," in *Leaves of Grass* (1881–2 edn), 161.
28 Whitman, 239, 241.
29 Whitman, 239, 242, 245, 257.
30 Whitman, 230, 231.
31 Whitman, 243.
32 Whitman, 256.
33 Whitman, 251.
34 Whitman, 256.
35 Whitman, 255.
36 Whitman, 244.

37 Whitman, 256. 258.
38 Whitman, 230, 231, 242.
39 Kuebrich, "Religion and the Poet-Prophet," 203. See the discussion of Emerson in chapter 3 above.
40 Emerson, "The Poet" (1844), 8, 37, 38. See the discussion of Emerson in chapter 3.
41 Whitman, *Democratic Vistas*, 230.
42 Emerson, "The American Scholar" (1837), 93, 95.
43 Whitman, *Democratic Vistas*, 257.
44 Whitman, 239.
45 "In Whitman's Hand: Notebooks," leaf 1 verso. "There was a child went forth every day" became one of the early poems in *Leaves* (1855 edn), 90–1.
46 Whitman, preface to *Leaves of Grass* (1855 edn), xi. Subsequent page references are in parentheses. Ellipses are in the original throughout.
47 For example, see "Falling of the Pemberton Mills at Lawrence, Mass," *Frank Leslie's Illustrated Weekly*, January 21, 1860, 118–24. Internet Archive, https://archive.org/details/franklesliesillu00lesl/.
48 Whitman, *Leaves of Grass*, 1855 ed., 39. Subsequent page references are in parentheses, ellipses in the original.
49 Emerson, "The Poet," 37; Kuebrich, "Religion and the Poet-Prophet," 203. On Whitman reading Emerson, see also Loving, *Emerson, Whitman, and the American Muse*, especially chapter 3.
50 Emerson, "Goethe; or, The Writer," 290.
51 Whitman, "A Backward Glance O'er Travel'd Roads," in *Leaves of Grass* (1891–2 edn), 432–3.
52 Whitman, *Leaves of Grass* (1860–1 edn), 23. See also Harris, "Whitman's *Leaves of Grass* and the Writing of a New American Bible," 172–90. On Whitman "as a would-be religious founder" and "the value of reading the *Leaves* as a religious text," see Kuebrich, "Religion and the Poet-Prophet." Kuebrich also discusses Whitman's relative successes and failures as religion-maker in *Minor Prophecy*, chapter 8. Also see Herrero Brasas, *Walt Whitman's Mystical Ethics of Comradeship*, chapter 1.
53 Unsigned review, New York *Daily Times*, November 13, 1856, 2.
54 Whitman, preface to *Leaves of Grass* (1855 edn), iv.
55 Whitman, *Leaves of Grass* (1860–1 edn), 382–3. Subscript numbering follows the style of the original.
56 Psalm 137.
57 "In Whitman's Hand: Notebooks," leaf 1 verso. For additional background on Whitman's notebooks, see Miller, *Collage of Myself*, 11–20.
58 Reynolds, *Walt Whitman*, 31.
59 Whitman, "New York Dissected. V.—Street Yarn" (August 16, 1856), in Published Works: Periodicals.
60 Whitman, "Lo! Victress on the Peaks!," *Sequel to Drum-Taps*, in *Leaves of Grass* (1867 edn), 23b; Hutchinson, "Race and the Family Romance," 142.
61 See, for instance, the close descriptions of combat injuries in "The Dresser" (later retitled "The Wound-Dresser"), *Drum-Taps*, in *Leaves of Grass* (1867 edn), 31a–34a. The quoted line is from "A march in the ranks hard-prest, and the road unknown," *Leaves of Grass* (1867 edn), 44a.

62 See the discussion of this lecture in chapter 9 below.
63 Whitman, "Song of the Exposition," in *Leaves of Grass* (1881–2 edn), 159.
64 Henry Justin Smith, "The Day," 3, 4, 7.
65 Smith, 9–11.
66 Smith, 14, 15, 17–18.
67 Smith, 19, 21, 22. For a more detailed exposition of this essay, see Jeff Smith, "Things Appearing, Every Day."
68 Henry Justin Smith, "The Day," 6.
69 Whitman, "A Backward Glance O'er Travel'd Roads," 426, 427–8. Emphases throughout are in the original.
70 Whitman, 428, 429, 430.
71 Whitman, 434–5. Spelling is from the original.
72 See the discussion of the Divinity School Address in chapter 3.
73 Whitman, "A Backward Glance O'er Travel'd Roads," 427, 428, 430.
74 Whitman, 430, 436, 437, emphasis in original.
75 Whitman, 437, 438, emphasis in original.
76 Whitman, 427.
77 Harrison, "Gatekeeping and News Selection," 198, 200.
78 Kaplan, "Origins of Objectivity in American Journalism," 34.
79 Calcutt and Hammond, *Journalism Studies*, 17.
80 Henry Justin Smith, "The Day," 9.
81 Anderson, *Imagined Communities*, 33.
82 Anderson, 7. For a further discussion of Anderson's relevance to Whitman, see O'Reilly, "Imagined America."
83 Whitman, "A Backward Glance O'er Travel'd Roads," 434. 435.
84 Whitman in 1890, quoted in Folsom and Price, *Re-Scripting Walt Whitman*, 68. For extended discussions of comradeship in Whitman, see Herrero Brasas, *Walt Whitman's Mystical Ethics of Comradeship*, especially chapter 4, and Reynolds, *Walt Whitman*, chapter 6.
85 Whitman, "Opening of the Secession War," *Specimen Days*, 21. Others have noted the resemblance between this account and Anderson's observations on newspapers; see, for instance, Mancuso, "Civil War," 292–3.
86 That is, in the context of reading news. Anderson in *Imagined Communities* also presents other conditions as contributing to the emergence of national identities—for instance, the way in which service to a colonizing power brings together members of the colonized groups, who thus infer that they must all be part of one heretofore unrecognized "people."
87 Whitman, "A Backward Glance O'er Travel'd Roads," 438.
88 Whitman, *Democratic Vistas*, 244.
89 Whitman, footnote on 247–8.
90 Whitman, "A Backward Glance O'er Travel'd Roads," 438.
91 Whitman, *Leaves of Grass* (1855 edn), 46.
92 Folsom, "Whitman Making Books." See Figure 17.
93 See the discussion of the newspaper as political "Bible" in chapter 6 above.
94 Quoted by Noverr, "Journalism," 32.
95 Whitman, *Leaves of Grass* (1855 edn), 95.
96 "A Backward Glance O'er Travel'd Roads," 438.

Chapter 8

1. Watkins, *Slavery and Sacred Texts*, 18.
2. Watkins, 8–11, 16–17, 26–7.
3. Watkins, 331–2.
4. Garrison, "The Deed of Infamy Consummated." The 1854 case in question involved the escaped slave Anthony Burns. Garrison's protest, which included publicly burning the Constitution and other documents, is further discussed below.
5. Resolution adopted by the Massachusetts Anti-Slavery Society, January 27, 1843.
6. Ross, *Slavery Ordained of God*.
7. Weld, *Bible against Slavery*.
8. Quoted in Noll, *America's God*, 408.
9. Kraditor, *Means and Ends in American Abolitionism*, 93–4.
10. Stowe, *Key to Uncle Tom's Cabin*, 115–20; on Douglass's arguments, see the further discussion below. Paul's letter to Philemon in the New Testament seems to advocate the return of a fugitive slave.
11. Lee, *Erosion of Biblical Certainty*, epilogue, especially 176–9.
12. Quoted in Snay, *Gospel of Disunion*, 64.
13. Ross, *Slavery Ordained of God*, 96–7.
14. Parker, "Speech at the New England Anti-Slavery Convention in Boston" (May 29, 1850), 68, 79. For further details of Parker's views, see chapter 4 above.
15. Van Deburg, "Garrison and the 'Pro-Slavery Priesthood'," 224–37.
16. Kraditor, *Means and Ends in American Abolitionism*, 92–3.
17. Francis Jackson Garrison, *William Lloyd Garrison*, 383–8; Delp, "A Spiritualist in Connecticut," 356–8; *Proceedings of the Hartford Bible Convention*, 10, emphases in the original.
18. *Proceedings of the Hartford Bible Convention*, 35, 142–3, 339.
19. *Proceedings of the Hartford Bible Convention*, 26–7, 274, 369.
20. Francis Jackson Garrison, *William Lloyd Garrison*, 384–5.
21. Delp, *A Spiritualist in Connecticut*, 358; Francis Jackson Garrison, *William Lloyd Garrison*, 388.
22. William Lloyd Garrison, quoted in Van Deburg, "William Lloyd Garrison and the 'Pro-Slavery Priesthood'," 237.
23. Delany, *Condition, Elevation, Emigration, and Destiny*, 156.
24. Parker, "Speech at the New England Anti-Slavery Convention," 85. On debates involving Webster, Stuart, Parker, Garrison, and Douglass, see Watkins, *Slavery and Sacred Texts*, especially chapter 5.
25. Stowe, *Key to Uncle Tom's Cabin*, 37.
26. See the discussion of Dallas's views in chapter 5 above.
27. Phillips, *Constitution a Pro-Slavery Compact*.
28. See the discussion of these issues in Kraditor, *Means and Ends in American Abolitionism*, 185–217, especially 206–7 and 215–17, and in Tillery, "Inevitability of the Douglass-Garrison Conflict," 144–5.
29. Kraditor, 207.

30 Francis Jackson Garrison, *William Lloyd Garrison*, 412–13, citing the original report in *The Liberator* 24, July 7, 1854, emphasis in the original; also see Yacovone, "A Covenant with Death and an Agreement with Hell."
31 1 Chronicles 16:36, Psalm 106:48 and 2 Kings 23; Jannuzzi, "'And Let the People Say Amen'," 1–27, especially 9.
32 Francis Jackson Garrison, *William Lloyd Garrison*, 413, emphases in the original.
33 Garrison in 1842, quoted in Kraditor, *Means and Ends in American Abolitionism*, 197.
34 See the discussion of Lincoln and the war in chapter 9.
35 Quoted in Tillery, "The Inevitability of the Douglass-Garrison Conflict," 138.
36 On Douglass's evolving views, see Tillery, 137–49; Watkins, *Slavery and Sacred Texts*, 204–7 and 212–18; and James A. Colaiaco, *Frederick Douglass and the Fourth of July*, 73–107.
37 Douglass, *Oration* ["What to the Slave Is the 4th of July?"] (July 5, 1852), 20. Subsequent page references are in parentheses. Emphases are in the original throughout.
38 That was Senator John M. Berrien of Georgia, arguing before the Supreme Court in the 1824 *Antelope* case. See Noonan, Jr., *The Antelope*, 100.
39 Spooner, *Unconstitutionality of Slavery*; Barnett, "Was Slavery Unconstitutional before the Thirteenth Amendment?," 981. From this close look at Spooner's arguments and Wendell Phillips' reply, Barnett concludes: "In many ways, Spooner's interpretive approach has a very modern ring. In important respects, however, his approach is preferable to those commonly used today and worthy of study for this reason alone" (978). Spooner would also be involved in "conpiratorial efforts to free the captured John Brown" (980), and would later take more radical positions against the Constitution's authority altogether (1014).
40 Wendell Phillips, for instance, replied at length in his *Review of Lysander Spooner's Essay on the Unconstitutionality of Slavery*.
41 Weld, *The Bible against Slavery*, 90 (footnote), emphases in the original.
42 For examples of the complicated interplay of literalism and non-literalism in liberal but also conservative biblical interpretation, including the liberal appeal to "principles instead of explicit precepts" (p. 178), see Lee, *Erosion of Biblical Certainty*, 158–65 and 173–80.
43 Mark, "Luther's Speech at the Diet of Worms," paragraph 7 of Martin Luther's speech of April 18, 1521.
44 Banneker to Thomas Jefferson, August 19, 1791; Walker, *Walker's Appeal*.
45 Garrison, "Declaration of the National Anti-Slavery Convention."
46 Smith, "Speech on the Nebraska Bill" (April 6, 1854), 129–30, 133.
47 John Randolph, quoted in "Virginia versus Pennsylvania," 243; Rufus Choate and John Pettit, quoted in Maier, *American Scripture*, 200, 202.
48 Fitzhugh, *Sociology for the South*, 182.
49 Calhoun, "Speech on the Oregon Bill" (June 27, 1848).
50 Choate, Speech at Lowell, MA (October 18, 1856), 404–5, emphases in the original.
51 Ross, *Slavery Ordained of God*, 105, 116–40, emphasis in the original.
52 Ross, 97, 184.

53 *A Debate on Slavery*, 44.
54 Stuart, *Conscience and the Constitution*, 100, 102, 103–4, emphases in the original. On these debates and their larger context, see Noll, *Civil War as a Theological Crisis*, 36–45.
55 Quoted in Maier, *American Scripture*, 199.
56 Stuart, *Conscience and the Constitution*, 57, emphasis in the original.
57 Reynolds, *John Brown, Abolitionist*, 34, 77.
58 Sanborn, ed., *Life and Letters of John Brown*, 45–51, emphases in the original.
59 John Brown, November 21, 1834, quoted in Sanborn, 40.
60 John Brown's note of December 2, 1859, quoted in Sanborn, 517.
61 Onion, "John Brown's Passionate 'Declaration of Liberty'."
62 For accounts of the origins and contents of Brown's constitution and the debate over it at his trial, see Tsai, *America's Forgotten Constitutions*, chapter 3, and Zuck, *Divided Sovereignties*, 113–20.
63 Sanborn, *Life and Letters of John Brown*, 575; Zuck, *Divided Sovereignties*, 118–20.
64 Douglass, "John Brown Not Insane."
65 Emerson, "Relief of the Family of John Brown" (November 18, 1859); Bush, "Emerson, John Brown, and 'Doing the Word'," 206.
66 Emerson, "Relief of the Family of John Brown," 269–70.
67 DeCaro, Jr., "John Brown's Liberation Theology."
68 Sanborn, *Life and Letters of John Brown*, 614.
69 Sanborn, 147, 247, 444. Sanborn, who knew Brown personally, frequently compares him to a prophet and quotes others doing so too.
70 Quoted in Hahn, *A Nation under Our Feet*, 122.
71 Delany's extensive contributions to African American self-organizing are detailed in Ernest, *A Nation within a Nation*. On Delany's role in the "Negro" or "Colored" convention movement that was especially active from the 1830s through the 1860s, see chapter 5 of that book.
72 Delany, 13, 14, 18–22.
73 Delany, 13.
74 Delany, 11, 13, 14.
75 Delany, 209, emphasis in the original. On the questions of a collective African "diasporic identity," how it developed and declined, and Delany's role with respect to this, see Sidbury, *Becoming African in America*, especially 6–7 and 205–8.
76 Hitler, *Mein Kampf*, 165.
77 Delany, *Condition, Elevation, Emigration, and Destiny*, 7, 11–12, 209.
78 Delany, 209.
79 Delany, 210.
80 Delany, 212.
81 Delany, 215, emphases in the original.
82 Delany, 169–70.
83 Delany, 10, 210–12, 214, emphases in the original.
84 Delany, "Political Destiny," 249, 252–4.
85 Lists and records are available at the *Colored Conventions Project*.
86 Delany, "Political Destiny," 252–4.

87 Delany, *Blake, Corrected Edition*. On *Blake's* publishing history and its context within Delany's career, see Miller, introduction to *Blake or The Huts of America*, xi-xii, and McGann, "Rethinking Delany's *Blake*," 90. That essay is a revision of McGann's introduction to his *Corrected Edition*. Also see Chiles, "Within and without Raced Nations," 323–52.
88 Shreve, "Frederick Douglass's Feud," gives an overview of that controversy.
89 Novelist Samuel R. Delany (no relation) praised *Blake* as a strong example "of what is often referred to as proto-science fiction … about as close to an sf-style alternate history novel as you can get." Delany, "Racism and Science Fiction," 120. For a more detailed discussion of both *Blake* and its critical reception, see Smith, "The First American 'Superspy'."
90 Delany, *Blake, Corrected Edition*, 313.
91 Miller, Introduction to *Blake*, xiii; McGann, "Rethinking Delany's *Blake*," 83, 85, 86.
92 Delany, "Political Destiny," 248, 251, 253; *Condition, Elevation, Emigration, and Destiny*, chapter 4.
93 Delany, *Condition, Elevation, Emigration, and Destiny*, 7; Delany, *Blake, Corrected Edition*, 104.
94 Stowe, *Key to Uncle Tom's Cabin*, chapter 9, 244–50.
95 Delany, *Blake, Corrected Edition*, 43–4.
96 Delany, 104.
97 Delany, 220.
98 Delany, 18; Delany, *Condition, Elevation, Emigration, and Destiny*, 7.
99 Delany, *Blake, Corrected Edition*, 118.
100 Castiglia, *Interior States*, 226.
101 Delany, *Blake, Corrected Edition*, 291.
102 Delany had written a series of articles in 1849 on the complicated political position of Cuba. See Miller, Introduction to *Blake*, xxii–xxiii.
103 Delany, *Blake, Corrected Edition*, 243, 244.
104 On the special case of the superspy-influenced "action-hero president," see Smith, *The Presidents We Imagine*, 216–23.
105 Delany, *Blake, Corrected Edition*, 86, 102, 127, 291.
106 Arendt, *Origins of Totalitarianism*, 3002. Ivan Hannaford likewise contrasts the "brutish" oppression of those "locked in the private world" with life according to the "civic idea" or "political way" that he traces to ancient Greece. Hannaford, *Race*, 10–13, 50–7. Both writers link racism to attempts to deny those classical political ideals. As noted in Chapter 7 above, "imagined community" is the well-known term for the essential precondition of nationhood in Benedict Anderson's *Imagined Communities*. See 5–7, 22–36 and chapters 3 and 4. Blake's informative "seclusions" with isolated slaves resemble the nation-making function that Anderson assigns to newspapers. Similarly, Katy Chiles argues that the "seriality" of *Blake's* original appearance in print involves a "reconceptualization" of Anderson's "historical time of the nation." Chiles, "Within and without Raced Nations," 337.
107 Delany, *Condition, Elevation, Emigration, and Destiny*, 14, 210.
108 While it seems the Grand Council is planning a violent attack, both Robert S. Levine and Jerome McGann speculate that the novel's lost ending might not have been a race war but the new nation's peaceable emergence.

Levine sees Blake and his comrades creating "a regenerated society" in Cuba, where it would serve "as a daily refutation of whites' racist beliefs in black inferiority," while McGann sees them leading an emigration to found "a black city on an African hill." Levine, *Representative Identity*, 215–16; McGann, "Rethinking Delany's *Blake*," 88–9. With the failure of Reconstruction and the onset of Jim Crow, Sutton E. Griggs, another African American pamphleteer-turned-novelist, revisited the theme of Black-nationalist secret societies and underground nations in his 1899 novel *Imperium in Imperio*. Griggs's "Imperium" is an entire parallel government of, by and for African Americans, and his fable, too, reaches its climax when the clandestine organization's leaders confront the difficult, but essential, question of how to surface and make their proto-nation known to the world.

109 Even before Brown's raid greatly increased Southern anxieties, says Donald E. Reynolds, "slave panics" were common in the South, and "southern whites were unwavering in their conviction that Garrisons and Browns lurked in every shadow, ready at the slightest opportunity to seduce other Nat Turners from their natural loyalties and use them to destroy the South and its social system." Reynolds, *Texas Terror*, 6, 18.
110 "Ordinances of Secession of the 13 Confederate States of America."

Chapter 9

1 Lincoln, "Fragment on Pro-Slavery Theology" (October 1, 1858?), 204–5. On Ross's *Slavery Ordained of God*, see chapter 8 above.
2 Lincoln, Speech at Chicago, Illinois (July 10, 1858), 501.
3 Arnold, *History of Abraham Lincoln*, 120.
4 Lincoln, Speech at Springfield, Illinois (June 26, 1857), 407; Speech at Chicago, 499–501; "Fragment: Notes for Speeches," 553, emphasis in original.
5 Lincoln, Speech at Chicago, 499–501.
6 Lincoln, Speech at Springfield, 406–7.
7 Lincoln, 406–7.
8 Lincoln, Speech at Chicago, 501.
9 Shelly, "Pope to immigrants."
10 *Address Delivered by Abraham Lincoln at the Dedication of the National Cemetery*. For other efforts in this vein over the years, see "Lincoln's Gettysburg Address in Print."
11 Elmore, *Lincoln's Gettysburg Address*. In reviewing other scholarship on the address (14–17), Elmore sees attention to the biblical language as surprisingly lacking—but see also Daniel Dreisbach, "The Sacred Sounds of Lincoln's Gettysburg Address." Contrarily, argued an earlier critic, Glen E. Thurow, "The similarities of language and style to the Bible by themselves prove nothing about the religious qualities of Lincoln's speech." In Thurow's ingenious analysis, what matters most is Lincoln's recourse to the geometrical terminology of axioms and proofs. Thurow, *Abraham Lincoln and American*

Political Religion, 69 and chapter 4. Also see Apostolos Doxiadis' analysis, described in a further note below.
12 Stanton is quoted in Nelson, "Fighting for Lincoln's Soul," section 1.
13 Wills, *Lincoln at Gettysburg*, 169–71.
14 Everett, "Gettysburg Address."
15 Elmore, *Lincoln's Gettysburg Address*, 11.
16 Boritt, *The Gettysburg Gospel*, 165–86.
17 John Hay, quoted in Boritt, 185.
18 *Address of Hon. Edward Everett, at the Consecration of the National Cemetery.*
19 Boritt, *The Gettysburg Gospel*, 81–3; Elmore, *Lincoln's Gettysburg Address* (17–18), also says it was carefully prepared, like all Lincoln's public statements, as does David Herbert Donald in his biography *Lincoln*, 460–1.
20 Poore, in *Reminiscences of Abraham Lincoln*, 228. Also see Peterson, *Lincoln in American Memory*, 114–16.
21 Andrews, *The Perfect Tribute*, 4–5.
22 Andrews, 5–9.
23 Andrews, 17, 21.
24 Andrews, 40. The actual response of Lincoln's original audience is a matter of sharply conflicting reports. See Glenn LaFantasie, "Lincoln and the Gettysburg Awakening," 80–3.
25 Elmore, *Lincoln's Gettysburg Address*, 24–35, 47–51; Wills, *Lincoln at Gettysburg*, 62.
26 Fig. 2 and the analysis that follows rely on the text of the address at *Voices of Democracy: The U.S. Oratory Project*. Spellings are modernized. For the variants among the extant manuscripts, see "The Gettysburg Address," *Abraham Lincoln Online*.
27 Lincoln, Speech at Chicago, 500.
28 Frye and Macpherson, *Biblical and Classical Myths*, 22–3 and chapter 2; Frye, *The Great Code*, 79, 128, 169–71, and chapters 4 and 5. Donald says the address has "an hourglass form" (*Lincoln*, 461), which is also correct but misses the biblical parallels—as did other critics: Donald also notes that an opposition newspaper mocked Lincoln's birth and rebirth imagery as "obstetric analogies" (462). With some differences of detail, Apostolos Doxiadis notes the same internal patterning described here, which he labels "chiasmus," but relates it to Lincoln's study of Euclid, whose *Elements*, he suggests, had a large influence on Lincoln's rhetoric. According to Dioxiadis, the Gettysburg Address differs from Lincoln's earlier speeches in treating the Declaration's "all men are created equal" no longer as the self-evident axiom it claimed to be, but as a "proposition" that newly needed demonstrating because of the challenge the war posed to it. Doxiadis, "The Geometry of Gettysburg," 36:05–48:25.
29 Noll, "The Image of the United States as a Biblical Nation," 43, 51. See also the discussion of these issues in chapter 1 above.
30 Noll, 45–6.
31 As an example, see Everett, "Gettysburg Address," paragraph 38.
32 On Snowden's work, see chapter 5 above.
33 Auerbach, *Mimesis*, 40–9.
34 Lincoln, "Reply to Oliver P. Morton" (February 11, 1861).
35 Wills, *Lincoln at Gettysburg*, 105.

36 Wills, 109.
37 Wills, 108.
38 Lincoln, "The Perpetuation of Our Political Institutions" (January 27, 1838).
39 Maier, *American Scripture*, 191–208.
40 See the discussions of these ideas in chapters 3 and 7 above.
41 Taylor, "Gettysburg Ode."
42 Though scored in various ways, the tune is often played in a marching tempo with alternating dotted notes that also get vocal emphasis: "MINE EYES ● have seen ● THE GLOR●y of ●THE COM●ing of ● THE LORD …" "Thor-Hammer" is quoted in Gamble, *Fiery Gospel*, 126.
43 Wills, *Lincoln at Gettysburg*, 184.
44 Tierney, "'The Battle Hymn of the Republic'."
45 Howe, *Reminiscences*, 273–6.
46 Lincoln, Second Inaugural Address (March 4, 1865).
47 Lutz, *Colonial Origins*, xvi, xxiv.
48 Lutz, *Origins of American Constitutionalism*, 16.
49 McCalla, *The Creationist Debate*, 45, 119. See the discussion in chapter 1 above.
50 Joseph Mede to W. Twisse, March 23, 1634.
51 Mather, *Essay on the Golden Street of the Holy City*, 30–5, emphases and typography as in the original.
52 Psalm 104; Whitman, "The Return Of The Heroes" and "Thou Mother With Thy Equal Brood." *Leaves of Grass*, 1881–2 edition.
53 Smith, *The Presidents We Imagine*, 84–96, 113–19, 150–5. For book-length discussions of this phenomenon, see Peterson's *Lincoln in American Memory* and Fox, *Lincoln's Body*.
54 Hodes, *Mourning Lincoln*, 196; Nelson, "Fighting for Lincoln's Soul," section 1.
55 Arnold, *History of Abraham Lincoln*, 424.
56 Wood, "Visitor Center Script"; Gregory Eiselein, "Lincoln's Death [1865]."
57 Whitman, "Death of Abraham Lincoln," 310. Subsequent pages references are in parentheses. Emphases are in the originals.
58 Whitman, "When Lilacs Last in the Dooryard Bloom'd," in *Leaves of Grass*, 1867 edn.
59 Here and elsewhere, Whitman idiosyncratically spelled the name "Shakspere."
60 Blanchard, *Type of American Genius*.
61 Lewis Gannett reviews the evidence and the Rutledge legend's changing scholarly reputation in "'Overwhelming Evidence'," 28–41; for the Rutledge story itself, see Herndon and Weik, *True Story of a Great Life*, vol. 1, chapter VI.
62 Herndon and Weik, 139.
63 Herndon and Weik, vii–xii.

Conclusion

1 On Christian millenarians in history, see Cohn, *Pursuit of the Millennium*, and Court, *Approaching the Apocalypse*.
2 Doan, *Miller Heresy*, 10, 18.
3 Rowe, *Thunder and Trumpets*, x–xi; Miller, *William Miller's Apology and Defence*, 22–4.

4   Rowe, 5; Miller, 4. On Ethan Allen, see chapter 1 above.
5   Hatch, *Democratization of American Christianity*, 13.
6   Hatch, 71.
7   See Buell, *Dream of the Great American Novel; Beloved* is the subject of chapter 10. On *The Road,* see Lake, "Christ-Haunted."

BIBLIOGRAPHY

"The Baptist Faith and Message." 2000 revision. Southern Baptist Convention. Accessed August 20, 2022. https://bfm.sbc.net/.

"Book of Mormon Plagiarism Accusations." FAIR: Faithful Answers, Informed Response. Accessed August 20, 2022. https://www.fairlatterdaysaints.org/answers/Book_of_Mormon/Plagiarism_accusations.

"Comparison of 9 First Vision Accounts." Joseph Smith Foundation. Accessed August 20, 2022. https://josephsmithfoundation.org/docs/comparison-of-9-first-vision-accounts/.

"Comparison of the Inspired Version to the King James Version." Centerplace.org. Accessed August 19, 2022. http://www.centerplace.org/hs/iv2kjv/default.htm.

"In Whitman's Hand: Notebooks." The Walt Whitman Archive. http://whitmanarchive.org/manuscripts/notebooks/transcriptions/loc.00005.html.

"Latter Day Saints, Idol Worship, and the U.S. Government." *Mormon Chronicle*, December 10, 2017. https://www.mormonchronicle.com/latter-day-saints-idol-worship-and-the-us-government/.

"Lincoln's Gettysburg Address in Print." June 13, 2016. Lincoln Financial Foundation Collection, Indiana State Museum and the Allen County Public Library. http://lincolncollection.tumblr.com/post/145872657819/lincolns-gettysburg-address-in-print.

"Old Testament Orientation 1." Course syllabus. Liberty University. Accessed August 26, 2022. http://www.liberty.edu/media/1162/2013f_syllabi/OBST_515_Yates_F13.pdf.

"On Biblical Scholarship and the Doctrine of Inerrancy" (Resolution 7). *Annual of the 2012 Southern Baptist Convention*. Nashville, TN: Executive Committee of the Southern Baptist Convention, 2012.

"Ordinances of Secession of the 13 Confederate States of America." Civil War Photos. Accessed August 20, 2022. https://www.civilwarphotos.net/files/ordinances_of_secession.htm.

"Our Platform." *Woodhull & Claflin's Weekly*, June 15, 1872. Victoria Woodhull: The Spirit to Run the White House. Accessed August 20, 2022. http://www.victoria-woodhull.com/wc061500.htm.

"Sketches of Religious History [Disciples of Christ]." In *The Millennial Harbinger, New Series* III, edited by Alexander Campbell. Bethany, VA: A. Campbell 1839. 164–68.

"Treasure Seeking, Money Digging and Joseph Smith, Jr." FAIR: Faithful Answers, Informed Response. Accessed August 20, 2022. https://www.fairlatterdaysaints.org/answers/Joseph_Smith/Money_digging.

"Virginia Versus Pennsylvania." *Niles' Weekly Register*, June 9, 1827.

"Walt Whitman's Leaves of Grass." *Putnam's Monthly*. September 1855. In *Leaves of Grass Imprints: American and European Criticisms on Leaves of Grass*. Boston: Thayer and Eldridge, 1860.

"What Adventists Believe about Christ's Ministry in the Heavenly Sanctuary" (Belief 24). Seventh-day Adventist Church. https://www.adventist.org/christs-ministry-in-the-heavenly-sanctuary/.

"What Do You Know about the Political Kingdom of God?" *Mormon Chronicle*, May 10, 2018. https://www.mormonchronicle.com/what-do-you-know-about-the-political-kingdom-of-god/.

Abbott, Lyman. "What Is a Prophet?" In *The Prophets of the Christian Faith*. New York: Macmillan, 1896.

Adams, John to Benjamin Rush, March 14, 1809. Founders Online. National Archives. http://founders.archives.gov/documents/Adams/99-02-02-5319.

Address Delivered by Abraham Lincoln at the Dedication of the National Cemetery, Gettysburg, Pennsylvania, November 19th, 1863. Boston: Tudor Press, 1919. http://www.archive.org/details/addressdeliveredlinc.

Address of Hon. Edward Everett, at the Consecration of the National Cemetery at Gettysburg, 19th November, 1863, with the Dedicatory Speech of President Lincoln, and the Other Exercises of the Occasion. Boston: Little, Brown & Co., 1864.

Allen, Joseph Henry. *Our Liberal Movement in Theology: Chiefly as Shown in Recollections of the History of Unitarianism in New England*. Boston: Roberts Brothers, 1882.

Anderson, Benedict. *Imagined Communities: Reflections on the Origin and Spread of Nationalism*, 2nd edn. London: Verso, 2006.

Andrews, Mary Raymond Shipman. *The Perfect Tribute*. New York: Charles Scribner's Sons, 1906.

Arasola, Kai. *The End of Historicism: Millerite Hermeneutic of Time Prophecies in the Old Testament*. Upssala: University of Upssala, 1990.

Arendt, Hannah. *The Origins of Totalitarianism*, new edn. San Diego: Harvest/Harcourt Brace, 1979.

Armenius, Theophilus [Thomas S. Hinde]. "Account of the Rise and Progress of the Work of God in the Western Country, No. VI." *The Methodist Magazine* II (September 1819). https://archive.org/details/methodistmagazin02meth_0.

Arnold, Isaac N. *The History of Abraham Lincoln, and the Overthrow of Slavery*. Chicago: Clarke & Co., 1866.

Auerbach, Erich. *Mimesis: The Representation of Reality in Western Literature*, 50th anniversary edn. Translated by W. R. Trask. Princeton, NJ: Princeton University Press, 2003.

Baird, Robert. *Religion in America*. New York: Harper & Brothers, 1844.

Banneker, Benjamin to Thomas Jefferson, August 19, 1791. Founders Online. National Archives. https://founders.archives.gov/documents/Jefferson/01-22-02-0049.

Barnett, Randy E. "Was Slavery Unconstitutional before the Thirteenth Amendment? Lysander Spooner's Theory of Interpretation." *Pacific Law Journal* 28 (1997): 977–1014.

Barr, James. *The Scope and Authority of the Bible*. Philadelphia: Westminster Press, 1980.

Bartgis, M. [Matthias]. "To the Public." August 4, 1823. In Richard Snowden, *The History of the American Revolution; in Scripture Style*. Frederick County, Maryland: Matthias Bartgis, 1823.

Benson, Ezra Taft. "Fourteen Fundamentals in Following the Prophet" (February 26, 1980). *Liahona*, June 1981. Church of Jesus Christ of Latter-day Saints. Accessed August 20, 2022. https://www.lds.org/liahona/1981/06/fourteen-fundamentals-in-following-the-prophet.

Benson, Ezra Taft. "Our Divine Constitution" (October 1987). General Conference. Church of Jesus Christ of Latter-day Saints. Accessed August 20, 2022. https://www.churchofjesuschrist.org/study/general-conference/1987/10/our-divine-constitution.

Bentley, G. E. Jr. "A Swedenborgian Bible." *Blake/An Illustrated Quarterly* 24, no. 2 (Fall 1990): 63–4.

Bergmann, Hans. *God in the Street: New York Writing from the Penny Press to Melville*. Philadelphia: Temple University Press, 1995.

Bernstein, William J. *Masters of the Word: How Media Shaped History from the Alphabet to the Internet*. London: Atlantic Books/Grove Press, 2013.

Bittner, Terrie Lynn. "Critical Text Project Evaluates Changes in Book of Mormon." Book of Mormon Online, April 24, 2013. http://bookofmormononline.com/3301/critical-text-project-evaluates-mistakes-and-changes-in-book-of-mormon.

Blanchard, Rufus. *Abraham Lincoln, The Type of American Genius: An Historical Romance*. Wheaton, IL: R. Blanchard & Co., 1882.

Bliss, Sylvester. *Memoirs of William Miller*. Boston: Joshua V. Himes, 1853.

Bloom, Harold. *The American Religion: The Emergence of the Post-Christian Nation*. New York: Simon & Schuster, 1993.

Bloom, Harold. *The Western Canon: The Books and School of the Ages*. New York: Harcourt Brace, 1994.

The Book of Abraham. Scriptures. Church of Jesus Christ of Latter-day Saints. Accessed August 20, 2022. https://www.churchofjesuschrist.org/study/scriptures/pgp/abr/1?lang=eng.

The Book of Mormon Critical Text Project. BYU Studies. Accessed August 27, 2022. https://criticaltext.byustudies.byu.edu/critical-text-book-mormon-project-0.

Boritt, Gabor. *The Gettysburg Gospel: The Lincoln Speech That Nobody Knows*. New York: Simon & Schuster, 2006.

Bowen, Catherine Drinker. *Miracle at Philadelphia: The Story of the Constitutional Convention*. Boston: Little, Brown, 1966.

Braun, Frederick A. "Goethe as Viewed by Emerson." *The Journal of English and Germanic Philology* 15, no. 1 (January 1916): 23–34.

Brinkley, Alan. *The Publisher: Henry Luce and His American Century*. New York: Knopf, 2010.

Brodhead, Richard H. "Prophets in America Circa 1830: Ralph Waldo Emerson, Nat Turner, Joseph Smith." In *Joseph Smith Jr.: Reappraisals after Two Centuries*, edited by Reid L. Neilson and Terry L. Givens. Oxford: Oxford University Press, 2009. 13–30.

Buell, Lawrence. *The Dream of the Great American Novel*. Cambridge, MA: Harvard University Press, 2014.
Buell, Lawrence. "*Moby-Dick* as Sacred Text." In *New Essays on Moby-Dick*, edited by Richard H. Brodhead. Cambridge: Cambridge University Press, 1986. 53–72.
Buell, Lawrence. *New England Literary Culture: From Revolution through Renaissance*. Cambridge: Cambridge University Press, 1986.
Bush, Harold K. "Emerson, John Brown, and 'Doing the Word': The Enactment of Political Religion at Harpers Ferry, 1859." In *The Emerson Dilemma: Essays on Emerson and Social Reform*, edited by T. Gregory Garvey. Athens, GA: University of Georgia Press, 2001. 197–220.
Bushnell, Horace. *Christ in Theology; Being the Answer of the Author, Before the Hartford Central Association of Ministers, October, 1849, for the Doctrines of the Book Entitled "God in Christ."* Hartford, CT: Brown and Parsons, 1851.
Bushnell, Horace. *A Discourse on the Slavery Question* (January 10, 1839). Hartford: Case, Tiffany & Co., 1839.
Bushnell, Horace. *God in Christ: Three Discourses, Delivered at New Haven, Cambridge, and Andover, with a Preliminary Dissertation on Language*. Hartford, CT: Brown and Parsons, 1849.
Bushnell, Horace. *Nature and the Supernatural, as Together Constituting the One System of God*. New York: Charles Scribner, 1858.
Bushnell, Horace. "Our Gospel a Gift to the Imagination." 1869. In Bushnell, *Building Eras in Religion* [*Literary Varieties* III], Centenary edn. New York: Charles Scribner's Sons, 1909. 249–85.
Bushnell, Horace. *Women's Suffrage; The Reform Against Nature*. New York: Charles Scribner and Co., 1869.
Butler, Jonathan. "From Millerism to Seventh-Day Adventism: 'Boundlessness to Consolidation'." *Church History* 55, no. 1 (March 1986): 50–64.
Calcutt, Andrew and Philip Hammond. *Journalism Studies: A Critical Introduction*. New York: Routledge, 2011.
Calhoun, John C. "Speech on the Oregon Bill" (June 27, 1848). Teaching American History. Accessed August 20, 2022. https://teachingamericanhistory.org/document/oregon-bill-speech/.
Calvin, John. *Institutes of the Christian Religion*, vol. 1, edited by John T. McNeill. Translated by Ford Lewis Battles. 1536–59. Louisville, KY: Westminster, 1960, 2006. Ebook.
Campbell, Alexander [Biblicus, pseud.]. "Ancient Gospel—a Narrative of Facts." In *The Millennial Harbinger; and Voluntary Church Advocate*, vol. 1, edited by William Jones. London: G. Wightman, 1835.
Campbell, Alexander [Editor, pseud.]. "Anti-Campbellism." In *The Millennial Harbinger*, vol. 1. edited by Alexander Campbell, 1830.
Campbell, Alexander [Editor, pseud.]. "The Conversion of the World." In *The Christian Baptist*, vol. 1, 2nd edn, edited by Alexander Campbell. Buffaloe Creek, VA: Buffaloe Printing-Office, 1824.
Campbell, Alexander. "General Preface, an Apology for a New Translation" (January 29, 1826). In *The Sacred Writings of the Apostles and Evangelists of Jesus Christ, Commonly Styled the New Testament*, 2nd edn. Bethany, VA: Alexander Campbell, 1828.

Campbell, Alexander. "Millennium—No. 1." In *The Millennial Harbinger*, vol. 1, edited by Alexander Campbell. Bethany, VA: By the Editor, 1830.
Campbell, Alexander [Editor, pseud.]. "Reply" to R.B.S., April 3, 1826. *The Christian Baptist*, vol. 3. Buffaloe, VA: A. Campbell, 1825–1826.
Campbell, Alexander. "A Restoration of the Ancient Order of Things No. XVII." March 5, 1827. In *The Christian Baptist*, vol. IV, edited by Alexander Campbell. Bethany, VA: A. Campbell, 1827.
Capper, Charles. *Margaret Fuller: An American Romantic Life, Vol. 2: The Public Years*. New York: Oxford University Press, 2007.
Carafiol, Peter C. "James Marsh's American Aids to Reflection: Influence through Ambiguity." *New England Quarterly* 49, no. 1 (March 31, 1976): 27–45.
Carson, Hampton L. *History of the Celebration of the One Hundredth Anniversary of the Promulgation of the Constitution of the United States*, vol. 2. Philadelphia: J.B. Lippincott, 1889.
Castiglia, Christopher. *Interior States: Institutional Consciousness and the Inner Life of Democracy in the Antebellum United States*. Durham, NC: Duke University Press, 2008.
Cauldwell, William. "Walt at the *Daily Aurora*: A Memoir of the Mid-1840s" (July 1901). In Schmidgall, *Conserving Walt Whitman's Fame*, 80–2.
Channing, Dr. [William Ellery Channing]. "Letter on Creeds, &c." (January 11, 1837). London: Smallfield and Son, 1839.
Channing, Walter. "Reflections on the Literary Delinquency of America." *The North-American Review and Miscellaneous Journal* 2, no. 4 (November 1815). Boston: Wells and Lilly, 1816.
Channing, William Ellery. "The Present Age" (May 11, 1841). In *The Complete Works of William Ellery Channing, D.D.* London and New York: Christian Life/Routledge & Sons, 1884.
Channing, William Ellery. "Unitarian Christianity" (May 5, 1819). *Classical American Unitarian Christian Sermons and Writings*. American Unitarian Conference. http://www.americanunitarian.org/unitarianchristianity.htm.
Chauncy, Charles. *Seasonable Thoughts on the State of Religion in New-England*. Boston: Rogers and Fowle, 1743.
Cheney, Mary Bushnell. *Life and Letters of Horace Bushnell*. New York: Charles Scribner's Sons, 1905.
Cherokee Nation v. Georgia, 30 U.S. 1 (1831). Justitia/US Supreme Court. https://supreme.justia.com/cases/federal/us/30/1/.
Chiles, Katy. "Within and without Raced Nations: Intratextuality, Martin Delany, and *Blake; or the Huts of America*." *American Literature* 80, no. 2 (June 2008): 323–52.
Choate, Rufus. Speech at Lowell, MA, October 18, 1856. In *The Works of Rufus Choate*, vol. 2, edited by Samuel Gilman Brown. Boston: Little, Brown, 1862. Library of Congress. Accessed August 20, 2022. https://www.loc.gov/item/09004589/.
Clancy, Jonathan. *Transcendentalism and the Crisis of Self in American Art and Culture, 1830–1930*. Ph.D. diss., City University of New York, 2008.
Clavin, Matthew. "'Disciples of the Declaration': American Freedom and the Fugitive-Slave Rebellion at Rockville." *Journal of the Early Republic* 41, no. 2 (Summer 2021): 239–66.

Clavin, Matthew. "Slavery, Freedom, and the Fourth of July." *The Panorama*, July 2, 2021. http://thepanorama.shear.org/2021/07/02/slavery-freedom-and-the-fourth-of-july/.
Cohen, Charles L. and Paul S. Boyer, eds. *Religion and the Culture of Print in Modern America*. Madison, WI: University of Wisconsin Press, 2008.
Cohn, Norman. *The Pursuit of the Millennium: Revolutionary Millenarians and Mystical Anarchists of the Middle Ages*, revised and expanded edn. Oxford: Oxford University Press, 1970.
Colaiaco, James A. *Frederick Douglass and the Fourth of July*. New York: Palgrave Macmillan, 2006.
Cole, Phyllis. "Jones Very's 'Epistles to the Unborn'." In *Studies in the American Renaissance*, edited by Joel Myerson. Boston: Twayne Publishers, 1982. 169–83.
Coleman, Dawn. "The Unsentimental Woman Preacher of *Uncle Tom's Cabin*." *American Literature* 80, no. 2 (June 2008): 265–92.
Colored Conventions Project, co-founded by P. Gabrielle Foreman, Jim Casey and Sarah Lynn Patterson. University of Delaware Library. Accessed August 20, 2022. http://coloredconventions.org/conventions.
Complete Poetry and Collected Prose. New York: Library of America, 1982.
Congressional Record, vol. 144. Part 19, December 1998.
"The Constitution of the Kingdom of God." April 18, 1844. Latter-day Conservative. Accessed August 20, 2022. https://www.latterdayconservative.com/joseph-smith/constitution-of-the-kingdom-of-god/.
Conway, Moncure D. *Republican Superstitions: As Illustrated in the Political History of America*. London: Henry S. King & Co., 1872.
Cope, Kevin. "How General George Outlived His Own Funeral Orations." In *George Washington in and as Culture*, edited by Kevin Cope. New York: AMS Press, 2001. 65–98.
The Correspondence of Thomas Carlyle and Ralph Waldo Emerson, 1834–1872, 2 vols, library edn. Edited by Charles Eliot Norton. Boston: Ticknor, 1888.
Court, John M. *Approaching the Apocalypse: A Short History of Christian Millenarianism*. London: I.B. Tauris, 2008.
Cowdery, Oliver. *Latter Day Saints' Messenger and Advocate* 1, no. 5, February 1835. FAIR: Faithful Answers, Informed Response. Accessed August 20, 2022. https://www.fairlatterdaysaints.org/answers/Messenger_and_Advocate/1/5.
Crocombe, Jeff. *"A Feast of Reason": The Roots of William Miller's Biblical Interpretation and its Influence on the Seventh-day Adventist Church*. Ph.D. diss., University of Queensland, 2011.
Cross, Whitney R. *The Burned-over District: The Social and Intellectual History of Enthusiastic Religion in Western New York, 1800–1850*. Ithaca, NY: Cornell University Press, 1950, 1982.
Danner, Dan G. "The Millennium in the Restoration Movement: A Brief Historical Portrait." *Leaven* 7, no. 4 (1999): 189–93. https://digitalcommons.pepperdine.edu/leaven/vol7/iss4/6.
Darrow, Clarence. *The Story of My Life*. New York: Charles Scribner's Sons, 1932.
Davis, William L. "Hiding in Plain Sight: The Origins of the Book of Mormon." *Los Angeles Review of Books*, October 30, 2012. https://lareviewofbooks.org/article/hiding-in-plain-sight-the-origins-of-the-book-of-mormon/.

De Pillis, Mario S. "The Quest for Religious Authority and the Rise of Mormonism." *Dialogue: A Journal of Mormon Thought* 1, no. 1 (Spring 1966): 68–88.

A Debate on Slavery, Held on the First, Second, Third, and Sixth Days of October, 1845. Cincinnati: W.H. Moore, 1846.

DeCaro, Louis A. Jr. "John Brown's Liberation Theology: How and Why He Left Markings in His Jail House Bible." *John Brown the Abolitionist – A Biographer's Blog*, May 6, 2007. http://abolitionist-john-brown.blogspot.cz/2007/05/john-browns-liberation-theology-how-and.html.

Delany, Martin R[obison]. *Blake; or, the Huts of America: A Corrected Edition*, edited by Jerome McGann. Cambridge, MA: Harvard University Press, 2017.

Delany, Martin R[obison]. *The Condition, Elevation, Emigration, and Destiny of the Colored People of the United States, Politically Considered*. Philadelphia: Published by the Author, 1852.

Delany, Martin R[obison]. "Political Destiny of the Colored Race on the American Continent" (August 1854). In *Martin R. Delany: A Documentary Reader*, edited by Robert S. Levine. Chapel Hill, NC: University of North Carolina Press, 2003. 245–79.

Delany, Samuel R. "Racism and Science Fiction." *New York Review of Science Fiction*, August 1998. http://www.nyrsf.com/racism-and-science-fiction-.html.

Delp, Robert W. "A Spiritualist in Connecticut: Andrew Jackson Davis, the Hartford Years, 1850–1854." *The New England Quarterly* 53, no. 3 (September 1980): 345–62.

Detweiler, Philip F. "The Changing Reputation of the Declaration of Independence: The First Fifty Years." *William and Mary Quarterly* 19, no. 4 (October 1962): 557–74.

Dinius, Marcy J. *The Camera and the Press: American Visual and Print Culture in the Age of the Daguerreotype*. Philadelphia: University of Pennsylvania Press, 2012.

Dismore, David M. "Today in Feminist History: Suffragists Protest on Independence Day." *Ms.*, July 4, 2012. https://msmagazine.com/2012/07/04/the-suffragists-protest-on-independence-day-1876-you-are-there/.

Doan, Ruth Alden. *The Miller Heresy, Millennialism, and American Culture*. Philadelphia: Temple University Press, 1987.

Dobie, David. *A Key to the Bible: Being an Exposition of the History, Axioms, and General Laws of Sacred Interpretation*. New York: C. Scribner, 1856.

Doctrine and Covenants. Scriptures, Church of Jesus Christ of Latter-day Saints. https://www.churchofjesuschrist.org/study/scriptures/dc-testament?lang=eng.

Dodd, C. H. *The Authority of the Bible*. New York: Harper & Brothers, 1929.

Donald, David Herbert. *Lincoln*. New York: Simon & Schuster, 1995, 2011.

Dorrien, Gary. *The Making of American Liberal Theology: Imagining Progressive Religion 1805–1900*. Louisville, KY: Westminster John Knox Press, 2001.

Douglass, Frederick. "John Brown Not Insane." *Douglass' Monthly* 2, no. 6 (November 1859). Teaching American History. https://teachingamericanhistory.org/document/john-brown-not-insane/.

Douglass, Frederick. *Oration, Delivered in Corinthian Hall, Rochester, July 5th, 1852, to the Rochester Anti Slavery Sewing Society*. Rochester: Lee, Mann, 1852. [Modern title: "What to the Slave Is the 4th of July?"].

Doxey, Graham W. "New Jerusalem." In *Encyclopedia of Mormonism*, edited by Daniel H. Ludlow. New York: Macmillan, 1992. https://eom.byu.edu/index.php/New_Jerusalem.
Doxiadis, Apostolos. "The Geometry of Gettysburg: Abraham Lincoln's Rhetoric and Euclid's Method of Demonstration." Rhetoric in Athens conference, March 22, 2014. YouTube. https://youtu.be/LXsyrrhR7iA.
Dreisbach, Daniel. "The Sacred Sounds of Lincoln's Gettysburg Address." Online Library of Law & Liberty, November 19, 2013. http://www.libertylawsite.org/2013/11/19/thesacredsoundsoflincolnsgettysburgaddress/.
Driver, S. R. *An Introduction to the Literature of the Old Testament*. New York: Scribner, 1931.
Eagleton, Terry. *Literary Theory: An Introduction, 25th Anniversary Edition*. Minneapolis: University of Minnesota Press, 2008.
"The Early Nineteenth-Century Newspaper Boom." *The News Media and the Making of America, 1730–1865*. American Antiquarian Society. Accessed August 20, 2022. http://americanantiquarian.org/earlyamericannewsmedia/exhibits/show/news-in-antebellum-america/the-newspaper-boom.
Edwards, Phil. "Thomas Jefferson's Secret Reason for Sending Lewis and Clark West: To Find Mastodons." *Vox*, April 13, 2015. https://www.vox.com/2015/4/13/8384167/thomas-jefferson-mastodons.
Ehat, Andrew F. "'It Seems Like Heaven Began on Earth': Joseph Smith and the Constitution of the Kingdom of God." *Brigham Young University Studies* 20, no. 3 (Spring 1980): 253–79.
Eiselein, Gregory. "Lincoln's Death [1865]." In *Walt Whitman: An Encyclopedia*, edited by J. R. LeMaster and Donald D. Kummings. New York: Garland Publishing, 1998. The Walt Whitman Archive. https://whitmanarchive.org/criticism/current/encyclopedia/entry_30.html.
Eiselein, Gregory. "Whitman's Life and Work, 1819–92." In Kummings, *A Companion to Walt Whitman*. Malden, MA: Blackwell, 2006. 11–26.
Elazar, Daniel J. "The Political Theory of Covenant: Biblical Origins and Modern Developments." *Publius* 10, no. 4 (Autumn 1980): 3–30.
Elliott, Emory. *The Cambridge Introduction to Early American Literature*. Cambridge: Cambridge University Press, 2002.
Ellis, Arthur B., ed. *Memoir of Rufus Ellis, Including Selections from His Journal and Letters*, 2nd edn. Boston: William B. Clarke and Co., 1892.
Elmore, A. E. *Lincoln's Gettysburg Address: Echoes of the Bible and the Book of Common Prayer*. Carbondale, IL: Southern Illinois University Press, 2009.
Emerson, Ellen Tucker. *The Life of Lidian Jackson Emerson*, edited by Delores Bird Carpenter. East Lansing, MI: Michigan State University Press, 1992.
Emerson, Ralph Waldo. "An Address Delivered Before the Senior Class in Divinity College" (July 15, 1838). Cited as "Divinity School Address." In *Complete Works*, vol. 1.
Emerson, Ralph Waldo. "The American Scholar" (August 31, 1837). In *Complete Works*, vol. 1.
Emerson, Ralph Waldo. "Books." In *Complete Works*, vol. 7.
Emerson, Ralph Waldo. *The Complete Works of Ralph Waldo Emerson*, centenary edn, edited by Edward Waldo Emerson. University of Michigan Library Digital Collections, March 28, 2006. https://quod.lib.umich.edu/e/emerson/browse.html.

Emerson, Ralph Waldo. "The Fugitive Slave Law" (May 3, 1851). In *Complete Works*, vol. 11.
Emerson, Ralph Waldo. "The Fugitive Slave Law" (March 7, 1854). In *Complete Works*, vol. 11.
Emerson, Ralph Waldo. "Goethe; or, The Writer." In *Complete Works*, vol. 4.
Emerson, Ralph Waldo. *The Journals and Miscellaneous Notebooks of Ralph Waldo Emerson*, edited by William H. Gilman et al., 16 vols. Cambridge, MA: Harvard University Press, 1960–82.
Emerson, Ralph Waldo. "The Lord's Supper" (September 9, 1832). In *Complete Works*, vol. 11.
Emerson, Ralph Waldo. "Nature." In *Complete Works*, vol. 1.
Emerson, Ralph Waldo. "The Over-Soul." In *Complete Works*, vol. 2.
Emerson, Ralph Waldo. "The Poet." In *Complete Works*, vol. 3.
Emerson, Ralph Waldo. "Politics." In *Complete Works*, vol. 3.
Emerson, Ralph Waldo. "Remarks at a Meeting for the Relief of the Family of John Brown" (November 18, 1859). In *Complete Works*, vol. 11.
Emerson, Ralph Waldo. "Self-Reliance." In Emerson, *Complete Works*, vol. 2.
Emerson, Ralph Waldo. "Swedenborg; or, the Mystic." In *Complete Works*, vol. 4.
Emerson, Ralph Waldo. "The Transcendentalist" (January 1842). In *Complete Works*, vol. 1.
Ernest, John. *A Nation within a Nation: Organizing African-American Communities Before the Civil War*. Lanham, MD: Ivan R. Dee, 2011.
Eschner, Kat. "Without Edgar Allan Poe, We Wouldn't Have Sherlock Holmes." *Smithsonian Magazine*, April 20, 2017. https://www.smithsonianmag.com/smart-news/edgar-allan-poe-invented-detective-story-180962914/.
Everett, Eward. "Gettysburg Address. November 19, 1863." *Voices of Democracy: The U.S. Oratory Project*, University of Maryland. http://voicesofdemocracy.umd.edu/everett-gettysburg-address-speech-text/.
Fea, John. *The Bible Cause: A History of the American Bible Society*. Oxford: Oxford University Press, 2016.
The Federalist Papers. The Avalon Project. Yale Law School. Accessed August 20, 2022. https://avalon.law.yale.edu/subject_menus/fed.asp.
Fields, Annie, ed. *Life and Letters of Harriet Beecher Stowe*. Boston: Houghton, Mifflin, 1898.
Finney, Charles G. *Lectures on Revivals of Religion*. New York: Leavitt, Lord & Co., 1835.
Fitzhugh, George. *Sociology for the South, or the Failure of Free Society*. Richmond, VA: A. Morris, 1854. Documenting the American South. https://docsouth.unc.edu/southlit/fitzhughsoc/fitzhugh.html.
Folsom, Ed. "Whitman Making Books/Books Making Whitman: A Catalog and Commentary." 2005. The Walt Whitman Archive. Accessed August 20, 2022. http://whitmanarchive.org/criticism/current/anc.00150.html.
Folsom, Ed. and Kenneth M. Price. *Re-Scripting Walt Whitman: An Introduction to His Life and Work*. Malden, MA: Blackwell Publishing, 2005.
Foner, Philip S. *We the Other People: Alternative Declarations of Independence by Labor Groups, Farmers, Woman's Rights Advocates, Socialists, and Blacks, 1829–1975*. Urbana, IL: University of Illinois Press, 1976.

Fox, Richard Wightman. *Lincoln's Body: A Cultural History*. New York: W.W. Norton, 2015.

Frei, Hans W. *The Eclipse of Biblical Narrative A Study in Eighteenth and Nineteenth Century Hermeneutics*. New Haven, CT: Yale University Press, 1974.

Frick, John W. *Uncle Tom's Cabin on the American Stage and Screen*. New York: Palgrave Macmillan, 2012.

Frick, John W. "Uncle Tom's Cabin on the Antebellum Stage." In *Uncle Tom's Cabin and American Culture*, 2007. http://utc.iath.virginia.edu/interpret/exhibits/frick/frick.html.

Frye, Northrop. *The Great Code: The Bible and Literature*. 1983; Markham, Ontario: Penguin Books, 1990.

Frye, Northrop and Jay Macpherson, *Biblical and Classical Myths: The Mythological Framework of Western Culture*. 1962; Toronto: University of Toronto Press, 2004.

Fuller, Margaret et al. *Memoirs of Margaret Fuller Ossoli*, vol. 2. Boston: Phillips, Sampson & Co., 1852.

Furnas, J. C. *Goodbye to Uncle Tom*. New York: William Sloane Associates, 1956.

Gamble, Richard M. *A Fiery Gospel: The Battle Hymn of the Republic and the Road to Righteous War*. Ithaca, NY: Cornell University Press, 2019.

Gannett, Lewis. "'Overwhelming Evidence' of a Lincoln-Ann Rutledge Romance?: Reexamining Rutledge Family Reminiscences." *Journal of the Abraham Lincoln Association* 26, no. 1 (Winter 2005): 28–41.

Garrison, William Lloyd. "Declaration of the National Anti-Slavery Convention." Philadelphia, December 1833. Fair Use Repository. http://fair-use.org/the-liberator/1833/12/14/declaration-of-the-national-anti-slavery-convention.

Garrison, William Lloyd. "The Deed of Infamy Consummated." *The Liberator* 24, no. 23 (June 9, 1854): 2. Smithsonian Digital Volunteers: Transcription Center. Accessed August 20, 2022. https://transcription.si.edu/view/10287/NMAAHC-2016_166_41_4_002.

Garrison, Francis Jackson. *William Lloyd Garrison, 1805–1879: The Story of His Life Told by His Children*, vol. 3, 1841–60. New York: The Century Co., 1889.

Gee, John. "Joseph Smith and the Papyri." In *Introduction to the Book of Abraham*. Provo and Salt Lake City, UT: BYU Religious Studies Center, Brigham Young University, 2017. https://rsc.byu.edu/introduction-book-abraham/joseph-smith-papyri.

"The Gettysburg Address." Abraham Lincoln Online: Speeches and Writings. Accessed April 26, 2023. http://www.abrahamlincolnonline.org/lincoln/speeches/gettysburg.htm.

"The Gettysburg Address." Voices of Democracy: The U.S. Oratory Project. University of Maryland. http://voicesofdemocracy.umd.edu/lincoln-gettysburg-address-speech-text/.

Gilmore, Michael T. "*Uncle Tom's Cabin* and the American Renaissance: The Sacramental Aesthetic of Harriet Beecher Stowe." In Weinstein, ed., *Cambridge Companion to Harriet Beecher Stowe*, Cambridge, UK: Cambridge University Press, 2004. 58–76.

Gohdes, Clarence. "Some Remarks on Emerson's Divinity School Address." *American Literature* 1, no. 1 (March 1929).

Goldin, Claudia. *A Brief History of Education in the United States.* Historical Paper 119. Cambridge, MA: National Bureau of Economic Research, August 1999.
Goodrich, Samuel. *Recollections of a Lifetime, or Men and Things I Have Seen.* New York: Miller, Orton and Mulligan, 1856.
Gossett, Thomas F. *Uncle Tom's Cabin and American Culture.* Dallas: Southern Methodist University Press, 1985.
Graham, Stephen R. *Cosmos in the Chaos: Philip Schaff's Interpretation of Nineteenth-Century American Religion.* Grand Rapids, MI: Wm. B. Eerdmans, 1995.
Griggs, Sutton E. *Imperium in Imperio: A Study of the Negro Race Problem: A Novel.* 1899; New York: Arno Press, 1969.
Grusin, Richard A. *Transcendentalist Hermeneutics: Institutional Authority and the Higher Criticism of the Bible.* Durham, NC: Duke University Press, 1991.
Gura, Philip F. *American Transcendentalism: A History.* New York: Hill and Wang, 2007.
Gutjahr, Paul C. "The Bible-zine *Revolve* and the Evolution of the Culturally Relevant Bible in America." In *Religion and the Culture of Print in Modern America*, edited by Charles L. Cohen and Paul S. Boyer. Madison, WI: University of Wisconsin Press, 2008. 326–48.
Habich, Robert D. "Emerson's Reluctant Foe: Andrews Norton and the Transcendental Controversy." *The New England Quarterly* 65, no. 2 (June 1992): 208–37.
Hahn, Steven. *A Nation under Our Feet: Black Political Struggles in the Rural South from Slavery to the Great Migration.* Cambridge, MA: Belknap/Harvard University Press, 2003.
Hall, Harrison, ed. *Selections from the Writings of Mrs. Sarah Hall, Author of Conversations on the Bible: With a Memoir of Her Life.* Philadelphia: Harrison Hall, 1833.
Hall, Sarah. *Conversations on the Bible, between a Mother and Her Children,* 4th edn, 1818; Philadelphia: Harrison Hall, 1827.
Hankins, Barry. *The Second Great Awakening and the Transcendentalists.* Westport, CT: Greenwood Press, 2004.
Hannaford, Ivan. *Race: The History of an Idea in the West.* Washington: Woodrow Wilson Center Press, 1996.
Hansen, Klaus J. *Quest for Empire: The Political Kingdom of God and the Council of Fifty in Mormon History.* East Lansing, MI: Michigan State University Press, 1967.
Harris, W. C. *E Pluribus Unum: Nineteenth-Century American Literature and the Constitutional Paradox.* Iowa City: University of Iowa Press, 2005.
Harris, W. C. "Whitman's *Leaves of Grass* and the Writing of a New American Bible." *Walt Whitman Quarterly Review* 16, no. 3/4 (Winter 1999): 172–90. doi.org/10.13008/2153-3695.1622.
Harrison, Jackie. "Gatekeeping and News Selection as Symbolic Mediation." In *The Routledge Companion to News and Journalism*, edited by Stuart Allan. New York: Routledge, 2010. 191–201.
Hatch, Nathan O. *The Democratization of American Christianity.* New Haven, CT: Yale University Press, 1989.

Hedrick, Joan D. *Harriet Beecher Stowe: A Life*. Oxford: Oxford University Press, 1994.
Henderson, Desirée. "'What Is the Grass?': The Roots of Walt Whitman's Cemetery Meditation." *Walt Whitman Quarterly Review* 25, no. 3 (Winter 2008): 89–107.
Herbert, T. Walter Jr. "Calvinist Earthquake: *Moby-Dick* and Religious Tradition." In *New Essays on* Moby-Dick, edited by Richard H. Brodhead. Cambridge: Cambridge University Press, 1986. 109–40.
Herndon, William H. and Jesse William Weik. *Abraham Lincoln: The True Story of a Great Life*, vol. 1. Springfield, IL: The Herndon's Lincoln Publishing Company, 1888.
Herrero Brasas, Juan A. *Walt Whitman's Mystical Ethics of Comradeship: Homosexuality and the Marginality of Friendship at the Crossroads of Modernity*. Albany, NY: SUNY Press, 2010.
Hertzberg, Hendrik. "Framed Up: What the Constitution Gets Wrong." Review of Robert Dahl, *How Democratic Is the American Constitution? The New Yorker*, July 29, 2002. https://www.newyorker.com/magazine/2002/07/29/framed-up.
Hickey, W[illiam]. *The Constitution of the United States of America, With an Alphabetical Analysis*, 2nd edn. Philadelphia: T.K. & P.G. Collins, 1847.
Higgins, Brian and Hershel Parker, eds. *Herman Melville: The Contemporary Reviews*. Cambridge: Cambridge University Press, 2009.
Hill, Patricia R. "*Uncle Tom's Cabin* as a Religious Text." In *Uncle Tom's Cabin and American Culture*, 2007. Accessed August 20, 2022. http://utc.iath.virginia.edu/interpret/exhibits/hill/hill.html.
Himes, Joshua V., ed. *Views of the Prophecies and Prophetic Chronology, Selected from Manuscripts of William Miller: With a Memoir of His Life*. Boston: Joshua V. Himes, 1842.
Hitler, Adolf *Mein Kampf*. 1925; München: Zentralverlag der N.S.D.A.P., 1936.
Hodes, Martha. *Mourning Lincoln*. New Haven, CT and London, UK: Yale University Press, 2015.
Holmes, Oliver Wendell Sr. *Ralph Waldo Emerson*. Boston: Houghton, Mifflin, 1886.
Howard, Henry W. B., ed. *The Eagle and Brooklyn: The Record of the Progress of the Brooklyn Daily Eagle*. Brooklyn, NY: Brooklyn Daily Eagle, 1893.
Howe, Julia Ward. *Reminiscences, 1819–1899*. Boston and New York: Houghton Mifflin, 1899.
Hudson, Frederic. *Journalism in the United States, from 1690 to 1872*. New York: Harper & Brothers, 1873.
Hughes, Richard T., ed. *The American Quest for the Primitive Church*. Urbana, IL: University of Illinois Press, 1988.
Hughes, Richard T. and C. Leonard Allen. *Illusions of Innocence: Protestant Primitivism in America, 1630–1875*. Chicago: University of Chicago Press, 1988.
Hunt, G. J. *An Historical Reader; Containing "The Late War, between the United States and Great Britain, from June 1812, to February 1815. Written in the Ancient Historical Style." Altered and Adapted for the Use of Schools throughout the United States*. New York: Samuel A. Burtus, 1817.
Hurth, Elisabeth. *Between Faith and Unbelief: American Transcendentalists and the Challenge of Atheism*. Leiden: Brill, 2007.

Hutchinson, George. "Race and the Family Romance: Whitman's Civil War." *Walt Whitman Quarterly Review* 20, no. 3/4 (Winter 2003): 134–50. doi.org/10.13008/2153-3695.1709.
"Introduction to the New Edition." In *Uncle Tom's Cabin*. Boston: Houghton, Mifflin, 1879, 1888.
"Introduction to *The Pearl of Great Price*. Scriptures, 1986." Church of Jesus Christ of Latter-day Saints. Accessed August 20, 2022. https://www.churchofjesuschrist.org/study/scriptures/pgp/introduction.
Irons, Susan H. "Channing's Influence on Peabody: Self-Culture and the Danger of Egoism." In *Studies in the American Renaissance*, edited by Joel Myerson. Charlottesville, VA: The University Press of Virginia, 1992. 121–35.
Irving, Washington [Geoffrey Crayon, pseud.] "Rip Van Winkle." In *The Sketch Book of Geoffrey Crayon, Gent.*, edited by Susan Manning. 1819–20; Oxford: Oxford University Press, 2009. 33–49.
Jannuzzi, Lawrence. "'And Let the People Say Amen': Priests, Presbyters, and the Arminian Uprising in Massachusetts, 1717–1724." *Historical Journal of Massachusetts* 27, no. 1 (Winter 1999): 1–27.
Jefferson Papers. Founders Online. National Archives. https://founders.archives.gov/about/Jefferson.
Jefferson, Thomas. *The Life and Morals of Jesus of Nazareth*. Facsimile, Washington, 1904. Manuscript/Mixed Material. Library of Congress. Accessed August 20, 2022. https://www.loc.gov/item/mtjbib026581/.
Jefferson, Thomas. *Notes on the State of Virginia*. Query 6. Documenting the American South. Accessed August 20, 2022. https://docsouth.unc.edu/southlit/jefferson/jefferson.html. 24–79.
Jefferson, Thomas to Dr. Benjamin Waterhouse, June 26, 1822. In *Memoir, Correspondence, and Miscellanies: From the Papers of Thomas Jefferson*, vol. 4, edited by Thomas Jefferson Randolph. Charlottesville, VA: F. Carr, 1829.
Jefferson, Thomas to Samuel Kercheval, July 12, 1816. *Manuscript/Mixed Material*. Library of Congress. Accessed August 20, 2022. https://www.loc.gov/item/mtjbib022494/.
Johnson, Chris and Duane Johnson. "A Comparison of the Book of Mormon and the Late War between the United States and Great Britain." March 9, 2014. http://wordtree.org/thelatewar/.
Kammen, Michael. *A Machine That Would Go of Itself: The Constitution in American Culture*. 1986; New Brunswick, NJ: Transaction, 2006.
Kaplan, Richard. "The Origins of Objectivity in American Journalism." In *The Routledge Companion to News and Journalism*, edited by Stuart Allan. New York: Routledge, 2010. 25–37.
Keane, Patrick J. *Emerson, Romanticism, and Intuitive Reason: The Transatlantic "Light of All Our Day."* Columbia, MO: University of Missouri Press, 2005.
Keel, Terence. *Divine Variations: How Christian Thought Became Racial Science*. Stanford: Stanford University Press, 2018.
Knapp, Samuel L. *Lectures on American Literature, With Remarks on Some Passages of American History*, edited by Richard Beale Davis and Ben Harris McClary. 1829; Gainesville, FL: Scholars' Facsimiles & Reprints, 1961.
Kraditor, Aileen S. *Means and Ends in American Abolitionism: Garrison and His Critics on Strategy and Tactics, 1834–1850*. 1969; Chicago: Ivan R. Dee, 1989.

Kuebrich, David. *Minor Prophecy: Walt Whitman's New American Religion.* Bloomington, IN: Indiana University Press, 1989.
Kuebrich, David. "Religion and the Poet-Prophet." In Kummings, *A Companion to Walt Whitman.* Malden, MA: Blackwell, 2006. 197–215.
Kummings, Donald D., ed. *A Companion to Walt Whitman.* Malden, MA: Blackwell, 2006.
LaFantasie, Glenn. "Lincoln and the Gettysburg Awakening." *Journal of the Abraham Lincoln Association* 16, no. 1 (Winter 1995): 73–89.
Lake, Christina Bieber. "Christ-Haunted: Theology on *The Road.*" *European Journal of American Studies* 12, no. 3 (2017). Accessed August 20, 2022. doi.org/10.4000/ejas.12277.
Lawrence, Amelia W. *The Drawing-room Scrap Book: With Twenty Illustrations.* Philadelphia: Carey & Hart, 1850.
Lawrence, D. H. *Studies in Classic American Literature.* London: Martin Secker, 1920.
Lee, Michael J. *The Erosion of Biblical Certainty: Battles over Authority and Interpretation in America.* New York: Palgrave Macmillan, 2013.
Legaspi, Michael G. *The Death of Scripture and the Rise of Biblical Studies.* Oxford: Oxford University Press, 2010.
Letis, Theodore P. "From Lower Criticism to Higher Criticism: Joseph Priestley and the Use of Conjectural Emendation." *Journal of Higher Criticism* 9, no. 1 (Spring 2002): 31–48.
Lewis, Gladys Sherman. *Message, Messenger, and Response: Puritan Forms and Cultural Reformation in Harriet Beecher Stowe's Uncle Tom's Cabin.* Ph.D. diss., Oklahoma State University, 1992.
Lieberman, Jethro K. *A Practical Companion to the Constitution: How the Supreme Court Has Ruled on Issues from Abortion to Zoning.* Oakland, CA: University of California Press, 1999.
Lincoln, Abraham. *The Collected Works of Abraham Lincoln.* The Abraham Lincoln Association. University of Michigan Library. Accessed August 20, 2022. https://quod.lib.umich.edu/l/lincoln/.
Lincoln, Abraham. "Fragment: Notes for Speeches" (August 1858?), in *Collected Works*, vol. 2.
Lincoln, Abraham. "Fragment on Pro-Slavery Theology" (October 1858?). In *Collected Works*, vol. 3.
Lincoln, Abraham. "The Perpetuation of Our Political Institutions" (January 27, 1838). In *Collected Works*, vol. 1.
Lincoln, Abraham. "Reply to Oliver P. Morton at Indianapolis, Indiana" (February 1, 1861). In *Collected Works*, vol. 4.
Lincoln, Abraham. Second Inaugural Address (March 4, 1865). In *Collected Works*, vol. 8.
Lincoln, Abraham. Speech at Chicago, Illinois (July 10, 1858). In *Collected Works*, vol. 2.
Lincoln, Abraham. Speech at Springfield, Illinois (June 26, 1857). In *Collected Works*, vol. 2.
Lind, Michael. "Let's Stop Pretending the Constitution Is Sacred." *Salon*, January 4, 2011. https://www.salon.com/2011/01/04/lind_tea_party_constitution/.
Linton, Charles. *The Healing of the Nations*, 3rd edn. New York: Society for the Diffusion of Spiritual Knowledge, 1855.

Lipscomb, David. *Christian Unity, How Promoted, How Destroyed: Faith and Opinion*. Nashville, TN: McQuiddy Printing Co., 1916.

Loving, Jerome. *Emerson, Whitman, and the American Muse*. Chapel Hill, NC: University of North Carolina Press, 1982.

Lutz, Donald S., ed. *Colonial Origins of the American Constitution: A Documentary History*. Indianapolis: Liberty Fund, 1998.

Lutz, Donald S. "The Declaration of Independence as Part of an American National Compact." *Publius* 19, no. 1 (Winter 1989): 41–58.

Lutz, Donald S. *The Origins of American Constitutionalism*. Baton Rouge, LA: Louisiana State University Press, 1988.

Lutz, Donald S. "The United States Constitution as an Incomplete Text." *Annals of the American Academy of Political and Social Science* 496 (March 1988): 23–32.

Maffly-Kipp, Laurie F. *American Scriptures: An Anthology of Sacred Writings*. New York: Penguin Books, 2010. Ebook.

Maier, Pauline. *American Scripture: Making the Declaration of Independence*. New York: Vintage Books, 1998.

Mancuso, Luke. "Civil War." In Kummings, *A Companion to Walt Whitman*. Malden, MA: Blackwell, 2006. 290–310.

Mark, Joshua J. "Luther's Speech at the Diet of Worms." *World History Encyclopedia*, December 9, 2021. https://www.worldhistory.org/article/1900/luthers-speech-at-the-diet-of-worms/.

Markels, Julian. "Melville's Markings in Shakespeare's Plays." *American Literature* 49, no. 1 (March 1977): 34–48.

Marković, Helena and Biljana Oklopčić. "Edgar Allan Poe's Chevalier Auguste Dupin: The Use of Ratiocination in Fictional Crime Solving." *HUM* 15 (July 2016): 91–105. https://bib.irb.hr/datoteka/844523.Humjul2016_091_105.pdf.

Marquardt, H. Michael and Wesley P. Walters. *Inventing Mormonism: Tradition and the Historical Record*. Salt Lake City: Signature Books, 1994.

Marsh, James. "Preliminary Essay, and Additional Notes." In S. T. Coleridge, *Aids to Reflection, in the Formation of a Manly Character*. Burlington, VT: Chauncey Goodrich, 1829.

Martineau, Harriet. *Society in America*, vol. 2. New York: Saunders and Otley, 1837.

Mather, Cotton. "Theopolis Americana: An Essay on the Golden Street of the Holy City" (May 3, 1709). Edited by Reiner Smolinski. Electronic Texts in American Studies. Digital Commons. University of Nebraska-Lincoln. Accessed August 20, 2022. https://digitalcommons.unl.edu/etas/.

Matthews, Robert J. "Joseph Smith's Inspired Translation of the Bible." *Ensign*, December 1972. Church of Jesus Christ of Latter-day Saints. Accessed August 20, 2022. https://www.lds.org/ensign/1972/12/joseph-smiths-inspired-translation-of-the-bible.

Matthews, Robert J. "The JST: Retrospect and Prospect—A Panel." In Millet and Nyman, *The Joseph Smith Translation*. 291–305. Accessed August 20, 2022. https://rsc.byu.edu/joseph-smith-translation/jst.

Matthews, Robert J. "Major Doctrinal Contributions of the JST." In Millet and Nyman, *The Joseph Smith Translation*. 271–89. Accessed August 20, 2022. https://rsc.byu.edu/joseph-smith-translation/major-doctrinal-contributions-jst.

Mayhew, Jonathan. "Sermon IV: Objections against the Right and Duty of Private Judgment Considered." *Seven Sermons*, 1748, 1749. Classical American Unitarian Christian Sermons and Writings. American Unitarian Conference. Accessed August 20, 2022. http://www.americanunitarian.org/mayhewsermon4.htm.

McCalla, Arthur. *The Creationist Debate: The Encounter between the Bible and the Historical Mind*, 2nd edn. New York: Bloomsbury, 2013.

McCann, Sean. *A Pinnacle of Feeling: American Literature and Presidential Government*. Princeton, NJ: Princeton University Press, 2008.

McGann, Jerome. "Rethinking Delany's *Blake*." *Callaloo* 39, no. 1 (Winter 2016): 80–95.

McNaughton, John. "One Nation under God (Interactive)." 2009. McNaughton Fine Art Company. https://jonmcnaughton.com/one-nation-under-god-interactive/.

Mede, Joseph to W. Twisse (March 23, 1634). *The Works of the Pious and Profoundly-learned Joseph Mede, B.D.* Fourth book. 798–802. Early English Books Online. University of Michigan Library. Accessed August 20, 2022. https://quod.lib.umich.edu/e/eebo/A50522.0001.001/1:72?rgn=div1;view=fulltext.

Meer, Sarah. *Uncle Tom Mania: Slavery, Minstrelsy and Transatlantic Culture in the 1850s*. Athens, GA: University of Georgia Press, 2005.

Melville, Herman. *The Confidence-Man*, chapter 44. 1857. The Literature Network. Accessed August 20, 2022. http://www.online-literature.com/melville/confidence-man/44/.

Melville, Herman. "Hawthorne and His Mosses." 1850. In *Herman Melville: Pierre, Israel Potter, The Piazza Tales, The Confidence-Man, Billy Budd, Uncollected Prose*, edited by Harrison Hayford. New York: Library of America, 1984. 1154–71.

Midgley, Louis. "More Revisionist Legerdemain and the Book of Mormon." *Review of Books on the Book of Mormon* 3 (1991): 261–311.

Midgley, Louis. "Prophetic Messages or Dogmatic Theology?" *Review of Books on the Book of Mormon* 1 (1989): 92–113.

Miller, Floyd J. Introduction to *Blake or The Huts of America, A Novel by Martin R. Delany*. Boston: Beacon Press, 1970. xi–xxix.

Miller, Matt. *Collage of Myself: Walt Whitman and the Making of Leaves of Grass*. Lincoln, NE: University of Nebraska Press, 2010.

Miller, Perry, ed. *The Transcendentalists: An Anthology*. Cambridge, MA: Harvard University Press, 1950, 2001.

Miller, William. *Evidence from Scripture and History of the Second Coming of Christ, about the Year 1843*. Boston: Joshua V. Himes, 1842.

Miller, William. *Voice of Warning* 1, no. 1 (October 1, 1842). Boston: Second Advent Books, 1842.

Miller, William. *William Miller's Apology and Defence*, August 1, 1845. Boston: J.V. Himes, 1845.

Millet, Robert L. "Joseph Smith's Translation of the Bible: A Historical Overview." In Millet and Nyman, *The Joseph Smith Translation*. 23–47. Accessed August 20, 2022. https://rsc.byu.edu/joseph-smith-translation/joseph-smiths-translation-bible.

Millet, Robert L. and Monte S. Nyman, eds. *The Joseph Smith Translation: The Restoration of Plain and Precious Truths*. Provo, UT: Religious Studies Center, Brigham Young University, 1985.
Moby-Dick. "Contemporary Criticism and Reviews." In *The Life and Works of Herman Melville*, July 25, 2000. http://www.melville.org/hmmoby.htm#Contemporary.
Moritz, Fred. "The Landmark Controversy: A Study in Baptist History and Polity." *Maranatha Baptist Theological Journal* 2, no. 1 (Spring 2012): 3–28.
Myerson, Joel. "A Calendar of Transcendental Club Meetings." *American Literature* 44, no. 2 (May 1972): 197–207.
Neibaur, Alexander. "Journal, May 24, 1844, extract." The Joseph Smith Papers. Accessed August 20, 2022. http://josephsmithpapers.org/paperSummary/alexander-neibaur-journal-24-may-1844-extract.
Nelson, Michael. "Fighting for Lincoln's Soul." *VQR: The Virginia Quarterly Review* 79, no. 4 (Autumn 2003). https://www.vqronline.org/essay/fighting-lincoln's-soul.
Nichols, Charles. "The Origins of *Uncle Tom's Cabin*." *The Phylon Quarterly* 19, no. 3 (3rd qtr. 1958): 328–34. doi.org/10.2307/273254.
Noll, Mark A. *America's God: From Jonathan Edwards to Abraham Lincoln*. Oxford: Oxford University Press, 2002.
Noll, Mark A. *The Civil War as a Theological Crisis*. Chapel Hill, NC: University of North Carolina Press, 2006.
Noll, Mark A. "The Image of the United States as a Biblical Nation, 1776–1865." In *The Bible in America: Essays in Cultural History*, edited by Nathan O. Hatch and Mark A. Noll. New York: Oxford University Press, 1982. 39–58.
Noonan, John T. Jr. *The Antelope: The Ordeal of the Recaptured Africans in the Administrations of James Monroe and John Quincy Adams*. Berkeley, CA: University of California Press, 1990.
Nord, David Paul. *Faith in Reading: Religious Publishing and the Birth of Mass Media in America*. Oxford: Oxford University Press, 2004.
Norton, Andrews. *The Evidences of the Genuineness of the Gospels*, vols. 1–3. Boston: J.B. Russell, 1837–44.
Norton, Andrews. "The Latest Form of Infidelity" (July 19, 1839). Classical Unitarian Writings. American Unitarian Conference. Accessed August 20, 2022. http://www.americanunitarian.org/nortonlatestform.htm.
Norton, Andrews to the Editor of the *Boston Daily Advertiser*, November 5, 1836. Classical Unitarian Writings. American Unitarian Conference. Accessed August 20, 2022. http://www.americanunitarian.org/nortonletter1.htm.
Novalis. *Schriften*, vol. 2. Jena: Eugen Diederichs, 1907.
Noverr, Douglas A. "Journalism." In Kummings, *A Companion to Walt Whitman*. 29–41.
O'Reilly, Nathanael. "Imagined America: Walt Whitman's Nationalism in the First Edition of *Leaves of Grass*." *Irish Journal of American Studies* 1 (2009): 1–9. Accessed August 20, 2022. http://ijas.iaas.ie/index.php/imagined-america-walt-whitmans-nationalism-in-the-first-edition-of-leaves-of-grass/.
Oaks, Dallin H. "The Divinely Inspired Constitution." *Ensign*, February 24, 1992. Church of Jesus Christ of Latter-day Saints. Accessed August 20, 2022. https://

www.churchofjesuschrist.org/study/ensign/1992/02/the-divinely-inspired-constitution.
Oman, Nathan B. "'We the People of the Kingdom of God': Mormon Constitution Making and the Council of Fifty." September 8, 2016. *Mormon Studies*. University of Virginia. Accessed August 20, 2022. http://mormonstudies.as.virginia.edu/wp-content/uploads/2017/09/Full-Council-of-50-Paper-Oman.pdf.
Ong, Walter J. *Orality and Literacy: The Technologizing of the Word*, 3rd edn. Abingdon Park, UK: Routledge, 2012.
Onion, Rebecca. "John Brown's Passionate 'Declaration of Liberty,' Written on a Lengthy Scroll." *Slate/The Vault*, December 2, 2013. Accessed August 20, 2022. http://www.slate.com/blogs/the_vault/2013/12/02/john_brown_the_abolitionist_s_declaration_of_liberty_written_by_owen_brown.html.
Orvell, Miles. *The Real Thing: Imitation and Authenticity in American* Culture, *1880–1940*, 25th anniversary edn. Chapel Hill, NC: University of North Carolina Press, 2014.
Otter, Samuel. "Stowe and Race." In *The Cambridge Companion to Harriet Beecher Stowe*, edited by Cindy Weinstein. Cambridge: Cambridge University Press, 2004. 15–38.
Packer, Barbara L. "The Transcendentalists." In *The Cambridge History of American Literature, Volume Two: Prose Writing 1820–1865*, edited by Sacvan Bercovitch. Cambridge, UK: Cambridge University Press, 1995. 329–604.
Packer, Barbara L. *The Transcendentalists*. Athens, GA: University of Georgia Press, 2007.
Paine, Thomas. *The Age of Reason, Being an Investigation of True and Fabulous Theology*, Part II. 1795. New York: Cosimo Classics, 2005.
Parfait, Claire. "The Nineteenth-Century Serial as a Collective Enterprise: Harriet Beecher Stowe's *Uncle Tom's Cabin* and Eugene Sue's *Les Mystères de Paris*." *Proceedings of the American Antiquarian Society* 112 (April 2002): 127–52.
Park, Benjamin E. "Build, Therefore, Your Own World: Ralph Waldo Emerson, Joseph Smith, and American Antebellum Thought." *Journal of Mormon History* 36, no. 1 (Winter 2010): 41–72.
Parker, E. P. "Harriet Beecher Stowe." In *Eminent Women of the Age: Being Narratives of the Lives and Deeds of the Most Prominent Women of the Present Generation*, edited by James Parton. Hartford, CT: S.M. Betts & Co., 1869. 296–331.
Parker, Theodore. *A Discourse of Matters Pertaining to Religion*. Boston: Little and Brown, 1842.
Parker, Theodore. "Of Justice and the Conscience" (1852). In *Ten Sermons of Religion*, 2nd edn. Boston: Little, Brown & Co., 1855. 66–101.
Parker, Theodore. "A Sermon on the Public Function of Woman" (March 27, 1853). In *Woman's Rights Tracts*. Boston: Robert F. Wallcut, 1854. Tract no. 2.
Parker, Theodore. "A Speech at the New England Anti-Slavery Convention in Boston" (May 29, 1850). In *Speeches, Addresses, and Occasional Sermons*, vol. 3. Boston: Horace B. Fuller, 1867. 38–86.
Parker, Theodore. *The Transient and Permanent in Christianity*, edited by George Willis Cooke. 1841–58; Boston: American Unitarian Association, 1908.

Peabody, Elizabeth Palmer. "Egotheism, the Atheism of To-Day." 1858. In Peabody, *Last Evening with Allston, and Other Papers*. 1858; Boston: D. Lothrop and Co., 1886. 240–52.
Perkins, Keith W. "The JST on the Second Coming of Christ." In Millet and Nyman. 237–49. Accessed August 21, 2022. https://rsc.byu.edu/joseph-smith-translation/jst-second-coming-christ.
Persuitte, David. *Joseph Smith and the Origins of the Book of Mormon*, 2nd edn. Jefferson, NC: McFarland & Co., 2000.
Peterson, Merrill D. *The Jefferson Image in the American Mind*. New York: Oxford University Press, 1962.
Peterson, Merrill D. *Lincoln in American Memory*. New York: Oxford University Press, 1994.
Phelps, Austin. "Criticism of Revivals." In *Worth Keeping: Selected from the Congregationalist and Boston Recorder, 1870–1879*. Boston: W.L. Greene, 1880. 135–9.
Phillips, Wendell. *The Constitution a Pro-Slavery Compact: Or, Selections from the Madison Papers, &c.*, 2nd edn., enlarged. New York: American Anti-Slavery Society, 1845.
Phillips, Wendell. *Review of Lysander Spooner's Essay on the Unconstitutionality of Slavery*. Boston: Andrews & Prentiss, 1847.
Pillsbury, Parker. "'Uncle Tom's Cabin' at a Boston Theatre" (November 16, 1852). *The Liberator*, December 24, 1852. In *Uncle Tom's Cabin and American Culture*. Accessed August 21, 2011. http://utc.iath.virginia.edu/onstage/revus/osre02at.html.
Pisani, Bob. "Plundered by Harpies: An Early History of High-Speed Trading." *Financial History* 111 (Fall 2014): 20–4. Museum of American Finance. Accessed August 21, 2022. https://www.moaf.org/publications-collections/financial-history-magazine/111.
Poore, Benjamin Perley. "XI: Benjamin Perley Poor." In *Reminiscences of Abraham Lincoln by Distinguished Men of His Time*, collected and edited by Allen Thorndike Rice. New York: North American Review, 1888. 217–31.
Pratt, Orson. "Questions and Answers on Doctrine." *The Seer* 2, no. 2 (February 27, 1854).
Pratt, Parley P. *Key to the Science of Theology*. Liverpool: F.D. Richards, 1855.
Preus, J. Samuel. *Spinoza and the Irrelevance of Biblical Authority*. Cambridge: Cambridge University Press, 2001.
Prickett, Stephen. "The Bible and Literary Interpretation." In *The Blackwell Companion to Nineteenth-Century Theology*, edited by David Fergusson. Chichester, UK: Wiley-Blackwell, 2010. 395–411.
Priestley, Joseph. "A Comparison of the Institutions of Moses with Those of the Hindoos and Other Ancient Nations." 1784, 1799. In *The Theological and Miscellaneous Works of Joseph Priestley*, vol. 17, edited by J. T. Rutt. Hackney, London: George Smallfield, 1820. 129–319.
Proceedings of the Hartford Bible Convention, June 1853. New York: Published by the [Convention?] Committee, 1854.
Railton, Stephen. "Uncle Tom's Cabin on Film 1: The Silent Era." In *Uncle Tom's Cabin and American Culture*. http://utc.iath.virginia.edu/interpret/exhibits/utconfilm/utconfilm.html.

Reynolds, David S. *John Brown, Abolitionist: The Man Who Killed Slavery, Sparked the Civil War, and Seeded Civil Rights*. New York: Vintage Books, 2006.
Reynolds, David S. *Mightier Than the Sword: "Uncle Tom's Cabin" and the Battle for America*. New York: W.W. Norton, 2011.
Reynolds, David S. *Walt Whitman*. Oxford: Oxford University Press, 2005.
Reynolds, David S. *Walt Whitman's America: A Cultural Biography*. New York: Vintage, 1996.
Reynolds, Donald E. *Texas Terror: The Slave Insurrection Panic of 1860 and the Secession of the Lower South*. Baton Rouge, LA: Louisiana State University Press, 2007.
Reynolds, William M. *American Literature: An Address [at] Pennsylvania College* (September 27, 1845). Gettysburg, PA: H.C. Neinstedt, 1845.
Richardson, Robert. *Memoirs of Alexander Campbell*. Philadelphia: J.B. Lippincott, vol. 1, 1868; vol. 2, 1870.
Ripley, George. *"The Latest Form of Infidelity" Examined* (September 1839). Classical Unitarian Writings. American Unitarian Conference. http://www.americanunitarian.org/ripley1abridged.htm, capitalization in original.
Ripley, George. Review of James Martineau's *The Rationale of Religious Enquiry*, November 5, 1836. Classical Unitarian Writings, American Unitarian Conference. http://www.americanunitarian.org/ripleymartineaureview.htm.
Ripley, George to the Editor of the *Boston Daily Advertiser*, November 9, 1836. Classical Unitarian Writings. American Unitarian Conference. http://www.americanunitarian.org/ripleyletter.htm.
Ritner, Robert K. "'Translation and Historicity of the Book of Abraham' – a Response." In *Individual Scholarship – Robert Ritner*. Chicago: Oriental Institute, University of Chicago, 2014. https://oi.uchicago.edu/research/individual-scholarship/individual-scholarship-robert-ritner.
Roberts, B. H. *Studies of the Book of Mormon*. Edited by Brigham D. Madsen. Urbana, IL: University of Illinois Press, 1985.
Root, Deane L. "The Music of *Uncle Tom's Cabin*." In *Uncle Tom's Cabin and American Culture*. http://utc.iath.virginia.edu/interpret/exhibits/root/root.html.
Ross, Fred A. *Slavery Ordained of God*. Philadelphia: J.B. Lippincott, 1857.
Rowe, David L. *Thunder and Trumpets: Millerites and Dissenting Religion in Upstate New York, 1800–1850*. Chico, CA: Scholars Press, 1985.
Rubery, Matthew. *The Novelty of Newspapers: Victorian Fiction after the Invention of the News*. Oxford: Oxford University Press, 2009.
Sanborn, F[rank] B., ed. *The Life and Letters of John Brown*, 4th edn. Cedar Rapids, IA: The Torch Press, 1910.
Sanborn, F[rank] B. "Reminiscent of Whitman" (May 9, 1897). In Schmidgall, *Conserving Walt Whitman's Fame*, 65–71.
Sandoz, Ellis, ed. *Political Sermons of the American Founding Era: 1730–1805*, 2 vols., 2nd edn. Indianapolis: Liberty Fund, 1998.
Sarachik, Justin. "3 Doomsday Predictors Who Just Could Not Get It Right." *Christian Post*, October 3, 2013. Accessed August 21, 2022. http://www.christianpost.com/buzzvine/3-doomsday-predictors-who-just-could-not-get-it-right-107254/.

Sawyer, Leicester A. *The Elements of Biblical Interpretation*. New Haven, CT: A.H. Maltby, 1836.
Schaff, Philip. *The Principle of Protestantism as Related to the Present State of the Church*. Translated by John W. Nevin. Chambersburg, PA: German Reformed Church, 1845.
Schmidgall, Gary, ed. *Conserving Walt Whitman's Fame: Selections from Horace Traubel's Conservator, 1890–1919*. Iowa City: Iowa University Press, 2006.
Schudson, Michael. *Discovering the News: A Social History of American Newspapers*. New York: Basic Books, 1981.
Schwarzlose, Richard Allen. *The Nation's Newsbrokers, Vol. 1: The Formative Years, From Pretelegraph to 1865*. Evanston, IL: Northwestern University Press, 1989.
Shalev, Eran. *Rome Reborn on Western Shores: Historical Imagination and the Creation of the American Republic*. Charlottesville, VA: University of Virginia Press, 2009.
Shalev, Eran. "Written in the Style of Antiquity": "Pseudo-Biblicism and the Early American Republic, 1770–1830." *Church History* 79, no. 4 (December 2010): 800–26.
Shapiro, Barbara J. *A Culture of Fact: England 1550–1720*. Ithaca, NY: Cornell University Press, 2000.
Shelly, Kevin C. "Pope to Immigrants: 'Never Be Ashamed of Your Traditions'." *PhillyVoice*, September 26, 2015. https://www.phillyvoice.com/pope-pilgrims-gather-crowds-not-yet-heavy/.
Shreve, Grant. "Frederick Douglass's Feud." *JStor Daily* (blog), January 29, 2018. https://daily.jstor.org/frederick-douglass-feud-over-uncle-toms-cabin/.
Sidbury, James. *Becoming African in America: Race and Nation in the Early Black Atlantic*. Oxford: Oxford University Press, 2007.
Skousen, Royal. "A Brief History of Critical Text Work on the Book of Mormon." *Interpreter: A Journal of Latter-day Saint Faith and Scholarship* 8 (2014): 233–48. Accessed August 21, 2022. https://journal.interpreterfoundation.org/a-brief-history-of-critical-text-work-on-the-book-of-mormon/.
Slack, Reed D. "The Mormon Belief of [sic] an Inspired Constitution." *Journal of Church and State* 36, no. 1 (Winter 1994): 35–56.
Smith, Gerrit. "Speech on the Nebraska Bill" (April 6, 1854). In *Speeches of Gerrit Smith in Congress*. New York: Mason Brothers, 1855.
Smith, Henry Justin. "The Day." In *Deadlines: Being the Quaint, the Amusing, the Tragic Memoirs of a News-Room*. Chicago: Covici-McGee, 1923. 1–23.
Smith, Jeff. "The First American 'Superspy': Secret Agency and the Black Nation in Martin R. Delany's *Blake*." In *Silesian Studies in English 2018: Proceedings of the 5 International Conference of English and American Studies*, edited by Marie Crhová and Michaela Weiss. 157–66. https://www.slu.cz/fpf/cz/file/cul/2832f9b4-9e3c-4ffd-a5b4-756d1fc0c5b5.
Smith, Jeff. *The Presidents We Imagine: Two Centuries of White House Fictions On the Page, On the Stage, Onscreen, and Online*. Madison, WI: University of Wisconsin Press, 2009.
Smith, Jeff. "Things Appearing, Every Day: Walt Whitman and the Ubiquity of News." *ESQ: A Journal of Nineteenth-Century American Literature and Culture* 66, no. 1 (2020): 1–45.

Smith, Jeff. "'Where Genius Dies': The Debate Over 'Literary Delinquency' in the Early United States." In *Silesian Studies in English 2022: Proceedings of the 7th International Conference of English and American Studies*, edited by Marie Crhová, Filip Krajník and Michaela Weiss. Opava: Silesian University in Opava, 2022. Forthcoming.

Smith, Joseph Jr. *The Book of Mormon; an Account Written by the Hand of Mormon upon Plates Taken from the Plates of Nephi*. Palmyra, NY: E.B. Grandin, For the Author, 1830. Scriptures, Church of Jesus Christ of Latter-day Saints. https://www.churchofjesuschrist.org/study/scriptures/bofm?lang=eng.

Smith, Joseph Jr. "Church History" [The Wentworth Letter], *Times and Seasons* 3, no. 9 (March 1, 1842): 7–6–710. The Joseph Smith Papers. Accessed August 21, 2022. https://www.josephsmithpapers.org/paper-summary/times-and-seasons-1-march-1842/4.

Smith, Joseph Jr. "Extracts from the History of Joseph Smith, the Prophet." *The Pearl of Great Price, Scriptures*, Church of Jesus Christ of Latter-day Saints. Accessed August 21, 2022. https://www.lds.org/scriptures/pgp/js-h/1.

Smith, Samuel J. "Horace Bushnell: Advocate of Progressive Orthodoxy and Christian Nurture." In *A Legacy of Religious Educators: Historical and Theological Introductions*, edited by Elmer L. Towns and Benjamin Forrest. Lynchburg, VA: Liberty University Press, 2016. 359–80. Chapter Accessed August 21, 2022. https://works.bepress.com/samuel_smith/53/.

Smith, Susan Belasco. "Serialization and the Nature of *Uncle Tom's Cabin*." In *Periodical Literature in Nineteenth-Century America*, edited by Kenneth M. Price and Susan Belasco Smith. Charlottesville, VA: University Press of Virginia, 1995. 69–89.

Smith, Sydney. "Art. III: America" [unsigned book review]. *The Edinburgh Review, or Critical Journal* 33, no. LXV (January 1820): 69–80. Edinburgh: Archibald Constable, 1820.

Smolinski, Reiner, ed. *The Threefold Paradise of Cotton Mather: An Edition of "Triparadisus."* Athens, GA: University of Georgia Press, 1995. Electronic Texts in American Studies no. 48. Digital Commons, University of Nebraska – Lincoln. Accessed August 21, 2022. https://digitalcommons.unl.edu/etas/48.

Smoot, Stephen O. "The Council of Fifty and Its Minutes: A Review." *Interpreter: A Journal of Mormon Scripture* 23 (2017): 45–52. Accessed August 21, 2022. https://journal.interpreterfoundation.org/the-council-of-fifty-and-its-minutes-a-review/.

Smylie, James H. "*Uncle Tom's Cabin* Revisited: The Bible, the Romantic Imagination, and the Sympathies of Christ." *American Presbyterians* 73, no. 3 (Fall 1995): 165–76.

Snay, Mitchell. *Gospel of Disunion: Religion and Separatism in the Antebellum South*. Cambridge: Cambridge University Press, 1993.

Snowden, Richard. *The American Revolution: Written in Scriptural, or, Ancient Historical Style*. 1793; Baltimore, W. Pechin, n.d. [1802].

Spiller, Robert E., ed. *The American Literary Revolution 1783–1837*. Garden City, NY: Anchor Books, 1967.

Spooner, Lysander. *The Unconstitutionality of Slavery*, enlarged edn. 1845; Boston: Bela Marsh, 1860.

Standage, Tom. *The Turk: The Life and Times of the Famous Eighteenth-Century Chess-Playing Machine*. New York: Walker & Co., 2002.

Stearns, E. J. *Notes on Uncle Tom's Cabin: Being a Logical Answer to the Allegations and Inferences against Slavery as an Institution*, 2nd edn. Philadelphia: Lippincott, Grambo & Co., 1853.

Steiner, Mark E. "Abraham Lincoln and the Rule of Law Books." *Marquette Law Review* 93, no. 4 (Summer 2010): 1283–324. http://scholarship.law.marquette.edu/mulr/vol93/iss4/33

Stokes, Claudia. *The Altar at Home: Sentimental Literature and Nineteenth-Century American Religion*. Philadelphia: University of Pennsylvania Press, 2014.

Story, Joseph. *Commentaries on the Constitution of the United States*, vol. 1. Boston: Hilliard, Gray, 1833.

Story, Joseph. *A Familiar Exposition of the Constitution of the United States*. Boston: Thomas H. Webb, 1840.

Stowe, Charles Edward. *Life of Harriet Beecher Stowe Compiled from Her Letters and Journals*. Boston: Houghton, Mifflin, 1889.

Stowe, Harriet Beecher to Gamaliel Bailey, March 9, 1851. In *Uncle Tom's Cabin and American Culture*. http://utc.iath.virginia.edu/uncletom/utlthbsht.html.

Stowe, Harriet Beecher. "Introductory Essay." In Charles Beecher, *The Incarnation; or, Pictures of the Virgin and Her Son*. New York: Harper & Brothers, 1849.

Stowe, Harriet Beecher. *A Key to Uncle Tom's Cabin; Presenting the Original Facts and Documents upon Which the Story Is Founded. Together with Corroborative Statements Verifying the Truth of the Work*. Cleveland: John P. Jewett & Co., 1853.

Stowe, Harriet Beecher. Preface to the European Edition of *Uncle Tom's Cabin*. Leipzig: Bernard Tauchnitz, 1852. In *Uncle Tom's Cabin and American Culture*. http://utc.iath.virginia.edu/uncletom/uteshbsdt.html.

Stowe, Harriet Beecher. *Uncle Tom's Cabin; or, Life among the Lowly*, 2 vols. Boston: John P. Jewett & Co., 1852.

Stowe, Lyman Beecher. *Saints, Sinners and Beechers*. Indianapolis: Bobbs-Merril, 1934.

Stuart, M[oses]. *Conscience and the Constitution*. Boston: Crocker & Brewster, 1850.

Stuart, M[oses]. *Letters to the Rev. Wm. E. Channing, Containing Remarks on His Sermon ... at Baltimore*. Andover, MA: Flagg and Gould, 1819.

Sturtevant, J. M. Jr., ed. *Julian M. Sturtevant: An Autobiography*. New York: Fleming H. Revell, 1896.

Tanner, Jerald and Sandra Tanner. "B.H. Roberts' Secret Manuscript." *Salt Lake City Messenger* 41 (December 1979).

Tanner, Jerald and Sandra Tanner. "The Book of Mormon: Ancient or Modern?" *Salt Lake City Messenger* 84 (April 1993).

Taylor, Bayard. "Gettysburg Ode. Dedication of the National Monument, July 1, 1869." Poetry Nook. Accessed August 21, 2022. http://poetrynook.com/poem/gettysburg-ode-0.

Taylor, Isaac. *Ancient Christianity and the Doctrines of the Oxford Tracts*. Philadelphia: Herman Hooker, 1840.

Thoreau, Henry David. "Slavery in Massachusetts" (1854). African Studies Center. University of Pennsylvania. Accessed August 21, 2022. https://www.africa.upenn.edu/Articles_Gen/Slavery_Massachusetts.html.

Thoreau, Henry David. *Walden; or, Life in the Woods*. 1854; New York: Dover, 1995.

Thuesen, Peter J. *In Discordance with the Scriptures: American Protestant Battles Over Translating the Bible*. Oxford: Oxford University Press, 1999.

Thurow, Glen E. *Abraham Lincoln and American Political Religion*. Albany, NY: State University of New York Press, 1976.

Tierney, Dominic. "'The Battle Hymn of the Republic': America's Song of Itself." *The Atlantic*, November 4, 2010. https://www.theatlantic.com/entertainment/archive/2010/11/the-battle-hymn-of-the-republic-americas-song-of-itself/66070/.

Tillery, Tyrone. "The Inevitability of the Douglass-Garrison Conflict." *Phylon* 37, no. 2 (2nd quarter, 1976): 137–49. doi.org/10.2307/274765.

Tocqueville, Alexis de. *Democracy in America*, vol. 2. Translated by Henry Reeve, 1899. *American Studies Hypertexts*, University of Virginia. Accessed August 21, 2022. https://xroads.virginia.edu/~Hyper/DETOC/toc_indx.html.

Tompkins, Jane. *Sensational Designs: The Cultural Work of American Fiction, 1790–1860*. New York: Oxford University Press, 1985.

Torbett, David. *Theology and Slavery: Charles Hodge and Horace Bushnell*. Macon, GA: Mercer University Press, 2006.

Tsai, Robert L. *America's Forgotten Constitutions: Defiant Visions of Power and Community*. Cambridge, MA: Harvard University Press, 2014.

Turpin, Zachary. "Introduction to Walt Whitman's *Life and Adventures of Jack Engle*." *Walt Whitman Quarterly Review* 34, nos. 3/4 (Winter/Spring 2017): 225–61. doi: doi.org/10.13008/0737-0679.2247.

Uncle Tom's Cabin and American Culture: A Multi-Media Archive, directed by Stephen Railton. University of Virginia Electronic Text Center/Institute for Advanced Technology in the Humanities, 1998–2009. http://utc.iath.virginia.edu/.

Van Deburg, William L. "William Lloyd Garrison and the 'Pro-Slavery Priesthood': The Changing Beliefs of an Evangelical Reformer, 1830–1840." *Journal of the American Academy of Religion* 43, no. 2 (June 1975): 224–37.

van Liere, Frans. *An Introduction to the Medieval Bible*. New York: Cambridge University Press, 2014.

Versluis, Arthur. *American Transcendentalism and Asian Religions*. Oxford: Oxford University Press, 1993.

Vollaro, Daniel R. "Lincoln, Stowe, and the 'Little Woman/Great War' Story: The Making, and Breaking, of a Great American Anecdote." *Journal of the Abraham Lincoln Association* 30, no. 1 (Winter 2009): 18–34.

Walker, David. *Walker's Appeal, in Four Articles*. Boston: David Walker, 1830. Documenting the American South. Accessed August 19, 2022. https://docsouth.unc.edu/nc/walker/walker.html.

Watkins, Jordan T. *Slavery and Sacred Texts: The Bible, the Constitution, and Historical Consciousness in Antebellum America*. Cambridge: Cambridge University Press, 2021.

Watson, John F. [A Wesleyan Methodist, pseud.]. *Methodist Error; or, Friendly, Christian Advice, to those Methodists, Who Indulge in Extravagant Religious Emotions and Bodily Exercises*. Trenton, NJ: D. & E. Fenton, 1819.

Watts, Pauline Moffitt. "Prophecy and Discovery: On the Spiritual Origins of Christopher Columbus's 'Enterprise of the Indies'." *American Historical Review* 90, no. 1 (February 1985): 73–102.
Weld, Theodore. *The Bible against Slavery: An Inquiry into the Patriarchal and Mosaic Systems on the Subject of Human Rights*, 4th edn, enlarged. New York: American Anti-Slavery Society, 1838.
White, James. *Sketches of the Christian Life and Public Labors of William Miller*. 1875; New York: AMS Press, 1971.
Whitman, Walt. "An Afternoon at Greenwood." June 13, 1846. In Whitman, *The Gathering of the Forces*, vol. 2, edited by Cleveland Rodgers and John Black. New York: Putnam's, 1920.
Whitman, Walt. *Complete Prose Works*. The Walt Whitman Archive. Accessed August 19, 2022. https://whitmanarchive.org/published/other/CompleteProse.html.
Whitman, Walt. "Death of Abraham Lincoln." 1879, 1880, 1881. In *Complete Prose Works*.
Whitman, Walt. *Democratic Vistas*. In *Complete Prose Works*.
Whitman, Walt. *Leaves of Grass*, 7 eds. 1855–92. The Walt Whitman Archive. Accessed August 20, 2022. https://whitmanarchive.org/published/LG/.
Whitman, Walt. "Life and Adventures of Jack Engle: An Auto-Biography," edited by Zachary Turpin, *Walt Whitman Quarterly Review* 34, no. 3/4 (Winter/Spring 2017): 262–357.
Whitman, Walt. *Notebooks and Unpublished Prose Manuscripts*, vol. 1. Edited by Edward Grier. New York: New York University Press, 1984.
Whitman, Walt. "Opening of the Secession War." *Specimen Days*, in *Complete Prose Works*.
Whitman, Walt. Published Works: Periodicals. The Walt Whitman Archive. Accessed August 19, 2022. https://whitmanarchive.org/published/periodical/.
Williams, Florence. "A House, 10 Wives: Polygamy in Suburbia." *New York Times*, December 11, 1997.
Williams, Jeffrey. *Religion and Violence in Early American Methodism: Taking the Kingdom by Force*. Bloomington, IN: Indiana University Press, 2010.
Wills, Garry. *Lincoln at Gettysburg: The Words That Remade America*. New York: Simon & Schuster, 1992.
Wood, Tara [taraw, pseud]. "Visitor Center Script: Whitman's Lincoln Lectures." December 10, 2009. *Looking for Whitman*. Accessed August 19, 2022. http://twood.lookingforwhitman.org/2009/12/10/visitor-center-script-whitmans-lincoln-lectures/.
Woodbury, Levi. "Life and Character of Andrew Jackson" (July 2, 1845). In *Life and Writings of Levi Woodbury*, vol. 3. Boston: Little, Brown, 1852.
Yacovone, Donald. "A Covenant with Death and an Agreement with Hell" (July 2005). Massachusetts Historical Society. Accessed August 21, 2022. https://www.masshist.org/object-of-the-month/objects/a-covenant-with-death-and-an-agreement-with-hell-2005-07-01.
Zuck, Rochelle Raineri. *Divided Sovereignties: Race, Nationhood, and Citizenship in Nineteenth-Century America*. Athens, GA: University of Georgia Press, 2016.

INDEX

Abbott, Lyman 85–6
abolitionism 88–9, 94, 102, 115. *See also* slavery
Absolute Religion 95, 102
Abstract of New Bible 85
academic Bible 17
Adams, Charles Francis 86
Adams, John 18, 116
adventism 31–4
African American 185, 190–4
The Age of Reason (Paine) 18
Albany Gazette 131
Alcott, Bronson 83
Allen, Colonel Ethan 18, 224
  Reason, the Only Oracle of Man 18
American Anti-Slavery Society 102
American Bible Society 126
American Declaration and Constitution 89, 91, 113–15, 118–19
American Genius 220, 225
Anderson, Benedict
  comradeship 168
  Imagined Communities 167, 252 n.86
Andrews, Mary Raymond Shipman, *The Perfect Tribute* 205, 218
Anglican Book of Common Prayer 202
Anglo-American campaign 194
Anthony, Susan B. 115
apostolic succession 36
aspiration of society 71–2

Bailey, Gamaliel 143
Baird, Robert 20
Bancroft, George 212
Banneker, Benjamin 185
baptism 35, 36, 41

Barker, Joseph 178
Barr, James 53
Bartgis, Matthias 110
Battle Hymn of the Republic. *See* Howe, Julia Ward
Beecher, Charles, *The Incarnation; or, Pictures of the Virgin and Her Son* 142
Bennett, James Gordon 130
Bergmann, Hans 135
Bible 1–2, 9, 10, 12
  academic 17
  apocryphal 12
  Christianity and 10, 12
  Common Sense thinking 19–20, 24
  creationism in 103
  democratizing 18–26
  demonstrative science 25
  description of 9, 75
  evidence 13, 23, 24, 38, 68
  guides and handbooks 24
  inerrancy of 9
  interpretation of 13–15, 25, 59, 182
  liberal perception of 103–4
  modern science 15–16
  nation's authors and writing authority 4–5
  newspaper and 134–7
  in ordinary language 123
  original/autograph manuscripts 57
  orthodoxy 59
  plain sense of 14
  political 117–22
  readers 17, 33, 45
  record of the past 74
  replacements 56
  Self-Interpreting 10
  in the sixteenth to eighteenth

centuries 11–14
  on slavery 175–7
  spreading text 2, 20
  for teaching purpose 59–61
  textual authority 10–11, 14–17
  unintelligible book 175–8
  "U-shaped" 208–12
  writing 73–80
Bible-onlyism 19, 23
biblical canon 12
biblical stories 9
Black nation 192, 193
Blake, William 76
Blanchard, Jonathan 187–8
The Book of Abraham 47
Book of Mormon 44–7, 51–3, 75, 225
Book over Church 12
Booth, John Wilkes 219
Borges, Jorge Luis 152
Boritt, Gabor 204
Bowles, Samuel 130–1, 134
Brown, John 121–2, 189–91, 193
Brownson, Orestes 83
Buell, Lawrence 104, 139
  The Dream of the Great American Novel 226
Bunyan, John, *The Pilgrim's Progress* 70, 100
Bushnell, Horace 91, 225–6, 241 n.78
  and anti-slavery societies 102
  "Christian comprehensiveness" 98–9
  Christian Nurture 100
  Christ in Theology 101
  God in Christ 98, 100, 101
  on language 97–101
  The Reform against Nature 102
  religious papers 136
  theological father 91
  vision of Kingdom of God 102

Calhoun, John C. 186, 213
Calvinism 2, 71
Calvin, John 12–13
Campbell, Alexander 51, 52, 55, 224
  baptism 36
  biography 34–6
  language and text problems 37

lowercased "christian" 38, 49
  New Testament (Living Oracles) 40–2, 49
  on primitivism 36–42
  restoration 42
  The Sacred Writings of the Apostles and Evangelists of Jesus Christ, Commonly Styled the New Testament 40
  Scripture and 40–1
  Stone-Campbell/Restorationist 42
  teachings 42
  textuary system 37–8
Campbellism 38, 50
Campbell, Thomas 34–5, 41
camp meeting 28
canonical book 62. *See also* Bible
Carlyle, Thomas 64, 73, 83
Catholicism 83, 92
  biblical interpretation 13
  Roman Catholic Church 12
Channing, William Ellery 59–61
  Baltimore Sermon 59, 60, 63, 124
  "Letter on Creeds" 62, 63
  real-world practice 86
  on Unitarianism 61–2
Chauncy, Charles 27, 28, 30, 58, 59, 86
Clare, Augustine, St. 146–7
Coleridge, Samuel Taylor 98
  Aids to Reflection 64
Columbus, Christopher 14–15
commentary on scripture 13, 32, 59, 148, 188
Common Sense pamphlet 18
Council of Fifty 120
Council of the Kingdom of God 120
Cowdery, Oliver 44
Creationism 103
creeds and doctrines 58, 62
cultural authority 69–70
cultural defensiveness 4

Daily Eagle (Brooklyn) 132, 151, 152, 156
Daily News (Chicago) 165
Dallas, George 125, 179, 184
Daniel's prophetic vision in Old Testament 33

Darrow, Clarence 136
Davis, Andrew Jackson 121, 177–8
Day, Benjamin 130
Declaration of Independence and Constitution 1, 90, 95, 102, 104, 106, 113, 119, 121, 122, 149, 173–4, 185, 186, 190
Declaration of the Rights of Women 115
Delany, Martin R. 179
  Blake: or, the Huts of America 194–8, 256 n.87
  The Condition, Elevation, Emigration, and Destiny of the Colored People of the United States 192
  debates about a Black nation 192
  and National Confidential Council 193, 197
  and National Emigration Convention 193–4
  on nation within a nation 191–8
  nonfiction writings 216
The Dial 83
Disciples of Newness 66, 67
divine authority 60, 123
Dobie, David 25–6
doctrine of grace 58
Dodd, C.H. 12
Dorrien, Gary 56, 59, 64, 91
Douglass, Frederick 182–4
Doxiadis, Apostolos 258 n.28
Doyle, Arthur Conan 138

Eagleton, Terry 104
Egotheism 83
electioneer missionaries 120
Elliott, Emory 10
Ellis, Rufus 86
Emerson, Ralph Waldo 4, 64
  about Bible 73–80
  "The American Scholar" 69, 78, 225
  on American thinking 69–70
  on books 68–9
  to Christian imagery 76
  Divinity School Address 73, 75, 76, 81, 86, 166, 240 n.69
  on Goethe 78–9
  liberty 90
  "Man Thinking" 69
  Nature 66–9
  on new bibles 76–9, 84, 103
  new revelation 74
  on new Teacher 72, 74–5, 90
  "The Over-Soul" 82
  Parker on 81
  "The Poet" 77–8
  "Politics" 88
  prophetic mode 87
  on restorationism 75
  on Romanticism 64
  "Self-Reliance" 82, 85, 225
  social critique 70
  social responsibility 84
  and Swedenborg 76
  in traditional Christianity 65, 73
  "The Transcendentalist" 87
  writing style 84
  writing to Thomas Carlyle 83
ephemeral message, sacred history 214
Epistles 76, 84
epochal moment 15, 217
The Erosion of Biblical Certainty (Lee) 17
evangelical religion 20, 28
Everett, Edward 86, 203, 211
evidence and belief, Christianity 10, 12, 63

fallenness, human 10, 60, 65, 210, 211
false philosophy 61
Finney, Charles G. 20, 28–9
First Great Awakening 27
Fitzhugh, George 186
"fourth soil" 217–18
Frei, Hans W. 10
Frye, Northrop 208
Fugitive Slave Law 88–9, 115, 136
Fuller, Margaret 81, 86–7, 225
  on liberal Christians 105–6

Galileo 15–16
Garrison, William Lloyd 115, 174
  Lutheran incendiarism 178–82
Genesis 16, 47, 97, 175

genius 2–3, 64, 78, 81, 82, 113
American Genius 220, 225
genuine book 76–7, 79, 84
Gettysburg Address. *See* Lincoln, Abraham
The Gettysburg Gospel 202
Gilmore, Michael T. 149
God's Chosen People 47, 117, 209–10
Goodrich, Samuel 131
Gospel of Transcendentalism 81
Gospels, the 84, 85, 111. *See also* Bible
Great Awakenings 58
great reversal 217–18
Greeley, Horace 136, 138
Grimké, Sarah 20

Hall, Sarah 9–10, 24
Harmonial Brotherhood 121
Hartford Bible Convention 177–8
Hatch, Nathan O. 22, 27, 52, 130, 136
The Democratization of American Christianity 22
Hawthorne, Nathaniel 138
Hebrew Bible 10, 11, 34, 49, 72, 93, 176. *See also* Old Testament
Henry, Patrick 191
Herald (New York) 130, 134
Herndon, William H. 212, 220–1
Hickey, William 125–6
Hinde, Thomas S. 28
historical Christianity 71
history of the world, Bible 10
Hobbes, Thomas 17
Holmes, Oliver Wendell 104
holy writ 22, 74, 114, 115, 117, 218
Howe, Julia Ward 215
human failings 29. *See also* fallenness, human
Hunt, Gilbert J.
biblical-style storytelling 224–5
The Late War, between the United States and Great Britain 110
hyper-spiritualty, neo-super-visionary 83

indigenous tribes 45
industrial presses 1–2. *See also* penny press

Inspired Version of King James Bible 47
interpretation of Bible 13–15, 25, 59, 182
Irving, Washington, "Rip Van Winkle" 130

Jefferson, Thomas 2–3, 18, 111–12, 243 n.15
Life and Morals 242 n.8
rescuing the Bible 112–13
Jesus Christ in the Gospel 36, 111, 121
Jewish Scriptures 75, 178. *See also* Old Testament
John the Baptist 36
Joseph Smith Translation (JST) 47–8, 50

Kammen, Michael 118
Kant, Immanuel 64
Keel, Terence 10
Kent, James 131
Kepler, Johannes 15
Key to the Bible (Dobie) 25
Kingdom of God 48, 93, 96, 103, 105, 120–1, 125, 213, 224
King James Version (KJV) 40, 47–8, 195, 202

landmasses and human societies 15
LDS community 50
Lee, Michael J. 17, 19, 22, 23, 52
Erosion of Biblical Certainty 235 n.118
Legaspi, Michael G., *The Death of Scripture* 17
Levine, Robert S. 256 n.108
liberal Christianity 56, 62, 85–7, 102–6
liberals 56–7
liberal thinking 57
liberating gods, poets 77–8, 90
liberty 115–16, 185–8
Lidian Emerson, Jackson 84, 85
Lincoln, Abe 182
Lincoln, Abraham 124, 126–7, 199–200, 258 n.28
on Bible and the Declaration 202
Gettysburg Address 199–200,

202–7, 210, 212–18, 220, 257 n.11
  Herndon on 220–1
  and political religion 200
  on Revolution 201
  telegraphic messages 204
  "Thor-Hammer lines" 215
  U-shaped salvation history 217
  Whitman on 219–20
Linton, Charles 25
literary delinquency 2
literary scripturism 139
literature 102–106, 158
  creator 4
  import Great Britain's 3
  inherited bibles and 4
  lack of 2–3
  New World literature 156
  spiritualization 157
Lutheran incendiarism 178–82
Luther, Martin 12, 13
Lutz, Donald S. 114, 117, 216

Madison, James 122–3, 125, 126
Maffly-Kipp, Laurie F. 24
Maier, Pauline, *American Scripture* 115, 117, 118
Marcion of Sinope 11
Marsh, James 64, 65
Martineau, Harriet 4
Massachusetts Anti-Slavery Society 115
Mather, Cotton 217
Matthews, Robert 50
Mayhew, Jonathan 58, 59
Mayor Shinn 199–200
McCalla, Arthur 10, 13, 15, 16, 19
McGann, Jerome 256 n.108
mechanical printing 2
Mede, Joseph 217
Melville, Herman 135
  The Confidence-Man 139
  literary scripturism 139
  Moby-Dick 138
Mesoamerican societies' 15
Methodist Error (Watson) 28
Miller, William 31, 49, 51, 52, 55, 223
  adventism 31–4
  and Bible-readers 33
  biography of 31–2
  concordance-based method 34
  on news 129
  use of Cruden 33
Miracles Controversy 68, 71, 73
Mormonism 43–6, 50, 51, 120–1, 224
mysterious doctrines 60

National Confidential Council 193, 197
National Emigration Convention 193–4
The National Era 143
national identity 1
Natural Religion 73
nature and Religion 66–7
Negro Doctrine 47
Nevin, John W. 29, 30
new American scriptures 223–7
New Bibles 53, 76–9, 84, 85, 103, 106, 225
"New Church" 76
news/newspapers 129–34, 155
  and Bible 134–7
  culture of fact 138
  and disposable culture 135
  point of view 166–7
New Testament 11, 36, 40–3, 52, 56. *See also* Bible
  on abolition 176
  Kingdom of God 120
  miracles 68
Newton, Isaac 15
Nicene Creed 101
Noll, Mark A. 19, 20, 118, 209
Norton, Andrews 68, 73–4
Novalis 76, 79
novel, fictional facts 138

Old Testament 10, 33, 34, 45, 46, 110, 174, 229 n.3
  Chosen People's covenant 117
  on slavery 175, 176
Ong, Walter J. 135
On Religion: Speeches to its Cultured Despisers (Schleiermacher) 18
original/autograph manuscripts 57
Original Sin 60

Packer, Barbara L. 65
Paine, Thomas 18, 20–1, 56–7
  attacks on the Bible 62–3
pamphlet wars 61, 68, 73
parascriptures 114–17, 126, 216
Parker, Theodore 29, 81, 225–6
  Absolute Religion 95, 102
  and Bushnell 91
  on Christian practice 93
  deference to Scripture 91–3
  disciple of 212
  A Discourse of Matters Pertaining to Religion 91
  "Of Justice and the Conscience" 96
  poetical justice 96–7
  "Republic of Righteousness" 90–7
  on slavery 94, 177–9
  vision of Kingdom of God 96, 105, 213
partyism 35, 38, 50
Paul, St. 41, 71, 84, 177
Peabody, Elizabeth 83
pedobaptism 36
penny press 1, 106, 129, 130, 135–6, 148, 161
perpetual Scripture 4, 75, 79, 214, 225
Phillips, Wendell, *The Constitution a Pro-Slavery Compact* 179–80
Pillsbury, Parker 141
plain, common-sense rules 184–5
plural marriage, Old Testament 45
Poe, Edgar Allan 137
poets 2–3
  liberating gods 77–8, 90
political and social reform 88–9
political bible 117–22
political religion of the nation 122–7, 182, 200
political revolution 19
Poore, Benjamin Perley 205
Pope Andrews. *See* Norton, Andrews
Porter, Edwin S. 141
power
  abuse of 58
  astonishment and 71
  to read Scripture 75
precritical biblical interpretation 10, 17
Preus, J. Samuel 10

Prickett, Stephen 104
priesthood 13, 46
Priestley, Joseph 18, 62
Primitive Gospel 224
primitivism 34–42
printing and communications technology 1–2, 129. *See also* penny press
  accelerating print 156
Prophets 85–6
Protestant Reformation 2, 12–13, 21, 61
  biblical interpretation 14, 123
  movements of 21
pseudo-biblicism 110
pseudo-protestant 30

quasi-religious attributes 116

Radical Reformation 21
rapetissement 3
Reason, Romantic terms 64, 66, 74
Reformed, literal hermeneutic 19, 24
Religion in America (Baird) 20
Religious Democracy 106
religious evidences 68, 73
religious Phrenzy 27
religious pluralism 21–2
religious publications 135–6
Renaissance humanism 16
restorationism 42–8, 63, 75, 224
revelations 12, 19, 38, 44, 46, 66, 71, 74
reversing framework. *See* interpretation of Bible
revivalism 22, 27–8, 75. *See also* Second Great Awakening
  of religion 94–5, 100–1
  to ultraism 28–31
Reynolds, Donald E. 257 n.109
Ripley, George 66–8, 73–4, 83
Romanticism 18, 64, 104
Ross, Fred A. 178–9, 187, 200
  Slavery Ordained of God 177, 188
Rubery, Matthew 129–30, 138
Rush, Benjamin 18

sacralization 173, 218
sacred chronology, Bible 15

Sandburg, Carl 165
Sawyer, Leicester A. 24, 25
   The Elements of Biblical Interpretation 24
Schaff, Philip 29
Schleiermacher, Friedrich 18
Schudson, Michael 134
scientific revolution 15–16
Scottish Common Sense philosophy 19, 24, 50, 64
scripturalizing of the United States 20
Scriptures. *See* Bible
Scriptures, world 3, 9–15, 77
Second Great Awakening 18, 27–8, 42, 58
Self-Interpreting book 10
Shapiro, Barbara J. 138
Simon, Richard 17
slavery 58, 143, 173–4. *See also* abolitionism
   African America, nation within a nation 192–3
   on biblical grounds 175
   broken people 192
   plain, common-sense rules 184–5
   political analysis 193
   political identity 192
   slave factories 194
Smith, Gerrit 186
Smith, Henry Justin 165, 167
Smith, Joseph
   Kingdom of God 120–1
   on restorationism 42–6, 55–6, 224
   and revivalism 75
Smith, Sydney 3
Snowden, Richard 109–11, 113, 211, 224, 242 n.7
social responsibility 84–90
Sola scriptura 13
Spinoza, Baruch 17, 64
Spiritualism 71, 94
spiritual truth 63–5
Spooner, Lysander 184, 254 n.39
Stanton, Edwin M. 203
Stearns, Charles B. 176
Stone, Barton W. 42
story-telling 137–9

Stowe, Harriet Beecher 94, 226
   Gospel passages with novelistic detail 142
   The Incarnation; or, Pictures of the Virgin and Her Son 142
   A Key to Uncle Tom's Cabin 143–6, 148–50
   parascripture(s) of 139–50
   on slavery 143, 148, 226
   on theory of the Bible 147–8
   Uncle Tom's Cabin 139–41, 143, 146
Stuart, Moses 63, 179
   on slavery 176
Sun (New York) 130, 132
Swedenborg, Emanuel 76
Symposium 66

Taylor, Isaac 30
   Ancient Christianity 231 n.15
teachings 12, 22, 42, 59–61
textual authority 6, 10, 30, 49, 50, 227
textual criticism 16, 56–7
textual culture 106
textuary system 37, 39
theodemocracy 120
theological errors 60
Thoreau, Henry David 83, 133–4, 136, 238 n.12
Thuesen, Peter J. 12, 17
Times (New York) 133, 135
Tocqueville, Alexis de 3, 23–4
   Democracy in America 23
   democratic readerships 228 n.8
traditionalists 56, 73
Transcendental Bible 85
Transcendentalism 62–8, 70, 73, 74, 212
   antisocial 82
   Gospel of Transcendentalism 81
   meanings of 83
   political and social reform of 88–9
   and prophecy 85
Tribune (New York) 136, 138, 148
Trinity 60
the Turk 137–8
tyranny 58

ultraism 30–1, 55
Unitarianism 58–62
   to the United States 63

Very, Jones 76
View of the Hebrews (Smith) 45
Vulture's cargo, slaves 194, 196

Washington, George 114, 174
Watkins, Jordan T. 173
Webster, Daniel 89, 179
Weekly Tribune (New York) 136
Weld, Theodore 175, 185
Whitman, Walt 88, 106, 115, 132–3, 135, 214, 250 n.27
   Borges on 152
   career 166
   comradeship 168
   "Crossing Brooklyn Ferry" 152
   Democratic Vistas 156
   as editor of journals 151
   Emerson on 157–8
   Greenwood Cemetery 152
   Leaves of Grass 115, 152, 153, 168–9
   Life and Adventures of Jack Engle: An Auto-Biography 151–2, 155, 166
   on Lincoln 219–20
   lithographing the ancient gods 162–5, 168
   for loaferism 155
   on national bonding 168
   newspapers of 157, 161
   poems/stories 158–62
   on point of view 166–7
   "Religious Democracy" 157, 162
   and transformation of print culture 156
   on writing 152–5
Wilkes, John 115
Wills, Garry 212, 213, 215
Woodhull, Victoria Claflin 121–2
Word of God, Bible 12
Wright, Henry C. 177
writers and artists 3–4
written texts 52, 62, 90, 93, 96, 227

Year-Day schemes 33